Administrative History of India Since Independence

Surendra Nath Tripathi
Suresh Misra
Mamta Pathania
Jyotsana Mahor

Indian Institute of Public Administration

Prints Publications Pvt Ltd

Published by

Prints Publications Pvt Ltd
Viraj Tower-2, 4259/3, Ansari Road,
Darya Ganj, New Delhi-110002
Tel.: +91-11-45355555 Fax: +91-11-23275542
E-mail: contact@printspublications.com
Website: www.printspublications.com

Prepared by:
S.N. Tripathi, Suresh Misra, Mamta Pathania and Jyotsana Mahor
Administrative History of India Since Independence

Edition: 2024

ISBN 978-81-19972-00-5

Price Rs. 1495/-

Published and Printed by Mr Pranav Gupta (Managing Director) on behalf of Prints Publications Pvt Ltd, New Delhi.

डॉ. जितेन्द्र सिंह
राज्य मंत्री (स्वतंत्र प्रभार),
विज्ञान एवं प्रौद्योगिकी मंत्रालय,
राज्य मंत्री प्रधान मंत्री कार्यालय,
राज्य मंत्री कार्मिक, लोक शिकायत एवं पेंशन मंत्रालय,
राज्य मंत्री परमाणु उर्जा विभाग तथा अंतरिक्ष विभाग
भारत सरकार

सत्यमेव जयते

DR. JITENDRA SINGH
Minister of State (Independent Charge)
of the Ministry of Science and Technology
Minister of State in the Prime Minister's Office
Minister of State in the Ministry of Personnel
Public Grievances and Pensions
Minister of State in the Department of Atomic Energy and
Department of Space
Government of India

FOREWORD

Administrative History of India since independence is marked by significant political, economic and social changes. We became a republic in 1950 with the adoption of our Constitution. Our Constitution is a living document. Over the period, the needs of the country have grown that require various amendments to the Constitution.

Understanding the evolution of administrative practices is essential for interpreting constitution, laws and rules as it provides context for the intent and purpose behind legal framework. Administrative history clears the understanding regarding administrative ideologies, political decision making, administrative procedures and the role of bureaucracy. Additionally, it also helps to comprehend governance and good governance, interpret relationship between the government, state and society. It is an effort to channel the resources, aspirations and conflict resolution through formalized means of governance, which is established to provide stability and solve social problems.

In our democracy, the executive plays a major role in day-to-day governance. Several administrative decisions are taken, keeping in view the constitutional, judicial and legislative mandate to enable the government to provide better services to the citizens and also, ensure safeguard for marginalized groups. This helps to understand their strengths and weaknesses, learn from past mistakes, and identify best practices. It also contributes to organizational learning and continuous improvement. At present the government has initiated a number of administrative reforms to streamline governance, bureaucracy and make governance more effective and efficient.

To meet the administrative needs of a citizen friendly administration, a number of decisions have been taken to promote ease of living and ease of life which are the guiding principles. Government is working on one moto *'Sabka Sath Sabka Vikas aur Sabka Vishwas'* which aligns every section of the society in one. Many reforms reflect the government's dedication for citizen centricity.

I am happy that Indian Institute of Public Administration has taken the imitative to document the ***"Administrative History of India since Independence"***. It is a very important work in understanding the transformation that has taken place in providing Good Governance. This volume significantly depicts key aspects of India's administrative history since independence; all these events represent a broad perspective, and numerous other developments that have shaped the country's administrative landscape.

It is a valuable contribution to understand administrative history in nutshell. I congratulate the authors Shri Surendra Nath Tripathi, Prof Suresh Misra, Dr Mamta Pathania and Ms Jyotsana Mahor for undertaking this work. It will be useful to various stakeholders and particularly, policy makers, administrators, academicians, researches, law makers and all those interested in the theory and practice of administrative decision making.

(Dr. Jitendra Singh)
MBBS (Stanley, Chennai)
M.D. Medicine, Fellowship (AIIMS, NDL)
MNAMS Diabetes & Endocrinology

Anusandhan Bhawan, 2, Rafi Marg
New Delhi - 110001
Tel.: 011-23316766, 23714230
Fax: 011-23316745

South Block, New Delhi - 110011
Tel.: 011-23010191, Fax: 23017931
North Block, New Delhi - 110001
Tel.: 011-23092475, Fax: 011-23092716

Preface

Colonization of India spanned nearly 200 years – wiping out many of the medieval systems and replacing them with new ones to strengthen the British colonial rule in India. The British ruled India from 1858 to 1947 till India gained its independence on 15th August 1947. India was declared a republic in 1950 and the Constitution became the guiding principle of the country. It reflected the aspirations and desires of the country and its people to build a just and humane society.

Though many of Indian administrative systems and features are a legacy of the British times yet many new administrative, political and socio-economic alternatives have evolved since independence keeping in view the need of the new nation. The evolutionary process of Indian administration gave rise to numerous administrative organizations from time to time. After independence, India faced several challenges in the process of nation building, including effects of the partition of the country into two independent nations, India and Pakistan. The unification of the nation into one also posed a major challenge. The Constitution was never tested but reflected the vision and foresightedness of the founding fathers. An independent democratic India guided by its new constitution embarked on the journey of nation building as enshrined in the Preamble of the Constitution. While India emerged as a democratic republic at the same period many of the newly decolonized countries fell in the hands of dictators or despots. Indies's independent democratic status was a fallout of the foresight and tenacity of our leaders.

Over the years, India has made progress in various fields including agriculture, poverty reduction, economic development, education, healthcare and technology. It has become one of the world's largest democracies with a diverse and pluralistic society. In terms of foreign policy, India pursued a policy of non-alignment during the Cold War, maintaining independence from the major power blocs. India has developed diplomatic relations with various countries and played an active role in international forums. Economically, India underwent significant changes in the early 1990s with economic liberalization policies that opened up the economy to globalization and private investment. This period marked a shift toward market-oriented reforms and has contributed to India's economic growth. India continues to be a vibrant and dynamic nation, facing both opportunities and challenges on its path of development. Many of these reforms or developments preceded several administrative decisions, recommendations and legislative enactments. Apart from these, various commissions and committees set up have also helped shape the administrative structures and systems to promote good governance.

Administrative history is a branch of historical study that focuses on the development and evolution of administrative systems, structures, and processes within organizations, institutions, and governments. This knowledge is valuable for policymakers and decision-makers, allowing them to learn from historical successes and failures when crafting new policies. Administrative History of India is a culmination of passion, dedication and collaborative effort. We express sincere gratitude to our Honorable Chairman Dr. Jitendra Singh, Minister of State, Ministry of Personnel, Public Grievances & Pensions, Government of India for his support and encouragement. We would like to thank Shri. V Srinivas, Secretary, Department of Administrative Reforms, Public Grievances and Pension (DARPG), Government of India for his help in completing this work. We thank Shri Amitabh Ranjan, Registrar, IIPA for his administrative support and Ms. Meghna Chukkath for bringing out the volume in a short time. We acknowledge the support of our friends and colleagues at IIPA particularly the library for their help in completing the volume. We have used material from various sources which have been duly acknowledged.

In the recent past major administrative transformation has taken place both in theory and practices of administrative reforms in the country. This publication fills a lacuna in accessing material on administrative history of Independent India in a nutshell at one place. We are confident that this volume will be useful to policy makers, administrators, academicians, researchers and students of Public Administration.

Date: January 2, 2024
Place: New Delhi

Surendra Nath Tripathi
Suresh Misra
Mamta Pathania
Jyotsana Mahor

Contents

List of Tables

List of Figures

Background

Administration of independent India has undergone many transformations to get rid of British colonial administration that propagates the colonial need such as maintenance of law and order, Collection of revenue, tactics to holds the administrative power in British civil services. During the time of independence, India was facing political imbalance due to partition. Refugee crisis, incursion of millions of refugees and communal disturbances, posed a serious challenge to our administration. Famines in the forties leading to a shortage in supply of food grain coupled with price rise brought in an undue pressure on the administration to manage the crisis. Rationing was introduced to regulate supply and distribution of food grains. Subsequently, the introduction of rationing considered as necessary imperative and large-scale recruitment to several positions of public personnel.

This was a major unstable period for administration as configuration of cadres was depleted, and as a consequence, a large number of European and civil servants were relinquishing or leaving the country. The proportion of Indian service was 1064 in 1945 and 932 in early 1947. The British Indian Provinces were directly under the control of the British government Princely States covered one-third of the land area of the British Indian Empire and one out of four Indians lived under princely rule. Just before Independence it was announced by the British that with the end of their rule over India, paramount of the British crown over Princely States would also lapse. This meant that all these states, as many as 565 in all, would become legally independent. The British government took the view that all these states were free to join either India or Pakistan or remain independent if they so wished. This decision was left not to the people but to the princely rulers of these states. This was a very serious problem and could threaten the very existence of a united India. The process of nation-building did not come to an end with partition and integration of Princely States. Now the challenge was to draw the internal boundaries of the Indian states. This was not just a matter of administrative divisions. The boundaries had to be drawn in a way so that the linguistic and cultural plurality of the country could be reflected without affecting the unity of the nation. During the colonial rule, the state boundaries were drawn either on administrative convenience or coincided with territories annexed by the British government or the territories ruled by the princely powers.

India emerged as sovereign state on 15 August 1947 and 26 January 1950 announced new constitution. Adopted Parliamentary democracy, Federal structure with the Union and State levels, local administration, Financial administration and Public Services, these are the feature of British administration which were mention in Government of India Act 1935 because of imbalance between political scenario and public administration had to move with same British Administrative system after independence; however, its objectives and nature were quite different from those prevailing under the British rule. Public Service Commissions were set up at the union and the state levels for ensuring selection of meritorious candidates. Directive Principles of State Policy and the fundamental rights and fundamental duties for the citizens were laid down. These and such other provisions increased the responsibilities of public administration in the country and from here with time India was establishing a strong administrative and institutional framework.

Early in 1946, after examine the instability in the country and strong need for urgent administrative fulfillment country took a decision to continue with two services all India services namely the Indian Administrative Services and Indian Police service. Constitution approved them to proceed further and with it also start the procedure for creation of new services. Before independence, the officers of the ICS and other All India Services were appointed by the Secretary of State for India. After independence, under the India Independence Act, 1947, the ICS and other officers in All India Services, who continued in office, became officers in the service of the Government of India. At independence about two hundred and fifty European ICS officers retired, while about fifty of them opted to be in office here. Vallabhbhai Patel, India's Home Minister realized the dire need of the Indian members of the ICS continuing in service here after 1947. He assured to honor the existing terms and security of their tenure. They did contribute to the stability and continuity of the Indian administration. A new Constitution on January 26, 1950[1] and its objectives and nature were quite different from those prevailing under the British rule. The new Constitution established Parliamentary Democracy in the country. Federal governance with the Union and state governments was established. Public Service Commissions were set up at the union and the state levels for ensuring selection of excellent candidates. Directive Principles of State Policy and the fundamental rights and fundamental duties for the citizens were laid down. These provisions increased the responsibilities of public administration in the country.

When India became free from the colonial rule, the Constitution of India was written for the newly independent country. It started with a Preamble. The Preamble seeks to secure to all citizens social, economic, and political justice; liberty of thought, expression, belief, faith, and worship; equality of status and opportunity; and promote among them all fraternity assuring the dignity of the individual and sovereignty and integrity of the nation. Part IV of the Constitution, which deals with Directive Principles of State Policy provide for principles to give guidance to the government in making policies[2]. The State is to strive to minimize the inequalities in income and eliminate inequalities in status, facilities, and opportunities to its citizens. Both men and women will have equal right to an adequate means of livelihood. Equal pay for equal work is another directive to be adhered to by the states. The moral, mental, physical, and psychological health of children and youth are to be protected. Equal justice and free legal aid, right to work, education, and public assistance in old age, unemployment, etc. are secured by these Principles as guiding points in state programs.

The administrative work both at the Centre and State levels has, after Independence, become more complex and challenging. New forms of organization of these administrative activities have come up which did not exist before independence. The types of knowledge and skills required among the administrative personnel have also become more complex. The new economic social welfare, scientific and technical activities assumed by the state in India account for their variety and complexity. The growing international and defense responsibilities of the Indian state have also partly contributed to the strengthening and speeding up of this process.[3] The low levels of literacy and awareness of numerous people have also added to the responsibilities and tasks of the administration. Usually, the ministries at the central level will be having one or more departments, depending on the need for specialization. For instance, the Ministry of Personnel Public Grievances and Pension, as the name suggests, has three departments. The number of Ministries and their constituent departments go on increasing on both political and administrative grounds.

Need to accommodate many ministries leads to proliferation of Ministries and Departments. Also, specialization asks for creation of new ministries and departments. Science and technology, Atomic Energy, Non-Conventional Energy are such instances of new needs. In short terms, the Ministry of Social Justice and Empowerment exemplifies the need for new administrative set up to deal with social justice and empowerment. The new economic activities undertaken by the Union Government are reflected in the departments of coal, power and non-conventional energy sources in the Ministry of Energy, departments of chemicals and petrochemicals, industrial development and public enterprises in the Ministry of Industry, departments of planning and statistics in the Ministry of Planning, and Ministries of Petroleum and Natural Gas, Programmed Implementation and Steel and Mines. Nationalized banks are looked after by the Finance Ministry. Concerns for the development of Science and Technology are imbibed by the Ministries of Science and Technology and Department of Atomic Energy, Electronics and Space. The tremendous growth in the strength of Personnel administration has led to the creation of the new Ministry of Personnel, Public grievances and Pension. The new Departments of Family Welfare, Youth Affairs' and Sports and Women and Child Development mark the compulsions of a social awakening among the families, youth and women and the awareness of social responsibilities towards them, after independence.[4] The innovated forms of public corporations, government companies and joint companies have appeared on the post-independence administrative scene, giving rise to the demand for new categories of administrators. Involves offices like the National Academy of Administration at Mussoorie and subordinate office like the National Fire College at Nagpur are new off-shoots of administration. Numerous advisory bodies like the Central Board of Education and the Central Labor Advisory Board evoke the participation of concerned interest groups in the policy-making.

The pressures of the people in a democratic set up have brought the welfare state. Planning has guided the economic development of the country since the beginning of the first five-year plan from 1" April 1951. Plans formulated by the Planning Commission set up in March 1950, aimed at the rapid all-round economic development of the resources of the country. Planning Commission to enable it to frame the plans and check the progress in their implementation. Besides the national plan, state and district plans are also prepared by the administration at these levels. Plans set the targets of development in different sectors including industry, agriculture, electricity, minerals, transport and communication, education, health, etc. The administration at different levels, Central, State and local, is geared to the realization of the goals of the plans. It also furnishes data and statistics to the Planning Commission to enable it to frame the plans and check the progress in their implementation.

Post Independence: Institutional Building Phase

Constitution of India: Building Block of Modern India

The Constitution of India, adopted on 26th January 1950, is the supreme law of the country and lays down the framework that defines the political principles, establishes the structure, procedures, powers, and duties of the government institutions the fundamental rights, and directive principles. While the Constitution contains numerous features, some of its salient features, or underlying principles, include:

Sovereignty: The Constitution establishes India as a sovereign nation, meaning that it is independent and free from external control. It affirms the supremacy of the Indian people and their rights to determine their political, social, and economic fortune. The Doctrine of sovereignty is associated with the British Parliament, while the principle of judicial supremacy is with that of the American Supreme Court.

Secularism: The state does not promote any particular religion and treats all equally. India is a secular country, as enshrined in the constitution. The Constitution guarantees freedom of religion to all citizens and prohibits discrimination on religious grounds. The term 'Secular' was added to the Preamble of the Indian Constitution by the 42nd Constitutional Amendment Act of 1976.

Federalism: The Indian Constitution establishes a civil system of government, where powers are divided between the central government and the state governments. It outlines the distribution of powers between the Union and the states to ensure cooperation and collaboration. Indian Constitution contains a large number of unitary civil features, viz., a strong centre, single constitution, single citizenship, and strictness of Constitution, integrated judiciary, the appointment of State Governor by the Centre, All India services, and emergency provision and so on.

Fundamental Rights: The Constitution guarantees fundamental rights to all citizens, which include the right to equality, freedom of speech and expression, freedom of religion, right to life and personal liberty, and various other protections. These rights are enforceable by the courts and form the bedrock of individual freedoms in India. Part III of the Indian Constitution guarantees six fundamental Rights to all the citizens:

- Right to Equality (Articles 14- 19)
- Right to Freedom (Article 19 – 22)
- Right against Exploitation (Article 23 – 24)
- Right against Exploitation (Article 25 – 28)
- Cultural and Educational Right (Articles 25 – 28)
- Right to Constitutional Remedies (Article 29 – 30)

The Fundamental Rights are meant for promoting the idea of political democracy. They operate as limitation on tyranny of the executive and arbitrary laws of the legislature. The aggrieved person can directly go to the Supreme Court which can issue the writs of Habeas corpus, mandamus, prohibition, and certiorari and quo warranto for the restoration of his rights. The Fundamental Rights are not absolute and subject to reasonable prohibition, can be curtailed or repealed by the parliament through a constitutional amendment act. They can also be suspended during the operation of a National Emergency excluding the rights guaranteed by Articles 20 and 21.[5]

Directive Principles of State Policy: The Constitution includes directive principles, which are guidelines and principles that the government is anticipated to follow in making laws and policies. They cover a wide range of social, economic, welfare of State and political matters and aim to establish equal society. According to Dr.B. R Ambedkar, the Directive Principles of state Policy is a 'novel feature 'of the Indian Constitution. They are enumerating in Part IV of the Constitution.

Rule of Law: The Constitution upholds the principle of the rule of law, which means that all individuals, including the government, are subject to and accountable to the law. It ensures that no one is above the law and provides for an independent judiciary to interpret and enforce the laws.

Judicial Review: The Constitution grants the power of judicial review to the judiciary, allowing the courts to review the constitutionality of laws and government conduct. This power enables the judiciary to guard the rights and liberties of individuals and ensures the supremacy of the Constitution.

Universal Adult Suffrage: The Constitution provides for universal adult suffrage, granting every citizen who is 18 years of age without any discrimination based on gender, religion, caste or ethnicity. This principle ensures the democratic representation of the people in the country.

Social Justice and Equality: The Constitution emphasizes social justice and equality by prohibiting discrimination based on various grounds, including caste, religion, race, sex, or place of birth. It seeks to address historical injustices and promote equality of opportunity for all citizens.

Independent Institutions: The Constitution establishes independent institutions such as the Election Commission, Comptroller and Auditor General, and the judiciary to ensure checks and balances on the executive branch of the government. These institutions play a vital part in upholding democracy and ensuring transparency and accountability.

Preamble: Guarantee To Protect Social & Economic Security of Citizens

The Indian Constitution is one of the world's lengthiest written constitutions, consisting of a preamble and 470 articles divided into 25 parts. It reflects the principles of democracy, socialism, secularism, and social justice. The Preamble of the Indian Constitution declares India as a *sovereign, socialist, secular, and democratic republic* committed to *justice, liberty, equality, and fraternity*. The preamble is a set of ideals in whose framework of the Indian society to be moulded and socialized. The Preamble of the Constitution of India is an introductory statement that outlines the guiding principles and objectives of the Indian Constitution. It serves as a preface to the constitutional text and provides a glimpse into the vision and aspirations of the framers.[6]

The Preamble of the Indian Constitution reads as follows:

"We, the people of India, having solemnly resolved to constitute India into a sovereign, socialist, secular, democratic, and republic, and to secure to all its citizens:

Justice, social, economic, and political;
Liberty of thought, expression, belief, faith, and worship;
Equality of status and opportunity;
And to promote among them all
Fraternity assuring the dignity of the individual and the unity and integrity of the nation;

The Preamble declares India as a sovereign nation, emphasizing its independent status. It also defines India as a socialist nation, committed to achieving social and economic justice for its citizens. The term "secular" denotes that India does not endorse any particular religion as the state religion and ensures freedom of religion to all its citizens. The Preamble further highlights India's commitment to democracy, emphasizing the participation of the people in decision-making processes. It proclaims India as a republic, signifying that the head of state is an elected representative rather than a hereditary monarch.

Integration of Princely States Ushered Nation in One

At the time of independence, India comprised two categories of political units, such as British Provinces (under the direct rule of British government) and the princely states (under the rule of native princes but subject to the paramount of the British Crown). The Indian Independence Act 1947 created two independent and separate dominions of India and Pakistan and provides three options to the princely states joining India, joining Pakistan or remaining independent. Of the 552 princely states located within the geographical boundaries of India, 549 joined India and remaining 3 (Hyderabad, Junagarh and Kashmir) refused to join India. They were also integrated with India – Hyderabad by means of Police action, Junagarh by means of referendum and Kashmir by the Instrument of Accession. In 1950, the constitution contained a fourfold classification of the states and territories of the Indian Union – Part A, Part B, Part C State and Part D territories. They count as 29; Part A states comprised nine erstwhile governor's provinces of British India. Part B consisted of nine erstwhile princely states with legislatures. Part C, states consisted chief commissioner's provinces of British India and some of the princely states. Part C states were centrally administered; in which Andaman and Nicobar Islands were kept as solitary Part d territories.

State Part A	***State Part B***	***State Part C***	***State Part D***
Assam	Hyderabad	Ajmer	Andaman & Nicobar Islands
Bihar	Jammu & Kashmir	Bhopal	
Bombay	Madhya Bharat	Bilaspur	
Madhya Pradesh	Mysore	Coach Behar	
Madras	Patiala and East Punjab	Coorg	
Orissa	Rajasthan	Delhi	
Punjab	Saurashtra	Tripura	
United Provinces	Travancore Coachin	Kutch	
West Bengal	Vindhya Pradesh	Manipur	
		Himachal Pradesh	

Table 1 Territory of India in 1950[7]

Vitality of Fundamental Rights and Directive Principles of State in Democratic Nation

The Constitution guarantees some fundamental liberties to all individuals, both individually and collectively. These are safeguarded by the Constitution within the six rationalized categories of Fundamental Rights. Part III of the Constitution deals with Fundamental Rights under the Articles 12 to 35. These are: Right to equality, including equality before law, prohibition of discrimination on grounds of religion, race, caste, sex or place of birth, and equality of opportunity in matters of employment.

1. Right to Freedom of speech and expression, assembly, association or union, movement, residence and right to practice ant profession or occupation (some of these rights are subjects to security of the state, friendly relations with foreign countries, public order, decency or morality).
2. Right against exploitation, prohibiting all forms of forced labor, child labor and traffic in human beings.
3. Right to freedom of conscience and free profession, practice and propagation of religion.
4. Right of any section of citizens to conserve their culture, language and right of minorities to establish and administer educational institutions of their choice.
5. Right to constitutional remedies for enforcement of fundamental Rights.[8]

{Note: In 1978 the Right to Property was deleted from the list of Fundamental rights}

Directive Principles of State Policy

Directive Principles of State Policy are a set of guidelines or principles laid down in the Constitution that direct the government to pursue certain social, economic, and political objectives for the welfare of the people. Though not enforceable by the courts, they serve as a moral and political compass for the government. The Directive Principles cover a wide range of areas, including:

a. Social Welfare

- The provision of basic means of subsistence - the provision of equal remuneration to men and women

- Promotion of educational and economic interests of scheduled castes, scheduled tribes, and other economically disadvantaged groups - Protection of the health and strength of workers`

b. Fiscal policies Distribution of resources and wealth for the benefit of all.

- Safeguarding the rights of employees

c. Legal and Judiciary Reforms:

- Separation of the judiciary from the executive

- Promotion of justice on the basis of equal opportunity

d. Environment Protection

- Maintaining and improving the environment

- Adherence to international law and values comprises environmental protection

Directive Principles act as guidance for the government's policy- and decision-making, whereas Fundamental Rights are justifiable and subject to enforcement by the judiciary. However, over time, the courts have recognized the importance of Directive Principles in interpreting laws and ensuring social justice, and they may be considered while examining the constitutional validity of legislation. The welfare of the women, the scheduled castes and tribes and other backward sections had also to be advanced on the part of the administration in terms of the Directive Principles and also Fundamental Rights mentioned in the Constitution.[9]

Federal System of India Determine the Administrative Harmony

The parliamentary democracy in India has provided origin to a framework for representative administration, accountability, and peaceful transition of power. It allows for public participation, deliberation, and checks and balances to uphold democratic principles and protect the rights and interests of the citizens. The Act of 1919 introduced India 'diarchy', which can be regarded, as a first step towards federalism in British India. Further, the enactment of the Government of India Act, 1935 specifically provided for provincial autonomy.[10] When the Constituent Assembly met in 1946, it was agreed upon to have a federal form of government in India. The Constitution of India incorporated many provisions of 1935 Act, but without using the word 'federalism' anywhere in its text.

Legislature Process

The legislatives powers are divided into three exhaustive lists, as per the Seventh Schedule. These lists are Union List, State List, and Concurrent List. The Union List included 97 subjects and now has 100 subjects. Some of these include defense, war & peace, railways, foreign affairs, etc. The State list, which had 66 subjects initially and now, has 61 subjects, such as public health, agriculture, police, irrigation, prisons, etc. are the ones on, which the states are free to legislate. The Concurrent List, which earlier had 47 subjects and now include 52 subjects, are the ones on, which both the Union and State governments can legislate.

However, in case of conflict, the Centre prevails. Residuary subjects in the Constitution have been left with the Union government, which refers to a subject that is not included in any of the three lists. As per Article 249, the Rajya Sabha can pass a resolution by two-third majority of its members present and voting that a particular subject in the state list is of national importance and need to be transferred to Parliament to legislate. Moreover, during emergency Parliament gets power to legislate on the entire state subjects. As per Article 250, such legislation ceases to have any effect after expiry of six months of the ceasing of emergency. Similarly, the Union Parliament may also legislate on any State subject, if the legislatures of two or more States require the Parliament to do so.

Administrative Framework

Articles 257, 258, 262, and 263 of the Indian Constitution deals with the administrative arrangement between centre and states. Article 257 provides that the states will exercise their executive powers in such a way, as not to impede or prejudice the exercise of executive powers of the Union. The Government of India may give directions to a State, as may appear to it necessary for the purpose. Article 258 provides that the President can conditionally or unconditionally entrust to the states functions to, which the executive power of the Union extends. Article 262 empowers the President to provide the law for adjudication of any dispute among States with respect to the use, distribution, and control of river waters. Article 263 deals with the establishment of an Inter-State Council. All these provisions do ensure a cordial relationship between the two levels of government. However, during an emergency, the power to give directions to the state vis-à-vis the exercise of executive power relating to any matter rests with Centre.

Financial Structure

Under The federal set up, The Constitution's Articles 264 to 300 address how financial resources are distributed:

Exclusive Financial Sources of Union Government

The Union List lists the revenue streams that fall exclusively under the purview of the Union. The List includes corporate taxes, money, foreign exchange, customs and export fees, income taxes, estate taxes, posts and telegraphs, railroads, etc. Financial Sources of State Governments Taxes on consumption of electricity, revenue of goods other than newspapers, goods and passengers shipped by road or inland waterways, excise duty on goods produced or manufactured in the states, such as alcohol and opium, taxes on luxuries, and taxes on entertainment and amusements constitute some of the sources of revenue. Other taxes include duties on the succession of agricultural land, taxes on agricultural income, land revenue and taxes on land and buildings and land. Taxes Levied by the Union but Collected and Appropriated by States certain taxes are defined in Article 268 as being levied by the Union but collected and appropriated by the states. These are: Stamp duties on documents such as bills of exchange, checks, promissory notes, lending bills, letters of credit, insurance policies, transfers of shares, etc. Excise taxes on alcoholic and opium-containing pharmaceutical and toiletry products.[11]

Parliamentary Democracy Ensures Administrative Accountability

The Indian Constitution divides the government's power into three separate independent organs: the Legislature, the Executive, and the Judiciary. Again, the Indian Constitution established a parliamentary system of government at both the national and state levels. The Union of India's legislative authority is vested in Parliament. The President of India and the two Houses, the Rajya Sabha (Council of States) and the Lok Sabha, make up India's Parliament (House of the People). The Indian Independence Act of1947 declared the Constituent Assembly of India to be a fully sovereign body, and the Assembly assumed full governance of the country on the 14th and15th of August 1947, at midnight. The Constituent Assembly was given full legislative power under Section 8 of the Act.[11a] The Constituent Assembly agreed to the principle of a parliamentary executive that is collectively accountable to the House of Commons B.R. Ambedkar Chairman of the Drafting Committee, said in the Constituent Assembly on November 4, 1948, when introducing the Draft Constitution and recommending the parliamentary system, "The Draft Constitution in recommending the parliamentary system of executive has preferred more.

The parliamentary democracy which is enshrined in the Indian Constitution has numerous implications that have direct relevance to the accountability of public administration in the country:

1. The Supremacy of Parliament over the executive and the right of Parliament to review the working of administrative machinery;
2. The Collective responsibility of the council of Ministers to Parliament and the collaboration of major policies by the Cabinet;
3. The individual responsibility of each minister holding a portfolio for implementation and to ensure efficient working of the administrative machinery under his charge;
4. The Obligation of ministers as well as of civil servants to uphold the Constitution and rule of law;
5. The obligation of every civil servant to implement faithfully all policies and decisions of the ministers;
6. The freedom of civil servants to express themselves frankly giving advices to their superiors including ministers;
7. The observance by civil servants of the principles of political neutrality, impartiality and anonymity.

The Cabinet as Pinnacle of Administrative System

The Cabinet is the apex organ of the administrative hierarchy in a parliamentary democracy like In India. It formulates Policy of the Government, secure cooperation and coordination between different departments, and exercises general control over the entire administration. In the words of the Administrative Reform Commission (1966 – 70), the cabinet is responsible for the final determination of Policies and as well as the overall direction, coordination and supervision of the business of Government and its administrative organization. The function of Cabinet also reflected in Haldane Report of the machinery of Government Committee.

1) The supreme control of the national executive through parliamentary approval on certain policies.

2) Submission to the parliament is the Policy's ultimate destination.

3) The ongoing coordination and division of the various government agencies. The Cabinet is the inner core of the council of ministers, the provision for which is made under Article 74 of the constitution. This article provides for a council of ministers with the Prime Minister at the head to aid an advice the president in the exercise of his powers. The President is nominal head, real power hold in council of ministers with the Prime Minister at the head. The council of Ministers is collectively responsible to the Lok Sabha and comprises three categories of Ministers – Cabinet Ministers, Ministers of State and Deputy Ministers. The Council of Ministers necessarily includes the Cabinet ministers and has in it the other two categories of Ministers. The council of ministers never meets as a body but it is bound by the decision of the cabinet.[12]

Under the direction of N. Gopalaswami Ayyangar, cabinet committees were formed to relieve the pressure on the cabinet. In their 1949 report, ***Reorganization of the Government Machinery***, they recommended the creation of Standing Committees of the Cabinet in particular fields, alongside the strengthening of their secretariats and other organs.

Cabinet Secretariat Maintains Coherence in Execution of Policies

In India, the Prime Minister's Office is administered by the administrative entity known as the Cabinet Secretariat. It acts as the primary coordinating body for the operations of the Indian Central Government. The Cabinet Secretariat is essential to enabling efficient decision-making and effective governance within the government. It offers administrative assistance to the Cabinet and its committees, who are in charge of determining various policy issues. The secretariat assists in the preparation and dissemination of the Cabinet meeting agendas, minutes, and records. Senior civil officers and advocates are part of the Cabinet Secretariat, which reports to the Cabinet Secretary, the highest-ranking civil servant in India. The Cabinet Secretary is the highest advisor to the Prime Minister and the Cabinet and is in charge of managing the secretariat's operations.[13]

The Cabinet Secretariat is crucial for India's effective government at the national level in assisting the decision-making process. It provides a link between various government agencies, encouraging coordination and coherence in the execution of policies. The Cabinet Secretariat's primary responsibilities and duties are as follows:

- **Cabinet Coordination:** It fosters effective collaboration between the many government ministries and departments and coordinates their operations.

- **Policy Planning and Analysis:** The secretariat offers assistance in the creation and evaluation of government policies and initiatives. Regarding matters of policy, it offers suggestions and counsel to the Prime Minister and the Cabinet.

- **Administrative Support:** The Cabinet Secretariat offers the Cabinet and its committee's administrative support. It facilitates the development of Cabinet papers, keeps track of transactions, and ensures that decisions adopted by the Cabinet are carried out on schedule.

- **Inter-Ministerial Coordination:** This facilitates interaction and problem-solving between various departments and ministries. The secretariat fosters cooperation on policy problems and helps in the resolution of inter-ministerial disputes.

- **Intelligence and Security:** The Cabinet Secretariat is in charge of managing issues relating to intelligence and security. It collaborates with numerous intelligence agencies and offers the government advice on matters pertaining to national security.

Essential Decision Making Under Cabinet Committees

After the cabinet was established in the democratic system of India, cabinet committees constituted a development in cabinet government history. Cabinet committees are smaller government groups intended to examine particular policy concerns and make recommendations to the Cabinet. They are made up of senior ministers. These committees are significant decision-making bodies within the government and are created by the Cabinet or the Prime Minister. Depending on the requirements and goals of the government, the precise makeup and duties of the cabinet committees may change over time.

The Cabinet committees are a significant but informal innovation. The Cabinet in India has always operated through its committees; there were five cabinet committees in 1954.

1. The committee on foreign affairs
2. The Committee for Tele-communication
3. The Committee on Information and Broadcasting
4. The Housing Committee,
5. The Rehabilitation committee[13a]

Crucial Role of Prime Minister's Office in Government

The Prime Minister's Office (PMO) in India is the central administrative office of the Prime Minister of India. It serves as the nerve center for the Prime Minister's activities and plays a crucial role in coordinating and supporting the functioning of the government. Prime Minister's Office known as the prime Minister's Secretariat until 1977, was but a modest institution under the prime minister ship of Jawaharlal Nehru (1946 – 64). The Prime minister's office can be considered as an agency that helps the prime minister efficiently perform his role, responsibilities, and functions. Going back to the time, the first post of prime minister was created just after the independence of India in 1947.

Where the prime minister's office (PMO) can be considered as an extra-constitutional body that means there is no mention of PMO in constitution of India. For the first time in India, the PMO was considered as part of the Indian government in 1961 by the allocation of business rules in India. The PMO is headed by the secretary of the prime minister of India and the secretary has had this responsibility since 1977.

Functions of PMO

1. The PMO supports the Prime Minister in formulating policies, strategies, and programs for the government. It provides inputs, conducts research, and coordinates with various ministries and departments to develop comprehensive policies that align with the government's vision and priorities. The PMO also monitors and facilitates the implementation of government policies.

2. The PMO serves as a coordinating agency between different ministries and departments. It ensures effective communication, collaboration, and synergy among various government bodies to facilitate smooth governance. The PMO coordinates the flow of information, resolves inter-ministerial issues, and ensures timely decision-making.

3. The PMO acts as a liaison between the central government and the state governments. It facilitates cooperation, coordination, and collaboration between the two levels of government on policy matters, administrative issues, and development initiatives.[14]

Secretariat Serves as Operational Centre for Ministries and Departments

The entity that helps the government carry out its duties is called the Secretariat, which is an office. The secretariat has a crucial job to do. The administrative departments of the federal and state governments are referred to as the "secretariat" in everyday speech. It is the principal administrative entity in charge of assisting the government's operations and carrying out projects and policies. The Secretariat serves as the operational center for a number of ministries, departments, and agencies. It offers the tools, personnel, and resources required for the government to operate effectively. The number of departments and ministries expanded from 18 in 1947 to 78 in 1998.

The Secretariat performs a number of crucial tasks that are essential to the operation of the government, such as:

1. **Supporting the government's formulation of policies:** Programs and initiatives is the Secretariat's primary responsibility. It offers research, analysis, and administrative support for creating complete policies that are in line with the goals and priorities of the government.

2. **Facilitating Coordination and Communication:** The Secretariat helps departments and agencies coordinate and communicate. It serves as a forum for departmental cooperation, ensuring integration and coherence in the application of policies.

3. **Administrative Support:** Through the management of official records, facilitation of inter-ministerial correspondence, and planning of meetings and events, the Secretariat offers administrative support to the government. It helps with the creation and distribution of official documents such as notices, orders, and other papers from the government.

4. **Monitoring of Implementation:** The Secretariat keeps an eye on how government initiatives, programs, and policies are being carried out. To promote efficient execution and timely goal achievement, it monitors progress, identifies bottlenecks, and gives input to the relevant ministries and departments.

5. **Settlement with External Stakeholders:** The Secretariat acts as a point of contact for a range of stakeholders, including other governments, international organizations, and the general public. On behalf of the government, it communicates with these parties, sustains diplomatic ties, and plans global events.

A D Gorwala Committee Report (1951) Formed to Evaluate the Implementation Initiatives

The Committee on Plan Projects, popularly known as the A. D. Gorwala Committee, was established in India in 1951. It was given that name in honor of its chairman, the well-known economist and government official Ardeshir Dalal Gorwala. The committee was formed to assess the status of plan projects in India and offer suggestions for their successful execution. India was then beginning to put its first Five-Year Plan, which intended to encourage economic growth and development in the nation, into effect. Reports on Public Administration and Report on the Efficient Conduct of State Enterprises were the two reports he submitted. Among his crucial recommendations, the following stand out: (a) establishing a government O&M unit with a two-member board.

Designed to give management the inspiration and guidance it needs. (b) Training must not only encourage the civil servant to view his work in the broadest context and to continue with his own educational development, but also to encourage precision and certainty in the conduct of business and to boost staff morale. Gorwala's recommendations to establish an O&M branch within the government were accepted by the Indian government.

The A. D. Gorwala Committee was charged with evaluating the successes and difficulties encountered in the implementation of Plan initiatives across a range of industries, such as agriculture, industry, infrastructure, and social services. The committee offered suggestions for enhancing the execution of projects in light of its findings. Based on its findings, the committee made recommendations for improving the implementation of plan projects. It emphasized the need for efficient utilization of resources, the importance of balanced regional development, and the integration of social and economic objectives. The committee's recommendations aimed to strengthen the planning process and enhance the impact of development efforts in India. The A. D. Gorwala Committee played a significant role in shaping the early stages of India's planning process. The committee's work helped in refining the approach to economic planning and development in India, laying the foundation for future initiatives in the field.[15]

How Paul H Appleby's Report s enhance administrative operations and exercises

Two papers written in 1953 and 1956 by American public administration expert Paul H. Appleby marked a turning point in the history of administrative reforms. His group advocated the creation of an O&M division as one of the twelve recommendations he presented, which would enhance the nation's administrative practices. The Indian government only accepted two. The first involved creating an O&M (entity and Methods) entity within the national government, and the second involved creating a training facility, specifically the India Institute of Public Administration, which was created for promoting research in public administration. For the purpose of advancing administrative knowledge, the Indian Institute of Public Administration for India shall act as the hub of a professional journal, the extension of studies, and the creation of literature.[16]

The first report, **Public Administration in India: Report of Survey 1953** confirms the Indian administrative system's high ranking among global administrative systems but is highly critical of its organizational design, personnel policies, financial and administrative practices, and capacity for completing development tasks rapidly. A special reference to the management of the government's industrial and commercial businesses was made in the second report, RE - EXAMINATION OF INDIA'S ADMINISTRATION SYSTEM 1956. It was addressing issues related to optimizing organizational structure, operational processes, hiring, and training in these businesses.

Planning Commission Amplified Nation's Material Resources and Productivity

The most prominent planning institution in India is the Planning Commission. Two characteristics were noted during this organization's establishment. In order to prevent it from becoming stagnant, it was first placed outside of the conventional Ministries and Departments. Secondly, a commission-type organization was purposefully chosen to provide the necessary flexibility for developing an appropriate internal structure in response to emerging needs. The commission's original objective was to increase the standard of life for common Indians by effectively utilizing the nation's human and material resources, boosting productivity.

It was in charge of conducting yearly assessments of the nation's resources; creating five-year plans and implement it; and keeping checks on how the plans are being carried out, as well as suggesting policy changes. The country's first five-year plan was launched in 1951. It was established on 15 March 1950, The commission is chaired by India's prime minister and includes a deputy chairman and several full-time members. Each of the numerous divisions of the commission, corresponding to sectors of the national economy and society, is headed by a senior officer. The divisions include education, health, infrastructure, science, financial resources, industry, social welfare, rural development, and water resources. It was set up by a Resolution of the Central Government which mentioned its functions as:

1. Developing five-year plans for the most efficient and equitable use of the nation's resources.

2. Identifying measures to improve national resources and conducting an assessment of them.

3. Selecting the optimum equipment to guarantee the project's successful execution.

4. Setting the Plan's priorities.

5. Periodic assessment of the plan's development with a view to suggesting modifications, if necessary.

India's Planning Commission was a government organization tasked with creating five-year plans for the economic and social advancement of the nation. It was founded in 1950 and operated as an extra-constitutional body until 2014, when the National Institution for Transforming India, or NITI Aayog, took its place.[17]

The following were the commission's main duties:

1. Drafting five-year plans created detailed plans describing the nation's economic and social development objectives over five-year time frames. Sectors like agriculture, industry, infrastructure, education, health, and others were all addressed by these plans. The plans aimed to make an assessment of the nation's financial, material, and human resources, especially its technical workforce, and look into the potential for improving them.

2. Allocating resources for the nation's development; the Plan should be put into action and put forward the allocation of resources for the completion of every stage;

3. Based on the priorities and goals stated in the five-year plans, the Planning Commission distributed financial and other resources to various sectors to Make a capital, material, and human assessment.

4. To make the required corrections and alterations in succeeding plans, the commission analyzed the results of the plan's implementation and monitored its progress.[17a]

Finance Commission Imposes Financial Health of Nation

Finance Commission is a constitutional body for the purpose of allocation of certain revenue resources between the Union and the State Governments. It was established under Article 280 of the Indian Constitution by the Indian President. It was created to define the financial relations between the Centre and the states. It was formed in 1951. The core responsibility of the Finance Commission of India is to evaluate the state of finances of the Union and State Government, suggesting the share of taxes between them, formulating the principles determining the share of taxes between the States. The working of the Finance Commission of India is characterized by the seizable and rigorous consultation with all levels of government, hence reinforcing the principle of corporate federalism. The suggestions given by the Finance Commission were also regulated towards improving the quality of public spending and promoting fiscal stability. The First Commission was established in 1951 under The Finance Commission 1951. Fifteen Finance Commissions have been constituted since the promulgation of Indian Constitution in 1950.

Several provisions to bridge the fiscal gap between the centre and the states were already enshrined in the Constitution of India, including Article 268, which facilitates the levy of duties by the centre but equips the States to collect and retain the same. Similarly, Articles 269, 270, 275, 282 and 293, among others, specify ways and means of sharing resources between the Union and States. In addition to the above provisions, the finance commission serves as an institutional framework to facilitate Centre-State Transfers.[17b]

The purpose of the commission is described in Article 280 of the Indian Constitution as follows:

- The President shall establish a finance commission within two years of the Constitution's beginning and thereafter at the end of every fifth year or earlier, as deemed necessary by him/her;

• Parliament may by law specify the requirements for appointment as members of the commission and the method of selection.

• The commission was established to provide advice to the President regarding how to divide the net tax revenues between the Union and the States as well as among the States themselves. The finance commission has responsibility for defining the financial ties between the Union and the States. They also deal with the transfer of unexpected sources of income.[17c]

Pay Commission: Structure Duties and Compensation for Government Employees

The Government of India established the Pay Commission, to formulate recommendations for adjustments to the 1947-instituted compensation structure for its employees. Seven pay commissions have been established since India's independence on a regular basis to examine and propose modifications to the duties and compensation of all civil and military branches of the Indian government. The commission, which has its main office in Delhi (India), the commission, was given 18 months from date of its constitution to make recommendations. The pay commission is responsible for salary revisions of all the central government employees and pensioners and its decisions affect millions of people.

Pay Commission	Year	Chairman
First Pay Commission	1947-59	Srinivasa Varadachariar
Second Pay Commission	1959-73	Jaganath Das
Third Pay Commission	1973-87	Raghubir Dayal
Fourth Pay Commission	1987-96	P N Singhal
Fifth Pay Commission	1996-2006	Justice S Ratnavel Pandian
Sixth Pay Commission	2006-16	Justice BN Srikrishna
Seventh Pay Commission	2016-26	Justice Ashok Kumar Mathu

While reviewing the salary structure, the pay commission takes into account the prevailing economic conditions, inflation, fiscal position of government among various other factors. It is not mandatory for the government to accept the recommendations of the pay commission. The government may choose to accept or reject the recommendations. Pay commissions are usually constituted every 10 years and the first pay commission was set up in 1946. Since Independence, a total of seven pay commissions have been formed. The latest pay commission was set up in 2014 and its recommendations came into effect in 2016. Currently, central government employees and pensioners get the salaries based on recommendations of 7th pay commission.[17d]

National Development Council: Symbol of Federal Planning

The National Development Council (NDC) came into existence in August 1952 result issued from the cabinet secretariat. Its construction was recommended in the first five-year Plan. The National Development Council is one of the key organizations of the planning system in India. It symbolizes the federal approach to planning and is the instrument for ensuring that the planning system adopts a truly national perspective. The NDC has experienced numerous ups and downs in its fortunes. Its status has been determined by the prevailing political climate and the support provided to it by the government in power at the Centre and the effectiveness of the pressures exerted by state governments. Notwithstanding the vicissitudes that it has faced during the past six decades, its continuing presence in the apex policy structure has always been felt. Way back in 1946, the Planning Advisory Board under the chairmanship of KC Neogi, had recommended the setting up of an advisory organization that would include representatives of the provinces, princely states and other interests. Although this idea was not implemented before independence, its rationale was well appreciated.

The National Development Council's role:

- To periodically examine how the National Plan is operating.

- To take into account important social and economic policy issues that affects the development of the nation

- Periodic evaluation of the Plan's operation, including recommendations for improvements.

- Take measures that are required for achieving the goals and objectives in order to ensure that the populace actively participates and cooperates, increase the effectiveness of administrative services,

- The National Development Council was supposed to provide advice and recommendations to the Union and state governments.

- It has served as a powerful consultative group where the framework for the Five-Year Plans, significant issues affecting the Indian economy, and policies that have to be adopted for tiding over the urgent problems have been discussed and find solution for it. [18]

Administrative Reform Commission 1966 Evolve Methodical Public Administration System

The Government of India formed the Administrative Reforms Commission (ARC) in 1966 with the goal of researching the nation's public administration system and making recommendations for changes to increase its effectiveness and efficiency. Morarji Desai, who was serving as the Deputy Prime Minister and Minister of Finance at the time, served as the commission's chairman. The Indian government commissioned the Administrative Reforms Commission (ARC) in 1966 to research and make recommendations for the nation's administrative reform. It was the Indian government's first significant attempt to address problems with the way the administrative system and bureaucracy functioned.[19] On August 5, 1966, the ARC was founded, with Morarji Desai serving as its chairman. The commission included ten members, including lawmakers, government officials, and subject matter experts. The ARC's primary goal was to analyze the composition, administration, and effectiveness of the political system and make recommendations for improvements.

The main areas of attention for the ARC 1966 were as follows:

Organizational Structure: The commission examined the union, state, and municipal administrative structures in order to make recommendations for their rationalization and simplification to improve efficiency and coordination. Recruitment, training, promotion, and career development of civil officials were among the many facets of personnel administration that the panel looked into. It recommended actions to guarantee an effective and merit-based civil service.

Financial Management: The commission looked at how government agencies handled their finances and made reform recommendations to improve responsibility, openness, and effectiveness.

Administrative Procedures: The ARC 1966 examined bureaucratic practices and made recommendations for streamlining and standardizing administrative procedures to cut down on red tape, corruption, and delays.

Decentralization and Local Governance: The commission stressed the value of decentralization and made recommendations for ways to strengthen local governments' capacity for decision-making and service provision.

There were 537 significant recommendations in the 20 publications listed below. A report summarizing the implementation strategy based on these contributions from several administrative Ministries was sent to the Parliament in November 1977.

1. Problems of Redress of Citizens Grievances (Interim)

2. Machinery for Planning
3. Public Sector Undertakings
4. Finance, Accounts & Audit
5. Machinery for Planning (Final)
6. Economic Administration
7. The Machinery of GOI and its procedures of work
8. Life Insurance Administration
9. Central Direct Taxes Administration
10. Administration of UTs & NEFA
11. Personnel Administration
12. Delegation of Financial & Administrative Powers
13. Centre-State Relationships
14. State Administration
15. Small Scale Sector
16. Railways
17. Treasuries
18. Reserve Bank of India
19. Posts and Telegraphs
20. Scientific Departments

The following were the main factors that the first ARC report involved:

- Problems with the redress of citizens' complaints;
- The machinery of the Government of India and its processes or activities;
- The machinery for planning at all levels; Centre – State Relations
- Financial administration;
- Personnel administration;
- Economic administration;
- Administration at the State level;
- District administration;
- Agricultural administration.[19a]

Developing Unity and Integrity through Building Centre - State Relation

"The Indian Constitution is a federal Constitution in as much as it established what may be called a dual polity which will consist of the Union at the Centre and the States at the periphery each endowed with sovereign powers to be exercised in the field assigned to them respectively by the Constitution." - D.R. Ambedkar

The Sarkaria Commission, formally known as the "Commission on Centre-State Relations," was a government-appointed body in India established in 1983. The commission was formed to examine and suggest ways to improve the relationship and balance of power between the central government and the state governments in the Indian federal system. The commission was named after its chairman, Justice R.S. Sarkaria, a retired judge of the Supreme Court of India. The other members of the commission included Justice M.M. Punchhi and Shri B.Sivaraman. The Sarkaria Commission operated from 1983 to 1988 and submitted its report to the government in 1988. The primary objective of the Sarkaria Commission was to address issues related to the distribution of powers, responsibilities, and resources between the central government and the state governments. It aimed to provide guidelines and recommendations to strengthen cooperative federalism in India.[20]

Sarkaria Commission discusses 247 recommendations that are maintaining national integrity and unity and it was identified as the preventable problems in India. From this commission, the posting of judges of the High court before their permission. By this commission, article 263 stated that the performed duties of councils through the president. The Sarkaria commission suggested the following jurisdiction on the concurrent menu among the state governments before applying the legislation to them. This commission suggested federalism arrangements as a cooperative activity in administrative manners in the states of India.

The following list includes a few of the Sarkaria commission's recommendations:

- The zonal councils should be established, revitalized, and reorganized to support the federalist atmosphere.
- While it is preferable that the states be consulted, the central government should have the power to deploy its military forces even without their approval.
- The council of ministers has a majority in the parliament and is not subject to dismissal by the governor.

Through Part XI of the Indian Constitution, the Center-State is in control. Legislative and administrative alliances make up this group. Laws that apply to financial transactions are also found in Part XII. Continuing below is a thorough examination of each of the three components of the center-state relationship.

Legal Relations

The legislative relationships between the Union and the states, specifically the Parliament and state legislatures, are covered in Articles 245 and 255. It examines the range of legislative authority held by the Union and the states. When the provisions are examined, it becomes clear that the Parliament has supremacy over state legislatures. The various clauses specify a variety of topics, as well as the effects of inconsistencies between state and federal law, the residuary powers of the Parliament, and many other things. The Union List, State List, and Concurrent List are all covered in Schedule VII.

Administration Relations

The administrative relations between the Central Government and several state governments are covered in Articles 256 to 263. India is federal, although it also has unitary traits, as stated in Article 256. Governments are responsible for making sure they abide by the legislation established by Parliament and refrain from carrying out any executive or administrative duties in contravention of those laws. Controlling Center-State relations requires a strong focus on administrative relations. Articles 256 and 257, as well as 356 and 365, discuss the elements of relations between the Centre and the State. Under Articles 256 and 257, the Centre has the power to offer the State directives and instructions.

The entire goal of Article 356 is to ensure that a state is governed in cases where neither political party is able to do. Controlling Center-State relations requires a strong focus on administrative relations. Articles 256 and 257, as well as 356 and 365, discuss the elements of relations between the Centre and the State. Under Articles 256 and 257, the Centre has the power to offer the State guidelines and instructions.[21]

Financial Partnership

The Constitution's Articles 264 to 293 in Part XII deal with the Center's and the state's financial ties. Due to its federal structure, India upholds the principle of the separation of powers with regard to taxation, and it is the obligation of the federal government to distribute money to the states. The capacity of the Center and states to levy taxes is described in Schedule VII. It also includes several rules for the collection and distribution of taxes by the federal government and the states, as well as for grants to the states and surcharges. The Goods and Services Tax, a dual structure tax, is a current illustration of a link between financial centers and states.

Directives from the union to state governments

According to Article 256, the union has the authority to direct the states and require them to follow those directions. The Union has the ability to rule a state to the extent that it deems it necessary for the goal. For instance, the union may provide the state instructions on how to construct and maintain communication systems that have been given military or national importance, as well as how to safeguard the state's railways. This is essential for ensuring that laws are executed across the nation. If the instructions are not followed, the Union may invoke Article 356 to impose the President's rule in the state and take over the State administration.

Union duties being transferred to the states

According to Article 254, the President may assign to the state government duties pertaining to any topic coming under the jurisdiction of union executive power, either conditionally or unconditionally. In accordance with clause (2), Parliament may also delegate authority and responsibility to the state and employ the state apparatus to implement union laws. Additionally, a state may grant administrative responsibilities to the union with the agreement of the union government.

All India Services

In addition to national and state services, Article 312 of the Constitution calls for the creation of "All-India services" that are available to the union and the states alike. The state has the authority to revoke the Joint Public Service Commission's Constitution for Two or More States. The Constitution establishes a Joint Public Service Commission in addition to the Union Public Service Commission (UPSC) and the State Public Service Commission. The Parliament may enact legislation establishing a joint commission when two or more states concur to its formation by adopting a resolution in their respective legislatures. Intergovernmental interaction is encouraged by the Commission's organizational design. A provision in the Constitution also allows states to ask the UPSC for help in creating and carrying out joint recruitment strategies for any service that needs applicants.

Judicial Mechanism

Our federal government's integrated judicial system is one of its distinguishing characteristics. Despite having a federal form of government with two levels of administration and separate spheres of authority, there is no separate system for administering justice. The existence of a single integrated chain of courts, with the Supreme Court at the top of the hierarchy of courts, to administer both union and state legislation makes this evident.

Inter-State Council

India is a federation of states where the center plays a significant role but is also reliant on the states for the execution of policies. The Constitution has provisions to encourage intergovernmental collaboration and efficient state-federal discussions, guaranteeing that all significant national policies are developed through consultation, debate, and agreement. One such strategy is the creation of the Inter-State Council. The President is given the authority to define the nature of the Council's duties under Article 263 of the Constitution.[22]

Lokpal and Lokayukta for Effective Remedial System for Corruption

An important step in the history of Indian politics was the establishment of the Lokpal and Lokayukta, which provide a remedy for the corruption problem. It offers a strong and effective way to fight corruption across the board in government. The idea of a constitutional Ombudsman was first put out in Parliament by the former law minister Ashok Kumar Sen in the early 1960s. Dr. L. M. Singhvi also came up with the terms Lokpal and Lokayukta. The First Administrative Reform Commission issued proposals later in 1966 recommending the creation of two autonomous bodies at the union and state levels.

The Lokpal bill was enacted by the Lok Sabha in 1968 following the commission's recommendations, but it expired because of the dissolution of the Lok Sabha. The measure has since been introduced numerous times in Lok Sabha but has expired. Up to 2011, there were eight attempts to pass the Bill, however they were all unsuccessful. A commission to assess the operation of the Constitution was also established prior to 2011 and was led by M.N. Venkatachaliah. The Lokpal and Lokayukta were recommended for appointment by this commission. The commission further suggested that the Prime Minister be excluded from the Lokpal's purview.[23]

Later in 2005, the Veerappa Moily-led Second Administrative Reforms Commission made the suggestion that the Lokpal office be constituted right away. Despite the fact that none of these suggestions received the proper consideration, the administration established a group of ministers in 2011 under the leadership of the late President Pranab Mukherjee. These ministerial task forces studied the Lokpal Bill proposal and proposed countermeasures to combat corruption.[24]

The Lokpal and Lokayukta Bill, 2013, were passed by both Houses of Parliament as a result of the demonstrations and campaign. On January 1, 2014, the President gave his assent to the bill, which was then given the name "The Lokpal and Lokayukta Act 2013" and went into effect on January 16, 2014.

Emergence of Local Government: Distribute Authority and Decision Making

In India, the term "local self-government" refers to a system of government that gives local bodies the authority to run and control their particular domains. It is a crucial part of India's democratic system and strives to distribute authority and decision-making to the populace at large.[25] Local self-government is acknowledged as a basic component of the Indian government system in the constitution.

The Panchayati Raj organizations and the Municipalities are the two main types of local self-government in India.

Institutions of the Panchayati Raj (PRIs): Local self-government organizations known as panchayati raj institutions work at the village, block, and district levels. They are essential in rural areas. PRIs' essential elements are:

A. **Gram Panchayat** is the institution at the village level in charge of local governance in rural areas. There are elected officials in it known as Panchayat members, and a Sarpanch (village chief) serves as its leader.

B. **Panchayat Samiti:** A Panchayat Samiti, also known as a Block Development Council, is constituted at the block level. It is made up of elected officials from the block's several Gram Panchayats.

C. **Zila Parishad:** At the district level, the Zila Parishad is made up of elected officials from the district's Panchayat Samitis. It coordinates and supervises how lower-level institutions run.[26]

Municipalities are the local self-government entities in charge of urban areas. They oversee and control towns and communities all around the nation. The following three categories of municipalities exist:

A. **Municipal Corporation**: In bigger urban areas, municipal corporations are founded. They have elected councilors who represent several wards within the city and a mayor person municipal commissioner who serves as the administrative head.

B. **Municipal Council:** In smaller urban areas, municipal councils are established. They elect a chairperson or President to serve as the administrative leader in addition to councilors.

C. **Nagar Panchayat:** These local governments are found in smaller towns. They have elected members representing several wards and a president who serves as the administrative head.[27]

Municipalities and Panchayati Raj institutions both have certain roles and responsibilities. These consist of local development project planning and execution, the provision of essential utilities like water supply, provision of healthcare and sanitary services, the collecting of local taxes, the upkeep of local facilities, and the promotion of social and economic wellbeing in their particular regions. The functioning and specific powers of local self-government bodies vary across states in India, as they have the flexibility to enact their own laws and regulations regarding local governance within the framework provided by the Constitution.

LOCAL SELF GOVERNMENT BEFORE INDEPENDENCE

Lord Mayo's Resolution (1870) and Lord Rippon's Resolution (1882) led to the current concept of democratic decentralization (rural local government). The Government of India Acts of 1919 and 1935, as well as the Report of the Royal Commission on Decentralization (1909), had made additional contributions in this area (Malik, 2002). To maintain and stabilize its political sway, the British government implemented a number of policies and recognized village panchayats. A special commission on local self-government was established in 1909, and its recommendations included the need to revitalize village Panchayats for managing local matters. In its 1909 report, the Decentralization Commission made some comprehensive recommendations to fix some of the flaws in how the Local Boards operated. A Government decision from 1915 endorsed the Commission's recommendations. However, once more, the provincial administrations did nothing about the situation. Following the Montague Declaration of 1917, which called for the gradual introduction of responsible government starting with local bodies, the government issued a Resolution in 1918. By 1919, rural self-government had been transferred under the provincial dyarchy system to the Indian ministries. We made some progress. In practically all provinces, laws were introduced to establish Panchayats in villages in addition to the Municipal and Local Boards Acts (Henry, 1970). Several Acts followed, including the United Provinces Village Panchayats Act of 1920, the Madras, Bombay, and Bengal Village Self-Government Acts, and the Bengal Village Self-Government Act of 1919. To address village difficulties and some issues pertaining to their development, various acts have been passed, including the Punjab Village Panchayats Act of 1935, the Bihar and Orissa Village Administration Act, the Assam Rural Self-government Act of 1926, and others. Provincial autonomy began operating in the provinces as of April 1937 under the Government of India Act, 1935.[28]

Figure 1: Local Self Government before Independence

Committees Related Panchayati Raj

A committee was established by the Indian government in January 1957 to review the performance of the National Extension Service (1953) and Community Development Programme (1952) and make recommendations for improvements. In November 1957, the committee published its findings and proposed the implementation of the "democratic decentralization" plan, subsequently known as Panchayati Raj. Balwant Rai Mehta served as this committee's chairman.

Committee of Balwant Rai Mehta

Gram Panchayats at the village level, Panchayat Samitis at the block level, and Zila Parishads at the district level make up the three tiers of the Panchayati Raj system that the committee advocated. Decentralized governance and effective representation were goals of this arrangement. The Panchayat Samiti and Zila Parishad should be made up of members who were elected indirectly, but the Village Panchayat should be made up of representatives who were directly elected. The Zila Parishad should serve as the advising, coordinating, and supervisory body, with the Panchayat Samiti serving as the executive body. The chairman of the zila parishad should be the district collector.

Democratic Elections: The committee stressed the significance of holding fair elections at all Panchayati Raj institution levels. It was suggested that adult suffrage be used for these elections, granting the right to vote to every adult citizen.

Devolution of Powers: The committee emphasized the necessity to transfer sufficient authority and accountability to governmental organizations. It suggested giving these organizations control over specific duties, resources, and employees currently performed by the state government so they can make decisions and carry out local development initiatives. Transfer of authority and accountability to these democratic entities is necessary.

Committee of Ashok Mehta

A committee on the Panchayati Raj institution was established by the Janata Government in December 1977, with Ashok Mehta serving as its head. It presented suggestions to strengthen and resuscitate the nation's ailing Panchayati raj system when it published its report in August 1978. Its suggestions are:-

Constitutional Status: In order to ensure the stability and independence of Panchayati Raj institutions, the committee suggested giving them constitutional status. To do this, the Constitution would need to be amended to establish explicit guidelines for their operations and authority.

Two Tier Systems of PRIs: The committee endorsed the three-tier system of Panchayati raj should be replaced by the two tier system, that is, zila parishad at the district level, and below it, the mandal panchayat consisting of a group of villages with a total population of 15000 to 20,000. A district should be the first point for decentralization under popular supervision below the state level. Zila parishad should be the executive body and made responsible for responsible for planning at the district level.

Devolution of Powers and Functions: The committee emphasized the significance of giving Panchayati Raj institutions sufficient power, responsibility, and funding. It suggested giving local organizations control over planning and overseeing development projects as well as financial resources.

Democratic Elections: The committee stressed the importance of holding legitimate elections on a regular basis at all Panchayati Raj institution levels. It suggested holding these elections with adult suffrage and making sure reservation of seats for underrepresented groups in society, such as women and members of scheduled castes and tribes.

State Election Commissions: To hold free and fair elections for Panchayati Raj institutions, the committee suggested creating State Election Commissions. These commissions would be in charge of monitoring the electoral procedures, drawing up constituency lines, and resolving any conflicts arising in elections. The

Panchayati raj elections shall be organized and run by the state's chief electoral officer in coordination with the chief election commissioner. Seats for SCs and STs should be reserved on the basis of their institutions.

Financial Resources: The committee stressed the requirement for institutions under the Panchayati Raj to strengthen their financial foundation. It suggested giving local bodies' access to their own sources of income, such as taxing authority, grants from the state government, and a cut of money coming from the federal government. PRIs should be granted mandatory taxing authority so they can raise money on their own.

G.V.K Rao Committee

The Committee to review the existing Administrative Arrangement for Rural Development and Poverty Alleviation Programmes in 1985 under the chairmanship of G.V.K Rao was appointed by Planning Commission in 1985. The Committees came to conclusion that the developmental process was gradually bureaucratized and separated from the Panchayati Raj. This phenomenon of bureaucratization of development administration as against the democratization weakened the Panchayati raj institutions Hence, the committee made the following recommendation to strengthen and revitalize the Panchayati Raj system:

1. The zila parishad, a district-level body, shall play a key role in the democratic decentralization plan. "The district is the proper unit for planning and development of the zila," it was mentioned.

2. All development programs that can be managed at that level should be managed by Parishad as the primary body.

3. The planning, execution, and oversight of programs for rural development should be delegated to the Panchayati Raj Institution at the district and lower levels.

4. For efficient decentralized district planning, some state-level planning responsibilities should be shifted to district-level planning units.

5. A District Development Commissioner position has to be established. He should serve as the zila Parishad's main executive officer and be in charge of all the district-level development agencies.

6. Panchayati Raj institutions should be elected on a regular basis. It was discovered that 11 states had elections that were past due for one or more tiers.

Committee for L M Singhvi

The L.M. Singhvi-led committee was established by the Rajiv Gandhi administration to draft a concept paper on "Revitalizing Panchayati Raj Institutions for Democracy and Development." The following suggestion was made.

1. The Panchayati raj institutions ought to be acknowledged, safeguarded, and maintained by the constitution. The Indian Constitution should be amended to include a new chapter for this purpose. Their identity and integrity will become reasonably and significantly inviolate as a result. Additionally, it proposed constitutional clauses to guarantee frequent, fair, and open elections for Panchayati Raj bodies.

2. Nyaya Panchayats should be established for the cluster of villages.

3. To increase the viability of Gram Panchayats, the villages should be reformed. Additionally, it highlighted the significance of the Gram Sabha and referred to it as the epitome of direct democracy.

4. The village panchayats ought to receive more funding.

5. Judicial courts should be formed in each state to resolve disputes relating to Panchayati raj institutions' election, dissolution, and other operational issues.

Constitutionalization of Local Government

In an effort to strengthen Panchayati raj institutions, Rajiv Gandhi introduced the 64th constitutional Amendment Bill in the Lok Sabha in July 1989. Although the measure was adopted by the Lok Sabha in August 1989, the Rajya Sabha did not do so. The opposition fiercely opposed the law on the grounds that it aimed to increase centralization within the federal system. Soon after taking office in November 1989 as the National Front Government led by V.P. Singh as Prime Minister, the government declared that it would establish institutions. Under the leadership of V.P. Singh, a two-day meeting of state chief ministers was conducted in June 1990 to discuss issues pertaining to the development of the Panchayati raj bodies. [29]

The ideas for the presentation of a new constitutional amendment bill were adopted by the conference. As a result, in September 1990, a constitutional change bill was presented to the Lok Sabha. However, the bill expired as a result of the collapse of the administration. Narasimha Rao Administration issued the Constitutionalization of Panchayati raj bodies was once more taken into consideration under P.V. Narasimha Rao's premiership. In order to remove the contentious elements from the proposals, it significantly altered them. In September 1991, it filed a constitutional reform bill in the Lok Sabha. On 24 April 1993, this bill finally became law as the 73rd Constitution Amendment bill Act, 1992.[30]

Emergency Provision Protect Nation's Sovereignty, Unity and Integrity

Articles 154 to 360 of Part XVIII of the Constitution contain the emergency measures, which give the central government the ability to respond to any exceptional circumstance in an efficient manner. To protect the country's sovereignty, unity, integrity, and security as well as the democratic political system and the Constitution, this clause was incorporated into the Constitution. In times of emergency, the central government assumes absolute power, and the states are completely under its control. It formally amends the Constitution to change the federal system into a unitary one. The Indian Constitution is unique in that it allows for this kind of shift in the political system from federal in normal times to unitary in times of emergency.[31] In the Constituent Assembly, BR. Ambedkar made the following observation:

All federal systems including American are placed in a tight mould of federalism. No matter what the circumstances, it cannot change its form and shape. It can never be unitary. On the other hand, the Constitution of India can be both unitary as well as federal according to the requirements of time and circumstances. In normal times, it is framed to work as a federal system. But in times of Emergency, it is so designed as to make it work as though it was a unitary system.

Three categories of emergency are listed in the Constitution:

1. An emergency due to war, external aggression or armed rebellion (Article 352). This is popularly known as National Emergency. However, the Constitution employs the expression; proclamation of emergency to denote an emergency of this type.

2. An emergency due to the failure of the constitutional machinery in the states: (Article 356). This is popularly known as 'President Rule'. It is also Known by two other names – 'State Emergency' or 'Constitutional Emergency'. However, the constitution does not use the word 'emergency' for this situation.

3. Financial Emergency due to a treat to the financial stability or credit of India (Article 360).

National Emergency

Under Article 352, the President can declare a national emergency when the security of India or a part of it is threatened by war or external aggression or armed rebellion. It may be noted that the president can declare a national emergency even before the actual occurrence of war or external aggression or armed rebellion, if he is satisfied that there is an imminent danger. The President can also issue different proclamations on grounds of war, external aggression, armed rebellion, or imminent danger thereof, whether or not there is a proclamation already Issued by him and such proclamation is in operation. This provision was added by the 38th Amendment Act of 1975. When a national emergency is declared on the ground of war or external aggression, it is known as External Emergency. On the other hand, when it is declared on the ground of armed rebellion it is known as Internal Emergency. A proclamation of the national emergency may be applicable to the entire country or only a part of it. The 42nd Amendment Act of 1976 enabled the president to limit the operation of a National Emergency to a specified part of India.

India during Emergency (1975 -1977)

THE TIMES OF INDIA

STATE OF EMERGENCY DECLARED

Several leaders arrested

Security in peril, says P.M.

Rights suspended

Situation peaceful

Barooah blames opposition

When Prime Minister Indira Gandhi declared Emergency in India 1975

The Constitution lists internal disturbance as the third justification for declaring a national emergency, but the wording is too ambiguous and has a broader meaning. Thus, the 44th Amendment Act of 1978 changed the phrase "internal disturbance" to "armed rebellion." As a result, it is no longer possible to declare a national emergency based on domestic unrest, as the Congress administration led by Indira Gandhi did in 1975. However, the President cannot declare a national emergency without the cabinet's explicit approval. This means that the emergency may only be proclaimed with the cabinet's approval and not just on the prime minister's recommendation. In 1975, the president was counseled by the then-prime minister, Indira Gandhi. This precaution was included by the 44th Amendment Act of 1978 to completely rule out the idea of the prime minister acting alone in this matter.[32]

The declaration of a national emergency is exempt from judicial review under the 38th Amendment Act of 1975. This clause was later removed, nevertheless, by the 44th Amendment Act of 1978. Additionally, the Supreme Court ruled in the Minerva Mill case (1980) that the declaration of a national emergency might be contested in court on the theory of malafide or that the assertion is ludicrous or twisted, or that it is entirely unnecessary and irrelevant. There have already been three declarations of this kind of Emergency: in 1962, 1971, and 1975.

Impact of National Emergency

The political system is drastically and broadly affected by a declaration of emergency. Three categories can be made from these effects:

Center-State Relationships

While the Emergency Proclamation is in effect, the normal framework of relations between the Center and the State changes fundamentally. Three categories, namely executive, legislative, and financial, might be used to analyze this.

(a) **Executive:** During a national emergency, executive power of the Centre extends to directing any state regarding the manner in which its executive power is to be exercised. In normal times, the Centre can give executive directions to a state only on certain specified matters, however, during a national emergency; the centre becomes entitled to give executive directions to a state on any matter. Thus, the state governments are brought under the complete control of the centre, though they are not suspended.

(b) **Legislative:** During a national emergency, the Parliament becomes empowered to make laws on any subject mentioned in the State List. Although the legislative power of a state legislature is not suspended, it becomes subject to the overriding power of the Parliament. Thus, the normal distribution of the legislative powers between the Centre and states is suspended, though the states Legislature are not suspended. In brief, the Constitution becomes unitary rather than federal. The laws made by Parliament on the state subjects during a National Emergency become inoperative six months after the emergency has ceased to operate. Notably, while a proclamation of national emergency is in operation, the President can issue ordinances on the state subjects also, if the Parliament is not in session. Further, the Parliament can confer powers and impose duties upon the Centre or its officers and authorities in respect of matters outside the Union List, in order to carry out the laws made by it under its extended jurisdiction as a result of the proclamation of a National Emergency.

(c) **Financial:** while a proclamation of national emergency is in operation, the President can modify the constitutional distribution of revenues between the Centre and the states. This means that the president can either reduce or cancel the transfer of finances from Centre to the states. Such modification continues till the end of the financial year in which the Emergency ceases to operate. Also, every such order of the President has to be laid before both the Houses of Parliament.[33]

Parliament Consent and Duration

The proclamation of Emergency must be approved by both the Houses of Parliament within one month from its date of its issue. Originally, the period allowed for approval was reduced by the 44th Amendment A of 1978.However, if the proclamation of emergency is issued at a time when the Lok sabkha has dissolved or dissolution of the Lok Sabha takes place during the proclamation, then the proclamation survives until 30 days from the first sitting of the Lok Sabha after its reconstitution, provided the Rajya Sabha has in the meantime approved it. If approved by both the Houses of Parliament, the emergency continues for six months, and can be extended to an indefinite period with an approval of the Parliament indefinite was also added by the 44th Amendment Act of 1978. Before that, the emergency, once approved by the Parliament, could remain in operation as long as the Executive (cabinet) desired parliamentary approval However, if the dissolution of the Lok Sabha takes place during the period of six months without approving the further continuance of Emergency, then the proclamation survives until 30 days from the first sitting of the Lok Sabha after its reconstitution, provided the Rajya Sabha has in the mean-time approved its continuation.

Every resolution approving the proclamation of emergency or its continuance must be passed by either House of Parliament by a special majority that is, (a) a majority of the total membership of that house, and (b) a majority of not less than two-thirds of the members of that house present and voting. This special majority provision was introduced by the 44th Amendment Act of 1978. Previously, such resolution could be passed by a simple majority of the Parliament. Effect on the Life of the Lok Sabha and State Assembly While a proclamation of National Emergency is in operation, the life of the Lok Sabha may be extended beyond its normal term (five years) by a law of Parliament for one year at a time (for any length of time). However, this extension cannot continue beyond a period of six months after the emergency has ceased to operate. For example, the term of the Fifth Lok Sabha (1971-1977) was extended two times by one year at a time.

Suppression of Fundamental Rights

The impact of a National Emergency on Fundamental Rights is discussed under Articles 358 and 359 of the Constitution. Other Fundamental Rights (apart from those guaranteed by Articles 20 and 21) are suspended by Article 359, whereas the Fundamental Rights guaranteed by Article 19 are suspended under Article 358. Here is a description of these two clauses:

The six essential rights under Article 19 are immediately suspended with the declaration of a national emergency, according to Article 358. Their suspension does not require a separate court order. The limitations imposed by Article 19 do not apply to the state when a proclamation of a national emergency is in effect. In other words, the state is free to enact any law or exercise any executive authority that undermines the rights protected by Article 19. Automatically, Article 19 is reinstated and is put into effect. When the National Emergency is lifted and normal operations resume, any law passed during the Emergency that is in conflict with Article 19 is revoked.

The measures made by the executive and legislative branches during the emergency cannot be contested even after it has ended, however, because there is no redress for anything done during the emergency even after it has ended. The 44th Amendment Act of 1978 placed two limitations on the application of Article 358. First, only when the National Emergency is declared on the basis of war or external attack and not on the basis of armed revolt, may the six Fundamental Rights under Article 19 be suspended. Second, no other laws—only those that are relevant to the Emergency are shielded from legal review. Also protected is executive action that is only taken in accordance with such a statute.

Suspension of other fundamental Rights **Article 359** authorizes the president to suspend the right to move any court for the enforcement of Fundamental Rights during a National Emergency. This means that under Article 359, the fundamental Rights are such not suspended, but only their enforcement. Rights are theoretically alive but the right to seek remedy is suspended. The suspension of enforcement relates to only those Fundamental Rights that are specified in the presidential order. It should be laid before each House of Parliament for approval. While a Presidential order is in force, the state can make any law or can take any executive action abridging or taking away the specified fundamental Right.

44th Amendment Act of 1978 restricted the scope of Article 359 in two ways. Firstly, the President cannot suspend the right to move the court for the enforcement of fundamental rights guaranteed by Articles 20 to 21. In other words, the right to protection in respect of conviction for offences remains enforceable even during emergency. Secondly, only those laws which are related with the emergency are protected from being challenged and no other laws and the executive action taken only under such a law, is protected.[34]

How Articles 358 and 359 Works

- While Article 359 covers all Fundamental Rights whose execution is suspended by the Presidential Order, Article 358 is limited to only those under Article 19 of the Constitution.
- As soon as an emergency is proclaimed, Article 358 automatically suspends the fundamental rights under Article 19. However, Article 359 does not compel the suspension of any Fundamental Rights. The president is only given the authority to halt the application of the specific Fundamental Rights.
- In contrast to internal emergencies, which are those that are announced due to armed revolt, article 358 only applies in cases of external emergencies (i.e., when the emergency is declared due to war or external aggression).
- Article 359, on the other hand, is applicable to both internal and external emergencies.

Article 358 allows the State to pass laws or carry out executive orders that are in conflict with Article 19's Fundamental Rights, while Article 359 allows it to do so in conflict with those Fundamental Rights whose enforcement the President has suspended. Additionally, there is a similarity between Articles 358 and 359.[35]

Difference between 42nd and 44th Amendment Act

42nd Amendment Act

1. 42nd Amendment Act also known as the "Mini Constitution" or "Constitutional Coup," it was enacted during the period of Emergency (1975-1977) in India.
2. It was introduced by the Indira Gandhi-led government and aimed to strengthen the power of the central government.
3. The 42nd Amendment Act made several changes to various parts of the Constitution, including the Preamble, Fundamental Rights, Directive Principles of State Policy, and the distribution of powers between the center and the states.
4. It added the words "Socialist," "Secular," and "Integrity" to the Preamble of the Constitution.
5. It curtailed certain Fundamental Rights, such as the Right to Property (Article 31) was removed from the list of Fundamental Rights and was made a legal right.
6. It gave precedence to the Directive Principles over Fundamental Rights.
7. It increased the term of the Lok Sabha and State Legislative Assemblies from 5 to 6 Years.
8. It restricted judicial review and curtailed the power of the judiciary.

44th Amendment Act

1. The 44th Amendment Act was enacted after the end of the Emergency, during the Janata Party government led by Morarji Desai.
2. It aimed to undo some of the changes made by the 42nd Amendment Act and restore democratic principles and fundamental rights.
3. The 44th Amendment Act sought to reinstate and strengthen several fundamental rights that were curtailed during the Emergency.
4. It restored the right to property as a fundamental right and limited the power of the government to acquire and confiscate property.
5. It removed the provision that gave precedence to Directive Principles over Fundamental Rights.
6. It restored the power of judicial review and strengthened the independence of the judiciary.
7. It amended Article 352 to ensure that a state of emergency can only be declared in case of an armed rebellion or an external aggression and not for internal disturbances.
8. It made several other changes, including limiting the term of the Lok Sabha and State Legislative Assemblies to 5 years, and reducing the minimum voting age from 21 to 18 years

Figure: Difference between 42nd and 44th Amendment Act

NOTE: Overall, the 42nd Amendment Act was seen as a controversial amendment that expanded the powers of the central government and restricted individual rights, while the 44th Amendment Act aimed to restore and protect fundamental rights, democratic principles, and judicial independence.

Supersession of Supreme Court Judges

The five o'clock news on All India Radio had reported that A.N. Ray had been named the new 14th Chief Justice of India in 1973, the day following the Kesavananda ruling. Justice Shelat, Hedge, and Grover had been overlooked by the President. After Chief Justice Shikri's retirement, they were next in line for the job according to the seniority system. Justice Beg was named CJI after Ray retired, replacing Justice Khanna, the senior-most judge on the court, probably in reprisal for Khanna's harsh dissent in ADM Jabalpur v. Shivakant Shukla 1976. Under Prime Minister Indira Gandhi, there were two well-known supersessions.

The Prime Minister had also dealt a blow to democratic constitutionalism by trying to subjugate the judiciary to her rule, which tipped the balance of power between the three arms of government. Extreme power centralized was what it was. During the 21-month period between 1975 and 1977, there were strikes by attorneys' associations, anti-government rulings from several high courts, judge transfers, demotions, demolitions, and supersession so serious that it rendered the judge immortal. Resolutions were adopted in October 1975 at the "All India Civil Liberties Conference," denouncing the Emergency's arbitrary detentions and censorship and calling for the release of detainees and the restoration of civil liberties.[36]

Despite recommendations from the chief justice of the high court, the chief minister of Maharashtra, the CJI, and law minister H.R. Gokhale, another additional judge, Justice U.R. Lalit of the Bombay High Court, who had also ordered the release of a few detainees, was not confirmed as a permanent judge. Judges who made decisions in comparable habeas corpus cases experienced a similar outcome. Some examples were Justices D.M. Chandrashekar and M. Sadananda Swamy, who overturned the detention of political leaders from several different parties during the Emergency, including BJP leaders A.B. Vajpayee and L.K. Advani.

The majority decision said that since the fundamental right to personal liberty had been suspended, no one could seek any relief from a court, regardless of whether the order of detention was unlawful, malicious, or applied to the incorrect individual. The case was heard by Chief Justice of India A.N. Ray, Justices H.R. Khanna, M.H. Beg, Y.V. Chandrachud, and P.N. Bhagwati over the period of 37 working days from December 1975 to February 1976. Justice Khanna, however, disagreed with the majority ruling, disagreement with emergency costing him the position of chief justice. Although Justice Beg succeeded him as Chief Justice in 1977, he remained the senior Supreme Court judge. Justice Khanna submitted his resignation on the same day. Prior to this decision, Ram Jethmalani, who was the Bar Council of India's chairman at the time, had a MISA arrest warrant issued for him because of comments he made during the Palghat Lawyers Conference in Kerala on January 25, 1976.

Implementation of family planning policy

Congress Government Opted for Sterilization to Lower the Growth of Population

Mass sterilization became enmeshed in the main political problem India was facing during the 1970s, known as "the Emergency"— 21-month era that is regarded as the darkest in post-1947 Indian history. Family planning in India should be viewed in the broader framework of the effort to manage global population, which began in 1951 and reached its peak in 1977. The family planning program in India received the most foreign aid. Between 1972 and 1980, the World Bank loaned the Indian government US $66 million for sterilization. In truth, Western democracies pressured Indira Gandhi to start a mass sterilization campaign to reduce India's population.

After the Emergency was declared, the Western countries' lobby supported the sterilization program, despite the fact that her own advisors were opposed to it. The pressure from the outside world was so strong that in 1965, President Lyndon B. Johnson refused to give food aid to India, which was facing famine, until it agreed to provide incentives for sterilization. As a result, actions performed by the Indian government, including pushing

IUDs and sterilizations, can be considered as a reaction to pressure from institutions like the World Bank, International Planned Parenthood Federation, United Nations Fund for Population Activities, and USAID.[37]

Prime Minister Indira Gandhi changed the Constitution after declaring an emergency. National government was authorized to carry out family planning initiatives under the 1976 Constitution Act. Soon after, the central government organized the political leadership of the states and took prompt action, such as establishing camps and sterilizing targets. Force was indirect as well as physical in nature. The government sent out circulars informing workers that promotions and salary were on hold until they underwent sterilization or reached their allocated quota of those, who are successfully persuaded to get sterilized. To receive their salary or even renew their driving licenses, rickshaw, scooter, or sales tax registration, people had to present a sterilization certificate. Students who did not have sterilized parents were held in detention.

Curbing freedom of Press and Censorship

THE HINDU

President Proclaims National Emergency

"Security of India Threatened by Internal Disturbances"

Preventive Arrests: Press Censorship Imposed

PM Explains Action

During Emergency Ruling party-imposed Press censorship and curbs freedom

Prime Minister Indira Gandhi suspended civil rights, including the freedom of the press, and changed and revised the Constitution. Under the draconian administration of the Indira Gandhi regime, journalists, opposition figures, and activists were imprisoned during the emergency. The emergency dealt the nation's democratic values, which it had cherished since gaining independence, a severe blow. In order to manipulate and control the press and stifle public opinion, the administration proclaimed an emergency and invoked press censorship. In India at the time, the Press was the only privately owned mass media outlet because the government had control over both radio and television.

"The President issued an Emergency Proclamation. There is no need for concern, Indira Gandhi said on All India Radio. While circumstances drastically altered and India faced a constitutional crisis during the Emergency, press freedom took a severe turn. The printing facilities were raided and the publications were taken off the streets for the following two days as the right to free expression was curtailed. Newspaper bundles were seized as newspaper presses were raided and stopped. All of the nation's leading newspapers were unable to be published for the following few days. Several foreign correspondents were ejected by Gandhi, and more than 200 journalists were detained. [38]

Constitutional Bodies Promote Efficiency of Government

The three branches of government—executive, legislative, and judicial—are only briefly described in the very comprehensive writings known as Constitution. It was common practice for those who drafted the constitution to consider some institutions with such special significance that they were given their own section and were included in the final version of the law. The societies create the necessary institutional organizations, but these institutions must not be impacted by current political fervor and moods, which highlights the need for their control. The constitution's inclusion of these organizations shows how important they are to maintaining democratic values and promoting effective government.

The following institutions were established by the Indian Constitution.

1. The Comptroller and Auditor General of India (Articles 148 – 151)
2. The Election Commission (Article 324)
3. The Union Public Service Commission (Articles 315 -323)
4. The Attorney General of India (Article 76)
5. National Commission for Scheduled Castes (Article 338)
6. National Commission for Scheduled Tribes (Article 338 A)
7. National Commission for Backward Classes (Article 338 B)
8. The Special officer for Linguistic Minorities (Article 350 B)
9. The Finance Commission (Article 280 – 1)
10. The Official Language Commission (Article 344)
11. The State Public Service Commission (Articles 315 – 323)
12. The Advocate General for the State (Article 165)
13. Administrative Tribunals[39]

Liberalization Phase in 1991 as Renaissance of Indian Economy

Before Liberalization

Before the liberalization of 1991, the Indian economy followed a system of centralized planning and a mixed economy model, which was characterized by extensive government control, regulation, and protectionism. The result was that inflation reached its peak with daily use commodities becoming extremely expensive, striking people. Here are some key features of the Indian economy before 1991:

1. License Raj: A system known as the "License Raj," which involved an intricate network of industry licensing and permits, governed the Indian economy. Nearly every industry needed government licenses and permissions, which created bureaucratic red tape and corruption.

2. Limited Foreign Investment: Foreign investment in India was strictly regulated, and FDI was only allowed in certain areas.

3. State-led Planning: Through a number of Five-Year Plans, the government had a significant role in economic planning. These plans had three main objectives: resource distribution, production goal setting, and sector development priority setting. The government owned and ran many businesses and utilities, giving the public sector a considerable role.

4. Protectionism and Trade Barriers: The Indian economy was hampered by high import tariffs and onerous trade regulations. To shield native sectors from international competition, the government set import restrictions and licenses.

5. Import Substitution Industrialization (ISI): By restricting imports with high tariffs and quotas, the government pursued an import substitution policy with the goal of developing domestic industries. This strategy was designed to improve self-sufficiency and lessen reliance on imports.

Prior to 1991, the Indian economy was characterized by a highly controlled and protected economic environment with little involvement from the private sector and from foreign countries. The emphasis was on independence and import substitution, but these strategies produced a number of inefficiencies, administrative roadblocks, and a sluggish rate of economic expansion. In order to overcome these obstacles and expose the

Indian economy to market forces and global integration, liberalization reforms were implemented in 1991. India had to take a sizeable loan from the IBRD (International Bank for reconstruction and development) for $7 billion USD. It serves as the lending branch for both the World Bank and the IMF. A condition of receiving this financing was that India must liberalize its economic policy and allow for international trade.[40]

After Liberalization

The phrase "after the liberalization of 1991" refers to the government of India's 1991 economic opening and liberalization measures. Economic liberalization in India is often referred to as Neo liberalism and the opening up of the Indian economy. India had a system of centralized planning and a highly controlled economy prior to 1991. This economy was characterized by strong government control and protectionism. The Indian government implemented a number of initiatives to solve the crisis and revive the economy in 1991, when it was confronted with a serious balance of payments problem and a deteriorating economic condition. The Indian economy was significantly impacted by these policies.

They led to increased competition, improved productivity, and a greater integration of the Indian economy with the global markets. The liberalization policies played a crucial role in transforming India into a more open and market-oriented economy, attracting foreign investment, and fostering economic growth in the subsequent years. These reforms were primarily led by Dr. Manmohan Singh, who was the finance minister at the time.

The following were the main components of the liberalization policies:

1. **Abolition of the License Raj:** The government eliminated many administrative barriers and encouraged entrepreneurship by reducing the number of enterprises that needed industrial licenses. Capital goods imports and a reasonable governmental investment rate. With the exception of a few sectors like those producing alcohol, illegal narcotics, tobacco, hazardous chemicals, industrial explosives, aircraft, electronics, and medicines, the industrial licensing system was abolished.

2. **Deregulation and market-oriented reforms:** The government introduced efforts to deregulate a number of industries, including lowering limits on foreign investment (FDI), reducing government oversight of international trade and investment, and streamlining industrial and trade regulations. India permitted FII investment.

3. **International investment:** limitations were reduced, and the government urged international businesses to make investments in India. As a result, the nation experienced an injection of international cash and technology.

4. **Financial sector reforms:** Significant changes were made to the banking and financial sectors, including the construction of new private sector banks, the adoption of a more market-oriented interest rate structure, and the easing of foreign exchange controls.

5. **Budget reforms:** The government aimed to reduce the fiscal deficit by curbing public expenditure, rationalizing subsidies, and improving tax administration.

6. **Privatization:** To increase efficiency and lessen the burden on the public, the government began the privatization of state-owned firms.

Impact of Liberalization

The Indian economy and society were significantly impacted by the liberalization of 1991. It's crucial to remember that while liberalization sparked beneficial developments and economic progress, it also brought about a number of difficulties, including a rise in income disparity, environmental issues, and regional differences. These challenges remain crucial areas of emphasis for Indian policymakers. Here are a few important outcomes of the reforms for liberalization:

Economic Growth: The acceleration of India's economic growth was one of the most significant effects of liberalization. In the post-liberalization era, the average yearly GDP growth rate rose from an average of 3-4% in the pre-liberalization era to 6-7% on average. The reforms created new opportunities for investment, entrepreneurship, and competition, which boosted output and fueled economic growth.

Technology Inflow and Foreign Direct Investment (FDI): Liberalization measures drew foreign investment to India. International corporations were attracted to invest in India by the relaxation of FDI limits and the opening up of numerous sectors to foreign participation. New technologies, managerial know-how, and access to international markets were all made possible by this infusion of foreign finance.

Global Integration: Liberalization encouraged a greater degree of economic integration between India and the rest of the world. Import-export rules were loosened and trade obstacles were reduced. India's participation in international trade significantly increased, as did its economic ties to the rest of the world.

Industrial and Sectoral Transformation: Indian industry was restructured and modernized as a result of liberalization. The Permit Raj system was abolished, and the abolition of industrial licensing facilitated private sector participation and entrepreneurship. Many industries, including information technology, telecommunications, and services, grew quickly and entered the global marketplace.

Technological Development: India had a significant increase in the information technology (IT) and IT-enabled services sectors as a result of the entry of foreign businesses and the liberalization of the telecom sector. The expansion of the IT sector was essential in making India a center for software development and IT services on a worldwide scale.[41]

New Economic Policy 1991: Remove the Economic Rigidity in the Nation

India experienced a severe financial crisis in 1991. A critical Balance of Payments issue started the crisis. The crisis was used as a wonderful chance to overhaul the economy of the nation, its structure, and to implement significant reforms in economic policy. Stabilization measures and structural changes were implemented by the administration. While the former sought to reduce rigidities in the various Indian economic sectors, the latter sought to address deficiencies that had surfaced in fiscal and Balance of Payments advances. P V Narasimha Rao was India's Prime Minister at the time the New Economic Policy (NEP) was unveiled, and Dr. Manmohan Singh was the finance minister.

New Economic Policy's Objective

• Engage in 'globalization' and shift the economy toward a market-based system.

• Decrease inflation and correct payment imbalances. Boost the economy's growth rate and accumulate enough foreign exchange reserves.

• By removing unneeded regulations, stabilize the economy and turn it into a market economy.

• Remove unnecessary barriers to the free flow of commodities, capital, services, technology, human resources, etc. on a global scale.

• Increase the involvement of private parties in all areas of the economy.

The new economic strategy has three levels: liberalization, privatization, and globalization. During liberalization, there were several significant changes:

1) Commercial banks were given the authority to set interest rates. Previously, this was decided by the Reserve Bank of India.

2) The small-scale industry investment cap was increased to Rs. 1 crore.

3) The ability to import capital goods, such as machinery and raw materials, from other nations was granted to Indian enterprises.

4) The government already set the maximum production capacity for each industry. The industries now have the ability to diversify their production capacities and lower production costs. Industries are now free to make this decision depending on the needs of the market.

Major alterations took place during privatization:-

Sell PSUs shares to the general public and financial institutions. For instance, Maruti Udyog Ltd. shares were sold to private individuals.

1) A reduction in PSU investment 2) Selling PSUs to the Private Sector 3) The number of industries designated as public sector was bought down from 17 to just 3. These were transportation and railroads, nuclear energy, and mining of atomic minerals are these.

Globalization brought about significant alterations:-

1) A steady reduction in import and export taxes and customs duties will help India become more appealing to foreign investment.

2) Long-term commercial policy for longer periods of time saw the use of trade policy. The major aspects of the trade strategy are the removal of restrictions on international trade, a liberal policy, and encouragement of free competition.

3) Prior to 1991, a positive list of permissible imports governed imports into India. A condensed negative list took the place of the list starting in 1992. Nearly all capital and intermediate items were removed from the list of goods subject to import limitations.

4) The Indian rupee was given some degree of convertible status.

5) The foreign capital investment equity capital was increased from 40% to 100%. The harsh Foreign Exchange Regulation Act (FERA) was repealed and replaced with the Foreign Exchange Management Act (FEMA).[42]

Territorial Organization of States: To Foster Linguistic and Cultural Unity

Background

The nation of India was split up into a number of provinces and princely entities until it attained independence in 1947. After independence, these administrative divisions were reorganized into states, with language playing a significant role. There is little doubt that an ad hoc approach was used to integrate princely states with the rest of India. In India, linguistic state reform started in the 1950s and lasted throughout the 1960s. In order to foster linguistic and cultural unity, the main goal was to establish states where the majority of the populace spoke the same or a related language. Demands from numerous linguistic communities demanding representation and recognition drove this process. In 1953, when the state of Andhra Pradesh was created by dividing Telugu-speaking regions from the Madras Presidency, the first significant linguistic restructuring took place. The States Reorganization Act of 1956, which was a thorough reorganization of states based on linguistic lines, came after this.[43]

There has been a demand from different regions, particularly South India, for reorganization of states on linguistic basis. In June 1948, the Government of India appointed the linguistic Provinces Commission under the chairmanship of S. K Dhar to examine the feasibility of the matter. The commission submitted its report in December, 1948, and recommended the reorganization of states on the basis of administrative convenience rather on the linguistic agenda. This created much resentment and led to the appointment of another Linguistic Provinces Committee by the Congress in December, 1948. It consisted of Jawaharlal Nehru, Vallabhbhai Patel and Pattabhi Sitaramayya and was popularly known as JVP Committee. It submitted its report in April, 1949 and formally rejected language as the basis for reorganization of states.

Linguistic Commission: Advances Geographic Continuity for Future Expansion

Dhar Commission

On June 17 1948, Rajendra Prasad, the President of the Constituent Assembly set up The Linguistic Provinces Commission with SK Dhar (retired Allahabad High Court Judge), JN Lal (lawyer) and Panna lal were members of the committee. The Commission recommended in report (10 December 1948) that "forming provinces solely or even primarily on linguistic considerations is not in the larger interests of the Indian nation. "Bilingual districts in border areas that have developed an economic and organic life of their own should not be broken up and should be disposed of on the basis of their own special needs," the commission continued. The commission recommended that India & states be reorganized based on geographical continuity, financial self-sufficiency, administrative convenience, and future development capacity.

JVP Commission

Later, when Dhar commission released its report, the Congress established the JVP Committee to study the Dhar Commission's recommendations at its Jaipur session. In addition to Congress president Pattabhi Sitaramayya, the committee included Jawaharlal Nehru and Vallabhbhai Patel. The committee shifted the focus away from language to security, unity, and economic prosperity, reversing the party's own election platform. This may have been influenced by the situation that existed immediately following the partition. Supporting federal demands as Patel put it, would obstruct India's growth as a nation, according to the three-member committee.

The committee stated in its report dated 1 April 1949 that time was not appropriate for the formation of new provinces and formally rejected languages as the basis for reorganization of states, but said, "if public sentiment is insistent and overwhelming, we as democrats must submit to it, subject to certain Limitations in regard to the good for India as a whole". However, in October, 1953, the Government of India was forced to create the first linguistic state, known as Andhra State, by separating the Telugu speaking areas from the Madras state. This provoked the agitation and death of Potti Sriramulu who was 56 days of hunger strike.

Fazl Ali Commission

The demand for linguistically-based states in other regions increased as a result of the founding of the state of Andhra. In order to re-examine the situation, the Indian government was compelled to form a three-member States Reorganization Commission, headed by Fazl Ali, with two members named K.M. Panikkar and H.N. Kunzru. In September 1955, it turned in a report that was widely regarded as the foundation for the reorganization of states. However, it disproved the notion of "one language, one state." When redacting the country's political divisions, extreme consideration should be made to maintaining India's unity. Any plan for state reorganization must take into account four key factors, according to the commission:

1. Maintaining and enhancing the nation's security and unity.

2. Cultural and linguistic uniformity.

3. The organization and promotion of the welfare of the citizens of each state and the overall country.

4. Administrative, financial, and economic considerations.

The commission suggested the abolition of the four-fold classification of states and territories under the original Constitution and creation of 16 states and 3 centrally administered territories. The Government of India accepted these recommendations with few modifications. By the States Reorganization Act (19560 and the 7th Constitutional Amendment Act (1956), the distinction between part A and Part B states was done away and Part C states were abolished. Additionally, some of them were merged with adjacent states and some other was designated as union territories. As a result of it, 14 states and 6 union territories were created on November1, 1956.[44]

State Reorganization Act (1956)

A significant milestone toward recognizing linguistic variety, fostering regional identities, and strengthening India's federal system was taken with the passage of the State Reorganization Act in 1956. In a nation like India with a wide variety of languages, it met linguistic desires and provided a framework for efficient governance and administration. As a result of the act, states were reorganized along linguistic lines to reflect India's linguistic and cultural diversity. In order to fulfill linguistic desires and support regional identities, it sought to establish states where the majority of the population spoke the same or closely related languages. Based on linguistic factors, the act resulted in the creation of many new states. For instance, Telugu-speaking regions were divided from the Madras region to create the state of Andhra Pradesh.

The act involved the redrawing of boundaries to align them with linguistic affinities. For instance, the boundaries of Punjab were redefined to create the states of Punjab and Haryana, separating Punjabi-speaking areas from Hindi-speaking regions. The act facilitated the transfer of certain territories and districts between states to ensure linguistic homogeneity. This involved the transfer of regions with significant linguistic populations to align them with the linguistic majority. The act also led to the consolidation of various centrally-administered territories into union territories. For instance, the French-speaking territories of Pondicherry, Chandernagore, Karikal, Mahe, and Yanam were merged with India and formed the Union Territory of Puducherry.[45]

By combining the states of Travancore-Cochin and Kasargode of South Canara, this Act created the new state of Kerala. It combined Hyderabad state's Telugu-speaking regions with Andhra Pradesh state. Additionally, it combined the states of Madhya Pradesh, Vindhya Pradesh, and Bhopal; Saurashtra, Kutch, and Mysore into the Bombay state; Coorg, East Punjab States Union, and Patiala into the Punjab state; and Ajmer, into the Rajasthan state. Additionally, it separated the area from Madras state, creating the new union territory of Laccadive, Minicoy, and Amindivi Islands.

States	Union Territories
Andhra Pradesh	Andaman and Nicobar Islands
Assam	Delhi
Bihar	Himachal Pradesh
Bombay	Laccadive, Minicoy and Amindivi Islands
Jammu & Kashmir	Manipur
Kerala	Tripura
Madhya Pradesh	
Madras	
Mysore	
Orissa	
Punjab	
Rajasthan	
Uttar Pradesh	
West Bengal	

Table 2 Territory of India (After state Reorganization Act, 1956)[45a]

Dadra and Nagar Haveli: Portuguese colonists lived in Dadar and Nagar Haveli from the 1520s till India conquered them on December 19, 1961. The Indian Army attacked Dadra and Nagar Haveli on August 11, 1961. After that, an administrator chosen by the populace itself continued to lead the country until 1961. The 10th Constitutional Amendment Act of 1961 made it an Indian union territory.

Gujarat and Maharashtra: The proposal to create a unified Marathi state saw bitter opposition from Gujaratis, especially around the question of the cosmopolitan Bombay city. While the city too consisted of a majority Marathi population and was surrounded by Marathi speaking districts from which it drew much of its resources, Gujaratis argued that it was their contributions which gave Bombay much of its financial might. Instead of handing over the city of Bombay to Marathis, Gujaratis argued for a trifurcation of the region – into a Gujarati state, a Marathi state and the union territory of Greater Bombay. Going against the principle of linguistic states, the SRC recommended the creation of a single, bilingual Bombay state which included all Marathi and Gujarati speaking territories. At the time of its creation in 1956, it was by far the biggest state in India, covering roughly one-sixth of India's total landmass. But the 'compromise' left both linguistic groups unsatisfied. Government succumbed to political pressure and acknowledged that the creation of the bilingual state had been a failure. Finally, on May 1, 1960, the states of Gujarat and Maharashtra were carved out of the united Bombay State.

Puducherry: The de facto transfer of the French Indian territories from French governance to the Indian union took place on 1 November 1954 and was established as the union territory of Pondicherry. The treaty affecting the de jure transfer was signed in 1956. However, due to opposition in France, the ratification of this treaty by the French National Assembly only took place on 16 August 1962 made union territory by the 14th Constitutional Amendment Act.

Goa, Daman and Diu: Daman and Diu were administered as part of the union territory of Goa, Daman and Diu between 1962 and 1987, becoming a separate union territory when Goa was granted statehood. These territories acquired by police action in 1961. They were constituted as union territory by the 12th constitutional amendment act, 1962. Later, in 1987, Goa was conferred a statehood. Consequently, Drama and Diu was made a separate union territory.

Himachal Pradesh, Haryana, and Chandigarh: Haryana remained a part of Punjab after India gained its independence in 1947, but the demand for separate states—supported by both Hindus and Sikhs—persisted unabatedly. The movement did indeed gain momentum, reaching its zenith in the early 1960s. Haryana was finally divided from Punjab in 1966 by the Punjab Reorganization Act, becoming India's 17th state. According to the Shah Commission's (1966) recommendations, the areas that spoke Punjabi were formed into the single-language state of Punjab, and the parts that spoke Hindi were formed into the states of Haryana and Himachal Pradesh. Himachal Pradesh became the 18th state of the Indian Union in 1971 after being elevated from a union territory.

Nagaland: After India's independence in 1947, the question of the Naga Hills's political status emerged. The Naga National Council led by Zapu Phizo demanded an independent Naga nation and launched an armed struggle for an independent state. The Indian Government, however, maintained that Nagaland was an integral part of India. The conflict between the Naga National Council and the Indian Government resulted in a protracted insurgency that lasted for several decades limiting its economic development. It became the 16th state of India on 1 December 1963. The state of Nagaland was formed by taking the Naga Hills and tuensang area out of the state of Assam. It was placed under the control of governor of Assam in 1961.

Manipur, Tripura, and Meghalaya: In 1972, significant changes were made to the political landscape of Northeast India. This led to the creation of the two union territories of Mizoram and Arunachal Pradesh as well as the statehood of the sub state of Meghalaya, Manipur, and Tripura. The Indian Union now had 21 states (Manipur is the 19th, Tripura is the 20th, and Meghalaya is the 21st). Meghalaya was established as an independent state or sub state inside the state of Assam under the 22nd Constitutional Amendment Act (1969), complete with a council of ministers and legislative body. Assam's territories were also used to create the union territories of Mizoram and Arunachal Pradesh.

Sikkim: A political movement in Sikkim was sparked by Indian Independence and the country's transition to democracy, and as a result, the pro-accession Sikkim State Congress (SSC) was created. The party presented the palace with a plate of demands, which included a request for accession to India. By assigning three secretaries from the SSC to the government and supporting a counter-movement under the guise of the Sikkim National Party, which was opposed to joining India, the palace tried to neutralize the movement. After that, Sikkim was made a protectorate of India, and the Indian government was in charge of Sikkim's defense, foreign relations, and communications.

The Sikkim Prime Minister requested that Sikkim become a state of India in a petition to the Indian Parliament in 1975. The Chogyal palace guards were disarmed by the Indian Army, who had taken control of Gangtok in April of that year. Thereafter, a referendum was held in which 97.5 per cent of voters supported abolishing the monarchy, effectively approving union with India. In a referendum held people voted for the abolition of the institution of chogyal and Sikkim becoming integral part of India. Parliament enacted 35th Constitutional Amendment Act (1974).

Mizoram, Arunachal Pradesh, and Goa: Three new states—Mizoram, Arunachal Pradesh, and Goa—became the 23rd, 24th, and 25th members of the Indian Union in 1987. Following the signing of a memorandum of settlement (Mizoram Peace Accord) in 1986 between the federal government and the Mizo national front, which put an end to the two-decade-old insurgency, the territory of Mizoram was given the status of a full state. Since 1972, Arunachal Pradesh has also been a union territory. The territory of Goa was divided from the Union Territory of Goa, Daman, and Diu to form the state of Goa.

Chhattisgarh, Uttarakhand, and Jharkhand: In 2000, three additional new states were formed from portions of Madhya Pradesh, Uttar Pradesh, and Bihar, namely Chhattisgarh, Uttarakhand, and Jharkhand. These three states joined the Indian Union as the 26th, 27th, and 28th. Chhattisgarh was primarily founded on the regional population's demand for a separate state because they believed the government was not giving them enough attention or investing in their development. The 16 districts that make up the new state of Chhattisgarh were formerly a part of Madhya Pradesh. On November 9, 2000, the hilly parts of the state of Uttar Pradesh were divided to form Uttarakhand.

A distinct state of Uttarakhand, which comprises of 13 districts, was demanded for a variety of political, economic, and cultural reasons. On November 15, 2000, the southern portion of Bihar was divided to create Jharkhand. Tribal people who lived in the area were the main proponents of the demand for Jharkhand to become a separate state because they wanted to preserve their cultural identity and exert more control over the area's mineral wealth. Natural resources like coal, iron ore, and copper are abundant in Jharkhand. There are 24 districts in the state.

Telangana: In 2014, the new state of Telangana came into existence as the 29th state of the Indian Union. It was carved out of the territories of Andhra Pradesh. The Andhra State Act (1953) formed the first linguistic state of Andhra, by taking out the Telugu speaking areas from the state of Madras (now Tamil Nadu). Kurnool was the capital of Andhra state and the state high court was established at Guntur. The State Reorganisation Act (1956) merged the Telugu speaking areas of Hyderabad state with the Andhra State to create & enlarged Andhra Pradesh State. The capital of the state was shifted to Hyderabad. The Andhra Pradesh Reorganisation Act (2014) bifurcated the Andhra Pradesh into two separate states namely, Andhra Pradesh and the Telangana.

Jammu & Kashmir and Ladakh: Up until 2019, Jammu and Kashmir, an extinct state in India, had its own constitution and was accorded unique status under Article 370 of the Indian Constitution. A presidential order titled "The Constitution (Application to Jammu and Kashmir)" eliminated this special status in 2019. The 2019 order extended all the provisions of the constitution of India to Jammu and Kashmir also. However, the inoperative Article 370 continues to remain in the text of the Constitution of India. Further, the Jammu and Kashmir Reorganization Act, 2019, bifurcated the erstwhile state of Jammu and Kashmir into two separate union territories, the union territory of Ladakh. The union territory of Jammu and Kashmir comprises all the districts of the erstwhile state of Jammu and Kashmir except the Kargil and Leh districts which have gone to the union territory of Ladakh. Thus, the number of states and union territories increased from 14 and 16 in 1956 to 28 and 9 in 2019, respectively.[46]

District Administration Serves as Boon at Federal Level

Shortcomings of British India help to sustain the District Administration

A district collector or deputy commissioner was in charge of each district and was in charge of preserving peace and order, collecting taxes, and running the district as a whole. At the district level, the district collector was seen as the hub of the British administrative system. Revenue administration and general administration were combined to form district administration. The British created the permanent settlement system in an effort to stabilize tax collection and give the government a steady stream of income. Land revenue was fixed and derived directly from farmers under this system. The district collector was crucial in overseeing agricultural practices, keeping track of land records, settling land disputes, and collecting taxes.

It's critical to recognize the administrative flaws in the British system. The autocratic nature, lack of representation, and resource exploitation of the system were condemned. The tax system burdened peasants and caused agrarian misery even though it was designed to stabilize collection of income. Despite having the intention to protect the rule of law, the judicial system had sluggish procedures and difficult accessibility. These problems served as the impetus for later reform movements and called for administrative reform in India. However, the district administration, which included local self-government institutions, judicial functions, and revenue collection, played a significant role.

The Governor-General of India and the British Crown held ultimate power in the highly organized British colonial administration. The lack of responsiveness to local needs and concerns was frequently a result of this centralized management. Racial discrimination was a hallmark of the British Raj, with Europeans receiving preferential treatment over Indians in many areas of governance. Indians were frequently denied access to senior administration jobs. The Permanent Settlement and later the Ryotwari and Mahalwari systems of collecting land taxes were implemented by the British. These arrangements frequently involved exploitation and resulted in farmers being evicted from their lands. To crush dissent and opposition, the British government frequently employed harsh tactics. The British response to the Jallianwala Bagh massacre in 1919 is a famous example of anti-colonial protests.

In India, the term **"District Administration"** refers to the system of local government and public administration at district level. The three level of the country's administrative structure, above the state/union territory level and below the sub-district level (tehsil/taluk), is made up of various administrative entities known as districts. At the local level, the district administration is in charge of putting different policies, plans, and schemes of the federal and state governments into action. It is essential to the provision of public services, the upkeep of law and order, and the district's overall development. Typically, district administrations are in charge of many different tasks, including local government, law enforcement, public services, education, and healthcare.[47] some common functions and responsibilities of district administrations include:

Local governance: Ensuring the efficient functioning of local government bodies, such as municipal corporations or councils, within the district. Overseeing the delivery of essential services like water supply, healthcare facilities, public transportation, and waste management. Planning and implementing projects related to roads, bridges, schools, hospitals, and other infrastructure within the district. Implementing social welfare programs, such as poverty alleviation schemes, women empowerment initiatives, and support for marginalized communities. These include education, public health, social welfare, and the welfare of underprivileged communities and groups. Each of these duties is handled by a different department in the district, which is led by a specialist officer. Supervising and supporting the functioning of schools and educational institutions within the district.

Law enforcement: Maintaining law and order, coordinating with the police force, and ensuring public safety and security. The first set of functions is concerned with tranquility and public safety. The Superintendent of

Police, who leads the district's police force and the District Magistrate are jointly responsible for maintaining law and order.

Revenue Administration: Managing district-wise revenue-related issues, keeping track of land records, and collecting local taxes are all part of revenue management. Revenue administration is the focus of the second group of tasks. The most significant part of this category is land administration, which includes managing land records. However, it also includes various public dues that are collected in addition to assessments and collections of land revenue.

Disaster Management: Management of catastrophic situation is the process of preparing for and handling calamities or natural disasters within a district. The district administration is ready to respond to threats like famines, earthquakes, accidental fires, floods, and other natural disasters. The DC is in charge of coordinating the efforts of the various departments and taking the necessary action to alleviate suffering. Gram Panchayat at the village level, Panchayat Samiti at the block level, and Zilla Parishad at the district level are the three levels of the Panchayati Raj system of rural local government in India. Each level has sufficient authority and funding, and they are each in charge of planning and devolution in their respective areas of responsibility.

Working Framework of Three Tier System

STRUCTURE OF PRI IN INDIA	
District Level	Zila Parishad
Block Level	Panchayat Samiti
Village Level	Gram Panchayat

Figure 3: Three tier System of PRIs

The Panchayat is the executive committee of Gram Sabha. It is known by a variety of names. The membership of the Panchayat varies from five to thirty-one. Members of the Panchayat are called Panches and are elected by the Gram Sabha by secret ballot. The President is directly elected by the people in Orissa; by the Gram Sabha in Assam, Bihar, Punjab, Uttar Pradesh and West Bengal, and by the Panches in Andhra Pradesh, Gujarat, Jammu and Kashmir, Kerala, Madhya Pradesh, Maharashtra and Karnataka. Several states provide for reservations of a specified number of seats for women as well as members of Scheduled Castes and Scheduled Tribes. The tenure of the Panchayat in various states varies from three to five years. Gram Panchayat consists of a village or a group of villages divided into smaller units called "Wards". Each ward selects or elects a representative who is known as the Panch or ward member. The members of the Gram Sabha elect the ward members through a direct election. The Sarpanch or the president of the Gram Panchayat is elected by the ward members as per the State Act. The Sarpanch and the Panch are elected for a period of five years. Gram Panchayat is governed by the elected body and administration.[48]

The Panchayat is looked up in as an instrument for execution of the Community Development Programme. Functions of Panchayat are obligatory and discretionary. The Panchayat may also be entrusted with any other functions given by the state government. To perform these functions the panchayat has been given certain sources of revenue. Gram Panchayat is responsible for local governance and administration in the village. It acts as a grassroots-level institution for decision-making, planning, and implementation of various development programs and welfare schemes.

Basic Service Delivery: The village's gram panchayat makes sure that inhabitants receive all necessary services and conveniences. These services include the provision of clean water and sanitary conditions, access to healthcare, facilities for primary education, street lighting, upkeep of local infrastructure, and other regional services.

Gram Panchayat: It is involved in the design and execution of projects for the village's development. It determines the community's needs and priorities and creates plans for infrastructure improvement, agricultural endeavors, the creation of rural jobs, the reduction of rural poverty, and other developmental activities.

Social Welfare and Justice: At the local level, settling conflicts and addressing social issues are essential functions of the Gram Panchayat. It encourages social welfare projects, supports community development initiatives, and serves as a village forum for resolving disputes and enforcing justice.

The Panchayat Samiti is the intermediate tier in the PRIs of rural local government in India. The term varies from three to five years. There is no uniformity in consists a Panchayat Samiti in different states. It consists of ex officio, associate and co-opted members. The Sarpanchs of the Panchayats are the ex-officio member. Members of State Legislatures and of Parliament are also members. Women members and members from Scheduled Castes and Scheduled tribes in Panchayats are also members. President of Panchayat Samiti can be removed from his office by a no-confidence vote of the Panchayat Samiti passed with a special majority. President exercises control over the Block Development Officer for implementing resolutions of the samiti or its standing committee. He has all access to all records of the Panchayat Samoti. He is empowered to demote, suspend or dismiss any member of the staff whose jurisdiction is less than the whole Block.

The focal point of the Panchayati Raj system of rural local administration is the Panchayat Samiti. With the exception of Gujarat and Maharashtra, it is the primary executive body in charge of carrying out Community Development Programs. Additionally, it performs activities that may be delegated to it as an agent of the state government. Additionally, it oversees and controls the Panchayats under its jurisdiction and offers them the technical and financial support they require. It examines the Panchayat budgets in the territory under its jurisdiction and offers recommendations. Functions can be divided into two categories: (i) supplying civic amenities and (ii) carrying out development functions.

Membership in Zila Parishads has been created in a fashion that connects it to Panchayat Samiti, the intermediate level of Panchayati Raj. Because of its ex-officio and co-opted membership, Zila Parishad is an official rather than a well-liked organization. The Zila Parishad has anything from forty to sixty members. To see and operate the ZP in a comprehensive, intelligent, and meaningful way, urban local governments must be represented in the districts. Three to five years make up the term. A chairman is the president that the ZP's members elect among one another.

He supervises the chief executive office administratively in order to carry out ZP decisions and instructions, and he sends a private report on the CEO to the Divisional Commissioner. Every statute contains a clause that allows the president to be removed by a vote of no confidence. A network of standing committees helps the ZP run. Most governments have given the ZP executive jurisdiction, especially in issues pertaining to planning and development, and they were intended to be the strongest tier of PRIs. ZP serves as a supervising and coordinating authority, with the exception of Gujarat and Maharashtra.[49]

Panchayati Raj Institute's Revenue

Real strength in terms of both autonomy and efficiency of these organizations depends on their financial status (including their potential to create own resources), which is covered in great detail in Part IX of the constitution. In India, panchayats typically receive funding in the methods listed below:

1) Grants from the Union Government in accordance with Article 280 of the Constitution and the Central Finance Commission's recommendations.

2) Devolution of state finances from the state government in accordance with Article 243-I

3) Government loans and grants.

4) Allocations for certain programs under programs with enhanced central support.

5) Production of internal resources (tax and non-tax)

6) Various state laws suggest that the village panchayats have authority over a range of taxes, charges, tolls, and fees. Include the following taxes and fees: octroi, property/house tax, profession tax, land tax/cess, taxes/tolls on vehicles, entertainment, tax/fees, license fees, tax on non-agricultural land, fee on cattle registration, sanitation/drainage/conservancy tax, water rate/tax, lighting rate/tax, education cess, and tax on fairs and festivals Grants.[50]

Role of District Administrators

Deputy Commissioner

The general administration of the district is vested with the Deputy Commissioner, who for administrative purposes, is under the Divisional Commissioner, Faridabad. He is at once the Deputy Commissioner, the District Magistrate and the Collector. As Deputy Commissioner, he is the executive head of the district with multifarious responsibilities relating to development, panchayats, local bodies, civil administration, etc. As District Magistrate, he is responsible for law and order and heads the police and prosecuting agency. As Collector, he is the chief Officer of the revenue administration and is responsible for the collection of land revenue, and is also the highest revenue judicial authority in the district. He acts as the district Elections Officer and the Registrar for registration work. He exercises over-all supervision on other government agencies in his district. He is, in short, the head of the district administration, a coordinating officer among various departments and a connecting link between the public and the government so far as he executes the policies, administers the rules and regulations framed by the government from time to time.

• The Deputy Commissioner, who serves as the district collector, serves as the chief revenue officer and is in responsibility of collecting revenue and other governmental obligations that can be recovered as land tax arrears. He deals with a variety of natural calamities, including seasonal rain, droughts, floods, hailstorms, and fires.

• For the elections for the Parliament, the Assembly, the Municipality, and the Panchayat, the Deputy Commissioner acts as the District Election Officer.

Deputy Commissioner Additional

To assist the Deputy Commissioner on a daily basis, the role of Additional Deputy Commissioner was created. The Additional Deputy Commissioner is granted the same authority as the Deputy Commissioner by the regulations. The Additional Deputy Commissioner post was created in 1979 to help with the Deputy Commissioner's ever-increasing workload.

Sub divisional Magistrate

The responsibilities of the Sub Divisional Magistrate in his Sub Division are very similar to those of the Deputy Commissioner in his district. In all administrative affairs, he must act as the Deputy Commissioner's main representative. He oversees all of the Sub Division's development initiatives in addition to coordinating the activities of several divisions.

Naib Tehsildars and Tehsildars

Financial Commissioners appoint Tehsildars, Revenue, and Naib Tehsildars are appointed by the Division Commissioner. Their responsibilities within the Tehsil or Sub Tehsil are nearly the same and varied. They have the authority of Executive Magistrate, Assistant Collector, and Sub Registrar. Tehsildar assumes the powers of Assistant Collector 1st grade. Their main task being revenue collection, the Tehsildar and Naib Tehsildar have to tour extensively in their areas. The revenue record and the crop statistics are also maintained by them. The Tehsildars and Naib-Tehsildars are responsible for the collection of land revenue and other dues payable to the Government. To remain in touch with the subordinate revenue staff, to observe the seasonal conditions and condition of crops, to listen to the difficulties of the cultivators and to distribute those active loans, the Tehsildar and Naib-Tehsildars extensively tour the areas in their jurisdiction. They decide urgent matters on the spot, like correction of entries in the account books, providing relief to the people faced with natural calamities, etc. On their return from the tour, they prepare reports and recommend to the Government remission or suspension of land revenue and bring the records up to date.

Administration of Autonomous Regions

Sixth Schedule of the Constitution

The Sixth Schedule of the Constitution of India allows for the formation of autonomous administrative divisions which have been given autonomy within their respective states. The Sixth Schedule of the Constitution deals with the administration of the tribal areas in the four northeastern states of Assam, Meghalaya, Tripura and Mizoram as per Article 244. The Governor is empowered to increase or decrease the areas or change the names of the autonomous districts. While executive powers of the Union extend in Scheduled areas with respect to their administration in VIth schedule, the VIth schedule areas remain within executive authority of the state. These areas have hitherto been anthropological specimens. The tribal people in other parts of India have more or less adopted the culture of the majority of the people, on the other hand, tribes of Assam, Meghalaya, Tripura and Mizoram still have their same roots in their own culture, customs and civilization.

The Sixth Schedule's many administrative aspects include the following:-

1. Autonomous districts have been created for the tribal areas in the four states of Assam, Meghalaya, Tripura, and Mizoram. However, they do not fall outside the executive authority of the state concerned.

2. The autonomous districts may be organized and disorganized by the governor.

3. The governor may split an autonomous district into multiple autonomous regions if there are various tribes present.

4. There are 30 district council members in each autonomous district, of which four are appointed by the governor and the rest 26 are chosen using the adult franchise. While nominated members serve at the governor's pleasure, elected members are in office for a five-year term. A distinct regional council is also present in each autonomous region.

5. The governor can appoint a commission to examine and report on any matter relating to the administration of the autonomous district or regional council on the recommendation of the commission.

6. The acts of Parliament or the state legislature do not apply to automous districts and autonomous regions or apply with specified modifications and expectations.[52]

Autonomous Administrative Division Council

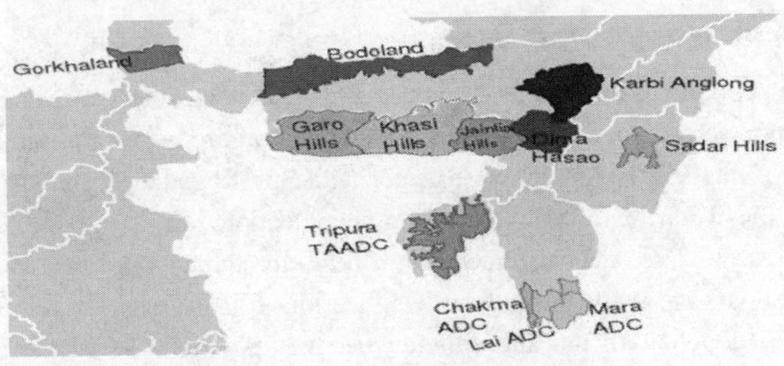

MAP: Autonomous Division of India

1. The district and regional councils oversee the regions that fall within their purview. They have the authority to enact laws regarding a number of specific topics, including inheritance of property, marriage and divorce, social norms, shifting agriculture, canal water, and land. But the governor must approve each of these legislations.
2. Within their respective territorial authorities, the district and regional councils may act as village councils or courts to hear disputes and cases involving the tribes. They hear their cries for help. The governor specifies the high court's jurisdiction over these lawsuits and cases.
3. The district and regional councils have the authority to assess, collect, and levy specific taxes as well as land revenue.
4. The district council has the authority to establish, build, or manage the district's primary schools, hospitals, marketplaces, ferries, fisheries, roads, and other facilities. Additionally, it has the power to enact laws governing non-tribal individuals' borrowing and trading of money. But the governor must approve such regulations.

The sixth schedule to the Constitution includes 10 autonomous district councils in 4 states which include:

States	Tribal Areas
Assam	The Karbi Anglong Autonomous District Council The Dima Hasao Autonomous District Council
Meghalaya	Khasi Hills Autonomous District Council Jaintia Hills Autonomous District Council The Garo Hills Autonomous District
Mizoram	The Chakma Autonomous District Council The Mara Autonomous District Council The Lai Autonomous District Council
Tripura	Tripura Tribal Areas District

Figure 4: Autonomous District Councils in 4 States[53]

Urban Local Bodies: Strong Hold on Governance of Cities

The term 'Urban Local Government' in India signifies the governance of an urban area by the people through their elected representatives. There are eight of urban local governments in India – Municipal Corporation, municipality, notified area committee, town area committee, cantonment board, township, port trust and special purpose agency. Urban spaces administration in India is primarily managed by urban local bodies, which are responsible for the governance and administration of cities and towns. These bodies are established under the provisions of the 74th Constitutional Amendment Act of 1992, which aimed to decentralize power and empower local self-government institutions in urban areas. In August 1989, Rajiv Gandhi government introduced the 65th Constitutional amendment Bill (i.e., Nagarpalika Bill) in the Lok Sabha. The bill aimed at strengthening and revamping the municipal bodies by conferring a constitutional status. Although the bill was passed in the Lok sabha, it was defeated in the Rajya Sabha in October 1989 and lapsed. P V Narasimha Rao's Government also introduced the modified municipalities Bill in the Lok Sabha in September 1991. It finalized as 74th constitutional Amendment act of 1992 and came into force on 1 June 1993.

Urban local government entities have the following duties and responsibilities:

• Providing fundamental services such as water supply, sanitation, solid waste disposal, street lighting, and public health.

• Infrastructure management and urban planning.

• Issuing licenses and permissions, such as building permits and trading licenses.

• The generation of income via property taxes, fees, and other fees.

• Regulation and enforcement of building codes, zoning regulations and land planning.

• Through citizen engagement initiatives and public consultations, the general public can participate in decision-making.

• Maintenance of local infrastructure, parks, gardens, and public areas.

For the management of urban regions, the following eight categories of urban local bodies were established:

Municipal Corporation: Municipal corporations are established in larger cities with a substantial population. They have a directly elected Mayor or Municipal Commissioner and elected councilors representing different wards. Municipal corporations have a wider range of functions and responsibilities, including providing civic amenities, infrastructure development, and overall governance of the city. Municipal corporations are created for the administration of big cities like Delhi, Mumbai, Kolkata, Hyderabad, Bangalore and others.

The standing committees are created to facilitate the working of the council, which is too large in size. They deal with public works, education, health, taxation, finance and so on. The municipal commissioner is responsible for the implementation of the decisions taken by the council and its standing committees. Thus, he is the chief executive authority of the corporation. He is appointed by the state government and member of the IAS.

Municipal Council: Municipal councils, also known as municipalities, are established in smaller urban areas. They are led by a chairperson or President and have elected councilors. Municipal councils focus on providing basic services, maintaining local infrastructure, and addressing the needs of the urban population. Municipalities are established for the administration of towns and small cities.

Nagar Panchayat: Nagar Panchayats are established in smaller towns and areas that do not qualify for municipal council status. They are headed by a President and have elected members representing different wards. Nagar Panchayats primarily focus on basic services and limited urban governance functions.

Cantonment Board: Cantonment boards are local bodies responsible for the administration of areas that fall under the jurisdiction of military cantonments. These areas are primarily inhabited by military personnel and their families. Cantonment boards provide civic amenities and infrastructure services to both the civilian population and military establishments. It works under the administration control of the defence ministry of the central government.

Notified Area Committee (NAC): Notified Area Committees are established for areas undergoing urbanization or those with transitional urban characteristics. They have limited administrative and governance powers and focuses on providing essential services and infrastructure to the residents. A notified area committee is created for the administration of two types of areas – a fast developing due to industrialization, and a town which does not yet fulfil all the conditions necessary for the constitution of a municipality, but which otherwise is considered important by the state government.

Township: This type of urban government is established by the large public enterprise to provide civic amenities to its staff and workers who live in the housing colonies built near the plant. The enterprise appoints a town administrator to look after the administration of the township. He is assisted by some engineers and other technical and non-technical staff. Thus, the township form of urban government has no elected members. In fact, it is an extension of elected members. It is an extension of the bureaucratic structure of the enterprises.

Post Trust: The port trusts are established in the port areas like Mumbai, Kolkata, and Chennai and so on for two purposes: (a) to manage and protect the ports and (b) to provide civic amenities. A port trust is created by an act of Parliament. It consists of both elected and nominated members. Its chairman is an official. Its civic functions are more or less similar to those of a municipality.

Special Purpose Agencies: In addition to the above types of ULBs, special purpose agencies may be established for specific functions or sectors such as transportation, water supply, solid waste management, urban planning, and development. These agencies are responsible for specialized services and work in coordination with the relevant ULB

Municipal Personnel System: Promotes Local Autonomy

There are three types of municipal personnel system in India:

1. **Separate Personnel System:** Under this system, each local body appoints, administers, and controls its own personnel. They are not transferable to other local bodies. It is the most widely prevalent system. This system upholds the principle of local autonomy and promotes undivided loyalty.

2. **Unified Personnel System:** In this system, the state government appoints, administers, and controls the municipal personnel. In other words, state services (cadre) are created for all the urban bodies in the state. They are transferable between the local bodies in the state. This system is prevalent in Andhra Pradesh, Tamil Nadu, Uttar Pradesh, Rajasthan, and Madhya Pradesh and so on.

3. **Integrated Personnel System:** Under this system, employees of local and state governments work together in the same service. In other words, the employees of local governments are state employees. They can be transferred not just among state local bodies but also between local bodies and state government departments. As a result, there is no separation between local and state civil services. This approach is common in many states, including Punjab, Haryana, Karnataka, Odisha, and Bihar.[54]

Municipal Revenue: Magnitude of Taxes

The urban local authorities receive funding from five different sources. These include:-

1. **Tax cash:** Local taxes such as property tax, entertainment tax, advertisement tax, professional tax, water tax, animal tax, lighting tax, pilgrim tax, market tax, toll on new bridges, and octroi are among those that generate cash locally. Additionally, the municipal authority levies a number of taxes, including beggary, education, and library taxes. Most governments have abolished octroi (taxes on the admission of commodities into a local region for consumption, use, or sale therein). Property tax is the most important tax revenue.

2. **Non-Tax Revenue:** This includes royalties, fees and fines, rent on municipal properties, Interest, user fees, profits and dividends, and other receipts. Water, sanitation, sewerage, and other fees are included in the user charges, which are payments for public facilities.

3. **Grants:** These grants include the various grants given to municipal bodies by the central and state governments for several development programmes, infrastructure schemes and urban reform initiatives.

4. **Devolution:** This refers to the transfer of funding from the state government to the urban local bodies. This devolution is made on the basis of the state finance commission recommendations.

5. **Loans:** The urban local bodies raise loans from the state government as well as financial institutions to meet their capital expenditure. They can borrow from the financial institutions or other bodies only with the approval of the state government.[55]

Apparatus for Capacity Building Period

How Power Expands by Accountability

Expansion of Power in State by Accountability

Administrative accountability ensures optimization of the available resources and at the same time to realize the organizational objectives. Administrative accountability is an organizational imperative because it purposes to evaluate an organization's performance in terms of its goals. The goal is split up into definite tasks and responsibilities, and it is the individual administrators who are called to render an account of how they are discharging their responsibilities. Accountability is intrinsic to any organization such as hierarchy, span of control, unity of command, supervision, etc., are all accountability promoting and enforcing mechanisms. Accountability has two facets, somehow separate but interrelated. The first one is basically political, and in a parliamentary system of government like the executive is kept under the obligation of giving an account of its performance to Parliament. The second facet is primarily administrative wherein the executive, in its turns, holds the administrators in departments and other public agencies accountable for how they carry out their responsibilities. These two are complimentary and together they constitute the foundation of a responsible government.[56]

The supreme executive authority in India is vested in the President of India, and the most important acts of state are performed in his name. However, the President of India has been put under a firm constitutional obligation to act in accordance with the 'aid and advice' given by the council of Ministers with the Prime Minister at its head. The Executives' accountability to Parliament is total and non-partisan; and to assert such a relationship the latter has many ways and many occasions. The executive is obliged to remove people's grievance. Indeed, the redressal of people's grievance precedes the grant of supply, through taxation. besides, before Parliament grants funds to the executive it must satisfy itself about the merit of its policies for which funds are needed. Parliament ensures that the money so granted is spent on purposes for which the grant was accorded.[57]

Accountability is ensured and made more specific by a complex system of organizational and procedural devices. Hierarchy is itself an exercise in accountability fixation. Therefore, without adequate control and supervision over the actions of the lower levels, accountability can hardly be enforced. Span of Control, unity of command, inspection, supervision etc., are well known accountability facilitating devices. For instance, to ensure financial responsibility, a financial advisory system is now a part of each Ministry. Agencies like the Ministry of Home Affairs, Ministry of Finance, etc., are other accountability mechanisms. One should not forget that an audit is a powerful tool of accountability, so powerful that the Comptroller and Auditor General is one of the topmost constitutional functionaries of India and is independent of the executive. Certain prerequisites must be met in order to make accountability a genuine, ongoing proposition. Decentralization, delegation, devolution and deconcentration are vital to accountability.

73rd Amendment Act granted the constitutional provision that the state shall take steps to organize village panchayats and endow them with such powers and authority as may be necessary to enable them to function as units of Self Government in a concrete form. The Directive Principles of State Policy include this article. The Indian Constitution now includes a new Part-IX as a result of this act. The provisions in this section, named the Panchayats, range in length from Articles 243 to 243O. A new Eleventh Schedule has also been added to the constitution as a result of the act. There are 29 operational panchayat items included in this schedule. The topic is Article 243G. The statute grants the Panchayati raj a constitutional status. The subject is Article 243G, statute grants the Panchayati raj institutions a constitutional status.

74th Amendment Act has added a new part IX A to the Constitution of India. This part is entitled as 'The Municipalities' and consists of provisions from articles 243 – P to 243 –ZG. In addition, the act has also added a new twelfth schedule to the constitution. This schedule contains eighteen functional items of municipalities. It deals with Article 243 – W. The act provides constitutional status to the municipalities. It has brought them under the purview of justifiable part of the Constitution. In other words, state governments are under constitutional obligation to adopt the new system of municipalities with the provision of the act. The act aims at revitalising and strengthening the urban governments so that they function effectively as units of local governments.[58]

States and Territories Exempt from Panchayat

The states of Nagaland, Meghalaya, and Mizoram, as well as a few other places, are exempt from the law. These areas include (a) the tribal and scheduled areas in the states; (b) the district councils for the Manipuri hills; and (c) the Darjeeling district in west Bengal, which is home to the Darjeeling Gorkha Hill Council. Through the passage of the "Provision of the Panchayats (Extension to the Scheduled Areas) Act", 1996—also referred to as the PESA Act or the Extension Act—Parliament extended part of this provision to the scheduled and tribal districts.

States and Territories Exempt from Panchayat

Scheduled areas and tribal areas in the states are exempt from the law. Additionally, it shall also affect the functions of the Darjeeling Gorkha Hill Council of the West Bengal.

Figure 5: Exempted states & Areas of Panchayats[58a]

Reservation of Seats Every panchayat at all three levels is covered by the 73rd Amendment Act provision for scheduled castes and scheduled tribes. In proportion of their population to the total population in the panchayat areas. The state legislature must also make provisions for the SCs and STs to be given priority in chair positions in panchayats at the village level or any further level. According to the law, women must be given at least one-third of all available seats. Additionally, it stipulates that not less than one-third of all seats (including those set aside for women who belong to the SC and ST groups) will be allocated for women. The state legislature may specify how to reserve chairs in municipalities for women and minorities. Additionally, it may stipulate that any municipality seats or chair positions be reserved for members of the underclass.[59]

State Election Commission The superintendence, direction and control of the preparation of electoral rolls and the conduct of all elections to ***the panchayats*** shall be vested in the state election commission. It consists of a state election commissioner to be appointed by the governor. He shall not be removed from the office except in the manner and on grounds mentioned for the removal of a judge of the state high court. The state legislature may make provision with respect to all matters relating to elections to the panchayats. ***Concerning of Municipalities,*** superintendence, direction and control of the preparation of electoral rolls and the conduct of all elections to the municipalities shall be vested in the state election commission.

State Finance Commission Every five years, the governor of a state must appoint a finance commission to assess the panchayats financial situation. It will advise the governor to take the following actions: The following principles should be taken into account: (a) the distribution of shares among the panchayats at all levels and the net proceeds of the state's taxes, duties, tolls, and fees among the states and the panchayats. (b) Deciding which taxes, tariffs, tolls, and other charges the panchayats will be responsible for collecting. (c) The grants-in-aid from the state consolidated fund given to the panchayats. Reviewing town's financial standing and making recommendations to the governor regarding (a) the division of the state & net revenue from taxes, duties, tolls, and other levies among the state and the municipalities, as well as the distribution of shares among the municipalities at all levels. (a) Determining the taxes, levies, tolls, and other charges that may be levied against municipalities (c) The grants from the state's consolidated fund provided as assistance to the municipalities.[60]

Pesa Act 1996 Strengthens the Autonomous States

The provision of Part IX of the constitution relating to the Panchayats is not applicable to the Fifth Schedule areas. However, the Parliament may extend these provisions to such areas, subject to such exceptions. Under this provision, the Parliament has enacted the "Provision of the Panchayats (Extension to the Schedule Areas) Act", 1996, that popularly Known as the PESA Act or Extension Act. In 2019, ten states have Fifth Schedule areas, Includes – Andhra Pradesh, Telangana, Chhattisgarh, Gujarat, Himachal Pradesh, Jharkhand, Madhya Pradesh, Maharashtra, Odisha and Rajasthan. All the ten states have enacted requisite compliance legislations by amending the respective Panchayati Raj Acts.

The Act's primary goal of PESA ACT:

1. To the scheduled territories the panchayat-related provisions of Part IX of the Constitution.

2. To grant the majority the indigenous population self-rule

3. To implement participatory democracy in village governance and make the gram sabha the hub of all operations.

4. To develop an appropriate administrative architecture that adheres to customary procedures.

5. To protect and uphold indigenous communities; traditions and customs.

6. To give panchayats more authority,

7. To grant special powers to panchayats at the appropriate levels that are suited to tribal needs.

8. To stop gram sabha panchayats at the higher level from taking the rights and authority of gram sabha panchayats at the lower level.[61]

Accountability: Ecosystem of Institutions

Right of Information

The right to information is a fundamental right under Article 19 (1) of the Indian Constitution. In 1976, in the Raj Narain vs. the State of Uttar Pradesh case, the Supreme Court ruled that Right to information will be treated as a fundamental Right under article 19. The Supreme Court held that in Indian democracy, people are the masters and they have the Right to know about the working of the government. Thus the government enacted the Right to Information act in 2005 which provides machinery for exercising this fundamental right. The act is one of the most important acts which empower ordinary citizens to question the government and its working. This has been widely used by citizens and media to uncover corruption, progress in government work, expenses-related information, etc. The primary goal of the Right to Information Act is to empower citizens, promote openness and accountability in government operations, combat corruption, and make our democracy truly function for the people. It goes without saying that an informed citizen is better equipped to keep a required track on governance instruments and hold the government responsible to the governed. The Act is a significant step in informing citizens about the activities of the government.

All constitutional authorities, agencies, owned and controlled, also those organiszations which are substantially financed by the government comes under the purview of the act. The act also mandates public authorities of union government or state government, to provide timely response to the citizens' request for information. The act also imposes penalties if the authorities delay in responding to the citizen in the stipulated time.

The RTI Act's goals include empowering citizens to challenge the government and fostering accountability and openness in working of the Government.

• The act also aids in better serving the needs of the populace and reducing corruption in government.

• The act aims to create more knowledgeable individuals who will maintain the essential vigilance regarding how the political system functions.[62]

Citizen Charter

A document called the Citizen Charter shows a methodical effort to concentrate on the organization commitment. On the level of services provided, information provided the ability to choose and consult with the government, non-discrimination, accessibility, complaint resolution, courtesy, and value for money. Citizen Charter emphasizes on citizens as customers by ensuring that public services are responsive to the citizens they serve. It comprises of the Vision and Mission Statement of the organization, stating the outcomes desired and the broad strategy to achieve these goals and outcomes. A Citizen's Charter is not legally enforceable and, therefore, is non- justifiable. The concept was first articulated and implemented in the United Kingdom by the Conservative Government of John Major in 1991 as a national Programme with a simple aim: To continuously improve the quality of public services for the people of the country so that these services respond to the needs and wishes of the users.

Nodal Department: In order to provide more responsive and citizen-friendly governance, the Department of Administrative Reforms and Public Grievances (DARPG) of the Ministry of Personnel, Public Grievances, and Pensions, Government of India, coordinates the efforts to develop and operationalise Citizen's Charter. The Citizens Right to Time-bound Goods and Services Delivery and Grievance Redress Bill, in order to provide a system for timely delivery of products and services to citizens, the Citizens Charter of 2011 was introduced.[63] the idea of a Citizen Charter formalizes the relationship of trust between service providers and their customers. The Citizens Charter movement initial six guiding principles were: **Quality, Choice, Value, Accountability, Transparency and Participatory.**

Public Interest Litigation

In the infamous & Hussainara Khatoon case, Kapila Hingorani petitioned in 1979 and won the release of around 40.000 undertrials prisoners from Patna jails. Lawyer Hingorani was arrested. This matter was brought before a SC bench presided over by Justice P N Bhagwati. Because of this victorious case, Hingorani is known as the mother of PILs. The court granted Hingorani permission to continue a case even though she lacked personal standing, making PIL an indispensable part of Indian legal doctrine Justice Bhagwati strived hard ensuring that the principle of PILs was articulated clearly.[64]

• It is typically employed to protect collective interests rather than individual interests, which are covered under Fundamental Rights.

• PILs may be filed with the High Courts and the Supreme Court of India.

• PILs have undermined the locus standi principle, which states that solely the person or party whose liberties have been violated may file petitions. PILs are derived from the authority of judicial review.

• It has most frequently and effectively been used to question the legality of a public body's decision, action, or inaction, as well as to challenge the authority of public authorities through judicial review. PILs have a significant impact on Indian politics.[65]

Local Government and Social Audit

Social Audit is the critical stock taking of any programme or scheme by the community with active involvement of the primary stakeholders. It includes audit of the quality of works being executed at different levels along with the details of disbursements made, the number of labourers employed and materials used. The people in coordination with local administration will conduct social audit. Programme Officer - PO shall ensure that all the required information and records of all implementing agencies are properly collated in the requisite formats; and provided along with photocopies to the Social Audit Unit for facilitating conduct of social audit at least fifteen days in advance of the scheduled date of meeting of the GS.

District Programme Coordinator: DPC is responsible for ensuring that PO provides the Social Audit Unit with all necessary records for the conduct of the social audit. Make sure that the social audit report receives time-bound corrective action, such as launching criminal and civil lawsuits or terminating services. Take action to reclaim the funds that were wrongly used, and then offer invoices or recognition for the funds that were. The Social Audit Unit (a) would gather the primary actors and other civil society organizations with knowledge and experience in advocating for the interests of the people to help select, train, and employ competent resource personnel at village, block, district, and state level. (b) Will educate workers about their legal rights and obligations under the Act and make it easier for records to be verified with key parties and job sites.[66]

Significance of Bureaucracy in India

The bureaucracy, or civil service system, was created in India during the British colonial era. The British took full control of India's government under the Government of India Act of 1858. This marked the beginning of the British Empire's control over India through a panel of approved experts. The British established a capable administration in less than a century that was primarily made up of Indians who swore allegiance to the British Government. This governing body might very well be considered essential to British Rule in India. Covenanted Civil Service (CCS) was founded by the East India Company in 1854.

In London, a civil service commission was established, and exams were routinely held there until 1855. Satyendranath Tagore was the first Indian to be accepted into the Indian civil service in 1864. There had been 12 civil servants in 1883. India started holding civil service exams in 1922. In the 1920 batch, Subhash Chandra Bose earned the fourth spot. Only 20% of the positions in the police force prior to 1931 were filled by Indians; however, this situation would change after the Second World War. Before the division, India had the most civil servants in 1947.

India's top bureaucracy adopted a hard and distinctive attitude after gaining its independence, when third-world nations were looking to build qualified and knowledgeable professional services. It gave India independence and continuity, which have remained unaffected even through times of political unrest and weak governmental control at the federal and state levels. India established the Indian Administrative Service (IAS) when the Civil Service was divided after Partition. By stating that civil services preserved India's unity, Sardar Vallabhbhai Patel stressed the importance of all India services.

"This administrative system has no substitute. The Union will not sustain, if you don't have good All India Services, India will never be united." - Sardar Vallabhbhai Patel

Coordinating a sizable group of people who must cooperate is the essence of bureaucracy. To effectively implement the laws passed by elected officials, bureaucrats assign government policy. These are members of the executive arm of government & permanent professional personnel.[67] although they work for the ministries; these people's main duty is to support the running of government institutions. Sukumar Sen, who was the Chief Secretary of West Bengal and was deputed as the Chief Election Commissioner of India in 1951, is an early example of good governance.

However, the fact that 85% of the population was unable to write or read made it necessary to hold an election for the first time. Sukumar Sen published a report on the entire process, which includes the number of people involved and how it was carried out because conducting an election required different people to play different roles (i.e., Electoral Registration Officers, Returning Officers, and Presiding Officers, who oversaw polling places). All of these tasks were carried out by civil servants. More than 1600 registration officers were hired; the majority of them were Tehsildars, collectors, and deputy collectors. India had more than 1 Lakh 32 thousand Polling Stations for this solution was adapted and only government employees were appointed on this Polling Stations.[67a]

The simplicity of management was facilitating administration by structuring the organization rationally into a hierarchical structure. A bureaucratic structure makes it easier to maintain management control, make necessary changes as and when necessary, and occasionally introduce new regulations. The Indian bureaucracy effectively carries out the government's plans for the welfare of the populace. Bureaucracy plays an important role in development of the nation, there are some more important roles carried out by the Indian Bureaucracy. These are as follows:

1. **Running the administration:** One of the important roles of bureaucracy is ensuring that the administration is running smoothly and as per the rules and regulations that have been implemented by the government, without any disturbances.

2. **Advisor to political executives:** Advisors to Government's decision-making for the development of the country is assisted by bureaucracy, who also helps the government run more efficiently. These bureaucrats advise political executives on their choices since they are unaware of how the government operates.

3. **Passing laws:** As they prepare the bills that are submitted to the legislature for consideration as laws; the bureaucracy indirectly participates in the process of creating laws. The ministers contact the civil servants for all the necessary information that they need to give to the legislation for passing of the bill.

4. **Policy formulation:** Policy formulation for the policies that are made to come into action, they need to be included in specific situations. This is a function of the political executives. However, the civil servants or bureaucrats play a major role in guiding these political executives in their role, the bureaucracy plays a major role in the whole process of policy formulation. [68]

Public Services Upholding National Integrity

India's civil services (also known as public services) are divided into three groups: All India Services, Central Services, and State Services.

Sarkaria Commission

The Sarkaria Commission analyzes the institution of All India Services in the context of emerging politico administrative issues and challenges of national integration and development administration. The commission was appointed for centre state relations in 1983 under the chairmanship of Mr. Justice Ranjit Singh Sarkaria. Its term was extended five times and then submitted in 1987. The commission examined in detail the various issues raised by the centre and state government on the role of All India Services. The commission supported the institution of All India Services as like Administrative Reform Commission. It emphasizes on importance of these services for maintaining national unity and integrity. It made the following recommendations as:

1) It suggested the establishment of three new All India Services: An All-India Service for Education, an All India Service for Engineers, and an All India Service for Medicine and Health.

2) It was suggested that before creating full-fledged All India Services in other sectors, such as industry, cooperation, agriculture, and so forth, a pool of officers made up of representatives from the Centre and the States be established in that sector first.

3) The establishment of an advisory board with the Union Cabinet Secretary as its head will allow the Center and the States to regularly discuss on the management of All India Services.[69]

All India Services

All India services are kind of services which are common to both Central and state governments. The members of these services occupy top positions under both the Centre and the state. In 1947, the Indian Civil Service (ICS) was replaced by IPS and were recognize by the constitution as all India services. In 1966, the Indian Forest service was established as third all India service. The All-India Services Act of 1951 authorized the central government to make rules in consultation with the state governments for regulation of recruitment and service conditions of the members of all India services. The members of these services are recruited and trained by the central government but are assigned to different states different states for work. They belong to different state cadres; the centre having no cadre government on deputation and after completing their fixed tenure they go back to their respective states.

The Central government acquired the services of these officers on deputation under the well-known tenure system. Each of these all-India services forms a single service with common rights and status and uniform scales of pay throughout the country. Their salaries and pensions are met by the states. The all-India services are controlled jointly by the central and state governments. The ultimate control lies with the central government while the immediate control is vested in the state governments. Any disciplinary action against these officers can only be taken by the central government. At present, there are three all India services. They are as follows:

1. Indian Administrative Service

2. Indian Police Services

3. Indian Forest Service

Central Services

The employees of the Central Services are solely under the control of the Central Government. They work in specialized roles across a number of Central government ministries. The Central services were divided into class I, class II, subordinate, and inferior services prior to Independence. Following Independence, class III and class IV services took the place of subordinate and inferior services in the nomenclature. The division of central services into classes I, II, III, and IV was revised once more in 1974, becoming group A, group B, group C, and group D, respectively.

There are 62 groups' central services as of right now. The Indian Audit and Accounts Service, Indian Economic Service, Indian Foreign Service, Indian Meteorological Services, Indian Postal Service, Indian Revenue Service (customs, Excise and Income Tax), Indian Statistical Service, Overseas Communication Service, and Railway Personnel Service are a few of them.[70]

State Public Service Commission

A constitutional body known as the State Public Service Commission was created in accordance with Articles 315 to 323 of Part XIV. Each state has a State Public Service Commission (SPSC), in addition to the Union Public Service Commission (UPSC) at the centre level. The Constitution visualizes the SPSC to be the watchdog of merit system in the state. It is concerned with the recruitment to the state services and advises the government, when consulted, on promotion and disciplinary matters. It is not concerned with the classification of services, pay and service conditions, cadre management, training and so on. These matters are handled by the Department of Personnel or the General Administration Department. Therefore, the SPSC is only a central recruiting agency in the state while the Department of Personnel or the General Administration Department is the central personnel agency in the state.

The role of SPSC is not only limited, but also recommendations made by it are only of advisory nature and hence, not binding on the government. It is up to the state government to accept or reject that advice. The only safeguard is the answerability of the government to the state legislature for departing from the recommendation of the Commission. Further, the government can also make rules which regulate the scope of the advisory functions of SPSC. Also, the emergence of State Vigilance Commission (SVC) in 1964 affected the role of SPSC in disciplinary matters. This is because both are consulted by the government while taking disciplinary action against a civil servant. The problem arises when the two bodies tender conflicting advice. However, the SPSC, being an independent constitutional body, has an edge over the SVC. Finally, the SPSC is consulted by the governor while framing rules for appointment to judicial service of the state other than the posts of district judges. In this regard, the concerned state high court is also consulted.

Joint State Public Service Commission

The Constitution makes a provision for the establishment of a Joint State Public Service Commission (JSPSC) for two or more states. While the UPSC and the SPSC are created directly by the Constitution, a JSPSC can be created by an act of Parliament on the request of the state legislatures concerned. Thus, a SPSC is a statutory and not a constitutional body. The two states of Punjab and Haryana had a JSPSC for a short period, after the creation of Haryana out of Punjab in 1966. The chairman and members of a JSPSC are appointed by the president. They hold office for a term of six years or until they attain the age of 62 years, whichever is earlier. They can be suspended or removed by the president. They can also resign from their offices at a time by submitting their resignation letters to any the president. The number of members of a JSPSC and their conditions of service are determined by the President. A JSPSC presents its annual performance report to each of the concerned state governor. Each governor places the report before the state legislature.

The UPSC can also serve the needs of a JSPSC - for two differed states on the request of the state governor and Po with the approval of the president. As provided by the Government of India Act of 1919, a Central Public Service Commission was set up in 1926 and entrusted with the task of recruiting civil servants. The Government of India Act of 1935 provided for the establishment of not only a Federal Public Service Commission but also a Provincial Public Service Commission and Joint Public Service Commission for two or more provinces. Articles 308 to 314 in part XIV of the Constitution contain provisions with regard to all-India services, Central services and state services. [71]

Administrative Posts at District level

In India, a number of significant government jobs are in charge of the administration and governance of the district. Here are a few crucial factors:

District Collector/Deputy Commissioner

The District Collector, also known as the Deputy Commissioner in some states, is the highest-ranking administrative officer in the district. They are responsible for overall administration, law and order, revenue collection, and implementation of government schemes. They act as the principal representative of the state government in the district. They coordinate with various departments and ensure the smooth functioning of administrative processes in the district.

Superintendent of Police (SP)

The Superintendent of Police is responsible for maintaining law and order in the district. They oversee the functioning of the police force, investigate crimes, and take necessary actions to prevent and control criminal activities.

District Judge

The District Judge is responsible for the administration of justice in the district. They preside over the district court and handle civil and criminal cases within their jurisdiction.

Director General (DG), Zilla Parishad

The CEO of the Zilla Parishad is responsible for the overall administration and implementation of rural development programs in the district. They work closely with elected representatives and supervise the functioning of various departments under the Zilla Parishad.[72]

Recruitment Process at District Level

Recruitment of District Collector

The appointment of a District Collector, also known as the District Magistrate or Deputy Commissioner, in India is governed by the rules and regulations set by the central and state governments. The process may vary slightly depending on the state, it's important to note that the specific details and procedures for appointing a District Collector can vary across states in India. The state government's rules and regulations, as well as the guidelines provided by the Union Public Service Commission, should be referred to for accurate and up-to-date information regarding the appointment process in a particular state; but the general procedure is as follows:

District Collector: The District Collector is normally an officer in the Indian Administrative Service (IAS) cadre. IAS officers are hired through the Union Public Service Commission (UPSC) Civil Services

Examination: Candidates who pass the test are assigned to a variety of cadres, such as the Indian Administrative Service and the state administrative service.

State Government Notification: The state government sends out a notification when a district collector is appointed. This announcement details the credentials, experience, and eligibility requirements for the Promotion.

Selection Process: The selection process for the District Collector may include a combination of written examinations, interviews, and assessments conducted by the state government. The details of the selection process may vary across states.

Posting and Appointment: Once the selection process is completed, the state government assigns the selected IAS officer to the district as the District Collector. The appointment is usually made by an official order issued by the state government.

Training: Before assuming the role of a District Collector, the appointed officer undergoes training at the Lal Bahadur Shastri National Academy of Administration in Mussoorie, Uttarakhand. The training program equips them with the necessary skills and knowledge to carry out their administrative responsibilities effectively.[73]

Recruitment of a Police Superintendent

Superintendent of Police (SP), also known as Deputy Commissioner in a Police Department, is a senior rank in the Indian Police Service (IPS) Superintendent of Police (SP) who is in charge of a police district is referred to as the District Police Chief (DPC). However, in certain other states, the title District Superintendent of Police (SP). Appointing a Superintendent of Police (SP) at the district level in India is typically done by the respective state government. The process may vary slightly from state to state. Some states may have additional stages such as medical examinations or physical fitness tests. Therefore, it is advisable to refer to the official notifications and guidelines issued by the state government or the concerned authority for precise information on the appointment process in a particular state.

Indian Administrative Services: IAS officers are hired through the Union Public Service Commission's (UPSC) Civil Services Examination. Candidates who pass the test are assigned to several cadres, such as the Indian Police Service and the state service.

Interviewing and Selection: Candidates who have passed the written test and have been shortlisted are contacted for an interview. The interview is conducted by a selection committee to determine which candidates are most qualified for the position. This group usually consists of senior police officers and government representatives. The committee assesses their expertise, experience, leadership qualities, and capacity for problem-solving.

Training: In India, the initial training for IPS (Indian Police Service) officers typically takes place at the Sardar Vallabhbhai Patel National Police Academy (SVPNPA) located in Hyderabad, Telangana. The SVPNPA is the premier training institution for Indian Police Service officers and is responsible for providing basic training as well as advanced and specialized courses for police officers at various stages of their careers. IPS officers undergo a rigorous training program that includes classroom lectures, physical fitness training, field exercises, and practical sessions. The training curriculum covers a wide range of subjects including law, investigation techniques, crime prevention, leadership, and administration.[74]

District Judge: Recruitment of District Judges

• The Governor of the state appoints them based on the Chief Justice of the High Court of the relevant state's recommendation.

• Both civil and criminal cases can be heard by district judges.

• To help with the burden of workload, there may be a number of Assistant District Judges and Additional District Judges.

Article 233 of the Constitution provides references to the appointment of district judges. It lists the requirements that must be satisfied in order to be given consideration for appointment as a district judge. Since they are not in compliance with Articles 233 and 235, Article 233A upholds the validity of Judge's appointments made before to the start of the Constitution (Twentieth Amendment) Act 1966. The High Court is given control over District courts and Subordinate courts by Article 235.

The candidate must have at least seven years of experience as an advocate or pleader in order to be considered for the position of district judge. They must have the High Court's authorization to be employed there and must not have any other positions of employment with the Union or the State. The High Court Panel of Judges would conduct interviews with the recommended applicants after the State Public Service Commission administered an exam. On the basis of the Chief Justice of the High Court's recommendations, the state's governor will choose the district judges.[75]

Amalgamation of Strong Executive and Laws: Necessary for Sustainability of Administration

The foremost requirement for democratic system is Strong Executive; this organ must follow inter-governmental relations with state and local Government. Due to changing subsistence pattern of society, globalisation, and privatization, Executive power needs to be re-visited in the light of provisions of the Constitution according to today's socio-economic scenario that will help to build the administration in accurate direction. The expression "Executive Power" is very wide. It depicts the residue of governmental functions that remain after the legislative and judicial functions are taken away. It includes actions are necessary for the carrying on or supervision of the general administration of the State.

Dr. BR Ambedkar& his remarks on the significance of the Union's executive power are as follows:

Article 11 of the Constituent Assembly eradicated untouchability. The Center enacts legislation outlining specific punishments and legal actions for impeding untouchables from exercising their civil rights. Is it logical to pass a law of that nature if, for example, the sentiment against untouchability is not as strong and intense in the specific region and the government is not concerned with ensuring that untouchables have all the civil rights that the Constitution guarantees? If the offense was designated an offense that can be charged the enforcement of such a legislation might necessitate the establishment of more police and particular machinery for bringing off. For criminal prosecution and all administrative costs necessary to make the law effective. Shouldn't the Center with the enactment of such a law have the power to carry it out? I'm curious if anyone can argue that the Centre shouldn't do anything more than pass a law on a subject of this magnitude.

How Executive use their power

The executive expresses themselves through the remaining members of the government that carry out judicial and legislative duties in accordance with the Constitution or any other law. The creation of policy and its implementation, upholding law and order, and promoting social and economic wellbeing are all considered executive tasks. Political and diplomatic pursuits are also included. The following are likewise covered by article 298: (a) frame trading operations; (b) the purchase, possession, and sale of property; and (c) contracts for any reason.

Operation of Executive Powers and laws together

It is one of the Executive's primary responsibilities to carry out laws, but this does not mean that it is the only function it has. For example, the Executive may need to enact laws in order to maintain the expenditure of public funds or to infringe on private rights, both of which are prohibited by the Constitution without the need for legislation. But beyond from this, it is inconceivable that the Executive must first receive legislative approval in order to carry out any function, such as starting a business or commerce. The Government may, in the exercise of its executive power, make administrative Rules, such as those relating to conditions of service under the Government, in the absence of statutory provisions or in cases where such Rules are silent. Such non-statutory Rules shall, to the extent are applicable, be binding upon parties.

Article 73: The Executive Power of the Union to better the governance

India's Constitution's Article 73 addresses Extent of the Executive Power of the Union. It outlines the purview and jurisdiction of the federal government (the Union), particularly with regard to areas where both the Union and the State governments have legislative authority. According to the provisions of this Constitution, The executive power of the Union must, extend to the areas with respect to which Parliament has the capacity to make laws as well as the exercise of such rights, leadership, and any power that the Government of India may exercise under a treaty or other arrangement. The Government may, in the exercise of its executive power, make administrative Rules, such as those relating to conditions of service under the Government, in the absence of statutory provisions or in cases where such Rules are silent. Such non-statutory Rules shall, to the extent applicable, be binding upon parties.

In a nutshell Article 73 gives the central government the authority to exercise executive control over issues that are under the purview of the Union (central) legislature, and in certain circumstances, pursuant to international conventions or agreements, even if such problems pass over into areas where both the Union and State governments may enact legislation. The clause clearly states that, unless the Constitution or particular laws passed by Parliament expressly stipulate otherwise, the federal Government's executive power does not extend to sectors in which the State legislature also has legislative authority.

How Executive power require to uplift particular subject

The Constitution itself stipulates that the act can be accomplished by legislation, such as when it comes to the imposition of tax under article 265 or the expenditure of money under article 266(3), or when it comes to equality before the law under article 14 or the infringement of fundamental rights under article 19(2) (6) or the protection of life and liberty according to article 21 of the Constitution or other legal rights under article 300A, legislation may be needed.[76]

Reforms Phase From 1947 - 2013

India undertook substantial reforms in a number of areas of its economy, society, and government after achieving independence from British domination in 1947. These reforms, which attempted to create a new nation and overcome the difficulties encountered by an independent nation with a diverse people, were crucial in determining India's course as a young country and in setting the groundwork for future growth and development. Under Jawaharlal Nehru's direction and that of succeeding leaders, the Indian government set out on a mission to address these issues and alter the social and economic climate of the country. To improve the standard of living of all its residents, the nation continues to address a variety of socioeconomic problems and strive for inclusive growth.[77] Following independence, India's growth in society and the economy can be summarized as follows:

Reform Phase: After Independence

First Prime Minister Jawaharlal Nehru addressing a newly independent India on 15 August 1947

(i) **Constitutional Reforms:** The Indian Constitution, which went into force on January 26, 1950, was the most important reform. The Constitution established a legislative democratic process, fundamental rights, and a guiding principle of state policy to direct the government's efforts in achieving social and economic justice. Dr. B.R. Ambedkar served as chair of the writing committee. In order to define and advance its governance structure, India has undergone a number of key constitutional modifications. These changes attempted to deal with numerous problems, uphold democratic values, and meet the many requirements of the country. Following India's independence, the major constitutional modifications were made:

• **The Constitution of India (1950):** The most significant constitutional reform after independence was the adoption of the Constitution of India on January 26, 1950. It replaced the Government of India Act 1935, which had served as India's governing framework during the colonial period. The Constitution of India established India as a sovereign, socialist, secular, and democratic republic. It enshrined fundamental rights and directive principles of state policy to safeguard individual liberties and promote social and economic justice.[78]

• **Abolition of Privy Purses (1971):** Privy purses were monetary allowances granted to the erstwhile rulers of princely states after they acceded to India following independence. The government decided to abolish privy purses through the 26th Amendment Act of 1971, thereby putting an end to the special privileges of the former rulers.

• **Panchayati Raj System (1992):** Part IX, which served as the framework for the Panchayati Raj system, was added to the Constitution by the 73rd Amendment Act of 1992, bringing about considerable changes. By introducing elected rural local councils and giving them control over administration and finances, this amendment transferred authority to the local levels.

• **Municipalities Reforms (1993):** Part IXA of the Constitution, which dealt with urban local bodies (municipalities), was added by the 74th Amendment Act of 1993. Decentralized urban government and the development of municipal bodies were both included.[79]

• **Constitution (Scheduled Castes) Order (1950) and (Scheduled Tribes) Order (1950):** For various states and territories, the President of India issued orders naming the Scheduled Castes (SC) and Scheduled Tribes (ST), giving them particular safeguards and equal opportunities in the form of reservations in employment and education. Following India's independence in 1947, there were some significant attempts in support of the Scheduled Castes and Scheduled Tribes (SCs and STs), the Other Backward Castes (OBCs) after the 1980s, and the impoverished in the general category in 2019.

(ii) Land and Agriculture Reforms: To solve issues concerned with land allocation and tenancy, the government launched land reforms. The intention was to get rid of middlemen and landlords and give vacant property to farmers in order to spread out land ownership. To safeguard the liberties of farmers and agricultural workers, several land reform laws were put into place by various governments. The following are a few of the significant agrarian reforms carried out in India after independence:

• **Zamindari Abolition:** The zamindari system was eliminated, which was one of the initial and most important agrarian reforms. In the zamindari system, a feudal form of land tenure, middlemen called zamindars would collect money from farmers and give an amount of it to the British colonial rulers.

• **Tenancy Reforms**: To protect the rights of tenant farmers, several states introduced tenancy reforms. These reforms aimed to provide security of tenure to tenants and regulate their relationship with landlords. Some of the common provisions included setting a maximum limit on rents, conferment of ownership rights to long-term tenants, and providing legal protection against arbitrary eviction.

• **Land Ceiling Laws:** Several states passed land ceiling legislation to address the problem of property accumulation and disproportionate land distribution. The most land that a person or family might own was constrained by these rules. The government purchased the extra land that was above the set ceiling limit and gave it to marginal or landless farmers.

• **Green Revolution:** India saw the Green Revolution in the 1960s and 1970s, which had a considerable impact on agricultural productivity without directly enacting an agrarian reform. It required the employment of high-yielding crop types, more fertilizer, and better irrigation systems. India went from having a food shortage to having a surplus of food as a result of the Green Revolution. The Green Revolution's main characteristics in India are:

Introduction of High-Yielding Varieties (HYVs) of seeds:

High-yielding wheat and rice cultivars created via scientific study were introduced during the Green Revolution. These HYVs responded well to contemporary interventions like fertilizers and irrigation, had shorter crop cycles, and was immune to pests and diseases.

Expansion of irrigation:

The Indian government made significant investments in expanding irrigation infrastructure to facilitate the growing of HYVs. To supply water to farmlands, dams, canals, and tube wells were constructed, thereby reducing reliance on monsoon rains and expanding the area under cultivation.

Services for agricultural research and extension: Agricultural research organizations and extension agencies helped the Green Revolution by educating farmers all around the nation about contemporary farming methods.[79]

Impact of the Green Revolution:

Enhanced farming effectiveness: The use of HYVs and modern farming techniques has resulted in a notable improvement in crop yields, especially in the case of wheat and rice, the two main dietary staples of India.

Food self-sufficiency: India transformed from a food deficient nation heavily reliant on food imports to a self-sufficient country capable of meeting its own food needs.

Reduced poverty and better quality of life: The Green Revolution had a favorable effect on the rural economy, raised farm earnings, and helped to reduce poverty in many areas.[80]

(iii) Economic Planning: After the Planning Commission was established in India in 1950, the country transitioned to a planned economy. Five-Year Plans were developed to direct economic growth and distribute funds to important industries, infrastructure, and education. India started a series of economic reforms after attaining independence in 1947 to address the difficulties of being a new sovereign state and to promote economic growth and development. These changes can be generally divided into the following phases:

• **Planning and Development (1951-1991):** The period from 1951 to 1991 was characterized by a planned economy, with the government playing an essential part in economic development and planning. The governmental and private sectors are both present in India's mixed economy model. The most important economic reforms and programs during this period were:

• **Five-Year Plans: Five-Year Plans** were first developed in India to set particular economic goals and distribute resources to various sectors. These initiatives attempted to industrialize, expand the infrastructure, and combat poverty by implementing various social schemes.[81]

Public Sector Undertaking (PSUs)

India had a less industrial base and was essentially an agrarian nation when it attained independence in 1947. There were only 18 government-owned Indian Ordnance Factories, which had been built in the past to lessen the British Indian Army's reliance on imported weapons. Jawaharlal Nehru, India's first prime minister proposed an industrialization-based economic strategy based on import substitution, as well as a mixed economy. He thought that the development and modernization of the Indian economy depended on the formation of heavy and basic industry.

PSUs (Public Sector Undertakings) are government-owned companies or enterprises that are run by the federal or state governments in India. In India, there are two primary categories of PSUs:

Public sector units (PSUs) that are owned and managed by India's central government are known as central public sector enterprises (CPSEs). Based on factors including their financial performance and other factors, CPSEs are further divided into Maharatnas, Navratnas, and Miniratnas. The most powerful and most financially stable CPSEs are known as Maharatnas. They exercise a great deal of decision-making and investment autonomy. Examples are National Thermal Power Corporation (NTPC), Oil and Natural Gas Corporation (ONGC), and Indian Oil Corporation Limited (IOCL).

Navratnas: Compared to Maharatnas, Navratnas have a little less financial autonomy. They are the next tier of CPSEs. They have the power to decide on investments up to a particular amount. Examples are Hindustan Aeronautics Limited (HAL), Bharat Heavy Electricals Limited (BHEL), and Bharat Petroleum Corporation Limited (BPCL).

Miniratnas: These are more financially and operationally flexible, smaller CPSEs. Examples are Rashtriya Ispat Nigam Limited (RINL), Power Finance Corporation (PFC), and Chennai Petroleum Corporation Limited (CPCL).

State Public Sector Enterprises (SPSEs): These PSUs are owned and managed by the state governments in which they are located. Depending on local demands and resources, every state could possess a distinct set of SPSEs engaged in a variety of business activities.[82]

(iv) Industrial Policy: India implemented an industrial policy to encourage industrialization and financial independence. The government concentrated on growing important industries, especially those deemed crucial for the expansion and prosperity of the nation. Here is a summary of the main industrial policies that India pursued following independence:

• **1948 Industrial Policy Resolution** Only a few years after independence, in 1948, the nation's initial industrial strategy was created. In order to promote quick industrialization and self-reliance, this resolution placed a strong emphasis on state involvement in industrial growth. The program was centered on designating specific industries as belonging only to the public sector and encouraging private businesses to join in non-reserved industries.

• **1956 Industrial Policy Resolution** This policy, often referred to as the "Socialistic Pattern of Society" policy, was a landmark in India's industrialization efforts. It emphasized the role of the state as the principal driver of industrial development. The policy aimed to achieve a mixed economy, with the public sector playing a dominant role in core and strategic industries, while the private sector was encouraged to participate in other areas.

• **1977 Industrial Policy Resolution:** The government implemented this program in response to economic difficulties and the requirement to revive industries. It aimed to increase the competitiveness of small-scale industries, support their role, and lessen regional inequities. The policy also aimed to promote modernization and technical developments while bolstering the public sector.

• **Industrial strategy of 1991 (Revised in 1998 and 2003):** To stimulate foreign direct investment (FDI) in a variety of sectors, the government updated the industrial strategy as economic reforms progressed. Particular attention was provided to industries including services, telecommunications, and information technology.[83]

(v) Education and Literacy: There have been initiatives to advance education and raise literacy rates all around the nation. The government set up schools, colleges, and universities and took steps to increase everyone's access to education. The government recognized that education and literacy were essential for the socio-economic development of the country and for empowering its citizens. Over the years, India has made substantial progress in these areas, but challenges still remain. Here's an overview of the developments in education and literacy after independence:

• **Educational Reforms**: Various educational reforms were implemented by the Indian government to increase access to education and improve learning outcomes. Several important initiatives were:

• **The Kothari Commission (1966–1966):** This commission, led by educationist Dr. D.S. Kothari, provided recommendations for the development of education in India. Its report emphasized the need for free and compulsory education for children up to the age of 14, expansion of higher education, and the promotion of vocational education.

National Policy on Education (1968)

With the help of this policy, the nation's educational system was intended to become more uniform and accessible. It placed a priority on providing all children with free and required education, putting a strong emphasis on science and technology education, and encouraging the study of regional languages. In 1968, the government led by Prime Minister Indira Gandhi unveiled the first National Policy on Education, which was based on the conclusions and suggestions of the Kothari Commission (1964–1966). This policy called for a “restructuring of Radicalism" and suggested equitable access to education with the goal to accomplish national integration and higher cultural and economic development.

The **"three language formula"** to be used in secondary education—the teaching of Hindi, the official language of the state wherever the school was located, and English—was outlined in the policy, which called for a concentration on the acquisition of regional languages. In order to bridge the gap between the elite and the common people, language instruction was considered to be crucial. The National Policy on Education of 1968 included the following main goals and highlights:

• **Universalization of Education:** The policy aimed to provide free and compulsory education for all children up to the age of 14 (later increased to 18 years by the Right to Education Act, 2009).

• **Emphasis on Vocational Education:** The policy recognized the importance of vocational education and aimed to develop programs that would help students acquire skills and knowledge relevant to the world of work. The policy aimed to create programs that would assist students in acquiring knowledge and skills relevant to the workplace and acknowledged the value of vocational education.

• **Promotion of Indian Languages**: The policy recommended that schools implement a three-language curriculum and underlined the value of maintaining and promoting Indian languages.

• **Reorganization of the Higher Education System:** With a focus on raising the standard of higher education institutions, the program called for the creation of a three-tiered educational system made up of universities, colleges, and schools.[84]

National Education policy (1986)

Under the assistance of this policy, the nation's educational system was intended to become more uniform and egalitarian. It placed a priority on providing all children with free and required education, putting a strong emphasis on technological and scientific education, and encouraging the study of indigenous languages. A new National Policy on Education was announced in 1986 by the Rajiv Gandhi-led administration. According to the new policy, there should be "exceptional attention to the elimination of imbalances and to democratize academic opportunities," particularly for Indian women, Scheduled Tribes (ST), and Scheduled Caste (SC) populations.

In order to strengthen primary schools across the country, the NPE called for a "child-centered approach" in primary education and launched "Operation Blackboard." The policy added the 1985-founded Indira Gandhi National Open University to the system of open universities. In order to foster economic and social development at the local level in rural India, the strategy also called for the establishment of the "rural university" model, which was inspired by the ideas of Mahatma Gandhi. The 6% of GDP allocated to education in the 1986 education policy.

The key objectives of the National Policy on Education 1986 include:

Improvement in Quality: The NPE placed a strong emphasis on raising the standard of instruction at all levels, from elementary to higher education, in order to foster excellence and relevance.

Education Vocationalization: The policy acknowledged the value of vocational training in preparing students to meet the needs of the labor market and to acquire the necessary skills and abilities for gainful employment.

Adult Education: The NPE of 1986 placed a strong emphasis on the importance of adult education in eradicating illiteracy and ensuring that everyone has access to opportunities for lifelong learning.

Equitable and Socioeconomic Justice: The strategy attempted to lessen gaps in educational access between various social groups, geographic areas, and genders. It emphasized uplifting poor and marginalized groups in society through education.[85]

- **Literacy Programs:** In terms of literacy rates, India experienced major difficulties, particularly in the early years following the independence. Numerous literacy initiatives were started to solve this problem:

  Mission Saakshar Bharat**:** The goal of this initiative, which was introduced in 2009, was to improve adult literacy, particularly among women and members of Scheduled Castes and Scheduled Tribes.

  Higher Education**:** India focused on constructing fresh universities, Indian Institutes of Technology (IITs), Indian Institutes of Management (IIMs), and other specialized educational institutions in order to expand accessibility to higher education.

(vi) Women's Rights : India made achievements toward strengthening women rights and establishing gender equality. Equal rights for men and women have been established by the Constitution, and a number of laws were enacted to uphold the rights and interests of women.

Many initiatives were started by the Indian government, social reformers, and women's rights advocates to advance women's status and rights in the nation. After India gained independence, the following significant changes in women's rights occurred:

The Indian Constitution, which came into effect on January 26, 1950, enshrined several provisions to safeguard women's rights and promote gender equality. Some of the relevant articles include Article 14 (Right to Equality), Article 15 (Prohibition of Discrimination on grounds of religion, race, caste, sex, or place of birth), and Article 16 (Equality of opportunity in public employment). The Committee on the status of women (1974) provided the first comprehensive study on the rights and status of Indian women. Recently the department of Women and Child Development has drawn up a National Perspective Plan for Women (1988-2000 A.D.) The Prime Minister, Mr. P.V. Narasimha Rao, also announced the setting up of two commissions on women. Also, 'Women's studies' as a discipline is being encouraged in many universities, as well as by the U.G.C. Several pre-woman laws have been passed, to protect their rights.

• **Women's Suffrage:** Following India's independence, women were granted the right to vote. Women participated in the 1951–1952 general elections as voters and candidates, which was a crucial turning point for women's political emancipation.

• **The Hindu Succession Act of 1956:** This act reformed inheritance laws and granted daughters the right to inherit ancestral property on an equal basis as sons. Prior to this, daughters had limited rights to ancestral property.

• **The Maternity Benefits Act of 1961:** The act provides for certain benefits to women employees in India, including maternity leave and financial assistance during pregnancy and childbirth.

• **The Dowry Prohibition Act of 1961:** The act aims to combat the social evil of dowry, which has been a significant problem in India. It prohibits the giving or taking of dowry in marriage.

• **The Equal Remuneration Act of 1976:** This law guarantees that men and women in the same workplace receive equal pay for equivalent work. NCW, the National Commission for Women was established in order to protect the rights and interests of women in India, to examine laws and policies that impact women, and to recommend necessary reforms. , the NCW was founded in 1992.

• **Women in Politics:** Over the time, there have been progressively more women in politics. The President, Prime Minister, and numerous ministerial portfolios are just a few of the significant roles in the government that women have held. 73rd and 74th amendments established to make policies for women's equality.

• **Educational Empowerment:** To encourage females' education and raise female literacy rates, the government has taken action. Access has been made better by programs like the Sarva Shiksha Abhiyan (Education for All).[86]

(vii) Reservation Policy: In order to address historical social inequalities and caste-based discrimination, the reservation system was introduced, providing affirmative action for Scheduled Castes (SC), Scheduled Tribes (ST), and Other Backward Classes (OBC) in educational institutions and government jobs. The government introduced various policies to address historical and social injustices and to promote social equality. One such policy is the Reservation Policy, also known as Affirmative Action or Positive Discrimination, which aims to provide opportunities and representation to historically disadvantaged and marginalized communities. The Reservation Policy in India primarily focuses on reservations in education and public sector employment. 73rd & 74th initiated representation of marginalized community. Here's an overview of the Reservation Policy after Independence:

Scheduled Castes (SCs) and Scheduled Tribes (STs) Reservation:

Scheduled Castes: Historically, SCs, often referred to as Dalits, were the lowest caste and experienced extreme discrimination. To uplift them socially and economically, the Indian Constitution provided for reservation in education and public sector jobs for SCs.

Scheduled Tribes: Also known as Adivasis, STs are indigenous groups that have historically endured discrimination and exploitation. The constitution also included provision for reservation in education and public sector jobs for STs.

(viii) Foreign Policy: After the independence of India, Pt. Nehru observed and I quote "The preservation of world peace and the expansion of human freedom are the objectives of our foreign policy." He added that the idealism of today would give way to realism in the future. India adopted a non-alignment strategy, claiming its independence from the Cold War blocs and fostering cordial relations with all countries. India was a key player in the Non-Aligned Movement, which promoted harmony and collaboration among developing nations. Following are some of the main tenets of India's foreign policy after independence:

Non-Alignment: One of the cornerstones of India's foreign policy was the principle of non-alignment. India chose not to align itself with any major power bloc during the Cold War era and aimed to maintain strategic autonomy and independence in its international relations. This policy was articulated by India's first Prime Minister, Jawaharlal Nehru, who emphasized the need to remain neutral in global power struggles.

Panchsheel (Five Principles of Peaceful Coexistence): India, along with China, played a significant role in formulating the Five Principles of Peaceful Coexistence, also known as Panchsheel, in 1954. These principles emphasized mutual respect for sovereignty and territorial integrity, non-aggression, non-interference in internal affairs, equality, and peaceful coexistence.

Concentration on Multilateralism: India has been a major proponent of multilateralism and has taken an active role in a number of international forum, including the World Trade Organization (WTO), the Non-Aligned Movement (NAM), and several regional alliances. India has made an effort to interact with the world community on global concerns including climate change, sustainable development, and disarmament.

Priorities in the territory: India places a high value on its connections with its neighbors and the larger South Asian region. For the sake of regional stability and prosperity, programs like the "Neighborhood First" strategy seek to strengthen economic and political relations with neighboring nations.[87]

(ix) Healthcare and Public Services: To meet the requirements of the expanding population, the government extended public services and healthcare facilities. The public health and sanitation were improved. India faced enormous difficulties in 1947 when it became independent; in trying to ensure its people had access to quality healthcare. The Indian government has put a lot of effort towards enhancing healthcare delivery, expanding access to medical services, and improving healthcare infrastructure. Here is a overview of the changes to India's healthcare system after independence:

National Health Programs: In order to address the country's serious health problems, the Indian government launched a number of national health programs. The National Malaria Eradication Program, which began in 1958, the Family Planning Program, which began in the late 1950s, the National Tuberculosis Control Program, which began in 1962, and the Universal Immunization Program, which began in 1985, are a few of the important programs.

National Health Policy (1983): The Government of India published the National Health Policy in 1983 as a key document outlining the nation's approach to health and healthcare delivery. This strategy sought to offer an all-inclusive framework for healthcare growth and planning in India. Here are some of the National Health Policy of 1983's major highlights:

Primary Health Care: As the cornerstone of the healthcare system, primary health care (PHC) was emphasized as being crucial in the strategy. It acknowledged the value of fundamental curative, preventive and promotional health services at the community level to raise the general public's level of health.

Inter-Sectoral Collaboration: The strategy placed a strong emphasis on inter-sectoral coordination since it recognized that variables outside the healthcare industry have an impact on health. In order to fully address health determinants, it planned to work with other industries including education, farming, cleanliness, and women's and children's development.

National Malaria Eradication Program: Originally known as the National Malaria Control Program (NMCP), the National Eradication Program (NMEP) was established in 1958. The NMEP was incredibly successful between 1958 and 1965, reducing the frequency of malaria to only 1 lakh cases and prevented any deaths in 1965.

National Tuberculosis Control Programme: The National Tuberculosis Control Programme was established in 1962 with the objective of reducing the disability and death from TB by effective treatment. The Govt. of India, WHO and World Bank together reviewed the NTP in 1992. Based on the findings a revised strategy for NTP was evolved. In order to attain a DOTS (Direct Observation Treatment Short course) cure rate of at least 85%, short-term chemotherapy has been established in 5 districts. Volunteers like teachers, anganwadi workers, former patients, and social workers carry out this activity. NGOs work in the fields of communication, education, and information.[88]

Declaration of Alma Ata: The Alma Ata Declaration, which stressed the value of primary healthcare as the key to achieving "Health for All" by the year 2000, was signed in 1978 by India and other World Health Organization (WHO) members. This statement reaffirmed India's commitment to enhancing healthcare for all of its residents.[89]

(x) Banking and Financial Reforms: India's banking industry experienced changes to improve the stability of the financial system. Major Banks were nationalized by the government in order to promote financial inclusion and assure credit flow to various economic sectors. The goal of nationalizing banks was to promote financial inclusion, implement economic reforms, and dedicate banking resources toward social development.

Here is overview of the significant occasions surrounding the nationalization of banks in India:

Indian Imperial Bank: The Imperial Bank of India was the biggest and the oldest commercial bank in the nation during the British rule when it was founded in 1921. Under the State Bank of India Act, the Indian government changed it into the State Bank of India (SBI) in 1955. The nationalization of banks in India began with SBI.

Nationalization's initial phase (1969): The announcement of the nationalization of 14 significant commercial banks in India was made by the Indian government on July 19, 1969, under the direction of then-Prime Minister Indira Gandhi. At the time, these banks accounted for almost 85% of all deposits in the banking industry. Punjab National Bank, Bank of India, Bank of Baroda, Canara Bank, Central Bank of India, United Bank of India, Dena Bank, Syndicate Bank, Union Bank of India, Allahabad Bank, Indian Bank, Indian Overseas Bank, Bank of Maharashtra, and UCO Bank were among the banks nationalized during this time.

The main goals of this nationalization were to: Promote financial inclusion by expanding banking services to rural and semi-urban areas; Ensure that banks meet the needs of priority industries, such as agriculture, small-scale manufacturing, and other sectors essential to economic development; prevent the concentration of economic power in the hands of a small number of private players.

Second stage of nationalization (1980): On April 15, 1980, the government undertook a second stage of nationalization, taking control of six more private banks. Andhra Bank, Corporation Bank, New Bank of India (which merged with Punjab National Bank in 1993), Oriental Bank of Commerce, Punjab and Sind Bank, and Vijaya Bank were among the banks nationalized during this time.[90]

Reform Phase: Early 1990s

Reform Phase initiated in 1991 as LPG Theory

In India, the process of liberalization, globalization, and privatization reform phases started in the early 1990s and lasted till the early 2000s. The economic reforms associated with privatization, globalization, and liberalization have significantly impacted India. They aided in boosting economic growth rates, boosting foreign investment, developing the services industry, and joining the worldwide supply chain. These reforms were not without difficulty, though, since worries concerning inequality and regional inequalities persisted as issues of policy focus for succeeding governments. These are the primary elements of this reform phase:

In Liberalization government controls and regulations on many economic sectors were loosened as a result of liberalization. This included removing trade restrictions, liberalizing private enterprise freedom, and simplifying industrial licensing. India's economic reform was aided by its 1985 balance of payments crisis. Due to the crisis, the nation was unable to cover both its debt obligations and necessary imports. Therein, India was driven to the verge of bankruptcy. Dr. Manmohan Singh, India's then-finance minister, responded by introducing economic liberalization in his country.[91]

Some of the liberalization's initial characteristics, which were part of the 1991 economic changes, include:

• The elimination of the nation's former License Raj system. A permit or license between 1947 and 1990, a complex system of rules, permits, and restrictions called license Raj was applied to the operation of the establishment of businesses.

• A decrease in tariffs and interest rates. Curbing public sector's monopoly in several sectors of our economy.

• Approval of foreign direct investment in various sectors. Economic liberalization in India integrated the above features and in general waived off several restrictions to become more private sector-friendly.

• Diversification of Investor Portfolio - post-liberalization, investors has the liberty to invest a percentage of their portfolio into a diversified asset class, thus generating more profit. Improvement of Stock Market Performance - Relaxation of economic laws also leads to a rise in the stock market's value, thus encouraging more trading among investors.

Globalization: The goal of globalization was to incorporate the Indian economy into the international market. It involves fostering technology transfer and partnerships with foreign businesses, as well as supporting foreign direct investment (FDI) and global trade and investment. The goal of globalization is to eliminate borders so that one country's needs can be met by the rest of the world, creating a single, massive economy.

Outsourcing as an outcome of globalization:

Contracting is the key result of the globalization process. In the outsourcing model, a corporation from one nation engages an expert from another nation to complete work that was previously completed by an internal resource from that nation. The benefit of outsourcing is that work may be performed more cheaply and competently from any location in the world. In India, a number of contact centers or BPO firms have emerged with their own models of voice-based business processes. Services like banking, accounting, and bookkeeping are all being outsourced from industrialized nations to India as well as medical Tele- Consultation.

Privatization: The goal of privatization was to lessen the role of the government in economic activity and to increase private sector involvement across a range of industries. To increase productivity and competitiveness, state-owned businesses were either sold off or divested. The reasons for privatization are:

• Make the government's financial situation better.

• Lighten the pressure on businesses in the public sector.

• Collect money through disinvestment.

• Boost the effectiveness of government agencies.

• Offer the consumer better and enhanced products and services.

• Promote FDI (foreign direct investment) in India.[92]

During this reform phase, important policy initiatives and benchmarks include:

1991 Economic Reforms: In 1991, the Indian government unveiled a comprehensive program of economic reforms in response to a balance of payments problem. Trade liberalization, currency devaluation, and the elimination of the industrial licensing system were all included in this package.

Industrial Policy Reforms: To lessen bureaucratic constraints, foster competition, and attract private investment, industrial policies were updated. The New Industrial Policy of 1991 sought to improve the climate for investors. Import tariffs were gradually lowered to encourage competition and broaden access to foreign goods as part of trade policy reforms.

Financial Sector Reforms: To liberalize interest rates, bolster the banking system, and promote private sector involvement in banking, considerable reforms were made in the financial and banking industries.

Foreign Investment Policy: FDI regulations were relaxed and industries were made more accessible to FDI. Additionally, India created SEZs, or special economic zones, to promote international business and companies that focus on exports.

Information technology and telecommunications: The opening of the telecommunications industry to private investment resulted in a sharp increase in the use of mobile phones. India became a hub for international IT services.

Budget Stabilization: To promote a stable macroeconomic environment, measures were implemented to control budget deficits and strengthen fiscal restraint.

National Telecom Policy 1994

The Department of Telecommunication (DOT), Government of India, created the National Telecom Policy 1994 as a result of the rapid change in the overall situation of the Indian telecommunication industry. Additionally, the Indian National Telecom Policy of 1994 introduced a number of changes to the country's earlier telecommunications policy. The two primary regulatory authorities for the Indian telecommunications sector are the "Telecom Regulatory Authority of India" (TRAI) and the "Department of Telecommunication" (DOT).[93]

The following are the goals of India's National Telecom Policy of 1994:

• To make telecommunication easier for everyone

• Ensuring prompt telephone connectivity via effective service networks

• Establish affordable universal service access for all Indian villages.

• Offering telecommunication services of the highest caliber.

• Addressing customer concerns, resolving disagreements, and paying special attention to public interaction

• To offer the broadest choice of goods and services, at competitive prices to all Indians

National Telecom Policy 1999

The study of the Group on Telecommunication served as the foundation for the 1999 New Telecom Policy. A high-level group on telecommunications (GoT) was established by the government to examine the National Telecom Policy of 1994, which is the current telecom policy. A new telecom policy was primarily necessary since the objectives of the National Telecom Policy of 1994 were not met within the allotted time frame, and on the other hand, there had been tremendous advancements in information and communication technology. The Government of India developed the National Telecom Policy (NTP) in 1999 as a fundamental policy framework to address the expanding telecommunications industry and its development in the nation.

The New Telecommunications Policy of 1999 has the following goals:

•Ensure access to cost-effective and effective telecommunications for all citizens. Establish a balance between high level services and universal services provided to all untapped areas.

•Promote the construction of telecommunications infrastructure in the nation's isolated, mountainous, and tribal regions.

Restructuring of the Department of Telecommunication (DoT)

Prior to the 1999 Policy, DoT was in charge of licensing, policy creation, and service providing. The proposal stated that the government will divide the DoT's tasks of policy and licensing from those of service providing. Additionally, it was announced that the corporatization of the DoT will occur by 2001, bearing in mind the interests of all stakeholders. Additionally, it was planned that all future interactions between DoT, MTNL, and BSNL will be guided by the best commercial practices.

Spectrum Control

The Policy noted that with the introduction of new technologies into the market the demand for spectrum has increased. It also recognized the need for utilizing spectrum efficiently, economically, rationally and optimally. Under the Policy, the Government intended to revise the National Frequency Allocation Plan. The allocation plan would be in conformity with the International Telecommunication Union (ITU) regulations.

USOF or Universal Service Obligation Fund

In accordance with the Policy, the Government intended to meet a number of objectives in order to offer fundamental telecommunications services at a fair and acceptable cost. The targets were:

• Provide voice and low speed data service to the balance 2.9 lakh uncovered villages in the country by the year 2002

• Achieve Internet access to all district headquarters by the year 2000

Role of Regulator

The Policy clarified the role of TRAI in the telecom sector. This was done with regard to the problem where the DoT refused to accept the TRAI's jurisdiction over some legal questions. The Policy expressly mentions that TRAI is envisioned to be an independent regulator with comprehensive powers. It stated that TRAI has the authority to hear disputes regarding telecommunication and also issue directives to the Government.

National Education Policy (1992)

The P. V. Narasimha Rao administration modified the National Policy on Education from 1986 in 1992. The "Common Minimum Programme" of his United Progressive Alliance (UPA) administration served as the foundation for a new strategy that Former Prime Minister Manmohan Singh adopted in 2005. Under the National Policy on Education (NPE) of 1986, the corresponding Program of Action (PoA) of 1992 envisioned holding a common entrance exam for admission to professional and technical programs across the nation.

Early childhood education and care is a feature of the 1992 New Education Policy.

• Universalization of Elementary Education – UEE

The POA also had the goal of achieving the UEE targets. For kids who are unable to attend full-time schools, it proposed a number of innovations and revamped programs including "Non-Formal Education.

• Navodaya Vidyalayas to Improve the Quality of Education

The POA of 1992 envisioned the establishment of Navodaya Vidyalayas all over the country. These institutions were designed to support outstanding achievers regardless of their socioeconomic status.[94]

Reform Phase: UPA Government

(I) Agriculture and Farmers Welfare reforms

In order to expand the Indian economy and open it up to the world market, reforms were started in 1991. These changes had a substantial impact on the agricultural and farmers' welfare sectors even though they were primarily directed at the industrial and service sectors. Numerous efforts and policy changes implemented in India as a result of the LPG reforms had an impact on agriculture and farmers' welfare. Dr. Manmohan Singh's policy changes from 1991 also sought to change India's trade policies.

India also signed the UR (Uruguay Round) trade agreements, which cover agriculture. All of the countries were required to liberalize agriculture as part of the UR pledges. The majority of agricultural products had very high tariffs. Dr. Manmohan Singh relieved the farmers in 2009 by waiving the loan (worth INR 65,000 crore). Additionally, he changed the law so that farmers can now seek bank loans up to Rs. 3 lakhs. Some of the important projects and reforms include:

Agricultural Marketing Reforms: By permitting contract farming and private players, the authorities have taken moves to liberalize the agricultural markets. With these measures, the market would be more competitive and farmers' produce would fetch a higher price.

National Agricultural Policy: The nation's government has put out a number of measures to enhance the agricultural industry as a whole, including boosting funding for irrigation, rural infrastructure, and agricultural R&D. On July 28, 2000, the Indian government released its National Agricultural Policy. It was created in accordance with World Trade Organization (WTO) rules.

The following are main goals of National Agricultural Policy:

1) To realize Indian agriculture's enormous latent potential

2) Achieve an agricultural sector growth rate greater than 4% annually.

3) Concentrate on the home market and increase the revenue from agricultural exports.

4) Achieve growth that is equitable and sustainable in terms of technology, the environment, and the economy.[95]

RKVY (Rashtriya Krishi Vikas Yojana): This program was developed to aid the states in providing them with flexibility and autonomy when developing and carrying out programs for the agricultural and related sectors. To assist the agricultural industry in achieving 4% annual growth, the Rashtriya Krishi Vikas Yojana was launched.

Direct Benefit Transfer (DBT) in Agriculture: In an effort to cut down on leaks and ensure that welfare programs are more effectively targeted, the government has started using DBT to send incentives as well as benefits directly to farmers' bank accounts. On December 12, 2014, DBT was further extended throughout the nation.

Agricultural Credit: Through a number of programs, including the Kisan Credit Card (KCC) and interest subvention, the government has increased the amount of credit available to farmers. The Kisan Credit Card (KCC) scheme was introduced in 1998 and calls for banks to issue Kisan Credit Cards to farmers based on their holdings. The Kisan Credit Card initiative intends to provide farmers with flexible and streamlined financial assistance through financial institutions through a single window for their farming and other requirements as listed below:

To meet the following short-term credit needs:

- Post-harvest costs;
- Produce marketing loan;
- Working capital for upkeep of land assets and activities associated with agriculture;
- Investment credit need for agriculture and related activities.

National Food Security Act (NFSA): The National Food Security Act, passed by the UPA government in 2013, sought to give subsidized food grains to around two-thirds of the Indian populace. The Act was designed to protect farmers and other vulnerable groups in society from food insecurity. Up to 75% of the rural population and up to 50% of the urban population are covered by the National Food Security Act of 2013 (NFSA) for getting substantially subsidized food grains.

Mahatma Gandhi National Rural Employment Guarantee Act (MGNREGA): Although this plan was started under the previous NDA administration, it was further expanded by the UPA administration. MGNREGA provided a safety net for landowners during difficult agricultural seasons by guaranteeing 100 days of pay work annually to rural households.

Agricultural Debt Waiver and Debt Relief Scheme: The UPA administration introduced a significant program of debt alleviation for farmers in 2008. In accordance with this plan, a sizeable portion of agricultural loans were forgiven to aid struggling farmers who were drowning in debt.

National Horticulture Mission (NHM): The NHM was established to increase horticulture productivity and develop the infrastructure for post-harvest management and selling of horticultural crops. The primary goals of the NHM are to increase production of all horticultural goods (fruits, vegetables, flowers, coco, cashew nuts, plantation crops, etc.) and to expand horticulture to the full extent of the state's capacity.

Pradhan Mantri Krishi Sinchai Yojana: In order to create PMKSY, the ongoing irrigation programs, notably the Accelerated Irrigation Benefit Program (AIBP), were combined in 2015 by the NDA government.

(II) Affordable Accessible Healthcare

The UPA administration worked to increase access and affordability of healthcare in India from 2004 to 2014, when Dr. Manmohan Singh served as Prime Minister. During this time, a number of programs and policies were put into place to address various healthcare issues and improve population healthcare services.

During the Manmohan Singh administration, some of the major measures for accessible and inexpensive healthcare included:

National Rural Health Mission (NRHM): To improve the healthcare system in rural areas, the UPA government introduced the NRHM in 2005. NRHM is to serve the rural population, particularly the most vulnerable populations, with equitable, cheap, and high-quality healthcare. The Empowered Action Group (EAG) States, North Eastern States, Jammu and Kashmir, and Himachal Pradesh have received special attention under the NRHM. This mission concentrated on the well-being of mothers and children, family planning, and access to affordable, high-quality healthcare for the rural population.[96]

National Health Policy (2002)

The National Health Policy-2002 (NHP) places a high priority on ensuring equitable access to health care throughout the nation's social and geographic diversity. The central government's contribution has been significantly boosted in order to improve the overall public health investment. By increasing the sectoral share of funding, preventive and curative programs at the fundamental health level would be given priority.

Janani Suraksha Yojana (JSY): The JSY was created as part of NRHM to encourage institutional deliveries among expectant women in rural regions. It reduced the rates of maternal and neonatal mortality by giving pregnant women financial support for giving birth in hospitals.

Rashtriya Swasthya Bima Yojana (RSBY): The UPA government introduced RSBY, a health insurance program for families living below the poverty line (BPL), in 2008. The program's goal was to protect financially vulnerable households by paying for hospital bills. The Government of India's Ministry of Labour and Employment has introduced RSBY to offer Below Poverty Line (BPL) families to access health insurance.

Free Drugs and Diagnostics Initiative: The UPA government began a Free Drugs and Diagnostics Initiative in a few public health facilities as part of NRHM. This had the goal of giving people seeking medical care in those facilities access to necessary medications and diagnostic services without charge. The Free Essential Diagnostics Initiative was started by the Indian government as part of the National Health Mission to address the high out-of-pocket costs for diagnostics (10% OOPE on cost of tests).

National Urban Health Mission: In order to meet the healthcare demands of urban people and to improve the healthcare system in urban regions, the UPA government created NUHM. The National Urban Health Mission (NUHM) aims to improve the general health of urban residents, but especially of the underprivileged and other disadvantaged groups, by enabling equitable access to high-quality healthcare through a redesigned public health system, collaborative efforts, and community-based mechanisms with the active participation of urban local governments.

Accredited Social Health Activists (ASHAs): The ASHA program, which entailed training and hiring female community health workers at the village level to act as a link between the community and the healthcare system, was expanded under the UPA government. Female community health activist with the designation of Accredited Social Health Activist (ASHA) were appointed. This involves a variety of activities, such as promoting knowledge of health care entitlements, particularly among the poor and enabling them to access the health care services.[97]

Affordable Medicines and Reliable Implants for Treatment (AMRIT) Program: To provide patients with access to high-quality, reasonably priced medications and implants, the UPA government developed the AMRIT program. AMRIT pharmacies were established all across the nation to offer implants and medications at discounted rates.

National Mental Health Program (NMHP): The NMHP was started by the UPA government to enhance the provision of mental healthcare and raise awareness of mental health problems in the nation. Government of India has been conducting National Mental Health Program (NMHP) beginning 1982 to address the enormous burden of mental diseases and lack of skilled experts in the field of mental health. The Program included the Manpower Development Scheme (Scheme-A & B) in 2009.

(III) Economic Development

From 2004 until 2014, Manmohan Singh presided as prime minister of India, during which time the country had substantial economic growth. A number of significant programs and policies were introduced to support India's economic development were put into place while he was in power. With the exception of 2007–2008, while the worldwide severe recession occurred, Singh oversaw typical annual growth rates of around 7.5%–8% from 2004–2014.

Here are some of the notable economic developments under the Manmohan Singh government:

Economic Liberalization: As Finance Minister in 1991, Manmohan Singh was a key player in launching the economic reforms that expanded India's economy. The License Raj was abolished, trade restrictions were eased, and foreign direct investment (FDI) was promoted. The liberalization initiatives the promotion of economic expansion. Several crucial liberalization factors that supported economic expansion during his presidency include:

- **Fiscal Responsibility:** The administration implemented fiscal responsibility policies, which included limiting budget deficits and cutting back on unnecessary spending. This supported investor's confidence and economic stability.

- **Foreign Direct Investment (FDI):** Liberalization initiatives reduced the limits on FDI in a number of sectors, luring capital into the nation from abroad. This inflow of cash aided in the construction of infrastructure, the creation of jobs and technological innovations.

- **Industrial Reforms:** The government promoted strategies that promoted private sector involvement and lowered administrative barriers for firms. This stimulated investment in a variety of industries, which supported economic expansion.

- **Financial Sector Reforms:** To bolster the banking system, increase transparency, and promote financial inclusion, financial sector reforms have been adopted.

- **Trading Liberalization:** By lowering import tariffs and removing non-tariff barriers, India significantly opened its markets to foreign commerce. Exports increased and competitiveness was bolstered by this interaction with international markets.[98]

Infrastructure Development: The nation's infrastructure was a priority for the government, which made investments in power, ports, airports, and highways. The focus on infrastructure development enabled economic activity and improved connectivity. Project for the Development of the Golden Quadrilateral and National Highways during Manmohan Singh's tenure the Golden Quadrilateral project, started by the previous administration, continued to be a significant infrastructure improvement.[99]

Rural Infrastructure Development: Through programs like the Pradhan Mantri Gram Sadak Yojana (PMGSY), the government concentrated on enhancing rural infrastructure. In order to improve accessibility, connectivity, and economic prospects for those living in remote locations, PMGSY sought to create all-weather road connectivity to rural communities. The Rajiv Gandhi Grameen Vidyutikaran Yojana (RGGVY) sought to electrify villages all throughout the nation and give access to energy to rural households.

- **Development of urban infrastructure:** The Jawaharlal Nehru National Urban Renewal Mission (JNNURM) was a pioneering initiative designed to enhance urban administration and infrastructure in Indian cities. It put a special emphasis on initiatives for sanitation, transportation, and urban renewal. Enlargement of the Delhi Metro Rail system continued all throughout this time.

• **Bharat Nirman:** This time-limited program was started to hasten the building of infrastructure in rural India. It includes initiatives for rural connectivity, housing, water supply, and irrigation.

• **Telecom and information technology:** The government pushed to enlarge and update the infrastructure for these two sectors. The mobile and internet industries had substantial expansion during this time period, promotion of digital accessibility and connectivity.

• **Modernization and Expansion of Ports and Airports:** To promote trade and tourism, the government concentrated on renovating and enlarging ports and airports nationwide.

• **Indira Awaas Yojana (IAY):** This housing program was first introduced in 1985 but was given increased attention and money under the Manmohan Singh administration. The program was designed to give low-income households in rural areas financial support so they could build homes.

• **Rashtriya Krishi Vikas Yojana (RKVY):** RKVY was a centrally supported program that was introduced in 2007–2008 to promote different state-level agriculture and related activities. It aimed to support the agricultural industry, raise productivity, and guarantee sustainable growth.

• **Pradhan Mantri Gram Sadak Yojana (PMGSY):** Although the PMGSY was launched in 2000, it was given more financing and momentum under the Manmohan Singh administration. The project's goal was to connect isolated rural settlements with a population of 500 or more people to all-weather roads.

• **National Rural Livelihood Mission (NRLM):** NRLM, also referred to as Aajeevika, was established in 2011 with the goal of reducing rural poverty by encouraging self-employment and giving the underprivileged a sustainable means of subsistence.

• **Inclusive Growth in Agriculture:** To boost farmer production and income, the government undertook a number of agricultural reforms, including the Rashtriya Krishi Vikas Yojana (RKVY) and the National Food Security Mission (NFSM).

• **Inclusive Finance:** To foster entrepreneurship and give underprivileged people more power, the government sponsored microfinance organizations and encouraged the flow of credit to small and medium-sized enterprises (SMEs).

• **Information technology (IT) and IT-enabled services (IteS):** India emerged as a major global center for software development, IT outsourcing, and back-office operations during this time. The development of infrastructure and legislative initiatives by the government helped the IT businesses to grow actively.

• **Public-Private Partnerships (PPPs):** To utilize public and private sector strengths and resources for the advancement of infrastructure, technology, and research activities, the government supported PPPs.

{NOTE: Its focus on economic reforms and development initiatives contributed to India's economic progress during the 2004-2014 periods. Despite these economic achievements, the Manmohan Singh government also faced challenges, including issues related to corruption, policy implementation, and high inflation during certain periods.}[100]

(IV) National Security

From 2004 to 2014, Dr. Manmohan Singh served as the prime minister of India. During his term in office, the UPA administration undertook a number of initiatives and programs to solve national security issues and advance the interests of the nation. During this time, there were a number of security challenges to India, including terrorism, insurgency, and outside pressure. The government's strategy for ensuring national security included both local and foreign components. It is significant to remember that India's national security environment is dynamic and complicated, and that overcoming security difficulties necessitates ongoing efforts and policy adaptation.

Some of the key aspects of national security during the Manmohan Singh government's tenure were:

Counter-Terrorism Efforts: The government used several strategies to combat terrorism. It improved information coordination, updated security measures, and enlisted the assistance of foreign allies in the fight against international terrorism and extremist activities.[101]

Internal Security Reforms: To improve the security forces' ability to successfully address challenges to internal security, the UPA government moved to modernize and equip them.

Strengthening Border Security: To prevent infiltration and handle security issues along India's borders, the government concentrated on enhancing border security. The India-China Border Roads (ICBR) initiative was developed, planned, and carried out by the United Progressive Alliance (UPA) as part of a larger build-up against a growing China. Up to the June–August 2017 Doklam crisis, the policy remained consistent. However, following that, alarm bells began to ring in South Block, and the Modi administration increased funding for the ICBR program. The 1,850-km Trans-Arunachal Highway will be built by UPA along the Brahmaputra's northern bank.

Nuclear Doctrine: The UPA government upheld India's nuclear doctrine, which placed a strong emphasis on a minimum credible deterrent and a no-first-use nuclear weapons policy. The doctrine, also referred to as "India's Nuclear Doctrine," is a set of rules and values that describe India's position on the creation and employment of nuclear weapons. Under the administration of Manmohan Singh, India's nuclear doctrine had the following main components:

Policy for No First Use (NFU): According to India's Nuclear Doctrine, it will not be the first country to use nuclear weapons in a fight, reiterating its commitment to the No First Use policy. The nation swore that it would only use nuclear weapons as retaliation for a nuclear strike on its soil or on its military troops anywhere.

Credible Minimal Disarmament: The idea of credible minimum deterrence served as the foundation for India's nuclear strategy. In order to prevent any possible opponent from attacking India with nuclear weapons, it intended to retain a substantial and effective nuclear deterrent capacity. India's Nuclear Doctrine made it plain that it would not use nuclear weapons against nations that do not possess nuclear weapons or in areas where such use is prohibited.

Continued Strict Civilian Control: The doctrine reiterated that civilian authority continued to exercise strict control over India's nuclear weapons.

Negative Security Reassurances: According to India's Nuclear Doctrine, it would not use nuclear weapons against any nation that follows a similar No First Use policy.

Retaliation Policy: The doctrine said that in the case of a nuclear assault on Indian or its armed forces, the retaliation would be enormous and aimed at causing the aggressor intolerable harm.

(V) Foreign Policy

The UPA government maintained a proactive and active foreign policy that attempted to improve India's reputation internationally, advance economic interests, and create harmonious relations with regional allies and powerful nations. The foreign policy of the UPA administration aimed to balance India's national interests, regional dynamics, and international obligations. It sought to uphold India's dedication to the values of peace, non-alignment, and respect for one another while positioning India as a responsible and significant global participant. During the administration of Manmohan Singh, the following were the main tenets of Indian foreign policy:

Strengthening Relations with Major countries: The UPA administration aimed to intensify India's relations with major countries like the US, the EU, Russia, and China. It put a lot of effort into establishing strategic alliances and increasing economic cooperation with these nations.

Partnership with Neighbors: The administration placed a strong emphasis on enhancing ties with nearby nations through diplomatic efforts, economic collaboration, and interpersonal contacts. To improve India's relations with Southeast Asian nations, the "Look East Policy" was refocused as the "Act East Policy."

Regional Cooperation: To promote regional cooperation and address shared challenges, India actively participated in regional forums like the South Asian Association for Regional Cooperation (SAARC), Bay of Bengal Initiative for Multi-Sectoral Technical and Economic Cooperation (BIMSTEC), and the Indian Ocean Rim Association (IORA).

Track II diplomacy: The UPA government promoted Track II diplomacy, which entails unofficial conversations and discussions between non-governmental players, to promote inter-personal interactions and handle sensitive issues with neighbors, particularly Pakistan.

The signing of the civil nuclear agreement with the United States in 2008 was one of the major triumphs of India's foreign policy during this time. Due to the fact that India is not a party to the Nuclear Non-Proliferation Treaty (NPT), this agreement made it easier for India to get civilian nuclear technology and fuel. India regularly participated in international peacekeeping missions, humanitarian aid programs, and disaster relief operations as a means of responding to global disasters.[102]

(VI) Alleviation of business in India

Government of India wants to make it easier to conduct business there and to foster a climate that is more welcoming to both domestic and foreign companies. Among the major projects and reforms carried out are:

Liberalization of Industrial Licensing: To liberalize the industrial licensing system, the Indian government launched a number of economic reforms in the 1990s and early 2000s. It became simpler for firms to start up and run because many industries were relicensed and the number of licenses required for different sectors was decreased.

Foreign Direct Investment (FDI) Liberalization: To attract more foreign capital, the Indian government gradually reduced FDI regulations in a number of sectors. As a result, there was a greater infusion of finance and participation from abroad.[103]

Company Law Reforms: To make it easier to start and run businesses in India, the Companies Act has undergone a number of revisions. The goal was to encourage improved corporate governance and streamline the business process.

Online Single Window Clearance: To cut down on red tape and give businesses more time, some Indian states have implemented online single-window clearance systems for company clearances and permissions.

Protection of Intellectual Property Rights (IPR): The Indian government has taken steps to increase the protection of IPR, which is essential for companies to function in a competitive environment.

E-Governance projects: To digitize procedures and cut down on paperwork, the government established a number of e-governance projects. This made it simpler for businesses to communicate with government agencies.

(VII) Environment & Sustainability

Strategies and programs to solve environmental issues and advance sustainability across the nation. India made efforts to address a number of environmental challenges, such as biodiversity preservation, natural resource protection, and sustainable development.

Before 2014, some of the major environmental and sustainability efforts include:

National Action Plan on Climate Change (NAPCC): In 2008, the Indian government introduced the NAPCC, which sought to address climate change and its effects through a number of missions concentrating on forestry, water, sustainable habitat, and renewable energy.[104]

JNNSM, or the Jawaharlal Nehru National Solar Mission Launched as a component of the NAPCC, the JNNSM had aspirational goals for increasing solar capacity while promoting the growth and usage of solar energy in India.

The National Mission for Enhanced Energy Efficiency (NMEEE), a part of the NAPCC, aimed to improve energy efficiency in buildings, appliances, and industry through legislative and market-based measures.

The National Green Tribunal (NGT) was created in 2010 as a specialized judicial body to deal with environmental disputes and hasten the resolution of issues involving environmental preservation and conservation.

National Mission for Sustainable Agriculture (NMSA): The NMSA was established in 2010 with the goal of encouraging soil health management, water usage efficiency, and sustainable farming methods to provide food security while protecting the environment.

Green India Mission (GIM): The GIM, which was a component of the NAPCC, sought to improve ecosystem services and expand forest cover in India.

National Water Policy: To encourage efficient use of water resources across many sectors and to direct sustainable water management, India enacted a National Water Policy.

National Biodiversity Strategy and Action Plan: The rich biodiversity of India was to be preserved and its sustainable usage was to be ensured through the NBSAP.

(VIII) Initiatives for integrating Indian Culture

To promote and conserve India's rich and varied cultural history, the Indian government and numerous cultural groups have launched a number of programs. These programs supported artists and artisans while preserving varied art forms, languages, traditional knowledge, and historical sites. Following governments have continued to build on these attempts to further develop Indian culture.

Before 2014, some of the major initiatives for a thriving Indian culture include:

National Cultural legacy Policy: To protect and advance India's cultural legacy, including tangible and intangible cultural assets, the government developed and put into effect a National Cultural Heritage Policy.

The National Mission for Manuscripts (NMM), which was established in 2003, sought to find, catalog, preserve, and promote Indian manuscripts in order to aid in the preservation of antiquity and cultural legacy.

Monument Preservation: The Archaeological Survey of India (ASI) worked to conserve and restore historical sites, monuments, and other heritage buildings across the nation.

Cultural Festivals and Events: To highlight India's unique traditions, arts, and crafts, the government organized a number of cultural festivals and events at the national and provincial levels.

Promotion of Indian Languages: The government launched programs to advance Indian languages, including institutes for language study and promotion of language for academies purpose.

Promotion of Cultural Tourism: To draw tourists interested in India's many cultures, the government promoted historical and cultural monuments, heritage walks, and cultural events.[105]

(IX) Infrastructure Initiatives

Government of India launched a number of measures to solve the nation's housing and infrastructural problems. These programs sought to increase physical connectedness, give everyone access to inexpensive housing, and raise standards of living generally. These initiatives, which catered to the requirements of both urban and rural areas, significantly contributed to the improvement of India's housing and infrastructure sectors. Among the major housing and infrastructural projects are:

Jawaharlal Nehru National Urban Renewal Mission JNNURM was established in 2005 with the goal of enhancing urban infrastructure and governance in particular cities. It concentrated on initiatives for urban poor housing, public transportation, water supply, and sanitation.[106]

The National Highway Development Project (NHDP) aims to promote road connectivity and facilitate the flow of goods and people throughout the nation by enlarging and modernizing the national highway network. Launched in 2005, the Urban Infrastructure Development Scheme for Small and Medium Towns (UIDSSMT) sought to provide small and medium-sized towns with essential urban infrastructure, with a particular emphasis on solid waste management, water supply, and sanitation.

Inexpensive Housing Programs: The government launched a number of programs and incentives to encourage the development of inexpensive housing for various segments of society, including the LIG and EWS (economically weaker sectors).

Smart Cities Mission: Although the Smart Cities Mission was introduced in 2015, the groundwork for it was established prior to 2014. By putting a strong emphasis on urban development that is sustainable and technology-driven, the project aspired to transform a few cities into smart cities.

The National Urban Housing and Habitat Policy (NUHHP), which was created in 2007, sought to advance the development of affordable, accessible, and durable urban housing.

(X) Science and Technology

Manmohan Singh served as the Prime Minister of India from 2004 to 2014. During his tenure, the government focused on several significant initiatives and policies in the fields of science and technology.

Here are some of the key highlights:

Nuclear Deal: One of the most prominent achievements during Manmohan Singh's government was the Indo-US civilian nuclear deal. It aimed to enhance India's nuclear energy capabilities by allowing access to civilian nuclear technology and fuel from other countries, despite not being a signatory to the Nuclear Non-Proliferation Treaty (NPT).

Space Research: The Indian Space Research Organisation (ISRO) achieved several milestones during this period. In 2008, India successfully launched the Chandrayaan-1 mission, its first lunar probe, which made significant discoveries, including the presence of water molecules on the moon's surface. Additionally, India's Mars Orbiter Mission (Mangalyaan) launched in 2013, made India the first Asian country to reach Mars orbit and the fourth space agency globally to do so.[107]

Space Experiment

Chandrayaan – 1

Chandrayaan-1 Mission was India's first interplanetary mission

The Indian Space Research Organization (ISRO), which was responsible for Chandrayaan-1, the country's first lunar probe, did reach some key milestones. On October 22, 2008, Chandrayaan-1 was launched with the purpose of orbiting the Moon and performing a number of scientific investigations to investigate the lunar surface. It made important discoveries, including as confirming the presence of water molecules on the surface of the Moon. On November 8, 2008, Chandrayaan-1 took off aboard the PSLV-C11 launch vehicle, which effectively placed the satellite into a lunar trajectory. India became the fourth nation in the world to raise its flag on the lunar surface on November 14, 2008, after MIP (Moon Impact Probe) had been successfully detached. MIP had previously made a controlled impact on the lunar South Pole.

Mars Orbiter Mission

NASA Solar System Exploration, Mars Orbiter Mission launch in 2013

The design, development, and deployment of a Mars Orbiter spaceship with the ability to performing with enough autonomy during the travel phase, Mars orbit insertion or capture, and in-orbit phase surrounding Mars are among the mission's primary technological goals. In order to research the Martian surface features, morphology, minerals, and environment, MOM carries five scientific payloads.

The five scientific payloads on board the Indian Mars Orbiter Mission were as follows:

- The Mars Color Camera
- Spectrometer for Thermal Infrared Imaging (TIS)
- Mars Methane Sensor (MSM)
- MENCA, the Mars Exospheric Neutral Composition Analyzer
- 104 Lyman Alpha Photometer

The Polar Satellite Launch Vehicle (PSLV) rocket C25 launched the Mars Orbiter Mission probe on the Initial Space Platform around Satish Dhawan Space Centre (Sriharikota Range SHAR), Andhra Pradesh, at 09:08 UTC on November 5, 2013. The launch window began on October 28, 2013, and it lasted roughly 20 days. Prior to its trans-Mars injection on November 30, 2013, (UTC), the MOM spacecraft spent almost a full month in Earth orbit105 performing a sequence of seven orbital maneuvers to rise. On September 24, 2014, it was sent into Mars orbit following a 298-day transit to Mars.[108]

National Telecom Policy 2012

In order to ensure that India fulfills this role efficiently and successfully transforms the socioeconomic environment with intensified sustainable and equitable growth in the economy, the National Telecom Policy-2012 place a special emphasis on delivering high-quality and reasonably priced telecommunications facilities to isolated and rural regions. The main goal of this strategy is to emphasize how crucial it is for continuous technology adoption to provide workable solutions for resolving developmental difficulties in a variety of areas, including education, health, job creation, financial inclusion, and many more.

The key objectives of the NTP 2012 were as follows:

As with any policy framework, its effectiveness and implementation depend on various factors, and subsequent policies may have been introduced or updated since 2012 to address emerging challenges and opportunities in the telecommunications sector.

Broadband for All: The policy aimed to provide affordable and reliable broadband connectivity to all citizens, especially in rural and remote areas. It set a target of achieving 175 million broadband connections by 2017 and 600 million by 2020. To develop an eco-system for broadband in close coordination with all stakeholders,

Inclusive Growth: The goal of the policy was to encourage inclusive growth by making sure that everyone, particularly underserved and disadvantaged part of the population, had the opportunity to utilize inexpensive and reliable Broadband services.

Green telecom: NTP 2012 established standards for promoting ecologically effective procedures in the telecom industry to lower carbon emissions and energy usage.[109]

(XI) Energy Development

The administration conducted a number of programs to address the nation's energy difficulties, concentrating on various facets of energy development. Here are some significant changes that have occurred in the energy sector since Manmohan Singh took office:

National Solar Mission: In order to promote solar energy in the nation, the government established the National Solar Mission in 2010. It established economic support and incentives to assist solar power plants as well as setting high goals for the expansion of solar capacity.

Encouragement of Wind Energy: The government kept up its promotion of wind energy activities by establishing wind power projects all throughout the nation and offering incentives. Expansion of Renewable Energy: India anticipated doubling the renewable energy capacity from 25000 MW in 2012 to 55000 MW by the year.[110]

(XII) Policy Reforms for Marginalized Section

Manmohan Singh served as India's prime minister from 2004 to 2014, during which time significant policy changes were put into place to promote and uplift society's most vulnerable groups. Within the Manmohan Singh administration, important policy changes for disadvantaged groups have included:

The Mahatma Gandhi National Rural Employment Guarantee Act (MGNREGA), a ground-breaking social welfare program, aimed to give rural households, including those in marginalized areas, work possibilities by promising 100 days of pay employment per fiscal year. MGNREGA had a significant role in reducing rural poverty and improving the standard of living for numerous underprivileged people.

The **National Food Security Act (NFSA)** was passed in 2013 to guarantee food security for the population's most vulnerable groups. Under this law, the system for public distribution (PDS) distributed subsidized food grains to qualified recipients, especially underprivileged households.

Scheduled Castes and Scheduled Tribes (Prevention of Atrocities) Act: To shield marginalized communities from prejudice, retaliation, and violence, the government seeks to reinforce the enactment of the Scheduled Castes and Scheduled Tribes (Prevention of Atrocities) Act.

Urban Housing and Slum Development: With a focus on underprivileged urban populations, the government launched a number of projects to enhance housing and living circumstances for urban slum dwellers.

National Minorities Development and Finance Corporation (NMDFC) were established to aid linguistic and religious minorities in their socioeconomic development through a variety of financial support programs.

Rashtriya Swasthya Bima Yojana (RSBY): To shield vulnerable households from overbearing medical costs, the RSBY provided health insurance coverage to families living below the poverty line.

Administrative Reform Commission 2005 Strengthen the Administrative Capacity

ARC reports, are published by the Administrative Reforms Commission, which is engaged by the Government of India. ARC is crucial resource for efficient public administration, governance, and much more. There are primarily two ARC reports: The first ARC released in 1966, and the second ARC report, which was released in 2005.

On August 31, 2005, the Indian government established the 2nd ARC Report in accordance with resolution K-11022/9/2004-RC. It was created to develop a comprehensive plan to reform India's public administration system. Veerappa Moily led the commission initially in his capacity as chair. However, once he stepped down in 2009, V. Ramachandran assumed leadership duties. In order to achieve a realistic, adaptable, accountable environmentally friendly and competent public administration throughout all levels of government of India, the 2nd ARC Report was given the authority to make some helpful recommendations. Additionally, 15 reports covering various public administration fields were released by the 2nd Administrative Reforms Commission.

The Government of India rejected the suggestions made by the 2nd ARC on issues including judicial reform and ties between the federal and state governments, as well as fields consisting of defense of the nation, security, and intelligence, among others. Two different types of improvements were suggested in the 2nd ARC report. Changes to administrative setups, processes, and practices are the first.[111]

Numbers Of Arc Reports	Names Of Arc Reports
1st Report	Right To Information: Master Key to Good Governance
2nd Report	Unlocking Human Capital : Entitlements And Governance
3rd Report	Crisis Management
4th Report	Ethics In Governance
5th Report	Public Order
6th Report	Local Governance
7th Report	Capacity Building for Conflict Resolution
8th Report	Combating Terrorism – Protecting by Righteousness
9th Report	Social Capital – A Shared Destiny
10th Report	Refurbishing Of Personnel Administration & Scaling New Heights
11th Report	Promoting E-Governance: The Smart Way Forward
12th Report	Citizen-Centric Administration
13th Report	The Organizational Structure of Government Of India
14th Report	Strengthening Financial Management Systems
15th Report	State And District Administration

Table 3: List of ARC Reports [112]

These reforms demand tenacious political will and ongoing oversight.

- District disaster management emergency and long-term moderation plan;
- Indian Citizens Commission, a group that supervises local organizations;
- Tenacious Lok Adalat and Lokayukta;
- Corporate social responsibility
- Promoting e-governance, MIPUI AW, and social audit.
- The districts must receive the funds directly.

Second ARC Reports Considered by Central Government

First Report: The Right to Information Is the Key to Effective Government

•It is necessary to repeal the Official Secret Act of 1923 (N)

•Keeping an official secret without exercising due care constitutes a crime (A).

•Governmental privilege in evidence (Section 123 of the Indian Evidence Act of 1872 has to be changed (N)

•Oath of Secrecy (N), Armed Forces Exempt Organization (N),

•Rules for the conduct of Central Civil Servants, (A)

•Office Procedures Manual (A)

•The SIC (A) Constitution

2nd Report (Unlocking Human Capital-NREGA)

•Ensuring Reach (A)

•Assuring Results (A)

•Making certain convergence (A)

•Extending the program (A)

•Setting Wage Rate Fixes (NA)

•System of Financial Management (A)

•Workers Payment Method (NA)

•Fund flow: the part played by banks and post offices (A)

•Monitoring (A) and using IT, among many other things

3rd Report (Crisis Management: From despair to Hope)

•A specific disaster clause in the Constitution (N)

•State governments should manage crises, with backing from the federal government (A)

•There is a specific state- or national-level ministry or department.

•Giving Relief Commissioners More Power (A)

•Support from institutions and use of IT (GIS) for prevention and solution (A)

•The subject of disaster management ought to be introduced (A)

•National Disaster Management Policy (A)

•A plan for disaster management and an awareness campaign

•System for Early Warning (A)

4th Report (Ethics in Governance)

•Political funding reform (action not required)

•Stricter enforcement of anti-defection laws (A)

•Exclusion of those who have charge sheets (A)

•Collegiums should pick Chief Election Commissioners and Commissioners (A)

•Special Election Tribunals: Expediting the Resolution of Election Petitions (Rejected)

•Criteria for membership exclusion (A)

•Ministers' ethical framework (duplication of the Code of Conduct)

•PM and CM should be accountable for ensuring the Code of Ethics

•Ethics Commissioner& Office recommended (A)

•Profit Office (A)

•All public employees should adhere to the following public service values: (A)

•National Judicial Council (A)

•Sanction for Prosecution (NA)

•Whistleblower protection (A)

•Articles 310 and 311 sought to be eliminated (NA)

•Lok Pal and Lok Ayukta (from the first ARC-reinforcement)

5th (Public Order) is thus far to be deliberated by means of the Government

6th (Local Governance) gives the impression to be out of perspective for State.

7th Report (Capacity Building for conflict resolution)

•New Land Acquisition Act, Section (A)

•SEZ shouldn't be situated on land used mostly for agriculture (NA)

•Tribal area-related issues (A)

•Concerns relating to water (A)

•Administration in the North East capacity building (A)

8th Report (Combating Terrorism) is presence processed/instigated through Ministry of Home Affairs.

9th Report (Social Capital-A shared destiny)

•New Legal Framework for Charities in India (A)

•Corporate Social Responsibility (A)

•Accreditation of Voluntary Organisations (National Accreditation Council (A)

•Regulation of Foreign Contribution (Bill needs to be amended) (A)

•SHGs movement needs to be enhanced in the rural areas and also to be extended to the urban and semi-urban areas (A)

•Integrated Social Policy (A)

10th Report (Refurbishing of Personnel Administration-Scaling new heights) – being considered by the Government

•11th Report (Promoting e-Governance-The smart way forward)

•Building a congenial environment (A)

•Identification of e-Governance Projects and Prioritization (A) – {2-3% of Plan budget for this}

•Business Process Re-engineering (A)

•Capacity Building and Creating Awareness (A)

•Monitoring and Implementation (A)

•Common Support Infrastructure (SDC, SWAN, CSCs etc.)(A)

•Mission Mode Projects for Land Records (A)

•Knowledge management (A) and the legal framework for e-government (A)

12th Report (Citizen Centric Administration-The Heart of Governance)

•Effective role of the government (A)

•Effectiveness of the Citizens Charter (A)

•The Seven Step ARC Citizen Centricity Model (A)

•Involvement of Women and People with Physical Disabilities (A)

•Creating an efficient system for resolving public complaints (A)

•Grievance Analysis and Grievance Prone Areas Identification (A)

•Making internal processes simpler (A)

•Evaluation and Monitoring (A)

•Rationalizing Procedures: Birth and Death Registration, Issuing of Driving Licenses (A)

•Construction permits and completion certificates (A)

13th Report (Organizational Structure of Government of India)

•Fundamental Ideas for Reforming the Governmental Structure (A)

•The notion of subsidiarity should serve as a guide for all levels of government (A)

•Recasting the Allocation of Business Rules (A)

•Rationalizing and Reorganizing the Ministries and Departments (A)

•Rationalizing and Reorganizing the Government Functions (A)

•Establishing Successful Executive Agencies (A)

•Mechanism for Coordination (A)

14th Report (Strengthening Financial Management Systems)

•Irrational budget projections (A)

•Delayed Project Implementation (A)

•Unbalanced Spending Pattern: Increase in Spending Near the End of the Financial Year (A)

•Adherence to the multi-year perspective and a lack of coordination between the plan and the budget (A)

•Places more emphasis on achieving financial budgetary targets than on outputs and outcomes (A)

•Capacity Development

15th Report (State and District Administration)

•The Council of Ministers & size should be decreased (A)

•After the proposed act is approved by the central government, states are urged to take similar action.(A)

•Executive Agencies & Departments (A); Civil Services Law (A); Regional Level Administration (A);

•Lokayukta/Vigilance Commission (A)

•Commission for State Public Service (A)

•Modernizing the office and redefining the Collector's Role (A) [113]

{Note: A for Accepted/NA* for Non-Accepted}*

During Manmohan Administration Policy Failure: Policy Paralysis

The period during which Dr. Manmohan Singh served as India's prime minister is referred to as the "Manmohan Administration". From 2004 until 2014, Dr. Manmohan Singh presided as prime minister. Several policies were put into effect under his administration, and the effectiveness of the government has come under discussion and criticism. The Manmohan Singh administration also encountered difficulties, including problems with policy implementation, corruption, and excessive inflation at times. The failure of government programs and the fall of Congress have been condemned in a number of areas, including:

Monetary Policy Even though Dr. Manmohan Singh was well-known for his role in opening up the economy of India in the early 1990s, the government came under fire for failing to maintain the high growth rates while he served as prime minister. The United Progressive Alliance's first term, from 2004 to 2009, saw better results than its second, from 2009 to 2014. A worse economic outcome, double-digit inflation, and a protracted period of policy paralysis were all present during the second phase, which made meaningful reforms challenging. The economy was confronted with a number of issues, including rising inflation, a budget deficit, and sluggish industrial expansion. The government's economic initiatives, according to critics, are insufficient to resolve these problems.[114]

Embezzlement and scandals: Dr. Manmohan Singh's UPA-II (United Progressive Alliance-II) administration was accused of corruption and involvement in a number of scandals. Some notable examples that sparked popular outrage and raised concerns about the government's actions included the 2G spectrum fraud, the coal allocation scam, and the Commonwealth Games scam.[115]

Governance and Decision-Making: According to some opponents, the government frequently struggles with poor decision-making and leadership at crucial junctures. There have been times when the government has come out as unsure, which has complicated administrative processes.

Policy stagnation: The government struggled to make substantial choices on important subjects during the later portion of Manmohan Singh's administration, which was characterized by a perception of policy stagnation. Conflicts within the coalition government were blamed for this, as well as a lack of effective leadership. A coalition government led by Manmohan Singh included a number of political groups.

Compromises and delays in decision-making have occasionally resulted from the difficulties in managing and satiating the expectations of various coalition members.

Security issues: Internal conflicts like Naxalism and the insurgency in Jammu and Kashmir presented the administration with security issues. The efficiency of the government's methods to deal with these security challenges has been criticized. However, governments must constantly pay attention to these complicated, diverse concerns and employ flexible responses. Government must adhere to the principles of good governance.[116]

Security and Terrorism: The administration came under fire for how it handled matters relating to internal security, particularly in light of terrorism. Terrorist attacks in Mumbai in 2008 exposed flaws in the nation's security system, and some people claimed that the government's response was insufficient. The terrorist attacks in Mumbai in November 2008 were among the most sad and significant events that occurred under Manmohan Singh's presidency. Additionally referred to as 26/11, Over 160 people were killed and hundreds were injured when a gang of ten heavily armed terrorists from the Pakistan-based Lashkar-e-Taiba militant organisation launched coordinated strikes throughout Mumbai.

Jammu and Kashmir insurgency: For decades, terrorism and insurgency have afflicted the state of Jammu and Kashmir. The area continued to see violent episodes under Manmohan Singh's leadership, including cross-border incursions and assaults on security personnel and citizens.

Maoist Insurgency (Naxalism): Maoist rebels, often known as Naxalites, posed a threat to India's internal security. The majority of the states where these insurgents operated were in central and eastern India. In order to defeat their military insurrection and address the underlying socio-economic problems that motivated their movement, the administration encountered difficulties.

Samjhauta Express Bombings (2007): In February 2007, a bombing occurred that was directed towards the Samjhauta Express, a train that runs between Pakistan and India. Investigations indicated that extremist groups were involved in the attack, which left 68 people dead.

Hyderabad Twin Blasts (2007): In August 2007, twin bomb explosions took place in Hyderabad, a significant South Indian metropolis, killing more than 40 people. Extremists were accused of carrying out the incident.

Delhi High Court Blast (2011): In September 2011, a bomb explosion outside the Delhi High Court claimed the lives of 17 individuals while also injuring a large number of others. The administration received flak for its inability to stop such attacks.

Food Security and Inflation: The administration came under fire for its inability to successfully combat food inflation, which negatively impacted the livelihoods of the general populace and raised the cost of living. India had a considerable increase in food and gasoline costs in the latter part of 2007 and the beginning of 2008. As a result, inflation increased, making it harder for government agencies to keep an eye on prices. (2008–2009)

Global Financial Crisis: India's economy was impacted by the financial crisis of 2008 worldwide, and inflation rates were unstable at this time. The Indian government put in place a number of steps to curb inflation and stabilize the economy as the crisis developed. Restoration and Temperance (2010–2013).[117]

Infrastructure and Power Sector: The government was under fire for the delayed construction of infrastructure, especially power generation and distribution, despite the improvements that were promised. Throughout its existence, problems with power shortages and inefficiency in the industry persisted. The issue of insufficient infrastructure development and maintenance in many sectors was one of the most significant difficulties during Manmohan Singh's administration. The government initiated a number of initiatives and projects intended to accelerate infrastructure development in order to address these concerns. Key areas of attention included:

Roads and Highways, Power and Energy, Urban Infrastructure and Railways: Notwithstanding these efforts, infrastructure construction was frequently criticized for moving too slowly and failing to keep up with the needs of the expanding economy. The actualization of projects was hampered by problems like bureaucratic delays, financing limitations, and difficulties in cooperation between the various levels of government. Similar problems have been faced by successive governments as they worked to create and maintain a reliable infrastructure to support India's economic development and prosperity.

It is crucial to remember that the UPA government prepared the structure. However, the country's policy reforms were dismantled while the implementation and evaluation were rather scandalous. Political evaluations are frequently subjective and based on a variety of variables, such as differences in ideology and the viewpoints of various stakeholders. While some opponents point out the shortcomings of the Manmohan administration's policies, there are also advocates who contend that the administration made beneficial contributions in a number of sectors, including social welfare programs, rural development, and education. The Manmohan Singh-led government experienced both achievements and setbacks during its term, as with any administration, and opinions about its policies continue to be divided.

Revival of Policies

Background

In 1947, India declared its independence from British rule, and the bureaucracy was a key factor in creating the country's structure and administrative framework. India's bureaucracy had been given the important task of developing the country. After India gained its freedom, the bureaucracy successfully lifted the country until it began to wither. The public services must be prepared to adapt to changing social mores and meet residents' needs. The Indian bureaucracy inherited the administrative structure established by the British colonial government. However, recognizing the need for reforms, the Indian government initiated various measures to streamline and modernize the bureaucracy recommendations are included in the Report on Public Administration by A.D. Gorwala, 1951; Report on the Public Services (Qualifications for Recruitment) Committee, 1956 – alternatively called Dr A. Ramaswami Mudaliar Committee Report; Report on Indian and State Administrative Services and Problems of District Administration by V.T. Krishnamachari, 1962; ARC's Report on Personnel Administration,1969; Report of the Committee on Recruitment Policy and Selection Methods, 1976 to suggest improvements in the functioning of the civil services.[118]

73rd and 74th Constitutional Amendments of 1992 required the creation of urban local authorities and Panchayati Raj organizations. At the local level, bureaucrats have assisted in sustaining and directing these institutions. The Indian bureaucracy has encountered issues with corruption and a lack of accountability over the years. To address these challenges, a variety of steps have been taken, including the creation of anti-corruption organizations like the Central Vigilance Commission (CVC) and the adoption of e-governance projects.

•Systemic rigidities, unnecessary complexities, and excessive centralization in the policy and management frameworks, and as a result, the Indian civil service is more focused on internal processes than results.

• The structures are based on hierarchies and there are a large number of veto points to be negotiated for a decision to eventually emerge. The size and the number of ministries and departments have both overloaded the decision-making system and diminished the capacities of the individual civil servants to fulfill their operational responsibilities.

•The nation is undergoing rapid and fundamental change, including rapid economic expansion, urbanization, environmental deterioration, technological advancement, and enhanced local knowledge and identity. The contribution of the private sector and civil society organizations to government and the provision of public services have improved over time.

Lateral Entry Reform for Increasing Bureaucratic Efficiency

The process of hiring people from outside the conventional bureaucratic structure to fill senior-level posts in the government is known as lateral entry. In India, the idea of lateral entrance into the bureaucracy has been growing in popularity recently in order to supplement the current civil service with specialized knowledge, domain expertise, and new viewpoints. It is vital to remember that lateral entry is a relatively new notion in the Indian bureaucracy and is still developing. Various government agencies and ministries may have various policies regarding the magnitude and breadth of lateral entry roles. The Indian government has started a number of initiatives to make lateral entry within the bureaucracy easier. The following are some crucial details about lateral entrance in India:

Positions: The main goal of lateral entry is to fill senior-level posts in different government agencies and ministries, such as Joint Secretaries and above.

Eligibility Requirements: The requirements for lateral entry differ according to the particular post and department. Candidates often need to have the necessary educational background, professional experience, and domain knowledge for the post.

Application Assessment: selection, written tests, interviews, and/or evaluations are frequently used in the hiring procedure for lateral entry employment. Depending on the division and the post, the specific procedure could change.

Selection Committee: To assess and choose qualified applicants for lateral entry employment, a selection committee made up of government representatives and outside specialists is frequently formed. The committee evaluates the applicants' credentials, experience, and skills for the prescribed role.

Contractual Appointment: Lateral entrance positions are normally made under a contract for a set period of time, usually between three and five years. Continuity of the contract is subject to performance and other considerations.

Integration with the Bureaucracy: Lateral entrants are expected to work in tandem with career government employees to promote efficient governance. The goal is to create beneficial outcomes by using the advantages for each lateral entry and the current bureaucracy.

Sectoral Expertise: Lateral entry attempts to recruit experts from a variety of sectors, including academia, business, the private sector, and non-governmental organizations. This makes it possible to bring in expertise and experience in particular policy fields.

Collaborative Governance: Participatory and varied governance is evolving which take different stakeholders assistance.

How Lateral Entry Is Breaking Bureaucratic establishment

Professionals hired outsiders in the conventional civil service through lateral entry into the government have the potential to significantly alter and transform the bureaucratic structure. It is crucial to remember that the commencement of lateral entry depends on a number of variables, including the selection procedure, the degree to which lateral entrants are successfully integrated into current structures, and the presence of an atmosphere of encouragement that fosters working together and exchanging information among lateral applicants and civil servants. A balance between outside expertise and the institutional understanding and experience of the current bureaucracy should be ensured by appropriate means. Here are some examples of how lateral entrance might undermine the status quo of bureaucracy:

Infusion of Specialized Skills and Expertise: The government can access the specific talents, information, and experience of experts from a variety of sectors through lateral entry. These people provide new viewpoints, creative solutions, and industry-specific knowledge that can be used to tackle complicated problems and put in place sensible regulations.

Altering Organizational Culture: Lateral entrance can also help the bureaucracy change its organizational culture. Professionals from all backgrounds can foster a change from a typical bureaucratic culture to one that is more dynamic and agile by encouraging an improved accessible, cooperative, and result-oriented work environment.

Faster Decision-Making: Lateral entrants frequently approach problem-solving and decision-making from a different perspective, which can result in quicker and more effective procedures. They are more able to adjust to change since they are used to functioning in dynamic circumstances.

Enhanced Efficiency and Performance: Professionals with expertise working in the private sector, where effectiveness and performance are essential for success, are frequently hired from outside the bureaucracy. Their presence can bring about performance-oriented procedures, goal-driven methods, and accountability systems that can enhance the overall effectiveness of the political system.

Closing the Awareness Gap: Lateral entrants contribute specialized knowledge and skills in areas where the bureaucracy may be deficient. This can close the information gap and guarantee that the government is knowledgeable about new trends, cutting-edge technologies, and industry best practices in various sectors.[119]

Indian Institute of Public Administration: Provide Training the Lateral Entry Candidates

The Indian Institute of Public Administration (IIPA) is a premier training and research institution in India that focuses on capacity building and professional development of public servants. Established in 1954, it plays a vital role in training and promoting excellence in public administration and governance. The IIPA offers a wide range of training programs and courses for government officials, public administrators, and professionals from various sectors. These programs aim to enhance the knowledge, skills, and competencies of participants in the field of public administration and governance. Some key training programs provided by the IIPA include:

Foundation Course for newly recruited civil servants: For newly hired civil workers through the Indian Administrative Service (IAS), Indian Police Service (IPS), along with other central and state civil services, the IIPA offers a thorough Foundation Course. The purpose of this course is to introduce the officers to the fundamental concepts of leadership, governance, and public administration.

In-service education courses: The IIPA offers various in-service training programs for mid-career civil servants looking to improve their skills and abilities in certain fields such public policy, public finance, the administration of human resources, e-governance, and social development.

International training initiatives: The IIPA works with institutions and international organizations to run training initiatives for government employees from other nations. These initiatives promote knowledge exchange, intercultural communication, and the dissemination of excellence in the government sector.

Workshops, seminars, and conferences: The IIPA hosts conferences, seminars, and workshops on a range of public administration and governance-related subjects. These gatherings offer a forum for administrators, practitioners, researchers, and professionals to exchange knowledge, talk about problems, and consider creative solutions.

Research and Consultancy: The IIPA undertakes research projects and consultancy assignments on issues related to public administration, governance, and public policy. The findings and recommendations from these research endeavors contribute to evidence-based policymaking and administrative reforms. [120]

The IIPA's training courses are created to meet the changing demands and difficulties of public administration. The training sessions are taught by knowledgeable practitioners, the subject matter specialists, and faculty members that contribute an extensive amount of expertise to the classroom.

The Indian Institute of Public Administration (IIPA) is an autonomous organization in India that plays a significant role in providing training and capacity building programs for government officials, including both career civil servants and lateral entrants. While IIPA does not exclusively train lateral entrants, it offers various programs and courses that cater to the needs of professionals joining the government through lateral entry. IIPA conducts training programs and workshops on public administration, governance, policy analysis, leadership, and other relevant areas. These programs aim to enhance the knowledge, skills, and capabilities of government officials, including lateral entrants, to effectively perform their roles and responsibilities in the government machinery.

The training provided by IIPA to lateral entrants focuses on equipping them with the necessary understanding of government processes, policies, and administrative practices. It aims to familiarize them with the nuances of public administration and governance in the Indian context. The training may also emphasize the development of leadership skills, problem-solving abilities, and effective decision-making in the public sector. Additionally, IIPA serves as a platform for knowledge exchange and networking among government officials, both lateral entrants and career civil servants. It provides opportunities for interaction, collaboration, and sharing of experiences and best practices. It's worth noting that while IIPA offers valuable training and capacity-building programs, lateral entrants may also receive training through other avenues, such as on-the-job training, mentorship programs, or specialized training programs organized by the respective government departments or ministries.[6] The specific training requirements and programs for lateral entrants may vary depending on the nature of the position and the department they are joining.

IIPA and its Capacity Building to Generate Specialist

Since 1959, IIPA is imparting training and capacity building to the government officials of India and other countries' officials. Every year, IIPA conducts more than 100 training programmes for the officials. The flagship programme of IIPA is 10-month Advanced Professional Programme in Public Ad- ministration (APPPA) which is attended by senior officials of All India Services (AIS), Central Civil Services and Defence Services mainly Indian Administrative Services (IAS), Indian Police Services (IPS), Indian Revenue Services (IRS), Indian Air Force, Indian Army and various other services. IIPA conducts training for the officials of different departments and ministries of Government of India and State Governments on various topics of governance, finance, communication, leadership, administration and management. Capacity building in the Indian Institute of Public Administration (IIPA) can play a significant role in generating employment and fostering specialization in various fields. The IIPA is a premier training institute in India that aims to enhance the capabilities of public administrators and policymakers.

The Indian Institute of Public Administration (IIPA) makes significant improvements to the creation of jobs and the advancement of specialists in India by emphasizing development of skills, entrepreneurial spirit, sector-specific training, policy research, industry linkages, and networking. These initiatives have the potential to close the skills gap, promote economic expansion and develop an employee base that is knowledgeable and skilled in a variety of industries.

Here are a few ways in which capacity building in IIPA can contribute to employment generation and specialization:

Skill Development Programs: IIPA design and implement skill development programs focused on key sectors of the economy. These programs can provide specialized training in areas such as project management, financial analysis, policy formulation, urban planning, healthcare management, and more. By equipping individuals with industry-relevant skills, these programs can enhance their employability and create opportunities for specialized jobs.

Instruction Specific Sector: IIPA collaborate with industry experts and organizations to provide sector-specific training programs. For instance, specialized training in areas such as information technology, renewable energy, e-governance, agriculture, and rural development can help individuals acquire the necessary skills and knowledge to excel in these sectors. This, in turn, can lead to employment opportunities and specialization in these industries.

Training Approach at IIPA

Training Strategy: Lectures, Discussion, Case study, Management Games, Simulation Exercises, Role Play, Team Training/Building Exercises, Quiz for self-Evaluation, Field Visits participatory, Capstone (real time projects) and Experiential learning etc.

Training design: The training is designed in house based upon training need analysis (TNA) and in consultation with the client Ministry/Department/Organisation as per the objectives.

Adult learning Methods: Andragogy Methods like Unlearning, Reasons/Output of training, Problem Solving, Experiential sharing are used in the training programmes.

Modes of Delivery: Both online and offline mode / Blended / Field Visits / Experiential Presentation.

Examples of Creative Learning: Role plays, case studies, field visits, talks by experts, Simulation games, using smart boards, experiential tours

Adoption of Training methods: Training method decided mainly by specific subject expert which is based on institutional defined principles.

Figure 6: Training Approach at IIPA
Source: IIPA Capacity Building Report

Training Design Pattern at IIPA

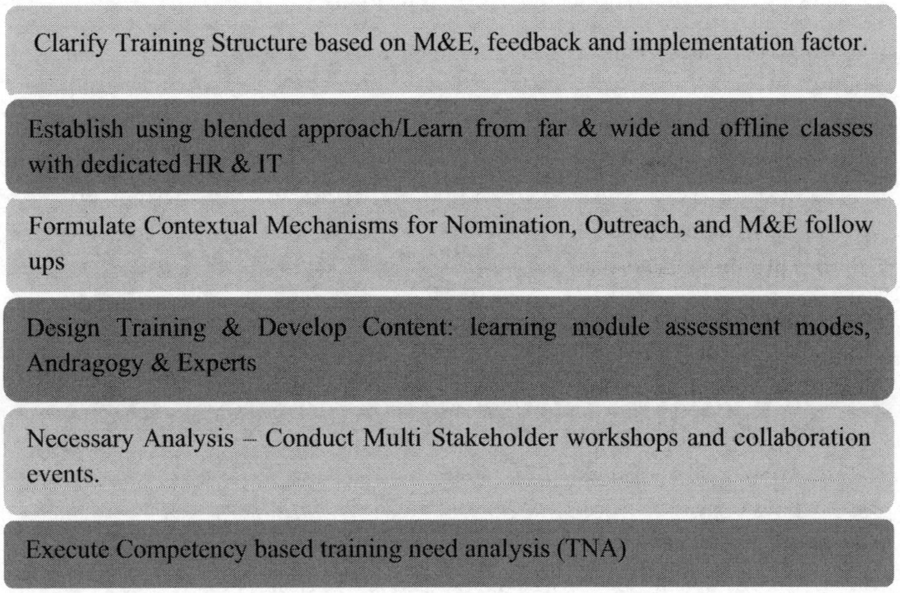

Clarify Training Structure based on M&E, feedback and implementation factor.

Establish using blended approach/Learn from far & wide and offline classes with dedicated HR & IT

Formulate Contextual Mechanisms for Nomination, Outreach, and M&E follow ups

Design Training & Develop Content: learning module assessment modes, Andragogy & Experts

Necessary Analysis – Conduct Multi Stakeholder workshops and collaboration events.

Execute Competency based training need analysis (TNA)

Figure 7: Training design at IIPA
Source: IIPA Capacity Building Report

Policy Research and Analysis: IIPA conduct research and analysis on various policy issues, including employment generation and specialist development. Through rigorous research, IIPA can identify the gaps and challenges in different sectors and develop policy recommendations to address them. This research can inform policymakers and stakeholders, leading to the formulation of effective policies that promote employment and specialization.

Partnership with Industries: IIPA establish partnerships and collaborations with industries, both in the public and private sectors. Such collaborations can facilitate knowledge transfer, industry exposure, and hands-on training opportunities for individuals undergoing capacity building programs at IIPA. Industry tie-ups can also help in aligning the training programs with the evolving needs of the job market, ensuring that the skills imparted are relevant and in demand.

Networking and Placement Assistance: IIPA can create a strong network of alumni, industry professionals, and policymakers, which can serve as a platform for knowledge exchange, mentorship, and job placements. By actively facilitating networking opportunities and providing placement assistance, IIPA can enhance the employability of its trainees and connect them with suitable employment opportunities.[121]

Capacity Building Commission Promoting Civil Services Capacity

On April 1, 2021, the Capacity Building Commission was established via the Indian Gazette. As the custodian of the civil services capacity building ecosystem, the commission is mandated to perform the following functions:

1. Aid departments, ministries, and agencies in creating annual capacity building plans.
2. Make policy suggestions to DoPT regarding human resources and capacity building.
3. Create a cohesive, de-siloed strategy to increase the capability of the civil service.
4. Examine learning and competency-related data from the online training platform iGOT-Karmayogi.
5. Promote uniformity, coherence, and a shared comprehension of capacity building activities.

6. Create shared learning resources, including internal and external faculty and resource centers.
7. Exercise functional supervision over all Central Training Institutions.[122]

National Programme Capacity Building – Mission Karmayogi

Prime Minister Narendra Modi Address about the Mission Karmayogi

The National Programme of Capacity Building (NPCB) in India is an initiative aimed at enhancing the skills, knowledge, and capacities of individuals and organizations across various sectors. The program focuses on capacity building activities to strengthen governance, improve service delivery, and promote sustainable development. Mission Karmayogi is the National Programme Capacity Building (NPCSCB). It is a reform in Indian Bureaucracy. Union Cabinet launched it on 2nd September 2020 The mission intends to lay down the foundations for the Indian civil servants' capacity building and aims to enhance governance.

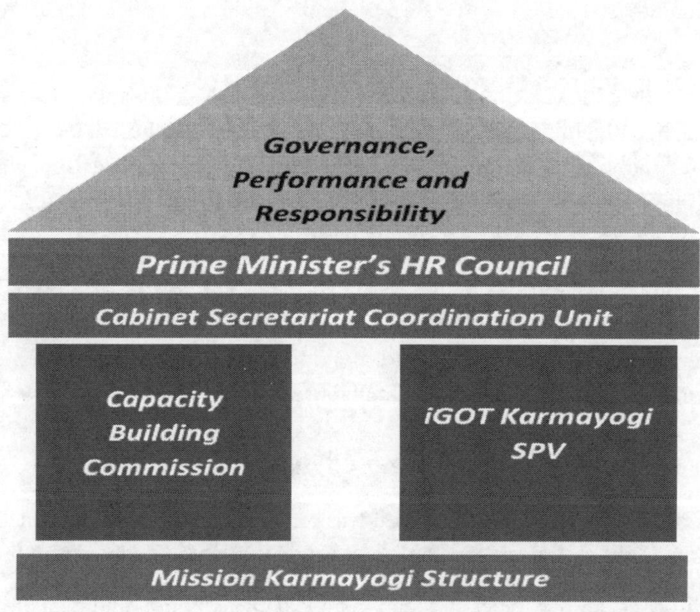

Figure 8: Mission Karmayogi Structure

Mission Karmayogi Structure

It was started by the Union Cabinet with the intention of creating a new national framework for enhancing the ability of the civil service at the individual, institutional, and procedural levels. Under the Companies Act of 2013, a special purpose vehicle (SPV) (non-profit corporation) is established to carry out this aim. This SPV is going to be in charge of managing the online training platform i- GOT Karmayogi. By significantly improving the citizen-government interface, NPCB is focused on boosting ease of living and ease of conducting business.

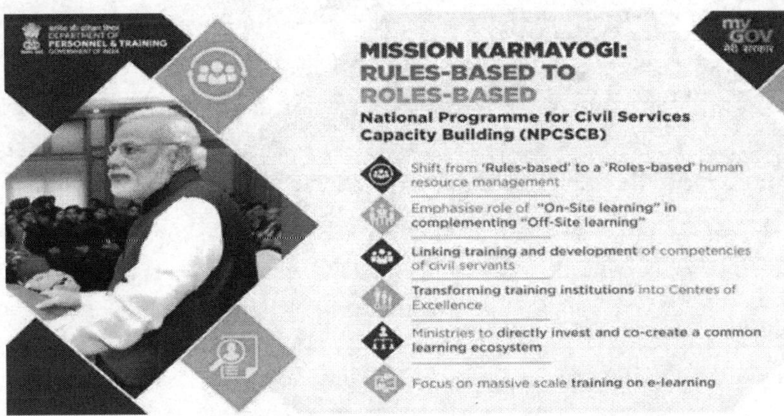

Mission Karamyogi Emphasize on Rules Based to Role Based Approach

In the Report of NITI AAYOG on India@75, has mentioned the need for reforms in training. The experience gained during the COVID 19 pandemic also brought forth the need for the civil service to be agile, capable of partnering with diverse stakeholders and to be up to date with new competencies, put forward the idea of Capacity Building for learn from the best practices across the world, while remaining connected to their roots for future generation of civil servants. Significant part of NPCB is to create an ecosystem of competency driven training and Human Resource (HR) management by ***transforming from a 'rules-based' system to the 'role-based' system.***

Following is a list of the six Pillars of Capacity Building:

- Frameworks for policies
- Institutions competencies
- Integrated Government Internet-Based Training Karmayogi Platform (iGOT-Karmayogi)
- Digital Learning Framework
- Technology Human Resource Management Systems (eHRMS) and
- The Framework for Monitoring and Evaluation.

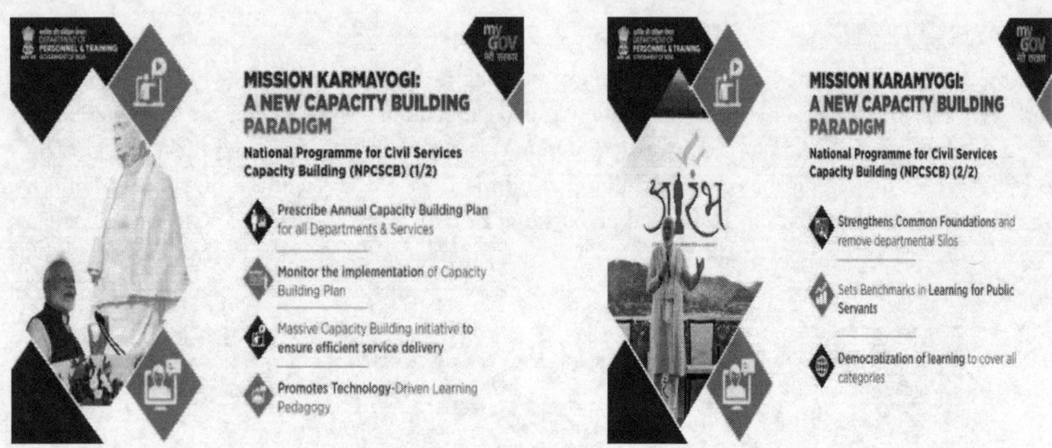

Mission Karmayogi: Capacity Building Paradigm (in two Parts)

Human Resource Management (HR) shift from a rules-based to a roles-based approach - The goal is to assign tasks to each of the civil servants in accordance with their qualifications. To supplement off-site learning, on-site training is provided for government employees. In order to implement such a human resources policy in the government, NPCB wants to develop a solid policy framework. The regulatory structure will also make it possible to adopt innovative technological instruments for monitoring and evaluating the entire program, especially the quality of the learning materials, customer input analysis, and competency evaluation. These tools include a digital medium, artificial intelligence, machine learning, and data analytics.

Institutional Framework

Prime Minister's Public Human Resource Council (hereinafter referred to as 'PMHRC'): A Council comprising of eminent public HR practitioners, thinkers, global thought leaders and representatives of the Indian political leadership under the Chair of the Prime Minister of India, is conceived to be the apex body for driving and providing strategic direction to civil services reforms and capacity building. It will identify areas for policy intervention and approve the National Capacity Building Plan.

Cabinet Secretariat Coordination Unit: A coordination unit under the Chairmanship of the Cabinet Secretary will monitor the implementation of the NPCSCB. It will align all stakeholders and provide mechanism for overseeing capacity building plans.

Capacity Building Commission: The Civil Service Capacity Building Commission is at the heart of the NPCSCB. It will coordinate the preparation of annual capacity building plans, monitor and evaluate their implementation and functionally supervise the training institutions (CM's etc.) for the purpose of creation of shared resources ecosystem. The Secretariat of the Commission will be headed by an officer in the grade of Joint (Designated as Secretary to the Commission) to Government of India.

Karmayogi Bharat is a Special Purpose Vehicle (SPV): For the purpose of owning, managing, maintaining, and improving the digital assets, i.e., iGOT Karmayogi the electronic learning system, which comprises the IPR of all software, content, process, etc., on behalf of the government, a not-for-profit organization under the administrative control of DoPT has been created as a 100% government owned entity. The SPV will be in charge of developing and launching the material onto the marketplace and regularly monitoring usage.

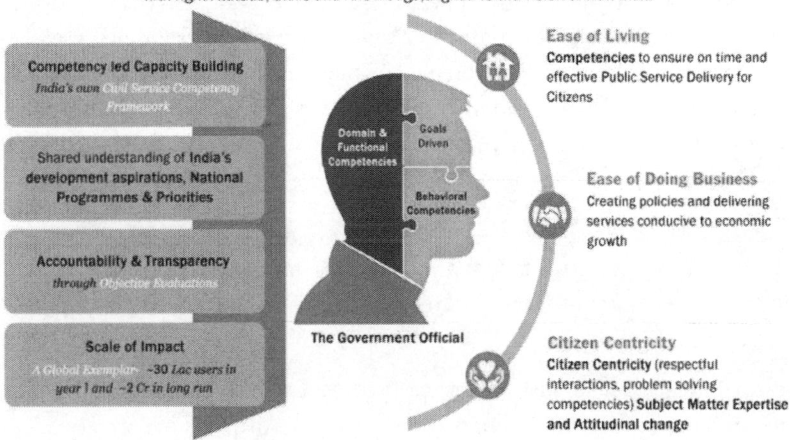

Mission Karmayogi: Concentrating on Building Competent Civil Servant

Competency Framework

- **Digital Learning Framework**

The Indian government created the digital learning framework known as the iGOT (Integrated Government Online Training) Karamyogi platform. It is made to offer government workers at all levels thorough training and possibilities for skill development. The following are the main characteristics and elements of the iGOT Karmayogi Structure. Portal for online learning: A variety of classes and educational programs are available through the iGOT Karamyogi platform, which acts as an online educational portal. It offers a central hub where government workers may access interactive modules, learning tools, and training materials.

The framework encourages a blended learning strategy that combines self-paced online modules with instructor-led instruction and virtual classrooms. This guarantees a well-rounded educational experience that takes into account various learning preferences and styles.

- **Human Resource Management (eHRMS)**

This pillar emphasizes supporting people in the workforce enhance their skills, knowledge, and capabilities. It seeks for ways to enhance their professionalism, productivity, and performance. Initiatives for human resource development under the NPCB include training courses, venues for information sharing, mentorship programs, and possibilities for career advancement.

Automation of HR operations: The eHRMS program intends to automate a number of HR operations, including hiring, on boarding new employees, tracking attendance and leaves, conducting performance reviews, providing training and development opportunities, as well as handling payments.

Centralized HR Network: This application makes it possible to build a centralized HR repository that houses detailed employee data, such as biographical information, credentials, job history, training logs, and achievement statistics.

Self-Service Portals: Self-service websites for managers, HR administrators, and employees are included in eHRMS. Employees can read their performance reviews, register for branches, modify their online identities, and access personal information.

- **Framework for Monitoring and Evaluation**

A national capacity development program needs to be monitored and evaluated (M&E) in order to determine its success, pinpoint areas for advancement, and confirm that the program's goals are being realized. Here are some important factors to think about when measuring and evaluating a national capacity-building program. A national capacity-building program could guarantee that finances are used efficiently, goals are reached, and continual enhancements are made by putting in place a strong M&E framework.[123]

Karmayogi Bharat

Karmayogi Bharat shall own, manage, maintain and ***improve the digital platform, iGOT Karmayogi,*** on behalf of Government for the implementation of National Programme for Civil Services Capacity Building (NPCSCB) – Mission Karmayogi

• To change the way the Indian civil services, improve their capacity by creating a strong digital environment that allows for continuous learning anywhere, at any time, so that the officials are prepared for the future.

• Create and maintain a thorough online platform to aid government employment administrators in their competency-driven capacity building journey. This platform should support on the internet, in person, and blended learning, discussion through topical forums, career path management, and dependable evaluations that credibly signal officials' competencies.

• Create, deploy, improve, and oversee the digital infrastructure

• Create, purchase, source internally, curate, and guarantee that every piece of material on iGOT-Karmayogi is validated.

• Control and provide services for proctored assessments

• Manage dashboards for all levels of viewing and the regulation of telemetry data.[124]

Recruitment Reforms to Enhance Equal Opportunity in Hiring Process

Recruitment reforms in India refer to the various initiatives and changes implemented to improve the recruitment processes in the country. These reforms aim to ensure transparency, efficiency, fairness, and equal opportunities in recruitment for government jobs and other sectors. Recruitment reforms in India have been an ongoing process aimed at improving the efficiency, transparency, and accountability of the bureaucracy. Over the years, the Indian government has implemented various measures to bring about these reforms. Some of the key initiatives include:

Civil Service Reforms: The Union Public Service Commission (UPSC) and other competitive exams have been used to find and select qualified applicants. Merit-based hiring has been prioritized, and political intervention in the hiring process has been minimized.

Productivity-based Appraisal: Systems that assess the performance of civil officials have been introduced. Having the use of these systems, good performance will be acknowledged, problem areas will be found, and suitable chances for training and growth will be offered.

E-Governance: To improve service delivery while lowering administrative processes, the Indian government has advocated the use of technology. Online services, automated administrative procedures, and a reduction in paperwork are all goals of programs like the National e-Government Plan (NeGP) and Digital India.

The government constantly organizes the Administrative Reforms Commission (ARC) to research and make recommendations for administrative reforms. The reform strategy in the government sector has been significantly shaped by the ARC's proposals.

Building capacity: A number of training and capacity-building initiatives have been launched to improve the abilities and education of civil officials. To increase bureaucrats' effectiveness, these programs put an emphasis on developing leadership, rules of conduct, decision-making, and other essential areas.[125]

To provide recommendations on various facets of the civil service, a variety of boards and committees were established. Below are a few of the pertinent suggestions made by these committees:

FOR RECUITMENT the 2001 Civil Services Examination Review Committee, which was presided over by Professor Yoginder K. Alagh, advocated testing the applicants on a common subject as opposed to optional subjects. Aptitude and leadership exams may be adopted for selection, according to the Committee on Civil Service Reforms 2004 (Hota Committee Report). The Basawan Committee (2016) advised doing a genuine assessment of the need for IAS officers annually in order to make the government a realistic request for Direct Recruits each year and to keep track of the openings below the promotion ceiling. Three mid-career training programs should be offered in the 12th, 20th, and 28th years of employment, according to a 2003 Yugandhar Committee suggestion.

DOMAIN EXPERTISE: 11 areas were recommended by the Surinder Nath Committee in 2003, including agriculture, rural development, social sectors, culture, and information, among others.

The Committee on Prevention of Corruption ***(Santhanam Committee*)** made a range of recommendations to fight the menace of corruption. It recommended the constitution of the Central Vigilance Commission. Changes were also suggested in Article 311 of the Constitution of India for conducting disciplinary Proceedings against government servants. It was also recommended that offering of bribes should be made a substantive offence.

The ***Hota Committee*** recommended that Sections of the Prevention of Corruption Act and the Code of Criminal Procedure may be amended to protect honest civil servants from malicious prosecution and harassment. It also recommended that a Code of Ethics should be drawn up for civil servants incorporating the core values of integrity, merit and excellence in public service. It also recommended that a ***Model Code of Governance*** should be drawn up benchmarking the standards of governance to be made available to the citizens.[126]

National Recruitment Agency Manages to Simplify Examination Process

In order to set up a common preliminary test for diverse employment in the central government, the Union Cabinet, which is presided over by the Prime Minister, has decided to establish the National Recruitment Agency. For the purpose of hiring employees for non-gazetted positions within government and banks in the public sector, the NRA will administer the Common Eligibility Test (CET). Every year, 1.25 lakh government positions are advertised, attracting 2.5 crore applicants to various tests. An organization incorporated within the Societies Registration Act of 1860 will be the National Recruitment Agency. A Chairman with the rank of Secretary to the Government of India shall serve as its leader.[127]

Requirement of Agency

This test intends to replace many exams administered by various recruitment agencies with solely one online exam for eligibility to government jobs announced each year. The government also intends to offer outreach and education services to help candidates in remote and rural locations become accustomed to the online testing process. A 24-hour helpline will be established to address complaints, questions, and other issues.

The current hiring organizations, including the Institute of Banking Personnel Selection (IBPS), Railway Recruitment Board (RRB), and Staff Selection Commission (SSC), will continue to operate. Final selection for recruitment is going to be made using distinct, specialized Tiers (II, III, etc.) of examinations, which is scheduled by the relevant recruitment agencies, based on the preliminary screening completed at the CET score level. Currently, applicants for government positions must show up for different exams held by numerous hiring organizations for various posts.

Tenure Based Hiring as Inventory Hiring Process

Lateral Entry

Lateral Entry means recruiting new entrants into a system from a pool of candidates who are outsiders to the system. In context of bureaucracy, Lateral Entry refers to the direct induction of domain experts at the middle or senior levels of administrative hierarchy, rather than only appointing regular recruits through promotion. The idea of lateral entry into civil services is seen by many as a panacea to the inertia that has crept in because of which it failed to respond to the need of the times. 1st ARC talked about need for specialization as early as in 1965. The 2nd ARC also recommended an institutionalized transparent process for lateral entry at both central and state levels. The Surinder Nath Committee and Hota committee in 2003 and 2004 made similar recommendations favoring lateral entry into the civil services. YK Alagh (2001) Committee also had recommended lateral entry into middle and senior levels of the government. In this context, the Central Government has taken a leap into the idea of inducting specialists to middle and senior level positions in the Indian Administrative hierarchy. After asking the Department of Personnel & Training (DoPT) to prepare a proposition on lateral entry into Civil Services, nine professionals were selected to work in the capacity of joint secretaries in the Government of India.

According to Shri Surendra Nath Tripathi, director-general of the Indian Institute of Public Administration (IIPA), who instructs lateral entrants before they join respective ministries, "The government seems to be delighted with them. Hiring industry experts and placing them in pertinent ministries was one of the main goals. That goal has been accomplished, he declared. Seven candidates about when they were admitted as lateral entrants, they were given 2 years of additional time, which was originally assign 3 years.[128]

Requirement for Lateral Entry to Address Officer Shortage: There are not enough IAS officers in the country, according to a report by the Ministry of Personnel, Public Grievances and Pensions. The larger states like Bihar, MP, and Rajasthan have a shortage of over 75 to 100 officers, according to the Basawan Committee (2016). Therefore, lateral induction is being viewed as a tiny step toward necessary cleanup in the staffing of the central government.

Changes in contours of policy making and need for specialization: It takes specialized knowledge and abilities to make informed policy decisions as we move away from the homogeneity of organized centrally economic policy and toward the various requirements of competitive federalism.

Enhanced governance and efficiency: In the IAS, career advancement is practically automatic, which may put officers in a rut. Additionally, lateral entry points could create competition inside the system. Sector specialists should be hired through lateral entry, according to Niti Aayog's Three-Year Action Agenda for 2017-2020, as doing otherwise would "bring pressure to the entrenched career bureaucracy."

Talent entry and retention in government: The Sixth Central Pay Commission, led by Justice BN Srikrishna, stated in its 2006 report that lateral entry may "ensure entrance along with retention of competence in the governing body regardless of those employment opportunities that have an abundance of demand and premium in the market."

Agnipath Scheme

Agnipath (Agnipath) Scheme 2022, The Union Cabinet made a momentous choice by approving an alluring recruitment program for young Indians to join three different branches of the armed forces. The program is open to both male and female candidates between the ages of 17.5 and 21. AGNIPATH (AGNIPATH) is the term given to the program authorized by the Government of India on June 14, 2022, for the recruitment of soldiers within each of the three services of the Indian military under the rank of commissioned officers. The program went into effect in September 2022. The national government has introduced a recruitment program called the Agnipath Scheme. Selected applicants would be enlisted as Agniveers for the Indian Armed Forces for a four-year period.[129]

The young people chosen for the Agneepath program will join the Indian Army, Indian Navy, and Indian Air Force as Agniveers. A chance for young people to serve for their country for four years has opened up with the launch of the Agnipath Scheme, if you desire to join the Indian Armed Forces as an Agniveer. After completing the four-year program, Agniveers will return to community as a focused, vibrant, motivated, and talented workforce for engagement in various industries so they can further their careers in the jobs of their choice.

Major features of Agnipath Scheme

1. It uses a merit-based recruitment procedure across all of India. That implies that anyone in India may apply for this position.

2. The job has tenure of four years.

3. Possibility of enlisting as an Agniveer in the military.

4. Attractive monthly pay and a dashing Seva Nidhi package.

5. There is a 100% chance to apply for enrolment indefinitely.

6. An Agneepath-based enrollment methodology.

7. After four years, 25% of Agniveers to be chosen in accordance with a central, rigorous approach that is transparent and is centered on fundamental organizational needs.

8. All India and All Classes are eligible.[130]

GEM Portal – Transparent Procurement Process

GeM stands for Government e-Market Place, which is operated by the Directorate General of Supplies and Disposal (DGS&D). GeM is a powerful, self-sufficient, user-friendly site that makes it simple for government officials to make purchases. The Public Sector Units (PSUs) and central and state government departments can access the Government e Marketplace, an innovation in public procurement. The GeM Portal makes the procurement process transparent, effective, and thorough. It serves as a single and unified platform for public procurement for both vendors of goods and services and government purchasing groups.[131]

Features of GeM Portal:-

Benefits: Improved openness, reduced expenses, quicker efficiency, a bigger market for sellers, and decreased corruption are just a few benefits of GeM. It streamlines the purchasing procedure and encourages honest competition amongst vendors.

Integration: To synchronize procurement procedures amongst several departments, GeM is integrated with other government platforms including the Ministry of Micro, Small and Medium Enterprises (MSME) and the Central Public Procurement Portal (CPPP).

E – Bidding: GeM enables government buyers to look for goods and services, evaluate costs, and make purchases directly through the site. E-bidding is another feature of the platform that enables vendors to compete and offer reasonable rates for particular goods and services.

Vendor Rating: Consumers can rate and comment on the efficacy of merchants using the rating system on GeM. This aids in ensuring the purchase process's dependability and quality.

Payment and Delivery: To ensure prompt and effective order fulfillment, transactions for goods placed through GeM are completed electronically. The platform also makes it easy to trace shipments.

Human Management in Public Sector to Improve the Governance Efficiency

A human manager in the public sector is responsible for overseeing and coordinating various activities within a government or public organization. They play a crucial role in ensuring the effective and efficient functioning of the organization, implementing policies and programs, managing resources, and leading a team of employees. A human manager in the public sector plays a critical role in overseeing the human resources function within a government or public organization. They are responsible for strategic planning, policy development, resource management, team leadership, stakeholder management, and other important tasks to ensure the organization operates efficiently and effectively.

Here are some key responsibilities and tasks typically associated with a human manager in the public sector:

Strategic Planning: creating and executing strategic plans to accomplish the goals and objectives of the organization. Analyzing existing trends, spotting areas for development, and aligning the personnel with organizational requirements are all part of this process.

Participating in the formation: It ensured implementation of the rules and regulations that direct the activities of the organization. This involves making sure that all legal and regulatory standards are met.

Budget management and material allocation: Managing the organization's budget and successfully distributing resources to support its activities. This entails keeping an eye on expenses, figuring out ways to cut costs, and maximizing resource use.

Managing the hiring process: Overseeing the recruitment process, including job posting, screening, interviewing, and selection of qualified candidates. Additionally, provide guidance and support for employee development, performance management, and training initiatives.

Team Leadership: Generating a healthy work environment, encouraging teamwork, and fostering effective communication among a group of employees. Task delegation, progress tracking, and conflict resolution fall under this category.

Risk management is the process of identifying and reducing risks that could have an influence on an organization's goals or operations. This includes identifying potential hazards, creating backup plans, and assuring adherence to risk management guidelines.

The field of public relations: Serving as an organization's spokesperson, advancing its mission, and preserving goodwill with the public. This entails responding to requests from the public, resolving issues, and interacting with the neighborhood.[132]

Human Manager as Administrator to Optimize the Administrative Tasks

The duty of a human manager in an organization as an administrator is to supervise and coordinate numerous administrative responsibilities. The roles of a human administrator in administration is to direct, coordinate, and optimize administrative tasks to ensure efficient operations, boost productivity, and support the organization's success. The following obligations could apply:

Team Leadership: Managing a team of administrative professionals, providing guidance, support, and feedback to ensure effective performance.

Management Strategy: Planning, planning, and prioritizing administrative duties to guarantee optimal use of resources and a smooth flow of business operations. In order to assure compliance, uniformity, and efficiency, operational rules, regulations and standards must be established and put into effect.

Problem Solving: Locating and resolving administrative problems, disputes, or bottlenecks through situation analysis, solution-proposal, and change-implementation.

Training and development: Determining the training requirements, setting up workshops, and giving administrative staff members that opportunity for professional growth. Supporting the process of strategic decision-making by partnering with senior management to provide administrative knowledge.[133]

Changing Role of Personnel Management to Boost the Employee Engagement

Over time, there has been a substantial evolution in the function of managing employees in the public sector. Personnel management has traditionally been centered on administrative responsibilities like hiring, payroll administration, and employee benefits. The responsibility for personnel management has changed recently, becoming more strategic and pro-active in character. A strategic and people-centered approach has replaced a transactional focus on the job of personnel administration in the public sector. Personnel administrators now play a crucial part in managing change, supporting employee growth and engagement, and advancing diversity and inclusion while also coordinating human resources with business goals. Following are some significant adjustments to the function of personnel management in public administration:

Strategic Workforce Planning: Strategic workforce planning currently places a significant emphasis on personnel management. It entails predicting the organization's future workforce requirements, identifying skill shortages, and creating strategies to find, keep, and develop the best employees. This makes it easier for public administrations to match their human resources to their aims and objectives.

Talent Administration and Growth: From purely administrative duties, management and growth of talent have taken the place of personnel management. It entails selecting high-potential workers, developing training and development plans, and mapping out career routes for staff members. Public administration may create a competent and motivated workforce equipped to handle future problems by putting money into talent management.

Performance Management: Performance management programs that go beyond standard annual reviews are the current emphasis of personnel management. It entails establishing precise performance standards, giving frequent feedback, and promoting a culture of continual development. Performance management procedures are being adopted by public agencies more frequently to boost worker efficiency and guarantee responsibility.

Wings-level Personnel Management: It makes sure that all labor laws, rules, and industry standards are followed. They are in charge of handling complaints, maintaining employee relations, and making sure that everyone is treated fairly. To reduce legal risks and create an environment that is compliant at work, they also keep up with changes in employment laws and regulations.[134]

Recruitment Agencies Require to Diverse Hiring Process

Government hiring organizations frequently implement pertinent changes through a methodical and organized manner. Although particular processes may differ based on the nation and organization in issue, the subsequent steps are often followed: Strategy Development: The government hiring organization recognizes the need for modifications to its hiring procedure. This may be brought on by changing legal requirements, altered policies, or organizational demands. To adopt new policies or update current ones, the agency frequently talks with pertinent parties, including government agencies, human resources specialists, and subject matter experts.

Planning for Implementation: The government recruitment agency identifies the need for changes in its recruitment process. This can be due to evolving legislation, policy changes, or organizational requirements. The agency typically consults with relevant stakeholders, such as government departments, human resources professionals, and subject matter experts, to develop new policies or update existing one.

Communication and Training: Effectively communicating the modifications to existing workers, prospective recruits, and the general public is an important first step. Public notices, online updates, circulars, and official announcements can all be used to accomplish this.

Government hiring organizations are aware that rules and procedures must be flexible in order to meet changing demands. On the basis of evolving requirements, stakeholder comments, or shifting legal and regulatory frameworks, they periodically examine the adjustments and implement any necessary adaptations.[135] A system of recruitment was devised as a result of numerous committee suggestions. Following are the committees:

1) Macaulay Committee
2) The Kothari Committee
3) Satish Chandra Committee

The main policy controlling the civil service was initially described in the Macaulay Committee to discuss the Indian civil service in 1854. The open competition method and the scholarly character of the exam were the two most important components of the policy. The Satish Chandra Committee and the Kothari Committee devised the current examination format to evaluate candidates' qualifications and suitability for recruiting directly to the All-India Service and higher Central Services. However, the Macaulay Committee is the primary source of influence on policy thought and had an impact on currently used system in India for hiring All India Service personnel as well as senior Central Service personnel. Recently, two additional Committees were constituted.[136] They were:

1) Alagh Committee

2) Hota Committee

Union Public Service Commission Brings Advances in Recruitment Process

Through the Royal Commission, which was established by the British crown in 1923 and was led by Lord Lee of Freeham requested an equal number of British and Indian members in a report that was submitted in 1924. The commission established a reserve of 49% for future British entrants, 40% for directly recruited Indians, and 20% for Indians who joined the provincial Services for advancement. Public Services Commission continues to be constructed with attention to Indian leaders and the freedom struggle. As a result, the Government of India Act of 1935 established the federal Public Service Commission.[137]

Constitutional Status

The primary hiring organization in India is the Union Public Service Commission, which was given the status of a constitutional authority. According to Part XIV of the Constitution's Article 315 to 323, the composition, nomination, and removal of members are covered. In accordance with Article 315, the UPSC operates independently; this institution is free to exercise all of its authority and functions as it sees fit. The independence of UPSC demonstrates its importance in the recruitment process.

To protect and guarantee the autonomous and unbiased operation of the UPSC, the Constitution has provided the following provisions, such as:

1) The President may remove the Chairman or any member of the UPSC from office only in accordance with the law and for the reasons specified in the Constitution. So they benefit from the security.

2) Even when the president sets the Chairman's or a member's terms of service, they cannot be changed to his detriment after the appointment.

3) Neither the Chairman nor a member of the UPSC is qualified for appointment to that position again (i.e., not qualified for a second term).[138]

Function of the UPSC:

1) The UPSC is described in the Constitution as India's "watch dog of the merit system." It oversees recruitment for Group A and Group B roles in the Central Services and All India Services, and it counsels the government on questions of discipline and advancement when required.

2) The categorization of services, compensation and working under certain circumstances, cadre administration, instruction, and other topics are unrelated to it. One of the three divisions of the Ministry of Personnel, Public Grievances and Pensions, the Department of Personnel and Training, is in charge of handling these issues. In India, the Department of Employment and Training serves as the central personnel agency, while UPSC is the principal central recruiting agency.

3) The UPSC's position is not only constrained, but it also only makes recommendations that are advisory in nature and so do not bind the government. The UPSC's role is to provide advice, not make decisions. The Union Government has the discretion to approve or reject that recommendation.[139]

Recruitment Process

The Union Public Service Commission (UPSC) establishes the eligibility requirements for the Civil Services Examination (CSE) in India. Each year, candidates are chosen for a number of civil services, notably the Indian Administrative Service (IAS), Indian Police Service (IPS), Indian Foreign Service (IFS), and various other central services through the highly competitive CSE exam. The following criteria must be met in order to participate in the CSE:

Nationality: Candidates must either be an Indian citizen, a subject of Nepal or Bhutan, a Tibetan refugee who arrived in India before January 1, 1962, with the intention of settling permanently there, or a person of Indian ancestry who relocated from Pakistan, Burma, Sri Lanka, East African nations Kenya, Uganda, or the United Republic of Tanzania.

Age Limit: According to the candidate's category, the age requirements change and are the following: As of August 1, of the examination year, candidates of the Indian Administrative Service (IAS) and Indian Police Service (IPS) must be between the ages of 21 and 32. B) Candidates from reserved groups, which include Scheduled Castes (SC), Scheduled Tribes (ST), and Other Backward Classes (OBC), are allowed to apply with age restrictions.

Number of Attempts: The maximum number of tries for the CSE is determined on the candidate's category: a) General category: 6 tries up to 32 years old. B) OBC category: nine tries up until age 35. C) SC/ST category: Up to 37 years old, no restrictions on attempts.

Eligibility Criteria: Candidates must fulfill the following requirements in order to be eligible for registration for the Civil Services Examination:

a. Nationality: The applicant must be an Indian national.

a. Age Requirements: The minimum age to take the CSE is 21, whereas the age limit differs based on the category and certain UPSC-provided relaxations.

c. Educational Requirement: The applicant must possess a bachelor's degree from an accredited institution. The area of research is unrestricted in any particular way.

Three Phases: The CSE is divided into three phases: Initial Assessment (Prelims): The Civil Services Aptitude Test (CSAT) Paper-II and the General Studies (GS) Paper-I are the two objective-type papers that make up the first stage of the exam. Preliminaries are a form of screening, and only qualified candidates are allowed to continue.

Main Examination (Mains): The Mains are for those who pass the Prelims. It consists of nine descriptive-type questions, comprising two papers on the candidate's selected subject from the section of alternative topics offered by the UPSC and one qualifying language question. The Mains test is a thorough assessment of a candidate's knowledge, analytical capabilities, and writing skills.

Personality Interview: Candidates who pass the main examination are invited for a personality test (interview). It determines if a candidate is suitable for a career in the civil services based on their personality traits, communication abilities, and other factors. Members of the UPSC board constitute the interview panel.[140]

Training of Candidates at LBSNAA

Lal Bahadur Shastri National Academy of Administration is known as LBSNAA. It is India's top training facility for civil workers. The LBSNAA, is based in Mussoorie, Uttarakhand, is the premier training facility for members of the Indian Administrative Service (IAS) and other civil services, such as the Indian Police Service (IPS), Indian Foreign Service (IFS), and Indian Revenue Service (IRS). The academy works to prepare students for their challenging jobs in the public sector by offering an all-encompassing training program. In honor of Lal Bahadur Shastri, India's second prime minister, the Academy was founded in 1959.

The following services have a training period:

1) Training of IAS

Training in Foundational Course	4 months

Training in Professional (first spell)	5 months
Training in District of the state	12 months
Training in Professional (second spell)	3 months

2) Training of IPS

Foundational Course	4 months
Professional Training Course (first spell)	12 months
District Training in the States	8 months
Professional Training Course (second spell)	3 months

3) Training of IFS (Foreign)

National Academy of Administration, Mussoorie imparted Foundational course	4 months
Professional Course at the Foreign Service Institute in New Delhi	12 months
Training with the Ministry of External Affairs	6 months
Linguistic preparation at an Indian mission abroad	14 months[141]

Here are some key aspects of training at LBSNAA:

Foundation Course: All civil service officers who are enrolled in the LBSNAA's training program must first complete the Foundation Course. It focuses on creating a solid foundation in a variety of areas, including decision-making, ethics, public administration, and government.

Domain-Specific Training: Officers are normally allocated into their respective cadre-specific instruction after completing the Foundation Course. These training courses concentrate on particular fields including tax administration, politics, economics, agricultural growth, and beyond. The training program is created to give officers the information and abilities they need to meet the difficulties of their individual roles.

Field Visits and Attachments: The LBSNAA places a strong emphasis on field trips and practical experience as essential components of training. Officers frequently visit various government agencies, groups, and operational sites during the training session to have a direct understanding of the difficulties and implementation on the ground.

Resolution of Public Complaints

The process of attending to and resolving grievances brought up by the public regarding the operation of public institutions or services is referred to as the redressal of public grievances in administration. Responsibility, openness, and citizen satisfaction are all ensured by it, making it a crucial component of efficient governance. To guarantee that citizen issues are addressed effectively and fairly, it is crucial for governments to develop a grievance redressal procedure that is both effective and responsive.

Administrative Tribunal Ensure Protection for Government Employees

Central Administrative Tribunals (CAT)

'Tribunals' were added to the constitution by Part XIV-A of the 42nd Amendment Act of 1976. There are two articles in it, 323A and 323B, which address administrative tribunals and other tribunals, respectively. The Administrative Tribunals Act was passed in 1985 with Article 323A. This law enables swift and affordable justice to be served to the wronged public employees. The creation of administrative tribunals for the resolution of disputes relating to the hiring and employment conditions of individuals appointed to public services by the Centers, the states, local bodies, public corporations, and other public authorities is authorized by Article 323A, which gives the parliament this power.

State Administrative Tribunals

On a specific request from the involved state governments, the Administrative Tribunals Act of 1985 gives the Central government the authority to create state Administrative Tribunals (SATs). Within the nine Indian states of Andhra Pradesh, Himachal Pradesh, Odisha, Karnataka, Madhya Pradesh, Maharashtra, Tamil Nadu, West Bengal, and Kerala, SATs have been established. SATs also have authority over state government employee recruitment and any service-related issues. After consulting with the governors of the relevant states, the president appoints the chairman as well as the members of a JAT. [142]

Central Information Commission

The Right to Information (RTI) Act of India created the Central Information Commission (CIC), an independent statutory authority. It was established to encourage accountability and transparency in the operation of public agencies and to render it attainable for citizens to access the information these institutions hold. Guaranteeing that public authorities adhere to the RTI Act's guidelines and making it easier for citizens to access the data the government possesses on themselves.[143] The Central Information Commission's salient characteristics are as follows:

Jurisdiction and establishment: The RTI Act's adoption led to the creation of the CIC in 2005. It is centrally controlled and has authority over all public agencies that fall under its purview.

Composition: A Chief Information Commissioner (CIC) and up to 10 Information Commissioners (ICs) make up the Central Information Commission. On the recommendation of a committee made up of the Prime Minister, the Leader of the Opposition in the Lok Sabha, and a Union Cabinet Minister the Prime Minister has nominated, the President of India appoints the Chief Information Commissioner and the Information Commissioners.

Functions: The CIC's main responsibility is to decide on appeals and complaints made in accordance with the RTI Act. It has the jurisdiction to take complaints from people who were refused access to sought information or who weren't happy with the response they got from a public entity and investigate them. Additionally, it has the power to impose sanctions.

1) The commission is required to take any complaint it receives and to look into it:

2) Who has not been able to put forward a request for information due to the lack of a Public Records Officer's appointment? Who has had information requests denied?

3) In accordance with the deadlines indicated, has not received an answer to his information request; who believes the costs levied are excessive?

4) Who believes the information provided is inaccurate, deceptive, or incomplete; and

5) Any additional information-related issues[144]

Assistance after Retirement

Pension

For as long as they are alive, retired government employees will receive a regular monthly payout. The following are the different pension options.

• A public employee who retired after reaching the age of pension savings, which is 58 or 60 years, is eligible for a superannuation pension.

• Retiring Pension, given to a public employee who left their position after the stipulated amount of time had passed but before reaching retirement age.

• An invalid pension is given to a public employee who retired due to a physical or mental condition that rendered him permanently unable to perform his prior duties.

Provident Fund

This is an additional retirement benefit that is given to the worker in a single lump sum. In that both the employee and the government contribute to the fund, it is a partially participatory system of retirement benefits.

Gratuity

Gratuity is a payment made to a public employee at the time of retirement. It might take the form of an administrative gratuity, retirement gratuity, or death gratuity.

Insurance Advantages

The Central Government Employees Group Insurance Scheme of 1980 offers the dual benefits of an insurance cover in the event the employee passes away while performing their duties and a lump sum payment to supplement their resources upon retirement, both at a cheap cost and on a contributory and self-financing basis.[145]

Strategies to Make Bureaucracy Accountable

For effective government and public trust, the bureaucracy must ensure accountability. It is crucial to remember that establishing transparency throughout the government system calls for a multifaceted strategy that includes effective leadership, institutional changes, and an environment of honesty. Combining these tactics can aid in fostering a bureaucracy that is more transparent and responsible. The following tactics can be used to encourage and improve accountability in bureaucracy:

Roles and responsibilities that are clear: It is essential to specify the duties and roles of bureaucrats. Bureaucrats should be held responsible for their conduct and choices by having straightforward duties and performance objectives. This will help them to comprehend their responsibilities.

Recruitment and Promotion Transparency: Ensuring that suitable people are chosen for bureaucratic posts is made possible by establishing open, merit-based mechanisms for recruitment and advancement. As a result, this encourages accountability throughout the system and reduces instances of corruption, favoritism, or nepotism.

Performance Evaluation and Incentives: Bureaucrats' performance should be regularly and impartially assessed. Evaluations must take into account KPIs and goals that are in line with the objectives of the firm. Bureaucrats can be encouraged to be more accountable by rewarding excellent performance and tackling underperformance with the proper sanctions.

Unbiased oversight organizations: Creating independent oversight organizations like anti-corruption commissions or ombudsman offices helps improve transparency throughout the bureaucracy. These organizations have the power to look into complaints, keep an eye on regulation, and holding administrators accountable for any infractions or rule-breaking.

Participation and Engagement of Citizens: Transparency and accountability are promoted through encouraging citizen involvement and engagement in decisions that are made. Mechanisms incorporate citizen participation, feedback channels, and public consultations

Robust Grievance Redressal Mechanisms: Citizens are able to express their concerns and seek redress against bureaucratic incompetence or wrongdoing when adequate and easily accessible grievance redressal processes are established. Grievances should be addressed promptly and openly since this fosters accountability.

Independent reviews and assessments: It is possible to spot loopholes, inefficiencies, and potential instances of corruption or misbehavior inside the bureaucracy with the use of routine audits and reviews by independent organizations or auditors. The results of these audits may result in improved accountability and corrective measures.[146]

Management of Cadres

For India to continue to have a sufficient and productive administrative structure, cadre oversight of the All-India Services is essential. It guarantees the distribution of competent officers among various states and gives officers chances to make a difference towards local and national governance. According to their abilities, qualifications, and responsibilities, government personnel in India are managed and divided into various cadres or services. It is a fundamental component of Indian civil services as well as is necessary to the operation of the legislative and executive branches of government. The Union Public Service Commission (UPSC) and numerous state public service commissions are largely responsible for regulating India's cadre management system. Candidates are chosen for prominent positions in the Indian Administrative Service (IAS), Indian Police Service (IPS), Indian Foreign Service (IFS), along with other central services through the UPSC's Civil Services Examination.

1. Cadre Allocation: After passing the Union Public Service Commission's (UPSC) competitive test, candidates are assigned to the All-India Services depending on their ranks and choices. The distribution of offices is decided by the national government. Candidates who pass the Civil Services Exam are assigned to various state cadres determined by their classification, preferences, and open positions.

2. The All-India Services: The IAS, IPS, and IFS are regarded as the pillars that comprise the Indian administrative system. These services function at both the federal and state levels, offering executive direction and preserving national governance homogeneity. Throughout their careers, officers nominated to these services may be placed in a variety of positions and are assigned to several state cadres.

3. Group A and Group B Services: India's civil services are divided under Group A and Group B categories. The All-India Services and other central services include the Indian Audit and Accounts Service, Indian Revenue Service, and Indian Forest Service are all considered to be Group A services. State civil services and subordinate operations are included in group B services.

4. Training and Development Course: Investment in All India Service officer education and professional growth is made by both the federal and state governments. To improve their administrative, leadership, and management abilities, they participate in foundational instruction, specialized instruction, and mid-career development courses.

5. Posting and Transfers: Cadre administration entails posting and moving officials among their designated cadres. Based on administrative requirements, rules and regulations, and personal career advancement, the federal and state governments have the power to transfer officials. The Ministry of Personnel, Public Grievances and Pensions is in charge of establishing the laws and regulations governing postings and transfers as well as overseeing the general cadre management.

6. Training and Capacity Building: Cadre management primarily involves strengthening officers' professional abilities and expertise through training and capacity building. For civil officials at various phases of their careers, the Lal Bahadur Shastri National Academy of Administration (LBSNAA) at Mussoorie offers training programs with other specialized training facilities.[147]

NITI Aayog as Consultant Helps to Bring Reforms

The National Institution for Transforming India Aayog, also known as NITI Aayog, is a government organization and policy think tank in India. It became the primary establishing policies institution of the Indian government on January 1, 2015, after the Modi government abolished the 65-year-old Planning Commission on August 13, 2014. India's development agenda is significantly shaped by NITI Aayog, which also supports sustainable and equitable development nationwide. It focuses on important topics such as eradicating poverty, learning, medical care, farming, amenities and technology. NITI Aayog's main goal is to promote cooperative federalism in India by incorporating the states in the formulation of fiscal policies. It serves as a forum for the federal and state governments to interact, work together, and produce national development plans and goals.[148]

It was guided by the following principles with the goal to execute and carry out the NITI Aayog-specified functions: [149]

1) Antyodaya: Pandit Deendayal Upadhyaya's concept of 'Antyodaya' calls for giving the poor, oppressed, and underprivileged priority service and uplift.

2) Inclusion: Strengthen marginalized and at-risk groups while addressing identity-based inequalities of all kinds, including those based on gender, region, religion, caste, or class.

3) Population's engagement: By fostering awakening and citizen engagement, the development process may be transformed into a process that is driven by the people, which is a key component of sound government.

4) **Governance:** Transparency, openness, accountability, proactive, and support purposeful governance, shifting emphasis from expenditure to consequence.

NITI Aayog introduced Seven Pillars for effective governance:

1. A pro-people program that satisfies both societal and personal objectives.
2. Proactive in identifying and addressing the needs of citizens.
3. Ensure participation through citizen involvement.
4. Put an emphasis on empowering women in all spheres.
5. Participation of every demographic with a focus on minorities, SCs, STs, and OBCs.
6. Youth opportunities are equal.
7. Using technology to increase government transparency and responsiveness.

Specialized Wings, NITI Aayog

Few Specialized Wings are available at NITI Aayog homes, including:

1) Research Wings: As a specialized think tank of exceptional subject matter experts, specialists, and academics, it produces in-house sectoral expertise.[150]

2. Consultancy Wing: It provides a marketplace of expert panels of expertise and funding, for the central and state governments to tap into matching their requirements with solution providers, public and private, national and international. By playing match maker instead of providing the entire service itself, NITI Aayog is able to focus its resources in priority matters, providing guidance and an overall quality check to the rest.

3. India's team Wing: It functions as a permanent forum for intergovernmental cooperation and includes officials of each state and ministry. Each delegate is responsible for: a) Maintaining that every state and ministry continues to have a voice and an interest in the NITI Aayog. (b) Establishes a dedicated liaison interface for all development-related communications between the concerned state/Ministry and NITI Aayog.[151]

NITI Aayog enabler of Cooperative federalism

The NITI Aayog was established with the intention of creating strong states that will form a strong nation in order to conceptualize the crucial aim of cooperative federalism and permit effective governance in India. It is a fact that achieving national goals without cooperation between the federal and state governments is challenging. Working together on an equal basis is crucial in a political setting. The two key components of cooperative federalism are (a) combining the center's and the states' attention on the National Development Agenda, and (b) promoting state viewpoints beneath the central ministries.

The NITI Aayog's engagement mechanisms have changed as a result of the government's policy of including State Governments in cooperative federalism design. To make certain that states are equal partners in the process of creating and implementing policies, NITI Aayog undertakes a number of vital activities. The prime minister emphasized the significance of NITI Aayog during the Governing Council meeting of NITI Aayog, focusing on the necessity of effective center-state collaboration to promote outcomes for development and accomplish substantial broad-based expansion for India.[152]

Models include the Centre-State Partnership model: Development Support to States (DSSS); and the sustainable Action for Transforming Human Capital (SATH) Program. NITI Aayog has introduced models and programs for the development of infrastructure and for Private Public Partnership (PPP), which are structured to help states improve their social sector indicators by ensuring to them technical support. By creating distinctive strategies to ensure sustainable development occurs in these parts of the country while safeguarding their natural habitat, NITI Aayog has already taken astounding steps to satisfy the needs of these regions, such as North Eastern States.

These steps include creating special forums to identify constraints. The following NITI Aayog initiatives are desirable under cooperative federalism: 1) Governing Council meetings; 2)Task Forces on certain issues; and 3) The NITI Forum for North East 4) Subgroups of chief ministers on various topics, 5) Sustainable Development in the Indian Himalayan Region, 6) Development Support Services to states, and 7) Sustainable Action for Transforming Human Capital (SATH) are some of the models and programs for infrastructure development and for Private Public Partnership (PPP) that NITI Aayog has introduced.

Why it was necessary to revive planning commission into NITI Aayog

The former Planning Commission began as a staff agency with a consultative role; with time, it developed into a strong and directive authority, and both the Union and the States took into consideration its suggestions. A "Super Cabinet," a "Economic Cabinet," a "Parallel Cabinet," the "fifth Wheel of the Coach," and other terms were used to describe it.

1. According to the Constitution, the minister, whether at the federal or state level, has the final say on matters of policy. First Administrative Reforms Commission (ARC) reflects Planning Commission has acquired a reputation as a Super Cabinet and a parallel cabinet.

2. K. Santhanam: He underlined that planning has replaced the federation as a constitutional expert and that our nation operates in many ways like a unitary system.

3. P.V. Rajamannar: He highlighted the overlap in duties and responsibilities between the previous Planning Commission and the Finance Commission in terms of federal fiscal transfers while serving as the chairman of the fourth finance commission.[153]

Determining Development of Policies and Programmes through two offices of NITI Aayog

National Institute of Labour Economics Research and Development

The National Institute of Labour Economics Research and Development, formerly known as the Institute of Applied Manpower Research (IAMR), is presently in operation. It is a centrally located independent entity connected with the NITI Aayog. Research, data gathering, teaching, and training in all facets of human capital organizing, human resource development, monitoring, and assessment are its main objectives.

Development Monitoring and Evaluation Office

Since the country's introduction of the policy process, planners and policy makers have recognized the need for an effective and independent evaluation mechanism. As a result, the program evaluation organization was established in 1952 to conduct impartial and objective impact evaluations of central government-funded programs. The former Programme Evaluation Organization and Independent Evaluation unit were combined to form the Development Monitoring and Evaluation Office (DMEO), which the government established in 2015 as an affiliated unit of the NITI Aayog. Up to 2017, Regional Development Monitoring and Evaluation (RDMEO) had 15 regional offices.[154]

Decentralization V/S Centralization Debate

Since India's independence in 1947, the conflict among centralization and decentralization has remained a persistent and complicated problem in the country's political system. The division of powers between the federal government and the state governments in India, a nation with a democratic system has been the topic of debate, negotiation, and conflict. India's delicate equilibrium between centralization and decentralization is a topic of ongoing debate as the nation faces new problems and aspirations. To achieve effective governance, encourage growth in the region, and maintain the values of democracy and federalism, the proper balance must be achieved.

Historical Context: The founders of the Constitution chose a federal structure with a division of responsibilities amongst the center and the states at the time of India's independence. In the early years, there was some centralization as the nation concentrated on forging a united front across its different areas.

Administrative Efficiency vs. Local Empowerment: Centralization proponents contend that a powerful central government can guarantee consistent policies, national advancement, and effective decision-making.

Fiscal Federalism: The essential question in the argument between centralization and decentralization is that of financial autonomy. In order to efficiently satisfy their unique demands, states frequently request greater autonomy over financial resources, but the federal government is careful about upholding fiscal restraint and a fair allocation of resources.

Decentralization's Evolution: India has made progress toward decentralization over time by putting in place the Panchayati Raj system.[155]

Pre Independence Decentralization Debate

The decentralization debate during colonial rule can be traced to the famous Ripon Resolution of 1882. To train the Indians in the art of governance, to enable them to learn from experience and to open up avenues for political participation of the educated class, Ripon strongly advocated the cause of decentralization of administration through the establishment of local self-governing institutions. The British administrators were not prepared to accept the Ripon thesis as they questioned the competence of Indians to manage local administration and feared a general weakening of field administration under a local self-government regime. The debate was essentially over the choice of values: democracy or efficiency. With the rising tempo of freedom struggle, the imperial policy had to however willingly concede Indian demands for self-government and participation in administration.[156]

Figure 9: Pre Independence-Decentralization Debate

Post Independence Decentralization Debate

The second phase of the decentralization debate in post-Independence India was staged on the floor of the Constituent Assembly. Panchayati Raj was an important component of Mahatma Gandhi's vision of future India in which economic and political power would be decentralized and each village would be self-reliant economically. It was in accordance with the wishes of the Mahatma Gandhi that Article 40 of the Constitution of India was adopted stipulating that "the state shall take steps to organize village panchayats and endow them with such powers and authority as may be necessary to enable them to functions as units of self-government."

Dr. B.R. Ambedkar, however, had a different view of the Indian rural society. He argued in the Constituent Assembly that the Indian social structure at the village Level was hierarchical, oppressive and insensitive to change. In his view, it would be dangerous to give powers to the panchayats as he thought that would mean giving powers to the prevailing rural power structure which would work to the detriment of the harijans and the rural poor. Two contrasting views about decentralization had thus surfaced in the Constituent Assembly; a visionary stand point of decentralization and a realistic view of decentralization. Any scheme of decentralization presupposes a harmonious society. As Dantwala has observed: "

The Gandhian vision of village society is a normative model that serves the purpose of a guidepost. But the reality of rural life and the experiences of Panchayati Raj in India seems to have' largely confirmed the belief of Dr. Ambedkar. It is interesting, in this context, to note the observations of the Asoka Mehta Committee on Panchayati Raj Institutions: "Panchayati Raj institutions are dominated by economically and socially privileged sections of society and have as such facilitated the emergence of oligarchic forces yielding no benefits to weaker sections."The decentralization debate has its roots at the conceptual level. The concept of Panchayati Raj has been far from clear and as the Asoka Mehta Committee commented: "Some would treat it just as an administrative agency; others as an extension of democracy at the grassroots level; and still others as a charter of rural local government.

Figure 10: Post Independence Decentralization Debate

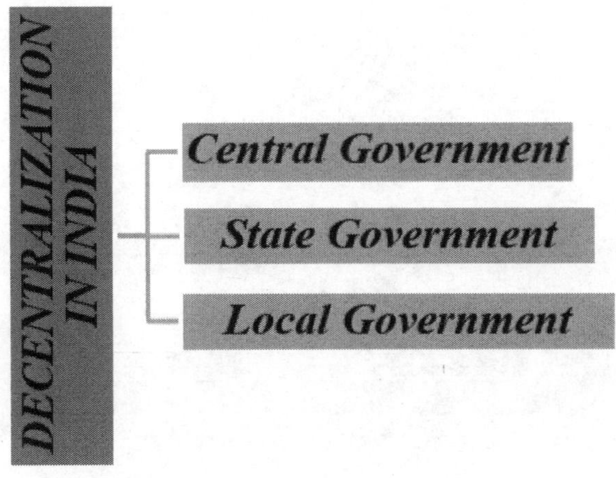

Figure 11: Decentralization structure of India

Features of Decentralization

Constitutional Amendment: Constitutional amendments have strengthened decentralization. Urban Local Bodies and Panchayati Raj institutions both received constitutional standing in 1992 as a result of the 73rd and 74th Amendments. These changes intended to strengthen local autonomy and provide local communities with greater authority over their own concerns.

Elections: To choose representatives for the village, block, district, and municipal levels, decentralized bodies hold elections on a regular basis. These elected officials have the power to make decisions and are incredibly essential for local government.

Financial Decentralization: Through a variety of financial commissions and grants, the federal and state governments distribute funding to Panchayati Raj organizations and municipalities. This financial devolution aids in funding initiatives and programs for local development.

29 Subjects: The 29 subjects that municipalities and Panchayati Raj institutions have been given authority over are outlined in the 73rd and 74th Amendments. Food and Agriculture, medical care, educational institutions, the management of water, and urban and rural planning are some of these topics.

Integrity and Accountability: Greater accountability and openness in government are goals of decentralization. Social audits are used to guarantee that finances and resources are used properly, and local politicians are accountable to the individuals they represent.[157]

Decentralization works in collaborative nature with Delegation, devolution and Deconcentration

The principles of decentralization, delegation, and devolution all pertain to how decision-making authority, power, and responsibility are allocated within a government or institution. Decentralization, delegation, and devolution constitute key ideas in India's governance system. They represent various strategies for gaining greater local autonomy and efficiency, although they have similarities. They are meant to transfer power and responsibilities across several levels of government and assure effective and efficient administration. Let's investigate each idea:

Devolution, Delegation and Deconcentration Framework with central Government

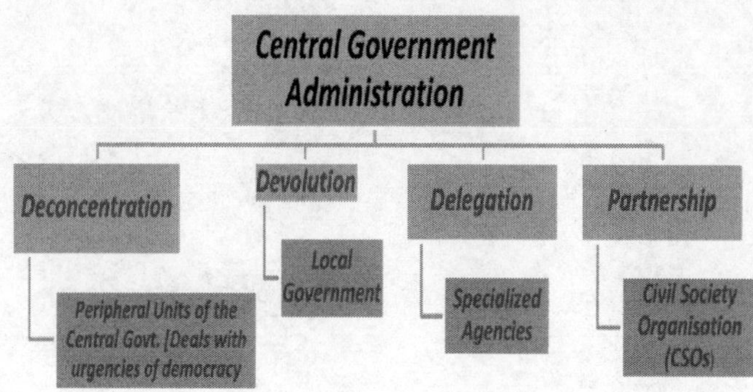

Figure 12: Central Government structure of Decentralization

Decentralization

The process of shifting authority, responsibility, and taking decisions from the governing body or greater degree of administration onto lower levels or local bodies is referred to as decentralization. The goal is to bring government closer to the individuals or groups that will be impacted by decisions so they can have more influence over their lives. Political, fiscal, or administrative decentralization are a few examples of the various ways that decentralization can manifest. Decentralization is the process by which administrative and decision-making responsibilities are transferred from the Union government to regional or local levels of government.

Delegation

A lower-level person, department, or institution within an organization is given particular duties, duties, or decision-making authority through the process of delegation from a higher authority. Although it expects those who are delegated to act on their behalf, the delegating authority nonetheless holds final responsibility for the results. In hierarchical systems, delegation is frequently employed to increase productivity, encourage specialization, and give power to subordinates. Delegation in politics can refer to elected authorities or top government officials giving specified tasks or obligations to government departments or agencies.

Devolution

Devolution is a type of decentralization where political power and decision-making authority are deliberately transferred beyond the national government to sub national or regional authorities. Though the central government still retains control over subjects of a national nature, it gives these sub national bodies greater autonomy in certain areas. Devolution is frequently viewed as a means of resolving regional inequalities and allowing for various cultural, linguistic, or historical variances within a nation. The Indian Finance Commission is essential to the decentralization process. It is established every five years to put forward proposals about the allocation of funds between the federal and state governments as well as between the several states. The Finance Commission's recommendations are legally enforceable and aid in ensuring a fair and equitable allocation of funds.[158]

Committees for Centre – States Relations to Consolidate National Unity

Rajamannar Committee

1) The DMK administration in Tamil Nadu established this committee in 1969. This committee also recommended the following in addition to calling for the immediate formation of the Inter-state Council:

2) The Union administration shall consult the interstate council before making any decisions that may have an impact on the objectives of a number of states.

3) Prior to being tabled in parliament, every law that concerns the well-being of the individual states should be referred to the inter-state council.

4) Article 356 should only be employed in extreme situations where there is a total loss of order and security in the state.

5) States should have the authority to levy residual taxes.

6) The union government utterly disregarded following proposals.[159]

Sarkaria Commission

1) Establishing a permanent intergovernmental council

2) Article 356 must be applied with caution.

3) The All-India Service Institution should be enhanced

4) The parliament should continue to have residuary power

5) When the President vetoes state legislation, the state should be informed of the president's reasoning.

6) Governors should be given the opportunity to complete their five-year terms.

7) Activate the Commissioner for Linguistic Minorities.[160]

Punchhi Commission

1) Giving the governors a set period of five years each and allowing for their impeachment

2) The Union should use extreme restraint when claiming the power of parliament over things that are the province of the states.

3) It stipulated a number of considerations for the appointment of governors, including: He should be well-known in a certain field, come from outside the state, be a distant figure unaffiliated with local politics,

4) The governor should have a fixed five-year term. Only a state legislature resolution could remove the governor.

5) The impeachment process for the president might be used for governors as well.

6) The Governor must urge that the Chief Minister demonstrate his approval rating for assembly.[161]

Cooperative Federalism Invigorates the Governance

The collaborative connection and division of duties and responsibilities between the national and state governments is referred to as cooperative federalism in India. It is a cornerstone of the Indian system of governance and ensures a cordial and collaborative style of governing. While "cooperative" emphasizes the spirit of cooperation and shared decision-making, the term "federalism" suggests a separation of responsibilities between the federal and state governments. In India, the idea of cooperative federalism has developed over time to take into account the changing demands of the country. In India, cooperative federalism has the following characteristics:

Division of Powers: The Seventh Schedule of the Indian Constitution explicitly defines the roles and responsibilities of the national government and state governments. It categorizes topics into three lists: the Union List, the State List, and the Concurrent List, which includes topics on which both the federal and state governments may enact legislation. The Union List pertains to matters that are solely within the purview of the federal government. Separation of Powers: Schedule 7 of the Constitution outlines a clear division of authority between the federal government and the states.

Distribution of Resources: Another feature of cooperative federalism is the fair distribution of financial resources between the national and state governments. The Finance Commission plays an essential role in developing suggestions regarding how taxes along with other policies should be implemented in order to guarantee balanced development. The Inter-State Council was a legal entity created to encourage coordination and collaboration between the federal and state administrations. Its duties include debating and settling disagreements, examining issues pertaining to the financial ties between the federal government and the states, and establishing rules for cooperative federalism.

Local government and decentralization: Cooperative federalism includes local government systems as well. The Panchayati Raj and urban local bodies, accordingly, essentially distribute power to the grassroots level, were established by the 73rd and 74th Amendments to the Constitution that booster of cooperative governance at local level.

Planning Commission (now replaced by NITI Aayog): By creating five-year strategies and synchronizing development initiatives between the central government and the states, the Planning Commission constituted a significant institution that promoted cooperative federalism. It has since been superseded by NITI Aayog, which upholds the collaborative planning philosophy. To help India achieve its paramount objective to achieve cooperative federalism and promote good governance, the NITI Aayog was established. NITI Aayog serves as the pivotal forum for the Government of India through uniting States as "Team India" to work toward the national development objective, based on the tenet that strong states build a strong nation.[162]

GST Council: The passage of the GST is an excellent instance of cooperative federalism, where the States and the Centre have given up their taxing authority and created one tax structure in order to achieve the goal of a single economic India with a "One Nation, One Market" that entails a single tax on the distribution of goods and services from the company that produces them to the consumer. It turned the nation into a single market. The indirect legislation in the nation is streamlined and harmonized by the GST. In the 2003 Kelkar Task Force report on indirect taxes, GST was first mentioned.

GST Council as Federal Innovation

The 101st Amendment Act of 2016 opened the door for the government to adopt the Goods and Services Tax, or GST. The center and the states have to collaborate and work together to administer this tax in an effective and efficient manner. The Goods and Services Tax Council's (GST Council) revision will be taken into account when evaluating this consultation process. The Council is responsible for deciding how to carry out its duties. The council adheres to the following Vision and Mission: VISION: The council is the first democratic federal body with the authority to make all significant decisions about the GST, and its mission is to uphold the highest principles of cooperative federalism in the council's operations. MISSION: Developing a user-friendly, information technology-driven GST structure through a process of broad consultation. A truly federal GST Council was set up with near-equal rights for the central and state governments to administer the new tax regime; this was the sanctum sanctorum of the Treaty of Faith, the guardian angel of the federal doctrine that underscored the new tax architecture.[163]

1) It is a value-based tax, with credits for taxes paid on inputs at each level being accessible at the next stage.

2) Only the GST assessed by the last retailer in the distribution chain is paid by the final consumer.

GST includes the following central taxes: Central Excise Duty, Additional Excise Duty, Octroi Entry Tax, Purchase Tax, Luxury Tax, and Taxes on Lotteries, Betting, and Gambling.

3)GST includes the following state-level taxes: sales VAT or sale tax; entertainment tax; octroi and entry tax; purchase tax; luxury tax; and taxes on lotteries, betting, and gambling.

Types of Goods and Services Tax

Under the GST form, four types of GST are:

1) Central GST (CGST): The CGST includes a provision to tax the Central Government's provision of goods and services. Prior to this, taxes levied by the central government included Central Excise, Excise (Drugs and Toilet Construction), Excise (Drugs and Special Duty of Custom Duty (SaD0), Service Tax, and Gratuity Surcharge relating to the provision of products or services. All of them were previously considered independent taxes, the CGST.

2) State GST (SGST): The state government imposes and collects taxes on goods and services under the state GST system. Previously, state governments employed to impose VAT under state taxes, particularly state excise and surcharges relating to purchase, admission, entrainment, and advertisement taxes.

3)GST Integrated (IGST, State Indemnification): The Goods and Services Tax (GST) is a global sales tax (GST) that is imposed on goods and services that are sold internationally. The central government imposes it and recovers it. From the loss of money created for the states, the state receives the sum of the amount of revenues collected under this arrangement.

4) Union Territory GST (UTGST): This arrangement or provision applies to the union territories, including Andaman and Nicobar Island, Daman and Diu, Dadar and Nagar Haveli, etc., which do not have their own legislative assemblies. The Central Government may impose and collect taxes in this Union Territories.[164]

{Taxes Out of GST}

Alcohol, real estate, crude oil, gasoline, natural gas, and turbine fuel are all items that aren't covered by any GST provision. These items are all exempt from the provisions of the GST; hence the previous taxes system will apply to them.

Figure 13: Taxes which are out of Goods & Services Taxes

Effect of GST on Economy

When GST is introduced, all of these extra charges will be incorporated into it. This would improve the indirect tax system's efficiency and reduce bureaucracy and corruption in India. Additionally, India would grow into a single, integrated market if all states have the same tax rates. Corporate rivalry will be encouraged as a result, and India will attract foreign investment. This will lead to increased economic growth in India.

Benefits for the Government

Due to the implementation of this, the tax system will become simple and detailed. As a result, India's tax to GDP ratio is expected to increase by 2%. Manufacturing expenses will go down.

Industrial Area and Merchant Profits

In addition to the benefits in this sector, the expense associated with production along with low tax rates are going to promote output and consumption, increasing competitiveness in the market for exported goods. For a total of seven North Eastern States (Assam, Meghalaya, Manipur, Nagaland, Mizoram, Arunchal Pradesh, and Sikkim) and three hilly States (Jammu Kashmir, Himachal Pradesh, Uttarakhand, etc.), this limit is decided to be 10 lakhs. Such traders who make up to 20 lakh annual turnover or less will be out of the GST preview.[165]

Gain for the Public

Taxes will only be levied in conjunction with the sale of the added tax system, and tax rates will become established in accordance with construction expenses. In addition, the GST preview has been omitted from numerous crucial expressions connected to consumption. As a result, those in the society who are most vulnerable will gain from this. Only the final retailer in the manufacturing chain adds GST, and the consumer is responsible for paying it. The rate of GST fixed by the Union Government in five slabs including 'No Tax'.

• 5%

• 12%

• 28%

• 18%

• No Tax[166]

Regulatory Bodies Enforce Accountability to Maintain Laws

Telecom Regulatory Authority of India (TRAI)

Following LPG, numerous private companies that had already been integrated into the administrative system necessitated autonomous regulation. Thus, on January 20, 1997, the Telecom Regulatory Authority of India (TRAI) was officially constituted with effect from the Telecom Regulatory Authority of India Act, 1997, an Act of Parliament. To control telecom services, including the setting or change of telecom service tariffs that were formerly under the control of the Central Government. The goal of TRAI is to foster the conditions necessary for the country's telecommunications sector to develop in a way and at a rate that will allow India to take the lead in the developing global information society.

TRAI's primary functions include:

• Controlling telecom services and rates to promote fair competition and safeguard the interests of customers.

• Controlling and enforcing telecom service providers' adherence to laws and licensing requirements.

• Resolving disagreements and complaints between customers and service suppliers.

• Promoting technological advancements and monetary investment in the telecom industry.

• Organizing and controlling how the communication frequency spectrum is distributed.[167]

Main objectives of TRAI are as follows:

1) Its goal is to create a fair and open political atmosphere that encourages equal opportunity and supports healthy competition.

2) To further the aforementioned goal, TRAI periodically issues a significant number of regulations, orders, and directives to address matters brought before it and give the Indian telecom market the necessary guidance as it transitions from a government-owned monopoly to a multi-operator, multi-service open competitive market.

3) The directives, orders, and rules made cover a wide range of topics, including tariff, interconnection, service quality, and the authority's management. A Telecommunications Dispute Settlement and Appellate Tribunal (TDSAT) was established to take over the adjudicatory and disputes functions from TRAI, and the TRAI Act was amended by an ordinance, which became effective on January 24, 2000.[168]

Insurance Regulatory and Development Authority of India (IRDAI)

The Insurance Regulatory and Development Authority of India is known by the initials IRDAI. It is the regulatory agency in charge of monitoring and controlling the Indian insurance market. IRDAI's main responsibilities include authorizing and overseeing insurance businesses, defending the rights of insurance customers, encouraging coverage from insurance, and assuring the expansion and advancement of the nation's insurance industry.

Objectives of IRDAI are:

- To set, promote, monitor, and enforce high standards of integrity, financial stability, fair dealing, and competence of those it regulates;
- To provide speedy and smooth expansion of the insurance sector , for the betterment of the common man;
- To provide long-term funds for accelerating growth of the economy;

Powers and functions of IRDAI with the introduction of Section 14 of IRDA Act, 1999

1) The Authority shall be charged with the responsibility of regulating, promoting, and ensuring the systematic development of insurance companies and re-insurance business, subject to the requirements of this Act and any other law now in effect.

2) Without limiting the broadness of the requirements in subsection the Authority shall have the following powers and duties: - Certify insurance firms; - Protect policyholder interests; and - Resolution of disagreements.

3) Provide the applicant with a certificate of registration; renew, modify, withdraw, suspend, or cancel such registration; protect the interests of policyholders in matters involving the assignment of policies, nomination of policies by policyholders, insurable interests, settlement of insurance claims, surrender value of policies, and other terms and conditions of insurance contracts; and specify the necessary credentials, code of conduct, and practical training for intermediaries.

4) Resolution of disagreements between insurers and brokers or insurance brokers.

Food Safety and Standards Authority of India (FSSAI)

The Food Safety and Standards Authority of India (FSSAI) is a stand-alone organization created by the Indian government's Ministry of Health and Family Welfare. It was established in accordance with the 2006 Food Safety and Standards Act, which unified several food safety legislation in India. To guarantee that food items are safe for ingestion and uphold the required quality standards, FSSAI is in charge of regulating and monitoring their safety and standards.

FSSAI's primary goals are as follows:

1) Formulating and enforcing food safety rules and regulations to guarantee the availability of healthy, safe food for consumption by human beings.

2) Licensing and registration: The authority is in charge of licensing and registering food firms, including producers, distributors, retailers, and importers, which operate in India.

3) Food safety training and capacity building: To educate stakeholders about food safety and to advance best practices, the FSSAI runs education initiatives and capacity-building exercises.

4) Food examination and assessment: To evaluate food samples and make sure they adhere to safety and quality requirements, the FSSAI operates food testing laboratories.

5) Consumer training: The authority runs a number of campaigns to inform the public about food safety, wholesome eating practices, and the significance of selecting safe food products.

6) Supporting R&D: The FSSAI supports R&D initiatives that are connected to food quality and safety, fostering entrepreneurship in the food sector.[169]

Bureau of Indian Standards (BIS)

The Department of Consumer Affairs, Ministry of Consumer Affairs, Food & Public Distribution, and Government of India oversee the Bureau of Indian Standards (BIS), which serves as the country's national standards body. BIS has benefited the national economy by means of its foundation operations of standardizing and evaluating compliance by providing safe, dependable, and quality goods; reducing health risks to consumers; protecting the environment; promoting exports and imports as alternatives; controlling over proliferation of varieties; and more.

Aside from helping customers and business, the BIS standards and certification program also supports a number of public policies, including those related to manufacture safety, consumer protection, food quality, environmental protection, building and construction, etc. Since October 12th, 2017, the Bureau of Indian Standards Act, 2016, has been in effect.

Positions and Objectives of BIS as the National Standards Body:

- It provides a variety of conformity assessment plans that are in compliance with international standards.
- Empowers the Government to delegate certification and enforcement of conformance to a standard to any agency other than BIS.
- Authorizes the government to compel product certification on the basis of national security, environmental protection, health and safety, and the avoidance of misleading practices.
- The establishment of standardization, marking, and product quality certification procedures in unison.
- To give regulation along with quality controls a boost in order to meet both the requirements of consumers and the industry's growth and development.

Reserve Bank of India (RBI)

The Reserve Bank of India (RBI) is the country's central banking organization and is in charge of overseeing the monetary and financial systems of the nation. The Reserve Bank of India Act established it on April 1, 1935. As the country's top banking institution, it is essential to the Indian economy.

RBI's duties and responsibilities:

1) Monetary Policy: To prevent inflation, stabilize prices, and promote economic stability, the RBI develops and implements monetary policies. To control liquidity and interest rates in the economy, it employs a number of mechanisms, including the repo rate, reverse repo rate; cash reserve ratio (CRR), and statutory liquidity ratio (SLR).

2) Currency Issuance: In India, only the RBI has the ability to issue and administer coins and currency notes. It makes sure there is a sufficient quantity of money to meet the needs of the economy.

3) Banking Regulation: To preserve the long-term viability of the financial system and safeguard depositor interests, the RBI controls and oversees the operation of banks and other financial institutions in India.

4) Foreign Exchange Management: The RBI is responsible for overseeing India's foreign exchange reserves and is a key player in enabling international payments and trade.

5) Banker to the Government: The RBI manages the accounts of the federal and state governments and facilitates interactions between them in its capacity as their banker.

6) Financial Stability: The RBI keeps an eye on and evaluates the overall stability of the Indian financial system, and it takes steps to minimize and avert hazards.[170]

Securities and Exchange Board of India (SEBI)

The SEBI Act, which was passed in 1992, granted legislative authority to SEBI, an autonomous organization that had been founded in 1988. Protecting the rights of shareholders in securities as well as fostering the development and oversight of the Indian securities industry is SEBI's two main goals. With considerable authority to uphold its rules and safeguard investors' interests, SEBI is essential to preserving the reliability and stability of India's securities market.

SEBI's primary duties and tasks are as follows:

1) Regulation of Stock Exchanges: SEBI monitors Indian stock market operations and makes sure they are fair and open. To maintain ethical behavior, SEBI oversees several securities market divisions, including bonds, stocks, debt instruments, and other financial instruments.

2) Registration and Regulation of Intermediaries: Brokers, depository participants, mutual funds, and other market intermediaries are among those that SEBI registers and regulates. Brokers, mutual funds, portfolio managers, investment advisers, and credit rating organizations are just a few of the securities market intermediaries that SEBI registers and regulates.[171]

3) Shareholder Security: SEBI promotes investor education and awareness while taking action to safeguard investors' interests.

4) Restriction of Insider Trading: SEBI enforces laws and procedures to stop insider trading, making sure that those with access to confidential information do not use it for their own benefit. Insider trading, that includes investing in commodities by individuals with access to confidential information with a potential to affect prices, is strictly prohibited by SEBI.

5) Issuance and Listing of Securities: In order to ensure that businesses abide by disclosure standards and transparency regulations, SEBI oversees the issuing and registration of instruments in the Indian capital market.

6) Marketplace Monitoring & tracking: In order to identify and stop market manipulation and unfair trading activities, SEBI conducts market monitoring. To identify price rigging, market manipulation, and other unfair acts that could be detrimental to investor interests, SEBI undertakes market monitoring.

7) Fostering Market Development: SEBI works to advance the expansion and development of the securities market by supporting new ideas and financial tools.[172]

Board of Control for Cricket India (BCCI)

Cricket in India is governed by the Board of Control for Cricket in India (BCCI). It is one of the wealthiest and most powerful cricket boards in the world. Cricket is organized and promoted at several levels in the nation, particularly domestic and international cricket, by the BCCI.

The BCCI has a number of important duties, including:

1) Hosting domestic cricket competitions: The BCCI is in charge of hosting a number of domestic competitions, including the Ranji Trophy (first-class cricket), the Vijay Hazare Trophy (one-day cricket), and the Syed Mushtaq Ali Trophy (T20 cricket).

2) Handling the Indian national teams: The BCCI is in charge of choosing and leading both the men's and women's national cricket teams in India.

3) Hosting international matches: One-Day International (ODI), Test, and T20 International cricket matches are all hosted in India by BCCI.

4) Player contracts and salaries: Depending on their achievements and experience, BCCI assigns national team players central contracts, which decides their compensation.[173]

Central Board of Film Certification (CBFC)

In India, a statutory organization called the Central Board of Film Certification (CBFC) is in charge of approving films for public viewing. It is run by the Indian government's Ministry of Information and Broadcasting. The CBFC's primary goal is to make sure that movies screened in India follow the rules and regulations established by the government.

Functions of CBFC:

1) Film certification: Based on a film's content, the CBFC evaluates and awards certification. The board gives movies particular age-based ratings, such as:

2) Universal (U), appropriate for all ages.

For children over the age of 12, with parental supervision. UA (Parental Guidance).

A (Adult) - Only suitable for adults above the age of 18.

S (Special) - Only available to professionals, such as scientists or doctors.

Content Analysis: To evaluate if a movie complies with government standards, the CBFC analyzes the movie's themes, language, visuals, and other components.

3) Censorship: In some circumstances, the CBFC may request that the filmmakers make necessary alterations or edits to the movie in order for it to adhere to the guidelines and receive the requisite certification.

4) Guidance Role: The CBFC also advises moviemakers on any problems that can come up during the certification procedure.[174]

Advent of NDA Government

Prime Minister Narendra Modi with union ministers at a cabinet meeting at the Prime Minister's Office, in South Block, New Delhi

"Reform is not the end in itself. Reform for me is just a way station on the long journey to the destination. The destination is the transformation of India" – Prime Minister Narendra Modi

There were BJP governments in 7 States when the Modi administration first took office in 2014. There were BJP Chief Ministers in five states: Gujarat, Rajasthan, Madhya Pradesh, Chhattisgarh, and Goa. The party was the NDA Government's junior ally in Punjab and Andhra Pradesh. The BJP now has a total of 15 States or UTs. In Uttar Pradesh, Maharashtra, Madhya Pradesh, Gujarat, Haryana, Uttarakhand, Assam, Tripura, Arunachal Pradesh, Goa, Manipur, Meghalaya, Nagaland, Sikkim, and Puducherry, the Party is either in charge on its own or as a member of the ruling coalition. The BJP has won the politically significant state of Uttar Pradesh not once, but twice, under PM Modi. We now have to consider how the Modi administration operates to secure a second victory. The BJP-led government's achievement can be attributed to the following main factors:

Strong Leadership: The BJP's nominee for Prime Minister, Narendra Modi, has emerged as a captivating and dynamic figure that has a strong ability to appeal to the masses. Voters seeking a leader who could deliver stable administration and decisive leadership were drawn to his image of strength and resolve.

Populist Programs and Schemes: The Modi government established a number of populist programs and schemes aimed at enhancing the lives of the underprivileged and marginalized groups in society. Initiatives like the Swachh Bharat Abhiyan (cleanliness campaign), Jan Dhan Yojana (financial inclusion program), and Ujjwala Yojana (LPG gas connections to poor homes) have all been successful in gaining support from a wide range of people.[175]

Development Agenda: The administration concentrated on a narrative that was centered on development, making promises of job growth, infrastructure improvement, and economic expansion. Other efforts tried to enhance housing, internet connectivity, and transportation, while the "Make in India" campaign promoted manufacturing and attracted international investment.

Foreign policy and national security: The Modi government adopted a firm stance on national security and defense matters, especially in response to cross-border terrorism. One of the innovative ideas of Modi government is the introduction of elements of Para diplomacy in India's foreign policy where each state and cities would be encouraged to forge special relation with countries or federal states of another country or even cities of their interest. It emphasized a more assertive foreign policy, strengthening India's position on the global stage.

Effective Use of Media and social media: The BJP and Narendra Modi's team successfully reached out to people personally and disseminated their message through social media and contemporary communication methods. This strategy assisted in creating a powerful brand and connecting with the youth market.

Opposition fragmented: In both elections, the opposition parties failed to present a unified and cohesive front to confront the BJP. The fact that Modi's leadership lacked a formidable national-level rival benefited the ruling party.

Positive Perception of Governance: In its first term, the Modi government garnered positive public perception regarding its efforts to address corruption and improve the ease of doing business. This contributed to the party's credibility and voter trust in their ability to govern effectively.

Effective Campaign Strategy: The BJP ran a well-organized and targeted campaign, focusing on issues that resonated with the electorate. The party's emphasis on nationalism, cultural identity, and development helped it build a strong electoral appeal .[176]

9 Years of Modi Government: Policy Initiatives

In the nine years that Narendra Modi has been in office, the nation has seen an important change in how politics is conducted. The nation's attitude toward development and growth has altered as a result of policy pronouncements that are mixed with decisions that are quite reformative. To rescue the nation's economy from a condition of policy gridlock, Prime Minister Modi has driven through a number of changes. Apathetic governance, high inflation, and a low growth rate were all burdens that the NDA government had to deal with. Exports were going south, which nearly caused stagnation in industrial output. By introducing initiatives like Make-in-India, which encourage lowering rules and enhancing the ease of doing business, the Prime Minister set the voice for development and progress. The government wanted to entice foreign corporations to establish manufacturing facilities in India.[177]

Start-up India is an initiative launched by the Government of India in January 2016 to promote and support startups in the country. The program aims to foster entrepreneurship, encourage innovation, and create a favorable ecosystem for startups to flourish. ***Skill development*** refers to the process of acquiring and enhancing the skills, knowledge, and competencies needed for employment, entrepreneurship, and personal growth. It is a crucial aspect of human capital development and plays a significant role in boosting economic productivity, reducing unemployment, and promoting inclusive growth.

The ***Pradhan Mantri Mudra Yojana (PMMY) or Mudra*** the Government of India announced the Scheme initiative in April 2015. The program aims to support financially and foster entrepreneurship among the nation's micro and small businesses. Micro Units Development and Refinance Agency is known as "MUDRA." The Mudra Scheme's main goal is to provide financial support to non-corporate, small enterprises like service providers, shopkeepers, traders, and small manufacturing units.

The Indian government launched the Direct Benefit Transfer (DBT) financial inclusion program in 2013 with the goal of directly transferring subsidies and benefits to eligible beneficiaries' bank accounts. DBT's main goals include minimizing leaks, getting rid of middlemen, ensuring that government welfare payments are distributed more effectively and transparently to the intended recipients, and many more.[178] ***Nine Years provided 14 engagements as One Goal – Seva, Sushasan, and Garib Kalyan*** under the leadership of Prime Minister Narendra Modi.

In the last nine years, this government has followed through on all of its assurances, Whether or not it was repealing Article 370, immunizing a billion people, outperforming in extremely difficult conditions, outlawing triple talaq, or placing the groundwork for the Ram Janmabhoomi temple, it has exceeded all of its own expectations. India achieved enormous goals for rural electrification and cutting-edge infrastructure while ensuring that everyone has access to basic services, such as food and healthcare. On the one hand, the country documented the greatest number of exports in history and gave birth to a digital revolution that is multiplying faster than one can blink.

The past nine years have proven that, if the resolution of "nation-first" is applied fully, political discourse and policy enforcement may be a match made in heaven while remaining faithful to ***"Sabka Saath, Sabka Vikaas"*** under PM Modi's inspirational leadership. This book is a compilation of all these nine years of assistance, regardless of whether it be making sure our farmers are well-off, helping the underprivileged, honoring our overlooked heroes, empowering women, getting rid of infrastructure, or Providing youth with limitless opportunities, enhancing national security, supporting an ethical foreign policy, preserving our natural resources, improving the quality of life of all our residents — ***Antyodaya — or honoring our vibrant and diverse culture are just a few of our goals.***

Public service delivery and operation have undergone a profound paradigm shift. We have observed the removal of obstacles. And we have seen the drive towards holistic development, which leaves no life unexplored. A culture of equitable development has emerged thanks vital contribution from the vast array of social programs that are empowering the formerly underprivileged and setting new standards for good government. Any individual is an essential component of India's growth story in this ***"Amrit Kaal."***

The Nation's Unstoppable Progress can be determined by its Approach to Policy Making. The majority of programs have advantages that go beyond the obvious; they promote secondary economic development and large-scale social transformation. Numerous revisions to one policy, numerous advantages (encompassing all beneficiaries) from one scheme. Many Jan Bhagidaaris emerged from a single initiative. Many lives are transformed by one change.

The PM's strategic agenda has preached this ***"gift of giving."*** Only dreams may be made of the tale of the new India, Atmanirbhar Bharat, and Ek Bharat Shreshtha Bharat. It's fortunate that we now anticipate realizing those dreams. In the past nine years, the government, led by Prime Minister Modi, has placed a laser-like focus on two things: first, reducing and eventually eliminating poverty; second, restoring dignity to those who have been oppressed in the past. Perhaps the definition of "serving the poor" in the true sense is redefined by the latter push, which aims to make everyone feel included, appreciated, and regarded for their involvement in societal progress. No other administration has been more closely matched to the demands and hopes of the underprivileged.

The direct benefits of plans and policies take on magnified significance when they are converted into second-order benefits that provide more inferred advantages and advantages than were initially suggested or envisaged, as PM Modi himself has said. As an example, consider the Swachh Bharat Mission-Gramin. By the second of October 2019, all villages in the nation had to declare themselves ODF under SBM-Gramin. Power policy that has a multiplier, continuous effect is the ODF aim, women's safety and hygiene, and the increasing enrollment of girls into educational institutions (and, consequently, in the next workforce and the country's economic success).

The choice to reach everyone, in every location (har ghar), through awas, ration, and clean energy has been one of the nine years' most distinctive aspects. The greatest nutrition program in the world***, Har Ghar Ration; PM-GKAY has been in operation since April 2020. More than 40 crore people in more than 8 crore rural families have benefited from the Har Ghar Jal (Jal Jeevan Mission) initiative. Nearly 3 crore homes—or more than 99.9% of all homes—were electrified as part of the SAUBHAGYA Yojana's Har Ghar Bijli project. In order to achieve the promise of the Har Ghar Gas Cylinder with Ujjwala Yojana, nearly 9 crore LPG connections*** will have been issued by March 2023.

The goal of these programs is to reach every home in order to help contribute to the economic growth of the socially and economically disadvantaged groups. As part of what is regarded as the largest vaccination program in history, India distributed more than 200 billion dosages of the COVID vaccine. India efficiently distributed over two crore shots of the COVID-19 vaccine across the country in just 18 months. This was done without any additional cost restrictions; thus, vaccinations were available to all people.

As evidenced in the aforementioned programs, the advantages that have benefitted to those in need are both transferable and perceptible; for instance, ***Numerous Pradhan Mantri Bhartiya Janaushadhi Kendras (PMBJKs)*** are being established to offer top-notch generic medications at competitive prices around the nation. Under the auspices of the Pradhan Mantri Mudra Yojana (PMMY), close to 41 crore loans have been approved since the scheme's inception, which is another fundamental necessity that enables bigger goals.[179]

The Creation of NITI Aayog (National Institution for Transforming India) is in keeping with the evolving requirements and expectations of an emerging country and "New India" in place of the Planning Commission.

(National Institution for Transforming India) is a government agency and policy think tank in India that acts as the principal body for developing and directing national development policies and initiatives. On January 1st, 2015, it was founded to take over from the Planning Commission and apply a more flexible and dynamic technique for India's development concerns.

The remarkable indirect tax reform, the boldest step since Independence, came with the introduction of ***GST (Goods & Services Tax)*** between June 30 and July 1 at midnight. The ***"One Nation, One Tax"*** system was implemented for the countrymen under the GST regime. The reform aims to increase tax transparency with the ultimate objective of protecting consumers' interests as well as those of businesses and industries. In India, a comprehensive indirect tax known as the Goods and Services Tax (GST) is imposed on the provision of goods and services. Value-added taxes have taken the place of numerous indirect taxes levied by the central and state governments, modernizing the tax code and fostering corporate accessibility. India's GST went into effect on July 1st, 2017.[180]

Capitalization of Banks: Resources were allocated to recapitalize banks in order to reinforce public sector banks and solve the problem of non-performing assets (NPA), allowing them to increase capacity and comply with regulatory capital requirements. Public sector banks should merge to increase efficiency, lower operating costs, and encourage their resistance to economic shocks. The Insolvency and Bankruptcy Code (IBC) 2016, which was enacted in 2016, provides a framework for the time-bound resolution of stressed assets and an organized approach for resolution of insolvencies and liquidation to address and resolve insolvency and bankruptcy issues.

E – Commerce Rules (2000) to effectively control internet marketplaces. These regulations were created to address problems with deceptive marketing tactics, fake goods, and unfair business practices. These regulations sought to control e-commerce platforms and guarantee consumer protection in India's quickly expanding electronic commerce market.[181]

These are only a few instances of the e-governance projects that the Modi administration has undertaken. The government continues to be working consistently to use technology to streamline procedures, enhance service delivery, and boost governance transparency. The government keeps looking for new, creative methods to improve the nation's e-governance as technology advances and new problems are encountered. For the most recent details on the Modi administration's e-governance projects are Digital India, which was launched in 2015. The objective of the Digital India effort is to make India into a knowledge-based society and economy. It focuses on enabling citizens a range of digital services, infrastructure, and literacy.[182]

The Aadhaar program is a special biometric identification system that issues inhabitants of India a 12-digit unique identity number. In order to simplify service delivery and eliminate duplications, it has been integrated into a number of government programs and social programs. An immediate time payment system called Unified Payments Interface (UPI) enables fast money transfers between banks using mobile devices. Cashless payments and digital transactions have significantly increased as a result. MyGov is a platform for citizen participation that enables anyone to take part in governance by offering recommendations, criticism on various government policy initiatives and programs.

E-NAM (National Agriculture Market) is a national network of online markets for agricultural products that enables efficient and transparent trade of agricultural goods.[183] ***a Smartphone app called UMANG***, or The Unified smartphone Software for New-age Governance (UMANG), gives users access to several government services and programs on a single platform. With the use of the e-Sign framework, citizens can electronically sign papers, doing away with the necessity for handwritten signatures and increasing the effectiveness of numerous procedures.

With the use of technology, state legislatures will become paperless and more effective by the e-Vidhan project. ***GeM (Government e-Marketplace)*** is an online platform for public procurement that enables government agencies to purchase products and services from authorized vendors while maintaining efficiency and openness. Mobile software called BHIM (Bharat Interface for Money) enables speedy and safe cashless transactions via UPI.

Implementing BharatNet TRAI recommended public-private partnerships (PPPs) that align private incentives with long-term service delivery, similar to the Build-Own-Operate Transfer/Build-Operate-Transfer models, as the preferred option for the national broadband network, BharatNet, in a February 2016 Broadband services through public ***Wi-Fi PM WANI*** participates in the broadband via WIFI in order to enhance Internet usage in the nation. In its most recent report from March 2017 titled "Proliferation of Bandwidth via Public Wi-Fi Networks," [184]

Government Approach to Integrate Entire Nation in one

Ek Bharat Shreshtha Bharat: Promoting Unity in Diversity

On the occasion of Sardar Vallabhbhai Patel's 140th birthday, the Hon'ble Prime Minister made the declaration "Ek Bharat Shreshtha Bharat" on October 31, 2015. An Indian government program called "Ek Bharat Shreshtha Bharat" seeks to foster harmony, intercultural understanding, and cooperation among the nation's many states and Union Territories. "One India, Excellent India" is the English translation of the slogan "Ek Bharat Shreshtha Bharat". The effort seeks to preserve and celebrate the distinctive cultural characteristics of India's many regions while fostering a stronger feeling of national identification and satisfaction amongst all residents. On the occasion of Sardar's 140th birth anniversary, Prime Minister Narendra Modi announced the project on October31, 2015.[185]

The key objectives of the Ek Bharat Shreshtha Bharat initiative include:

Cultural Exchange: The program promotes cultural exchanges between different states and Union Territories to foster mutual understanding, appreciation, and celebration of the diverse cultures, traditions, languages, and cuisines of India. To **CELEBRATE the Unity in Diversity** of our Nation and to maintain and strengthen the fabric of traditionally existing emotional bonds between the people of our Country;

Promoting Unity: The initiative seeks to strengthen the emotional integration and sense of belonging among people from different parts of India by encouraging interactions, collaborations, and exchanges. PROMOTE the spirit of national integration through a deep and structured engagement between all Indian States and Union Territories through a year-long planned engagement between States;

Collaboration in Various Fields: States and Union Territories are encouraged to collaborate in various fields such as art, literature, music, dance, sports, tourism, and other areas of mutual interest to share knowledge and experiences. To SHOWCASE the rich heritage and culture, customs and traditions of either State for enabling people to understand and appreciate the diversity that is India, thus fostering a sense of common identity;

Key themes of EK Bharat Shreshtha Bharat:

- *Cultural Interaction and Heritage: The Initiative's main goals are to foster cross cultural dialogue and to recognize the rich cultural diversity of the various states and Union Territories. It promotes people to become familiar with and supportive of the other cultures' works of art, music, dance, celebrations various language and food.*

- *The use of language and Multilingual Uniqueness: The program highlights the value of conserving and fostering the various languages used in the various states of India in light of the country's linguistic diversity. It promotes language acquisition and comprehension between those with various linguistic origins.*

- ***Hospitality and travel: The project encourages individuals to visit and travel inside the country, encouraging them to see the diverse states and Union territories' historical, artistic, and natural beauty. This promotes intercultural communication and understanding.***

- ***Participation of Youth and Education: Specific programs and events are held to involve young people in activities that support national harmony and a better knowledge of India's diversity. This includes volunteer work, cultural activities, and educational activities.***

- ***Interaction in a variety of sectors: States and Union Territories are urged to work together in a variety of field, including science, technology, sports, literature, the arts, and literature while exchanging best practices, expertise, and experiences. This cooperation improves regional ties and advances national growth as a whole.***

- ***The project encourages the promotion and preservation of regionally specific conventional crafts, art forms, and artistic manifestation. This aids in maintaining traditional skills and giving craftspeople opportunities for employment.***

- ***Unity in different kinds: The Initiative's central concept is to honor India's diversity while also recognizing its unity. It aims to build an awareness of national identity which embraces and values the diverse cultural fabric of the nation.***

Partnering states of Ek Bharat Shreshtha Bharat

- Tamil Nadu & Jammu & Kashmir
- Himachal Pradesh & Kerala
- Uttarakhand & Karnataka
- Haryana & Telangana
- Rajasthan & Assam
- Gujarat & Chhattisgarh
- Maharashtra & Odisha
- Goa & Jharkhand
- Delhi & Sikkim & Assam
- Madhya Pradesh & Manipur & Nagaland
- Uttar Pradesh & Arunachal Pradesh & Meghalaya
- Bihar & Tripura & Mizoram
- Chandigarh & Dadra & Nagar Haveli
- Puducherry & Daman & Diu
- Punjab & Andhra Pradesh
- Lakshadweep & Andaman & Nicobar[186]

Vikas Bhi Virasat Bhi

The idea of ***"Vikas Bhi, Virasat Bhi,"*** according to Prime Minister Narendra Modi, " bring traditional features together with modern technological elements to make the temple ecosystem even more vibrant" has been advocated by representatives of various temple managements. "This is the same idea that has driven many of our temple towns' transformational initiatives over the past few years. Whether it is Somnath, Kedarnath, or the city of Baba Viswanath, our temple towns are being modernized with facilities and infrastructure that are centered on the needs of the people, while maintaining the sanctity of the shrines. India has been blessed with an enormous variety of temples, which are a reflection of our diversity in artistic expression, theology, history, and cultural heritage.

"The 'Amrit Kaal' of the following 25 years—the era leading up to India's 100th year of independence—is also a 'Kartavya Kaal' (a period of duty) for the country and the people. We have a unique opportunity for temple administrations, architects, archaeologists, scholars, and enthusiasts to come together and exchange ideas, knowledge, best practices, and experiences to preserve and promote our cultural heritage. One of our most important duties is to work towards preserving and promoting our diversity in the spirit of "Ek Bharat, Shreshtha Bharat" (an initiative launched to promote national unity and integrity). For individuals who seek but also go beyond divine favor, our temples offer support and strength. For ages, our temples have served as the center of society as well as places of devotion, encouraging art, architecture, engineering, culture, economy and society. They are intimately connected with our past, present and future.[187]

Mann ki Baat

Prime Minister Narendra Modi broadcasting Mann Ki Baat

The Prime Minister of India, Narendra Modi, hosts a radio program in India called **"Mann ki Baat,"** which translates to **"Talk from the Heart"** or **"Words with the Heart"** signifying the program's intention to establish a relationship with people on a personal and empathetic level. The Prime Minister uses it as a stage to address the public and express his opinions on numerous topics and events. The program strives to engage Indian citizens by sharing government efforts, successes, and thoughts whilst also promoting citizen involvement in fostering the country. Every month's final Sunday, the program airs on All India Radio (AIR). Additionally, it broadcast live on a number of digital channels and dubbed into a number of indigenous languages.

The idea behind "Mann ki Baat" is to create a direct line of communication between the Prime Minister and the citizens of India. It aims to bridge the gap between the government and the public, allowing the Prime Minister to understand the aspirations, concerns, and suggestions of the people firsthand. It is a platform through which the Prime Minister can speak about important national events, policies, and initiatives, but also a space to celebrate the achievements and contributions of ordinary citizens. Launched on October 3, 2014, "Mann ki Baat" has become a popular medium for the Prime Minister to connect with citizens across the country and has been instrumental in conveying government initiatives and policies to a wide audience. The program is broadcasted on All India Radio, Doordarshan, and other digital platforms, reaching millions of people in different parts of India.[188]

The topics covered in "Mann ki Baat" are diverse, ranging from social issues, cultural heritage, environment, technology, education, health, to inspirational stories of ordinary citizens making extraordinary contributions. The show often features anecdotes and experiences shared by citizens from different parts of the country, highlighting their accomplishments and efforts in various fields. The program's interactive nature allows citizens to contribute their ideas, suggestions, and questions via letters, phone calls, or social media platforms. Some of the ideas or suggestions shared by citizens during "Mann ki Baat" have even led to policy changes and implementation by the government. "Mann ki Baat" has been well-received and has become a significant means of communication between the Prime Minister and the people of India, promoting a sense of unity and engagement in the nation's progress.

The main goals of "Mann ki Baat" are as follows:

•Promoting national unity through direct interaction with residents, the initiative seeks to advance inclusivity and unity across linguistic, regional, and religious divides.

•Encourages proactive citizen involvement and engagement in the process of developing the nation by providing a forum for residents to contribute their thoughts, experiences, and recommendations.

•Information dissemination acts as a conduit for communicating with individuals about government projects, campaigns, and policies, guaranteeing that people are informed about various national activities.

•A culture of positive transformation and creativity is promoted by "Mann ki Baat," which frequently tells the stories of regular people who have made important contributions to society.[189]

100th Episode of Mann ki Baat

The most popular program on All India Radio, Prime Minister, and Narendra Modi's 'Maan Ki Baat' was completed 100 episodes on the 30th of April 2023. To celebrate this milestone the 100th episode of the radio program telecasted Live by Doordarshan and a grand event will be hosted by Raj Bhavans across India. PM Narendra Modi Started the Telecast by saying;

My dear countryman, Namaskar, Today is the hundredth episode of 'Mann Ki Baat'. I have received thousands of letters from all of you, lakh of messages … and I have tried to read as many letters as possible, have a look at them and try to understand the messages a bit. Many a time while reading your letters, I got emotional, was filled with emotions, got carried away in emotions and then also composed myself. You have congratulated me on the 100th episode of 'Mann Ki Baat', but I say this from the core of my heart…that in fact, all of you, the listeners of 'Mann Ki Baat', our countrymen, deserve congratulations. 'Mann Ki Baat' is the 'Mann Ki Baat' of crores of Indians; it is the expression of their feelings.

The Raj Bhavan, Mumbai hosted a program with the Hon'ble Governor of Maharashtra, Shri Ramesh Bais as Chief Guest. The Central Bureau of Communication, Regional Office Pune organized a Photo Exhibition on'Azadi Ka Amrit Mahotsav' and 'Mann Ki Baat' on the lawns of the Raj Bhavan, on this occasion. Union Minister for Home Affairs and Cooperation, Amit Shah and Union Minister for Commerce & Industry, Consumer Affairs, Food & Public Distribution and Textiles, Piyush Goyal were also in Mumbai, on the occasion of the 100th episode of Mann Ki Baat.[33]

Prime Minister Narendra Modi addressed a historic 100th episode of the Mann Ki Baat radio programme on Sunday, in which he said that the preservation and promotion of education and culture have been an ancient tradition of India, adding that the country was working towards that through various means like the National Education Policy and the option of studying in regional languages.

The Prime Minister said that the people who have been mentioned in Mann Ki Baat over the years have been the heroes who made the programme come alive. He spoke to four of them on the 100th episode: Pradeep Sangawan, who ran a campaign to clean the mountains; Vijayshanti Devi from Manipur, who makes clothes from lotus fibres; Manzoor Ahmed, who makes pencil slates in Jammu and Kashmir; and Sunil Jaglan of Haryana, who had launched the Selfie with Daughter campaign.

Citizens from across Maharashtra who have been mentioned by Prime Minister, Narendra Modi, in previous editions of 'Mann Ki Baat' will be special invitees at the event. These include persons from different backgrounds and age groups. From Kamya Karthikeya who conquered Mount Aconcagua at the age of twelve to pensioner Chandrakant Kulkarni who has pledged to contribute five thousand from his monthly pension of sixteen thousand towards cleanliness drive. The achievements of these special invitees traverse the globe. From achievements of tribal persons from regions of Palghar, Chandrapur and Nashik to achievements of Hitendra Mahajan and Mahendra Mahajan in far off lands like United States. Persons from different professions and walks of life belonging to Maharashtra have participated enthusiastically in 'Mann Ki Baat'. Forty-Seven of them were have the unique privilege of attending the program in Raj Bhavan in the presence of the Hon'ble Governor of Maharashtra, Shri Ramesh Bais. Along with them Padma Awardees from Maharashtra and eminent social workers, businessman and film industry celebrities were also graced the event.[191]

Swacchh Bharat Mission

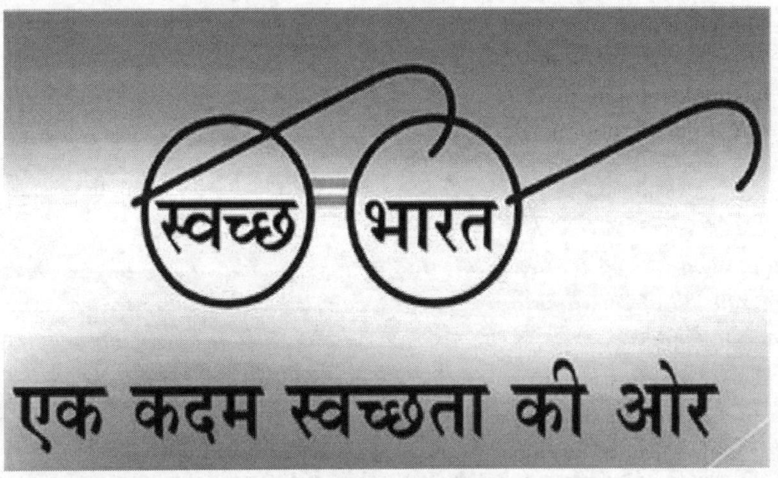

The Indian government started the "Swachh Bharat" or "Swachh Bharat Abhiyan" national cleanliness campaign on October 2, 2014. The campaign promotes cleanliness and appropriate sanitation practices throughout the nation in an effort to realize the objective of a healthy and safe India. Swachh Bharat Abhiyan has generated considerable strides in a number of sectors since its inception. Many villages and communities have been designated Open Defecation Free (ODF), and millions of toilets have been built. Additionally, the program has raised people's awareness regarding sanitation and hygiene. The Indian government continues to place a high premium on Swachh Bharat Abhiyan in order to maintain momentum and accomplish its objectives. It reflects a larger goal of making India an environmentally friendly and healthier country.[192]

Swachh Bharat Development: Propose changes in sanitation and cleanliness. In India, the Swachh Bharat Abhiyan has made tremendous progress in a number of sectors connected to sanitation and cleanliness. It's important to remember, though, that the circumstances may have changed. Here are some of the Swachh Bharat Abhiyan's most significant developments and accomplishments. The Swachh Bharat Abhiyan has made a huge contribution to the growth of India and the wellbeing of citizens by tackling the country's difficulties with cleanliness and sanitation.

Construction of Toilets: To end open defecation, the Swachh Bharat Abhiyan has concentrated on building bathrooms in both rural and urban regions. As a result, the nation now has thousands of privately owned household toilets in addition to community and public restrooms.

Status of Open Defecation Freedom (ODF): A considerable number of villages and cities were declared Open Defecation Free (ODF) under the campaign. ODF status indicates that all households in a village or city have access to toilets and no longer practice open defecation. One of the most significant achievements of the campaign in rural areas has been the declaration of thousands of villages as Open Defecation Free. The ODF status means that every household in these villages has access to a toilet, and open defecation practices have been eliminated.

Swachh Survekshan: Swachh Bharat Abhiyan introduced the Swachh Survekshan, an annual cleanliness survey to assess the cleanliness and sanitation levels of cities and towns across India. The survey aimed to encourage competition among cities to improve their cleanliness standards.

Waste management: Efforts were made to promote proper waste management practices and recycling to reduce the burden on landfills. Initiatives for waste segregation, composting, and promoting eco-friendly practices were undertaken. The campaign has also emphasized proper waste management in rural areas. Efforts have been made to raise awareness about waste segregation, composting, and recycling to reduce the burden on landfills.

School Sanitation: The campaign also focused on improving sanitation facilities in schools, ensuring that students have access to clean and hygienic toilets and washrooms.

Information and Awareness Campaigns: Swachh Bharat Abhiyan has conducted extensive information and awareness campaigns in rural areas to educate people about the importance of sanitation, hygiene, and the ill-effects of open defecation. These campaigns aimed to bring about behavioral change and promote the use of toilets.

Initiatives and Drives for Cleanliness: Swachh Bharat Abhiyan has encouraged the participation of local communities in cleanliness drives and initiatives. Villagers and local organizations have been involved in organizing cleanliness events and keeping public places clean.

India's cleanest cities ranking 2022

1. Indore, Madhya Pradesh

2. Surat, Gujarat

3. Navi Mumbai, Maharashtra

4. Vishakapatnam, Andhra Pradesh

5. Vijaywada, Andhra Pradesh

6. Bhopal, Madhya Pradesh

7. Tirupati, Andhra Pradesh

8. Mysore, Karnataka

9. New Delhi, Delhi

10. Ambikapur, Chhattisgarh[193]

Source: Swachh Bharat Abhiyan Portal

Celebration of 75 Years of Independence: Har Ghar Tiranga

Celebrating 75 years of Independence, Initiated Azadi Ka Amrit Mahotsav with Har Ghar Tiranga campaign

The Azadi Ka Amrit Mahotsav means elixir of energy of independence; elixir of inspirations of the warriors of freedom struggle; elixir of new ideas and pledges; and elixir of Aatma nirbharta. Therefore, this Mahotsav is a festival of awakening of the nation; festival of fulfilling the dream of good governance; and the festival of global peace and development.

Like the history of the freedom movement, the journey of 75 years after independence is a reflection of the hard work, innovation, enterprise of ordinary Indians. Whether in the country or abroad, we Indians have proved ourselves with our hard work. We are proud of our Constitution. We are proud of our democratic traditions. The mother of democracy, India is still moving forward by strengthening democracy. India, rich in knowledge and science, is leaving its mark from Mars to the moon.[194]

Narendra Modi
Prime Minister

'Har Ghar Tiranga' is a campaign under the aegis of Azadi Ka Amrit Mahotsav to encourage people to bring the Tiranga home and to hoist it to mark the 75th year of India's independence. Our relationship with the flag has always been more formal and institutional than personal. Bringing the flag home collectively as a nation in the 75th year of independence thus becomes symbolic of not only an act of personal connection to the Tiranga but also an embodiment of our commitment to nation-building. The idea behind the initiative is to invoke the feeling of patriotism in the hearts of the people and to promote awareness about the Indian National Flag. By encouraging citizens to hoist the national flag on Independence Day and beyond, "Har Ghar Jhanda" aims to create a strong sense of national unity, inspire patriotism, and strengthen the bond between the people and the nation.

"Har Ghar Tiranga" is an initiative proposed by Prime Minister Narendra Modi as part of the 75th Independence Day celebrations of India in 2021. The main idea behind the initiative is to instill a sense of pride and patriotism among Indian citizens by encouraging them to hoist the national flag (Tiranga) atop their homes. The phrase "Har Ghar Jhanda" translates to "Flag in Every Home," indicating the goal of having the Indian national flag proudly displayed in every household across the country. By doing so, the initiative aims to symbolize unity, national identity, and a collective spirit of patriotism among the diverse population of India.

The initiative is not only about celebrating Independence Day but also about fostering a continuous connection with the national flag and the values it represents. By hoisting the flag on their homes, citizens are encouraged to embrace the principles of liberty, equality, and fraternity enshrined in the Indian Constitution and to take pride in their Indian heritage. The "Har Ghar Jhanda" initiative also serves as a reminder of the sacrifices made by the freedom fighters during the struggle for independence and an acknowledgment of the nation's progress since gaining independence. During the launch of the initiative, Prime Minister Narendra Modi called upon every Indian to participate actively and make it a mass movement. Various government departments, civil society organizations, and educational institutions were also encouraged to promote and facilitate the initiative.[195]

International Yoga Day: Consolidation of Nations for Yoga under Modi Government

PM Narendra Modi on an earlier Yoga Day

Every year on June 21st, there is a celebration of international yoga, sometimes referred to as world yoga day. Prime Minister Narendra Modi first put up the idea in his September 2014 address to the UN General Assembly. The UN member nations unanimously backed the idea, and the 21st of June was declared International Yoga Day. As a result, International Yoga Day is observed as a representation of India's traditional knowledge and commitment to the wellbeing of the globe within the Narendra Modi administration. In order to live a better and more balanced lifestyle, people should incorporate yoga in their daily lives. Government attempts to spread yoga have helped to increase knowledge of its advantages and encourage people to do so.[196]

Here are some key aspects of the celebration of Yoga Day under the Modi government:

Global Recognition: The United Nations has formally recognized and adopted June 21st as International Yoga Day, demonstrating the government's achievement in promoting Yoga Day on a global scale. This has caused yoga to be widely celebrated all across the world. The Ministry of Ayurveda, Yoga & Naturopathy, Unani, Siddha, and Homoeopathy (AYUSH) was founded by PM Modi, and it has provided the entire sector a much-needed boost. As a result, the Allied Market Research predicts that the global Yoga market would develop at a CAGR of 9.6% and reach $66.2 billion by 2027.[197]

Mass yoga classes: Every Yoga Day, the Indian government plans numerous enormous scale yoga festivals around the nation, frequently with the Prime Minister serving as the host. These activities promote widespread involvement and knowledge

Promotion of Yoga: Yoga has been widely pushed by the Modi administration as a means of enhancing physical fitness, mental wellness, and general health. The significance of yoga in daily life has been stressed by a number of government initiatives and campaigns.

Yoga Integration in Schools: The government has taken steps to introduce yoga into school curriculums, aiming to instill the practice of yoga from a young age and promote a healthier lifestyle among children.

National Yoga Olympiad: The National Yoga Olympiad was organized by the Ministry of AYUSH and the NCERT (National Council of Educational Research and Training). Schoolchildren were encouraged to become interested in yoga early on by participating in the event and demonstrating their knowledge and skills in the discipline.

Yoga in Physical Education Curriculum: The government made efforts to include yoga in the physical education lessons taught in classrooms. Along with other sports and hobbies, yoga was acknowledged as a crucial part of physical wellness.

Assisting Yoga Teachers Abroad: The Indian government assists and supports yoga teachers and gurus in running courses and workshops in other nations through its embassies and cultural institutions. This not only increases yoga's appeal internationally but also solidifies intercultural ties.

Online yoga resources: In recent years, the government has introduced websites and mobile apps that offer articles, how-to videos, and other materials to promote regular yoga practice. Ayurveda, Yoga, Naturopathy, Unani, Siddha, and Homoeopathy (AYUSH) Ministry's Yoga Portal A special yoga portal (https://yoga.ayush.gov.in/) was created by the Ministry of AYUSH to offer online yoga resources, videos for instruction, and details on different yoga practices. The website provides information on the advantages of various yoga asanas (poses) and pranayama (breathing techniques).

COVID-19 Pandemic and Yoga: Yoga was marketed as a way to improve immunity, decrease anxiety, and preserve good health during the COVID-19 epidemic, and precise instructions were provided for performing yoga properly at home. Yoga has become more popular across the globe due to its many health advantages. Numerous diseases, such as insomnia, hypertension, digestive issues, diabetes, anxiety, depression, and psychosis, can be helped by yoga.[198]

Sabka Sath Sabka Vikas

"Sabka Saath, Sabka Vikas" is a Hindi phrase that translates to "Together with All, Development for All." It is a political slogan and philosophy that was popularized by the Government of India, led by Prime Minister Narendra Modi. The slogan reflects the government's commitment to inclusive and equitable development, where the progress and welfare of all sections of society are prioritized. The slogan "Sabka Saath, Sabka Vikas" represents the government's vision of fostering national unity and collective progress. It embodies the idea that inclusive development can only be achieved when all sections of society work together with a common goal of achieving prosperity and well-being for the entire nation.

The key principles and objectives of "Sabka Saath, Sabka Vikas" include:

Inclusive Growth: Regardless of caste, creed, religion, or socioeconomic status, the government wants to make sure that development programs serve all facets of society.

Empowerment of Marginalized Communities: The idea places a strong emphasis on giving opportunities and support for socioeconomic advancement to marginalized groups, such as the economically underprivileged, Scheduled Castes, Scheduled Tribes, and Other Backward Classes.

Infrastructure Development: To close the development gap and raise the standard of living for all inhabitants, concentrate on building infrastructure and providing essential amenities in both rural and urban areas. Encourage policies and initiatives that boost economic expansion and open up job possibilities, raising living standards and reducing poverty. Foster an inclusive and participatory approach to governance by including citizens in the process of making choices.

Education and Skill Development: Prioritize education and training initiatives to provide people the knowledge and abilities they need to succeed in a world that is changing quickly.

Healthcare and Social Welfare: To ensure the safety and well-being of all citizens, improve social welfare programs and healthcare facilities.

Environmental Sustainability: Emphasize sustainable development practices to safeguard the environment and ensure a better future for generations to come. [199]

Aspirational Districts as Innovation for Good Governance

Aspirational districts and blocks are terms often used in the context of development and governance in India. These terms are associated with government initiatives aimed at improving the socio-economic conditions of underprivileged and disadvantaged areas in the country. With the goal of accelerating development at the district level, NITI Aayog collaborates closely with the Ministries and a number of development partners. Additionally, the districts are urged to create and spread best practices that promote development across the socioeconomic categories. In essence, the Aspirational Districts Program seeks to localize the Sustainable Development Goals, resulting in the advancement of the country. Here's a brief explanation of both:

Aspirational Districts:

- Aspirational districts are regions in India that have been identified as lagging behind in various development indicators such as education, healthcare, infrastructure, and economic opportunities.
- The concept of aspirational districts was introduced by the Government of India in January 2018 as part of the "Transformation of Aspirational Districts" program.
- Under this program, specific districts were selected from across the country based on their development challenges and needs. The idea is to focus on these districts and accelerate their development to bring them at par with the rest of the country.

- Various government ministries and departments collaborate to implement targeted development interventions in these aspirational districts. These interventions aim to improve the quality of life, income levels, and overall well-being of the people in these areas.[199a]

Digital India: Transforming the Nation

I Dream of a Digital India Where Access to Information Knows No Barrier " – Narendra Modi

"Digital India" is an ambitious initiative launched by the Government of India under the leadership of Prime Minister Narendra Modi. The program was officially launched on July 1, 2015, with the vision of transforming India into a digitally empowered society and knowledge economy. The Digital India initiative aims to leverage technology to bridge the digital divide, improve governance, enhance citizen services, and foster economic growth and development. Digital India has seen significant progress since its launch, with increased internet penetration, the growth of e-governance services, and a surge in digital payments and transactions. The program has played a crucial role in transforming the way citizens interact with the government and access services, making governance more transparent, efficient, and accessible to all. [200]

Key components and objectives of the Digital India program under the Modi government include:

Broadband Connectivity: With this program, rapid internet and broadband access will be made available throughout the entire nation, especially in rural and distant places. The National Optical Fiber Network (NOFN) and BharatNet projects are used to accomplish this. The "Digital India" plan has been a major area of concentration for the Modi administration, with a focus on boosting the availability of broadband and digital infrastructure in every part of the nation. India is to be transformed into a knowledge-based society and economy. Throughout the Modi administration, a number of initiatives have been initiated, and substantial advancements in internet connectivity have been made. The following are some crucial elements of the Indian government's Digital India initiative's broadband connectivity:

BharatNet Project: One of the key programs under Digital India is the BharatNet project. It strives to deliver high-speed broadband internet for more than 250,000 village panchayats (local administrative entities) across the nation. To close the digital gap, the initiative entails installing broadband infrastructure and optical fiber lines in rural areas. One of the largest rural telecom projects within the world, BharatNet, was phased-in to all Gram Panchayats (about 2.5 lakh) in the nation in order to give all telecom service providers equal access to internet.

- **BharatNet Phase-I:**

The National Optical Fibre Network (NOFN, now BharatNet) project was approved by the Union Cabinet on October 25, 2011, and it will be built to deliver high-speed internet access at the Gram Panchayat (GP) level by connecting block headquarters (BHQs) to GPs using the existing fiber of CPSUs consisting of Bharat Sanchar Nigam Limited (BSNL), RailTel Corporation of India Limited (RailTel), and Power Grid Corporation of India Limited (PGCIL) and provide internet service at the Gram Panchayat (GP) level.

- **BharatNet Phase-II:**

On July 19, 2017, the Cabinet adopted a reworked BharatNet plan that incorporates the project's Phase I execution expertise and aligns its objectives with the objective of Digital India. Gram Panchayats (GPs) can be connected using the modified strategy's ideal combination of media (OFC, Radio, and satellite). Phase II calls for the connection of GPs using a variety of implementation options, including the State-led Model, the Private Sector Model, and the CPSU Model, as well as Last Mile communication in GPs using Wi-Fi or any other compatible broadband technology.[201]

Aadhaar based e-KYC norms

The government has been advised by TRAI to accept the electronic Aadhaar KYC as one of the acceptable documents when applying for a fresh cellular service. In order to speed up and simplify the registration and verification procedure for subscribers, the government introduced e-KYC regulations in August 2016.

National Optical Fiber Network (NOFN): The NOFN, later renamed BharatNet, laid the foundation for rural broadband connectivity by providing broadband access to various government institutions and enabling the delivery of e-governance services in rural areas. The National Optical Fiber Network (NOFN) is a crucial component of the Digital India initiative, which was launched by the Government of India under Prime Minister Narendra Modi. The primary objective of the NOFN is to provide broadband connectivity to rural and remote areas across the country, bridging the digital divide and enabling access to digital services and information for all citizens.

The National Optical Fiber Network, now known as BharatNet, has played a vital role in transforming the digital landscape of rural India, empowering citizens with digital access and opportunities. It has contributed significantly to the Digital India initiative's vision of creating a digitally inclusive and connected nation.[202]

PM-WANI (Wi-Fi Access Network Interface): PM-WANI, which was established as a component of the Digital India program, intends to offer Wi-Fi connectivity through open Wi-Fi hotspots. PM WANI constituted a crucial step in realizing the goal of an India that is empowered by technology. It aimed to use technology to improve internet accessibility and close the digital divide, giving individuals access to the advantages of the internet for economic opportunity, education, information, and e-governance.

***Accelerated Deployment of Broadband Infrastructure*:** To increase internet connectivity and speeds throughout the nation, the government has prioritized speeding the building of broadband infrastructure, particularly cell phone towers and fiber-optic networks. The "Digital India" plan was established by the Modi administration with the goal of transforming India into a knowledge-based society and economy.

National Digital Communication Policy (NDCP) 2018

Cabinet approves National Digital Communications Policy (NDCP) 2018; plans to propel India to top 50 Nations in IoT index

The NDCP 2018, launched by the government, aims to provide broadband connectivity to all citizens, including in rural and remote areas. It sets ambitious targets for broadband penetration and digital infrastructure development. The new National Digital Communications Policy - 2018 has been formulated, in place of the existing National Telecom Policy-2012, to cater to the modern needs of the digital communications sector of India. To introduce a 'customer focused' and 'application driven' policy for the Indian Telecom Sector, which can form the main pillar of Digital India by addressing emerging opportunities for expanding not only the availability of telecom services but also telecom-based services. a need was being felt to introduce a 'customer focused' and 'application driven' policy for the Indian Telecom Sector, which can form the main pillar of Digital India by addressing emerging opportunities for expanding not only the availability of telecom services but also telecom-based services.

The key objectives of the policy are:

Universal broadband

•Increasing the impact of the digital communications sector with India's GDP from less than 6% in 2017 to 8% in 2018

•Pushing India up to the Top 50 Nations in the ITU's ICT Development Index from 134 in 2017

• Enhancing India's contribution to Global Value Chains; and ensuring Digital Sovereignty.

It propagates in three Missions:

•**Connect India:** Creating Robust Digital Communications Infrastructure.

By 2022, every citizen will have access to universal internet connectivity at 50 Mbps according to the National internet Mission (Rashtriya Broadband Abhiyan).

- ✓ **BharatNet:** By 2020, it will offer 10 Gbps access to all of India's Gram Panchayats.

GramNet connects all significant institutions for rural development with a 10 Mbps connection that can be upgraded to 100 Mbps. NagarNet is creating 1 million free Wi-Fi hotspots throughout metropolitan areas.

- ✓ **JanWiFi:** Creating 2 million rural Wi-Fi hotspots.

By 2022, all important development institutions, including all educational institutions, will have access to 100 Mbps broadband on demand.

•**Secure India:** Ensuring Sovereignty, Safety and Security of Digital Communications.

- ✓ Create an all-encompassing safeguarding information legislation regarding digital communications that protects people's privacy, autonomy, and choice and enables India to participate effectively in the international digital economy.
- ✓ Guarantee that the principles of net neutrality are preserved and in line with service needs, bandwidth availability, and network capabilities, including next-generation access technologies.
- ✓ Create and implement strong frameworks for protecting digital communication networks.
- ✓ Increase security testing capabilities and set appropriate security guidelines.[203]

The characteristics of the national digital communications policy are:

High-speed and reasonably priced internet connectivity: Every Indian citizen was to have access to "broadband for all" under the Connect India strategy. It highlighted the development of additional towers and the placement of fiber optic cables as part of the growth of digital infrastructure.

Broadband for All: The NDCP sought to encourage the utilization of electronic services by all facets of society and enhance the prevalence of broadband in isolated and rural areas. Additionally, it attempted to raise service standards to improve the online experience.

Bandwidth administration and accessibility: The NDCP 2018 focused on the effective use of spectrum and emphasized the importance of ensuring that sufficient spectrum resources are made accessible to the development of new technologies, such as 5G. Internet service providers have to handle every internet connection equally, without making any exceptions or restricting any particular material or services, as required by the net neutrality principles advocated by the policy. To enhance connection and support digital services, it placed emphasis on the creation of a strong digital infrastructure, particularly the growth of optical fiber networks.

Consumer Protection: The NDCP attempted to establish suitable legislation for defending consumers' interests and underlined the significance of protecting consumers in digital technology communication industry.

Internet of Things and new Technologies: The policy acknowledged the importance of internet access of Things (IoT) along with other new technologies, and it sought to foster an environment that would support their advancement and implementation.

Universal Service Obligation Fund (USOF): To ensure a more equitable digital revolution, the USOF has been used to support initiatives that improve telecom and internet connectivity in distant and hard-to-reach locations. The government is still working close the digital gap and make sure that every part of the country benefits from the digital revolution, but the effort of delivering widespread and excellent broadband access is constantly ongoing.

E-Governance and Digital Services Through a variety of internet sites and mobile applications, Digital India aims to change the way that the government provides services to its citizens. Among these are programs like MyGov, Digital Locker, e-Hospital, and others. The Digital India project, which promotes e-government, has placed a strong emphasis on making government services available to residents online and through various digital channels. This has highlighted the requirement for reliable internet service even more.[204]

- **The NeGP, or National e-Government Plan**

The National e-Governance Plan (NeGP) provides a thorough overview of all e-Government initiatives across the nation. This idea is the foundation for the construction of a significant national infrastructure that will reach even the most isolated settlements, and extensive digitalization of records will be implemented to offer reliable and simple internet access. The central government has suggested adopting "e-Kranti: National Digital.[205]

•India's digital identity infrastructure

An ambitious e-Government project called Unique Identification (UID) has been started by the Unique Identification Authority of India. Using biometrics and demographic information provided by the Aadhaar number, the UID aims to offer an ongoing service for authentication of identity of every Indian resident. Aadhaar numbers have also been successfully linked by governments to a range of social programs, such as LPG subsidies, student scholarships, pensions, and the Public Distribution System (PDS).

- **The payment system in India**

Through ***Unified Payments Interface (UPI)*** almost every citizen has benefited from the development of unified platforms and applications that promote and facilitate digital financial transactions. The Unified Payments Interface (UPI) is one such system that combines many banking services, seamless fund routing, and merchant payments into a single mobile application (from any participating bank). The ***Bharat Interface for Money (BHIM)*** software has made digital financial transactions simpler, easier, and faster for the general public. The application is one-of-a-kind since the Aadhaar number is linked to a mobile number.

S.No.	Payment Modes
1.	AEPS
2.	BHIM Aadhaar
3.	BHIM UPI
4.	Closed Loop Wallet
5.	Credit Card
6.	Debit Card
7.	IMPS
8.	Internet Banking
9.	Mobile Banking
10.	NACH
11.	NEFT
12.	NETC
13.	Others
14.	PPI
15.	RTGS
16.	USSD

Many Options provided for online payment

•Electronic payment of (telephone & electricity) bills

✓ **Unified Mobile Application for New-age Governance (UMANG)**

The Maharashtra Electricity Corporation has implemented a system that allows citizens to pay their monthly electricity bills electronically, avoiding the need to go to the corporation's or post office's receipt counters and stand in long lines to pay their bills. So, it is with BSNL – Bharat Sanchar Nigam Limited, which offers its subscribers the option of paying their phone bills online from their homes. Subscribers who pay their bills electronically receive a 1% discount from BSNL.

- ✓ **Centers for Common Services**

Using Village Level Entrepreneurs (VLEs), CSCs provide digital government and commercial services in rural locations. These CSCs provide more than 400 digital services. 4.20 percent of the country's 5.31 lakh CSCs, which include both urban and rural areas, are currently operational. UMANG is offering citizens mobile access to governmental services. At UMANG, you can access over 22,000 payment options for bills as well as over 1,570 government services.

- ✓ **Mission Mode Project (MMP) for the E-District**

All States/UTs have implemented the E-District project at the district and sub-district levels, benefiting all citizens by providing a variety of e-Services like Electoral, Consumer Court, Revenue Court, Land Record, and services of various departments like Commercial Tax, Agriculture, Labour, Employment Training & Skill Development, etc. 4,671 e-services have currently been introduced in 709 constituencies of India.

- ✓ **DigiLocker**

The world is changing due to digitization, which makes life better by making things simpler. In India, the DigiLocker app is widely used. The most recent statistics shows that it has 156 issuing organizations and 36.7 million registered users. It is free, safe, and secure. Anyone may utilize it to save significant and official documents on your phone, namely passports, voter identification cards, birth certificates, PAN cards, and Aadhaar cards. A web browser can also be used to log into digilocker.gov.in.

- ✓ **National Electronic Toll Collection (NETC) system**

NETC system enables the customer to make electronic payments at NETC-enabled toll plazas on the highway without stopping at the toll, using Radio Frequency Identification technology.

- ✓ **Bill Payment System of India: Bill Payment System of India (BBPS)**

Customers can use Internet banking, mobile banking, mobile apps, BHIM-UPI, and other channels to access an interoperable and simple bill payment solution from BBPS. Through BBPS, citizens can easily pay their bills whenever and wherever they choose. DigiLocker provides access to 532 crore documents from 2,167 issuer organizations.

- ✓ **Online banking**

For cash withdrawals via ATM cards, the streamline Tailor-Made Machine technology is currently popular among bank account users at various institutions. In various cities and places, several banks operate a range of ATM counters.

- ✓ **E-Ticketing**

The Indian Railways introduce the opportunity to make reservations for every carriage by email will be very advantageous to commuters. This is offered for a small cost. For this service, many people use the Indian Railway Catering and Tourism Corporation (IRCTC) website.

- ✓ **GeM, or Government e-Marketplace**

The government has implemented GeM to improve public procurement transparency, efficiency, and speed. It offers technologies such as e-bidding, reverse e-auction, and demand aggregation to help government users get the most value for their money.[206]

✓ **National Digital Literacy Mission (NDLM)**

The government's National Digital Literacy Mission (NDLM) has also been instrumental in promoting digital literacy in India. Under the mission, the government aims to train at least one person from every family in India in digital literacy. The program covers various topics such as computer basics, internet browsing, email, and online safety and security. The program is implemented through a network of training partners nationwide, including NGOs, government agencies, and private companies. The number of Internet users in India has increased from 481 million in 2019 to 743 million in 2023, according to Internet and Mobile Association of India (IAMAI) data. This growth has been fueled by the increasing availability of affordable smart phones and mobile data plans. In addition, there has been a surge in digital adoption during the COVID-19 pandemic, as people have had to rely on digital services for work, education, and entertainment. This has led to a greater awareness of the importance of digital literacy and has created new opportunities for digital skills training.[207]

✓ **Pradhan Mantri Gramin Digital Saksharta Abhiyan (PMGDISHA)**

Pradhan Mantri Gramin Digital Saksharta Abhiyan (PMGDISHA) is a flagship digital literacy program launched by the Government of India under the Digital India initiative. The main objective of PMGDISHA is to empower rural communities by providing them with digital literacy skills and making them digitally literate. The program targets individuals in rural areas, especially those who have limited or no exposure to digital technologies. Through PMGDISHA, the government aims to bridge the digital divide between urban and rural populations, ensuring that the benefits of digital technologies reach every corner of the country.

The Pradhan Mantri Gramin Digital Saksharta Abhiyan has played a significant role in empowering rural communities with digital skills and promoting digital inclusion in India. By providing digital literacy, the program enables individuals to access government services, online education, financial services, and other opportunities available in the digital world. PMGDISHA contributes to the government's vision of building a digitally empowered society and knowledge economy in the country.

Note: ***During the years 2014 to 2016, Government of India had implemented two Schemes on providing digital literacy to the masses namely "National Digital Literacy Mission (NDLM)" and "PMG Digital Saksharta Abhiyan (DISHA)" with a cumulative target of 52.50 lakh persons (one person from every eligible household) across the country including rural India. Under these two schemes, a total of 53.67 lakh beneficiaries were trained, out of which around 42% candidates were from rural India.***[208]

Make in India Promoting India as Global Manufacturer

PRIME MINISTER NARENDRA MODI inaugurated Make in India Campaign

Encourage domestic electronic manufacturing and attract investments in the electronics industry to boost the "Make in India" campaign. Digital capabilities improve and connectivity becomes omnipresent, technology is poised to quickly and radically change nearly every sector of India's economy. That is likely to both create significant economic value and change the nature of work for tens of millions of Indians. India is well on its way to becoming a digitally advanced country. Propelled by the falling cost and rising availability of smart phones and high-speed connectivity, India is already home to one of the world's largest and fastest-growing bases of digital consumers and is digitizing faster than many mature and emerging economies.

Here are some key aspects and highlights of the Make in India initiative under the Modi government:

•**Focus on Key Sectors:** The campaign focused on 25 important economic sectors, including renewable energy, textiles, electronics, pharmaceuticals, aerospace, and the automotive industry. These industries were chosen because of their great growth potential and huge investment and innovation prospects.

•**Ease of Doing Business**: To make it easier to conduct business in India, the government launched a number of changes. To ease investment and business operations, steps were made such as streamlining regulatory processes, streamlining registration and regulating operations, and putting in place a single-window clearing system.

•**Investment Promotion:** Through targeted marketing initiatives, international road shows, and connections to foreign investors and business communities, the campaign effectively advertised India as an alluring investment destination.

•**Startup India:** The government started the Startup India initiative as a component of the Make in India drive to promote innovation and entrepreneurship in the nation. With a variety of incentives and legislative changes, this project intended to assist and grow businesses.

•**Manufacturing Infrastructure:** To provide a favorable environment for manufacturing industries, the government concentrated on creating and renovating production buildings, such as industrial corridors, special economic zones (SEZs), and industrial parks.

•**Skill Development:** The Make in India project placed a strong emphasis on skill development to produce a workforce with the specialized technical knowledge and skills required for the manufacturing industry.

•**Promotion of "Brand India:** The effort aimed to position India as a manufacturing powerhouse that stands for excellence, innovation, and dependability. To promote India's manufacturing capabilities, the Make in India logo and branding materials were widely employed.

•**Global Manufacturing Summits:** To highlight India's potential as a manufacturing hub and to entice investment from international firms, the government launched Global Manufacturing Summits.

•**Green and sustainable manufacturing:** The Make in India campaign also emphasized the promotion of green and sustainable manufacturing methods to solve environmental problems.

•**Sector-Specific Policies:** To create a favorable environment for manufacturing companies, the government created and updated sector-specific policies.[209]

Statistics of Make in India

1) By 2025, Indian market for appliance and consumer electronics is anticipated to rank sixth globally.

2) At a CAGR of 50.42%, the total amount of digital transactions rises from 1085 crore in FY 2016–17 to 5,554 crores in FY 2020–21.

3) From April to November 2021, the top 5 export destinations were the USA (18%), the UAE (16.6%), China (7.6%), the Netherlands (4.5%), and Germany (4.2%).

4) Between 2013–14 and 2021–22, India's exports of electronic items increased by over 88%, from USD 6600 million to USD 12,400 million. The main exports in this industry include mobile phones, IT hardware (laptops, tablets), consumer electronics (TV and audio), industrial electronics, and car electronics.

5) In the month of August, the country's total exports included 5.24% of electronic goods.

6) Electrical items represent 3.73% of the nation's total exports from April 21 to March 22.[210]

Sector Wise Make in India Policy

National Policy on Electronics

The National Policy on Electronics (NPE) 2019 envisions to position India as a global hub for ESDM by encouraging and driving capabilities in the Country for developing core components, including chipsets and by creating an enabling environment for the industry to compete globally. The NPE 2019 replaces the NPE 2012, which has successfully built the foundation for a competitive Indian ESDM value chain. The NPE 2019 targets to promote domestic manufacturing and export in the entire value chain of ESDM and achieve a turnover of USD 400 Bn by 2025.

2020 Electronics Manufacturing Plans:

The following programs have been announced by the Ministry of Electronics in order to further improve the ESDM ecosystem with a full value chain and establish India as the world's ESDM hub.

Electronic Components and Semiconductors Manufacturing Promotion Scheme (SPECS)

SPECS has been notified to strengthen the value chain for electronics manufacturing in India with the target segment comprising of downstream value chain products such as electronic components, semiconductor/ display fabrication units, ATMP units, specialized sub-assemblies and capital goods for manufacture of aforesaid goods. Under the scheme, 25% incentives will be provided on capital expenditure (on a reimbursement basis) in new units and expansion/ modernization/ diversification of existing units. The scheme will be open for applications for a period of 3 years from the date of notification. All investments made within 5 years from the date of acknowledgement will be eligible for receiving incentives under SPECS which has an outlay of about USD 440 Million.

Scheme for setting up of Semiconductor Fabs in India

The scheme provides fiscal support to eligible applicants for setting up of Semiconductor Fabs which is aimed at attracting large investments for setting up semiconductor wafer fabrication facilities in the country. Following fiscal support has been approved under the scheme:

- 28 nm or less - as much as 50 of the project cost

- A maximum of 40% of the project cost

- A maximum of 30% of the project cost - above 28 nm to 45 nm.[211]

Cybersecurity and Privacy: Strengthen cybersecurity measures to ensure the safety and privacy of citizens' data and transactions in the digital space. It is essential to note that the landscape of cybersecurity and privacy policies is continuously evolving, and new developments may have occurred since my last update. The government's efforts in this area are likely to continue as digital technology and online activities become increasingly integral to India's socio-economic development.

CERT-In: The Indian Computer Emergency Response Team (CERT-In) is the national nodal agency responsible for handling cybersecurity incidents and coordinating responses. The Modi government has strengthened CERT-In capabilities to handle and mitigate cyber threats effectively.

•**Data Protection Framework:** The Modi government took steps to draft and implement a comprehensive data protection framework to safeguard citizens' personal information and privacy. The Personal Data Protection Bill was introduced in Parliament and was under consideration for passage into law.

•**Strengthening Law Enforcement:** The government took measures to strengthen law enforcement agencies' capabilities to investigate and prosecute cybercrimes effectively.

•**National Cyber Coordination Centre (NCCC):** The government established the NCCC to generate comprehensive situational awareness and ensure timely responses to cyber incidents.

•**Digital Payments and Cashless Transactions:** Promote the adoption of digital payment methods and reduce the reliance on cash transactions through initiatives like BHIM (Bharat Interface for Money) and UPI (Unified Payments)

•**Unified Payments Interface (UPI):** The National Payments Corporation of India (NPCI) introduced the UPI in 2016. Users can utilize a smart phone application to instantly transfer money across banks. The landscape of digital payments in India has been completely transformed by UPI's widespread adoption.

•**Bharat Interface for Money (BHIM):** The NPCI created this UPI-based mobile app to enable safe and efficient cashless transactions. Without the requirement for account information, consumers can send and receive money by using their smart phones.

•**Promotion of Digital Wallets and Payment applications**: To enable cashless transactions, the government has actively promoted the application of digital wallets and payment applications. Numerous payment apps and wallet services have grown in popularity among consumers. The government promoted the Aadhaar-Enabled Payment System.[212]

•**QR Code-Based Payments:** To make digital transactions simpler for customers as well as companies, the government promoted the use of QR code-based payments.

Digital Healthcare and Education: Make better use of digital technologies to make healthcare and education more effective and accessible to citizens. Digital healthcare has become a key area for the Modi administration's Digital India project, which aims to use technology to enhance patient's satisfaction, availability, and healthcare services.[213]

Some key initiatives and components of digital healthcare under the Modi government's Digital India include:

•**National Digital Health Mission (NDHM):** The National Digital Health Mission (NDHM), which was introduced in August 2020, aims to build an ecosystem for digital health that would give Indian residents easy access to their medical records, a distinctive health ID, and healthcare services. It proposes a National Health Platform that offers health data interoperability across diverse healthcare stakeholders.

ESanjeevani Telemedicine Platform: The eSanjeevani platform was established by the government to offer telemedicine services to the public, particularly in rural and underserved areas. Instead of traveling to a healthcare center, patients can consult doctors online; get prescriptions, and access healthcare information.

•**Aarogya Setu App:** The Aarogya Setu app, which was introduced during the COVID-19 epidemic, quickly rose to prominence as a crucial resource for contact tracking and sharing COVID-19 information. Additionally, it provided self-assessment tools, pandemic updates, and a network of testing facilities and hospitals in the area.

•**Pradhan Mantri Jan Arogya Yojana (PM-JAY):** The Modicare Ayushman Bharat PM-JAY scheme leverages digital technology to give vulnerable families cashless and paperless medical insurance for secondary and tertiary healthcare services.

•**Online Drug Information System (ODIS):** This platform increases transparency in the pharmaceutical industry by providing data on medications, their availability, and costs in various locations.

•**National Cancer Grid (NCG):** The NCG is an internet-based community of Indian cancer treatment facilities that works together on clinical research.

•**Telemedicine and teleconsultation regulations:** The Indian government published regulations to support and develop telemedicine services in India, allowing doctors to consult with patients remotely and issue prescriptions online.

•**The Electronic Vaccine Intelligence Network (eVIN)** technology is used to digitally monitor vaccine stock and supply chain management, ensuring that immunizations are available at various healthcare facilities.

•**Healthcare applications and portals:** The government has supported and funded the development of these tools, which offer services including access to resources for healthcare, monitoring of one's health, and health education.

•**M-diabetes:** This is a website for diabetes messaging. http://mdiabetes.nhp.gov.in/

•Web gateway for donor registration and retrieval provided by the National Organ & Tissue Transplant Organization (NOTTO). Information on blood banks is available via the mobile application - National Health Portal Directory Services.

•**Nikshay:** TB patient tracking online.[214]

One Proof for Identification: Promote Simplification of Rules

Identity documents of India are increasingly used to transact and obtain government benefits in India. While there is no single mandatory document, the following documents are used in lieu of a national identity document. The unique ID also qualifies as a valid ID while availing various government services such as a LPG connection, a subsidized ration, kerosene from the PDS, or benefits under NSAP or pension schemes, e-sign, a digital locker, a Universal Account Number (UAN) under EPFO, and some other services such as a SIM card or opening a bank account. According to the UIDAI website, any Aadhaar holder or service provider can verify the genuineness of an Aadhaar number through a user-friendly service of UIDAI called the Aadhaar Verification Service (AVS), which is available on its website. Also, a resident already enrolled under the National Population Register is not required to enroll again for Aadhaar.[215]

Mera Aadhaar Meri Pehachan

The ***Aadhaar project*** has been linked to welfare schemes and unemployment benefit schemes such as the domestic LPG scheme and MGNREGA. In these Direct Benefit Transfer (DBT) schemes, the subsidy money is directly transferred to a bank account which is Aadhaar-linked. Previously, however, the direct-benefit transfer had been carried out quite successfully via the National Electronic Funds Transfer (NEFT) system, which did not depend on Aadhaar. Under the original policy for liquefied petroleum gas subsidies, the customers bought gas cylinders from retailers at subsidized prices, and the government compensated companies for their losses. Under the current Direct Benefit Transfer of LPG (DBTL), introduced in 2013, customers had to buy at full price, and the subsidy would be then directly credited to their Aadhaar-linked bank accounts. This scheme, however, did not take off, and in September 2013 a Supreme Court order put a halt on it.

The Aadhaar card is a unique 12-digit identification number issued by the Unique Identification Authority of India (UIDAI). It serves as proof of identity and address for Indian residents. While Aadhaar is widely accepted as a valid identification document, there are other documents that can be used for identification purposes in India, such as the Passport, Voter ID card, Driving License, and PAN (Permanent Account Number) card. The choice of identification document may vary depending on the specific requirements of the situation or institution. Aadhaar project has been widely praised for its potential to transform service delivery and improve governance, it has also faced criticism and concerns over issues related to privacy, data security, and potential misuse of personal information. The Supreme Court of India, in its landmark judgment in September 2018, upheld the constitutionality of Aadhaar.

The Aadhaar project's primary goals are:

Universal identity: The primary goal of the Aadhaar project is to provide a unique identification number to every resident of India, irrespective of age, gender, or nationality.

Financial inclusion: Aadhaar aims to promote inclusive governance by providing a robust identity infrastructure that can be used to deliver various government services and subsidies directly to the intended beneficiaries.

Simplified Service Delivery: Aadhaar facilitates the direct delivery of government services and benefits to eligible individuals, eliminating intermediaries and reducing leakages in subsidy and welfare schemes.

Digital Empowerment: Aadhaar is a crucial component of the government's Digital India initiative, enabling individuals to participate in the digital economy and access online services securely.

Reduction of Identity Fraud: The use of biometric data in Aadhaar helps reduce identity fraud and impersonation, ensuring that government services reach the right beneficiaries.

Key characteristics of the Aadhaar card as a form of identification:

Biometric authentication: The Aadhaar card includes biometric data such as fingerprints and iris scans, making it more secure and reliable for identification purposes.

Digital and Physical Form: Aadhaar cards are available in both digital and physical formats. Individuals can access their Aadhaar details online through the UIDAI portal and also receive a physical card by mail.

Banking and financial services: Aadhaar is commonly used for KYC (Know Your Customer) purposes in banks and financial institutions, making it easier for individuals to open accounts and avail of financial services.

Mobile SIM Card Verification: To increase security and lower the likelihood of abuse, mobile SIM cards are verified using Aadhaar.

Online authentication: Aadhaar-based online authentication is used in various government and private sector services to verify the identity of individuals.[216]

Personal Data Protection Bill 2019

The Personal Data Protection Bill, 2019 was introduced in Lok Sabha by the Minister of Electronics and Information Technology, Mr. Ravi Shankar Prasad, on December 11, 2019. The Bill seeks to provide for protection of personal data of individuals, and establishes a Data Protection Authority for the same. The Personal Data Protection Bill 2019 was proposed by the Indian government under the leadership of Prime Minister Narendra Modi. The bill aimed to provide a legal framework for the protection and regulation of personal data in India. It aimed to address concerns related to data privacy and security, as well as to establish guidelines for the collection, processing, and storage of personal data by both government and private entities.

The bill is being analyzed by a Joint Parliamentary Committee (JPC) in consultation with industry experts and stakeholders. The JPC which was established in December 2019 is headed by BJP Member of Parliament (MP) Meenakshi Lekhi.

Why Personal Data Bill was Introduced

In August 2017, the nine-judge bench of the Supreme Court of India affirmed the right to privacy in the K.S. Puttaswamy vs. Union of India (2017) "right to privacy case". The Court cited the right to life and personal liberty under Article 21 of India's Constitution.

During the case, the Indian government set up a Committee of Experts, chaired by Justice B.N. Srikrishna, to examine various issues related to data protection in India. After public consultation of the white paper, the Committee submitted a draft Personal Data Protection Bill and an accompanying report titled A Free and Fair Digital Economy: Protecting Privacy, Empowering Indians to the Ministry of Electronics and Information Technology in July.[217]

Some key provisions of the bill included:

Rights of the individual: The Bill sets out certain rights of the individual (or data principal). These include the right to: (i) obtain confirmation from the fiduciary on whether their personal data has been processed, (ii) seek correction of inaccurate, incomplete, or out-of-date personal data, (iii) have personal data transferred to any other data fiduciary in certain circumstances, and (iv) restrict continuing disclosure of their personal data by a fiduciary, if it is no longer necessary or consent is withdrawn.

Transfer of Data across Borders: The bill laid down conditions for the transfer of personal data outside India. Sensitive personal data may be transferred outside India for processing if explicitly consented to by the individual, and subject to certain additional conditions. However, such sensitive personal data should continue to be stored in India. Certain personal data notified as critical personal data by the government can only be processed in India.

Data Protection Authority: The creation of a Data Protection Authority of India (DPA) responsible for overseeing and enforcing data protection laws in the country. The Bill sets up a Data Protection Authority which may: (i) take steps to protect interests of individuals, (ii) prevent misuse of personal data, and (iii) ensure compliance with the Bill. It will consist of a chairperson and six members, with at least 10 years' expertise in the field of data protection and information technology. Orders of the Authority can be appealed to an Appellate Tribunal. Appeals from the Tribunal will go to the Supreme Court.

Consent for processing personal Data: The bill emphasized obtaining informed and specific consent from individuals before processing their personal data. The Bill allows processing of data by fiduciaries only if consent is provided by the individual. However, in certain circumstances, personal data can be processed without consent. These include: (i) if required by the State for providing benefits to the individual, (ii) legal proceedings, (iii) to respond to a medical emergency.[218]

Digital Personal Data Protection Bill 2022

The Digital Personal Data Protection Bill, 2022 introduces a new framework for personal data protection, making it paramount to comprehend and understand its applicability and functions. The Government of India sees this released bill as one of the parts of its larger vision of a Digital Economy, this vision will include a comprehensive "Digital India Act" that would in due course of time replace the existing Information Technology Act, 2000. Hence it becomes crucial to take a closer look at its provisions, implications and shortcomings considering its potential to impact our day to day lives.

Consent for processing personal data: Personal data may be processed only for a lawful purpose for which an individual has given consent. A notice must be given before seeking consent. Notice should contain details about the personal data to be collected and the purpose of processing. Consent may be withdrawn at any point in time. Consent will be deemed given where processing is necessary for: (i) performance of any function under a law, (ii) provision of service or benefit by the State, (iii) medical emergency, (iv) employment purposes, and (v) specified public interest purposes such as national security, fraud prevention, and information security. For individuals below 18 years of age, consent will be provided by the legal guardian.

Rights and duties of data principal: An individual, whose data is being processed (data principal), will have the right to: (i) obtain information about processing, (ii) seek correction and erasure of personal data, (iii) nominate another person to exercise rights in the event of death or incapacity, and (iv) grievance redressal. Data principals will have certain duties. They must not: (i) register a false or frivolous complaint, (ii) furnish any false particulars, suppress information, or impersonate another person in specified cases. Violation of duties will be punishable with a penalty of up to Rs 10,000.

Obligations of data fiduciaries: The organization deciding the purpose and method of processing, known as the data fiduciary, is required to: (i) take reasonable steps to ensure the accuracy and completeness of the data; (ii) put in place reasonable security measures to prevent a breach and notify the Data Protection Board of India and those impacted in the event of one; and (iii) stop keeping personal data promptly as the objective has been achieved and retention is no longer required for legal or business purposes.

Transfer of personal data outside India: Countries wherever a data fiduciary can transmit personal data shall be informed by the federal government. Transfers shall be governed by the terms and conditions specified.

Exemptions: The government can exempt certain businesses from adhering to provisions of the bill on the basis of the number of users and the volume of personal data processed by the entity. This has been done keeping in mind startups of the country who had complained that the Personal Data Protection Bill, 2019 was too "compliance intensive".

Indian Data Protection Board: The Data Protection Board of India established by the national government. The Board's main duties include (i) enforcing penalties for non-compliance, (ii) requiring data fiduciaries to take appropriate action in the case of a data breach, and (iii) listening to grievances brought forth by impacted parties.

Penalties: The Bill's schedule lists fines up to Rs. 250 crores for failing to take security precautions to avoid data breaches and up to Rs. 150 crores for failing to fulfill commitments to children. The Board will issue penalties following an investigation.[219]

SVAMITVA Scheme

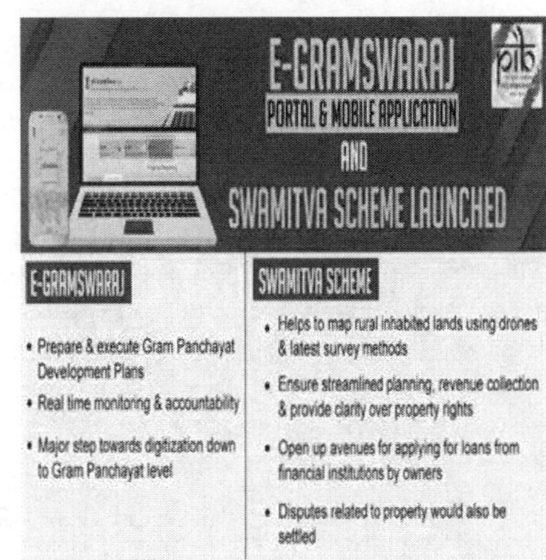

Under the direction of Prime Minister Narendra Modi, the Indian government began the Svamitva Scheme, a property survey program called Survey of Villages Abadi and Mapping with Improvised Technology in Village Area. On April 24, 2020, National Panchayati Raj Day, the program was introduced. Its primary goal was to offer rural India a comprehensive property certification service.

This program will survey about 6.62 lakh villages around the nation from 2021 to 2025, gathering property data using a variety of technologies, including drones. In several areas in Maharashtra, Karnataka, Haryana, Uttar Pradesh, Uttarakhand, Madhya Pradesh, Punjab, and Rajasthan, the scheme's initial phase was implemented between 2020 to 2021. The plan aims to increase financial liquidity while reducing ownership disputes by providing correct land records. The program aims to simplify construction and gathering revenue while also guaranteeing that locals are aware of their ownership rights in countryside regions.[220]

Objectives of SVAMITVA Scheme:

- To provide people in rural India with financial security by allowing them to use their real estate as a source of income for getting loans and receiving other financial benefits.
- Accurate land record keeping for rural planning.
- Property tax determination, which would go to the General Purposes (GPs) immediately in Provinces where it is delegated or else contribute to the State Exchequer.[221]

What is the SVAMITVA card?

Each landowner will receive an SVAMITVA property card within the Surveying of Villages and Mapping with Improvised Technology in Village Areas scheme.

In the event that they decide to use their piece of property as an investment in the future, they will be able to submit a legal document to the lending organizations.

Figure 14: Svamitva Card

Activities under SVAMITVA Scheme

The main activities under the Scheme are:

•Creation of the Continuous Operating Reference System (CORS), a network of reference stations that serves as a fictitious base station for long-range, high-accuracy network RTK corrections and real-time, centimeter-level horizontal positioning. The CORS network aids in precise geo referencing, ground truthing, and lands' delineation.

•Large-scale drone mapping - Survey of India will use drones to map inhabited rural areas (abadi). To grant ownership and property rights, it would produce detailed maps. The owners of rural homes would receive property cards built around these maps or data.[222]

E- Gram Swaraj

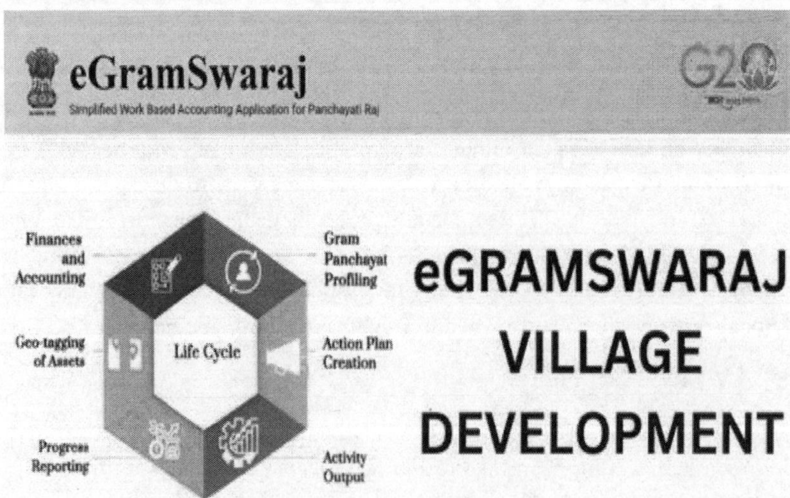

The Ministry of Panchayati Raj (MoPR) has introduced eGramSwaraj, a user-friendly web-based site, designed to reinforce e-Governance in Panchayati Raj Institutions (PRIs) throughout the nation. Better openness in decentralized planning, progress reporting, and task-based accounting are goals of E - Gram Swaraj. E-Gram

Swaraj is a digital effort started by the Indian government to improve and empower the use of technology in the operations for rural local bodies (Gram Panchayats). The amount of land conflicts in rural areas will decrease as a result of this central government initiative. Before it was even launched, the e-gram swaraj webpage was the subject of discussion of the town. The Indian Ministry of Panchayati Raj launched this programme. [223]

EGramSwaraj Architecture

With the subsequent 3 primary user groups in mind, eGramSwaraj was created:

• **Local Bodies:** Rural and Urban local bodies, together, forms up the primary end users of this application. These users, working at the field level, are primary custodians of numerous critical processes such as formulation of Gram Panchayat Development Plan (GPDP), Works progress monitoring, Vendor and employee management, and Financial Management.

• **Line Departments:** The GPDP spans 18 Ministries and 29 topics within the Indian government. These Division Departments are in charge of overseeing a number of social welfare projects and initiatives. Naturally, data-driven planning and monitoring lay the groundwork for effective last-mile service delivery, particularly for financial management.[224]

Merger of Banks

In recent years, there have been a number of bank mergers in India as a consequence of the government's initiatives to reinforce the financial system and consolidate the banking industry. The goals of mergers are to grow and strengthen banks, increase their operational effectiveness, and increase their capacity to respond to economic issues. The government's larger plan to modernize the banking industry and enhance financial stability includes these mergers.

The Indian bank merger was prompted by the country's emphasis on the economy, profitability, and cost-effectiveness. The economics and profitability were significantly impacted by the intensifying competition among the major competitors in the same industry. Even while the Indian bank merger has positively impacted the country's economy as a whole.[225]

Here are a few significant bank mergers that occurred in India:

State Bank of India (SBI) amalgamated with its partner banks, State Bank of Bikaner & Jaipur, State Bank of Hyderabad, State Bank of Mysore, State Bank of Patiala, and State Bank of Travancore in 2017, making the largest public sector bank in India. These affiliate banks vanished after the merger, and SBI took over their activities.

2019 saw the merger of **Dena Bank and Vijaya Bank with Bank of Baroda (BoB).** In terms of assets, this merger produced India's third-largest public sector bank.

Merger of Canara Bank and Syndicate Bank: The 2020 merger of Canara Bank and Syndicate Bank strengthened Canara Bank's status as one of the biggest government-owned banks in India.

Merger of Indian Bank with Allahabad Bank: This expansion of Indian Bank's range in 2020.

Merger of Corporation Bank and Andhra Bank with Union Bank of India

Punjab National Bank: Merger with **Oriental Bank of Commerce and United Bank of India**.[226]

Constitutional Amendments under Modi Government

- **Formation of National Judicial Appointments Commission (Insert Article 124A, 124B, 124C)**

The National Judicial Appointments Commission Act (NJAC) and the Constitutional (Ninety-Nine Amendment) Act, 2014 were deemed illegal in October 2015 by a five-judge Constitution Bench based on the 1993 verdict. NJAC will also suggest candidates for the positions of Supreme Court Judge and High Court Judge. The Law Minister of India, the Chief Justice of India, the two senior-most Supreme Court justices, and two renowned members appointed by the Committee of Selection constitute up the NJAC.

The Chief Justice of India, the Prime Minister of India, and the Leader of the Opposition in the Lok Sabha (or, in case of absence of a Leader of the Opposition, the Leader of the one Opposition Party alongside the greatest number of seats in the Lok Sabha), provided that one of the two notable people pertains to a Scheduled Caste, Scheduled Tribe, OBC, minority community, or women. The distinguished individuals are nominated for a three-year term and are not eligible for re-nomination.

- **100th Amendment of First Schedule - Exchange of certain enclave territories with Bangladesh**

In 2015, the Constitution (100th Amendment) Act formally recognised the boundary agreement between Bangladesh and India. In accordance with the bilateral LBA of 1974, the act revised the first schedule of the constitution in order to exchange the disputed regions occupied by both countries. In contrast to Bangladesh, which gained 111 Indian enclaves (containing 17,160 acres) in the Bangladesh mainland, India inherited 51 Bangladesh enclaves (covering 7,110 acres) in the Indian mainland. According to the LBA, 111 Indian enclaves would hypothetically be transferred to Bangladesh in exchange for 51 enclaves going to India.

• The Bill modifies the First Schedule of the Constitution to implement a May 16, 1974, agreement between India and Bangladesh regarding the acquisition and transfer of lands between the two nations.

•Each state and union territory's area, taken collectively to make up India, is specified in the first section of the Constitution.

•The territories involved are in the states of Assam, West Bengal, Meghalaya and Tripura. Many of these are enclaves (i.e., territory belonging to one country that is entirely surrounded by the other country), and there are even enclaves-within-enclaves. The enclave residents are to be allowed to either reside at their present location or move to the country of their choice

•Residents of the enclave will be given the option of staying where they are or relocating to another nation of their choosing.

•Between July 31, 2015, and June 30, 2016, the actual separation of enclaves will take place in stages.

• These enclaves were heavily populated with residents who were allowed to choose their residences. They could either continue to live at their present location or move to the country of their choice.[227]

- **Goods and Services Tax Act**

It was approved in May 2015 to enact the GST (122nd Constitutional Amendment) Bill, 2014. With effect from September 16, 2016, it was passed as the Constitution (101st Amendment) Act, 2016. The reform of indirect taxes in India has been delayed for thirty years, and this marks the first important step in that direction. On July 1st, 2017, the GST was introduced. The GST is further explained in the sections below.

This is a tax that customers pay when they purchase goods or services. It is intended to replace all other minor indirect taxes on consumption, such as service tax.

• It included 13 cesses and 17 major taxes.

• There is just one tax applied to the distribution of goods and services, from the producer to the final customer.

• Most industrialized nations conduct business in this manner. This taxation method is used in more than 160 nations.

• The GST does not impose taxes or cover particular commodities.[228]

➢ **102st Constitutional status to National commission for Backward classes**

The Supreme Court ordered the national government to establish an indefinite statutory body to investigate complaints or incorporation of any category of citizens in the backward classes in the Mandal Case judgment (1992). The National Commission for Backward Classes (NCBC) followed up in 1993. Later, the commission was granted constitutional legitimacy by the 102nd Amendment Act of 2018. A new Article 338-B was added to the constitution as a result of the modification. As a result, the Commission became a constitutional entity rather than a statutory one.[229]

- ✓ In August 2018, the 102nd Amendment Act became effective after receiving presidential assent.
- ✓ The Indian Constitution was amended to add Articles 338B and 342A.
- ✓ Article 342A deals with the President of India's authority to declare specific castes as a backward educational and social class (SEBC) and the power of the Parliament to change the list.
- ✓ Article 338B deals with the structure, responsibilities, and authority of the National Commission for Backward Classes (NCBC).

The following list of commission responsibilities is provided in the article:

The 102nd Amendment inserted **Article 338B** into the Constitution.

- This article provides for the establishment of a commission for the socially and educationally backward classes to be known as the National Commission for Backward Classes.
- The NCBC thus received a constitutional status after this amendment was passed.
- As per the article, the commission shall consist of the following members who would be appointed by the President:

✓ Chairperson

✓ Vice-chairperson

✓ Three other members

The article provides the duties of the commission as given below:

✓ Investigating and monitoring matters related to the safeguards provided for the socially and educationally backward classes under the Indian Constitution or under any other law or order of the Government and assessing the working of such safeguards.

✓ Inquiring into specific complaints regarding the deprivation of rights and safeguards of the socially & educationally backward classes.

✓ Participating and advising on the socio-economic development of the socially and educationally backward classes and appraising the progress of their development.

✓ Presenting to the President annually or whenever required reports about the working of those safeguards.

✓ Making recommendations of measures that should be taken by the central or state governments for the effective implementation of the safeguards and other measures for the protection, welfare and socio-economic development of the socially and educationally backward classes.

✓ Discharging any other functions with regards to the protection, welfare and development and advancement of the socially and educationally backward classes as decided by the Parliament.

- The article also gives the Commission all the powers of a civil court while enquiring into specific complaints regarding the deprivation of rights and safeguards of the socially & educationally backward classes.

Article 342A

The 102nd Amendment to the Indian Constitution added the provision known as Article 342A, which gives the President the authority to identify the academically and socially underprivileged groups within the boundaries of a state or union territory.[230]

➢ **103rd *Constitutional Amendment Extend Reservation seats for SCs and STs in the Lok sabha and state assemblies***

Lok Sabha on Tuesday passed the Constitution ***(One Hundred and Three Amendment) Bill, 2019***, which continues the reservation of seats for the Scheduled Castes and Tribes for another 10 years, upto January 25, 2030. Law Minister Ravi Shankar Prasad noted that the quota in legislatures was required to build a new political leadership of the two communities. The Bill was passed with 352 members in favour and none against. The reservation for SCs, STs and Anglo-Indians given for the past 70 years in Lok Sabha and State Assemblies was due to end on January 25, 2020. The amendment does not, however, extend the period of reservation of the 2 Lok Sabha seats and seats in State Legislative Assemblies reserved for members of the Anglo-Indian Community and thus the practice of nominating two members of the Anglo-Indian community by the President of India under the recommendation of the Prime Minister of India was effectively abolished.[231]

The reservation of seats for the Scheduled Castes and Scheduled Tribes was set to expire on 26 January 2020 as mandated by the Ninety Fifth Amendment but was extended for another 10 years with the given reason:

Although the Scheduled Castes and the Scheduled Tribes have made considerable progress in the last 70 years, the reasons which weighed with the Constituent Assembly in making provisions with regard to the aforesaid reservation of seats have not yet ceased to exist. Therefore, with a view to retaining the inclusive character as envisioned by the founding fathers of the Constitution, it is proposed to continue the reservation of seats for the Scheduled Castes and the Scheduled Tribes for another ten years i.e. up to 25th January, 2030 -Ravi Shankar Prasad, Minister of Law and Justice.

-Ravi Shankar Prasad, Minister of Law and Justice.[232]

➢ **105th Amendment Act To restore the Power the power of the state government to identify OBC**

The 105 Amendment of Indian Constitution, 2021, also known as the Constitution (One Hundred and Fifth Amendments) Act, revived the power of the State governments to identify SEBCs or socially and educationally backward classes. SEBCs include the community classes such as OBCs or Other Backward Classes for which the Indian state may provide specific provisions or affirmative steps. The 105th Amendment of Indian Constitution was signed into law by the President of India on 18th August 2021.

Significance of 105 Amendment of Indian Constitution

✓ The Bill aims to restore the power of State governments to recognize OBCs that are socially and educationally backward. The Union government has argued that the purpose of the 105 Constitutional

Amendment Act is to create a Central List that would be applied only to the Central Government and its institutions.

✓ It had nothing to do with the State Lists of backward classes or the State governments' powers to declare a community backward.

✓ The Bill will benefit around 671 OBC communities because if the state list got canceled, these OBC classes would have lost access to reservations in employment and academic institutions.

✓ This Bill promotes social empowerment.

✓ It also mirrors our Government's commitment to assuring pride, opportunity, and righteousness of the marginalized sections.[233]

➢ **The Muslim Women Act, 2019 (Protection of right on Marriage) Triple Talaq Act**

The Muslim Women (Protection of Rights on Marriage) Bill, 2019 was introduced in Lok Sabha by the Minister of Law and Justice, Mr. Ravi Shankar Prasad on June 21, 2019. It replaces an Ordinance promulgated on February 21, 2019.

Muslim Women (Protection of Rights on Marriage) Act, 2019 is an Act of the Parliament of India criminalizing triple talaq. In August 2017, the Supreme Court of India declared triple talaq, which enables Muslim men to instantly divorce their wives, to be unconstitutional. The minority opinion suggested the Parliament to consider appropriate legislation governing triple talaq in the Muslim community. The Bill makes all declaration of talaq, including in written or electronic form, to be void (i.e. not enforceable in law) and illegal. It defines talaq as talaq-e-biddat or any other similar form of talaq pronounced by a Muslim man resulting in instant and irrevocable divorce. Talaq-e-biddat refers to the practice under Muslim personal laws where pronouncement of the word 'talaq' thrice in one sitting by a Muslim man to his wife results in an instant and irrevocable divorce.

➢ **Offence and penalty:** The Bill makes declaration of talaq a cognizable offence, attracting up to three years' imprisonment with a fine. (A cognizable offence is one for which a police officer may arrest an accused person without warrant.) The offence will be cognizable only if information relating to the offence is given by: (i) the married woman (against whom talaq has been declared), or (ii) any person related to her by blood or marriage. The Bill provides that the Magistrate may grant bail to the accused. The bail may be granted only after hearing the woman (against whom talaq has been pronounced), and if the Magistrate is satisfied that there are reasonable grounds for granting bail.

The offence may be compounded by the Magistrate upon the request of the woman (against whom talaq has been declared). Compounding refers to the procedure where the two sides agree to stop legal proceedings, and settle the dispute. The terms and conditions of the compounding of the offence will be determined by the Magistrate.

Allowance: A Muslim woman, against whom talaq has been declared, is entitled to seek subsistence allowance from her husband for herself and for her dependent children. The amount of the allowance will be determined by the Magistrate.

Custody: A Muslim woman, against whom such talaq has been declared, is entitled to seek custody of her minor children. The manner of custody will be determined by the Magistrate.[234]

➢ **Aadhaar Act 2016**

The Aadhaar (Targeted Delivery of Financial and Other Subsidies, Benefits and Services Act), 2016 provides for good governance, efficient, transparent, and targeted delivery of subsidies, benefits and services, the expenditure for which is incurred from the Consolidated Fund of India, [or the Consolidated Fund of the State] to individuals residing in India through assigning unique identity numbers to such individuals and for matters connected therewith.

• On March 3, 2016, Finance Minister Arun Jaitley introduced the Aadhaar (Targeted Delivery of Financial and Other Subsidies, Benefits, and Services) Bill, 2016 in the Lok Sabha.

• The Bill aims to target the delivery of subsidies and other amenities to people living in India by allocating them special identification numbers, known as Aadhaar numbers.

• The Aadhaar Bill intends to send State subsidies effectively into beneficiaries' hands (or, more precisely, bank accounts) by using the identifying number provided by the Unique identifying Authority of India (UIDAI). [235]

➢ **Insolvency and Bankruptcy Code (2016)**

The Insolvency and Bankruptcy Code, 2016 (the "Code") was passed by the Parliament with the intention of establishing and modernizing the legal structure for solving insolvency in India in a timely manner as well as to encourage entrepreneurship, credit availability, and the balancing of the various interests of each and every stakeholder in a company. The Amendment Act aims to streamline the Corporate Insolvency Resolution Process ("CIRP") and provide protection to new owners of a loan defaulter company against prosecution for misdeeds of previous owners. By way of the Act, The Insolvency and Bankruptcy Code (Amendment) Ordinance, 2019 was also repealed.

Objects and Reasons of the Bill as under:

The Insolvency and Bankruptcy Code, 2016 (the Code) was enacted with a view to consolidate and amend the laws relating to reorganisation and insolvency resolution of corporate persons, partnership firms and individuals in a time-bound manner for maximization of value of assets of such persons, to promote entrepreneurship, availability of credit and balance the interests of all the stakeholders including alteration in the order or priority of payment of Government dues and to establish an Insolvency and Bankruptcy Board of India.[236]

➢ **Real Estate (Regulation and Development) Act, 2016**

The law was then passed by the Rajya Sabha on March 10, 2016, and the Lok Sabha on March 15, 2016. The Parliament enacted the Real Estate (Regulation and Development) Act, 2016, herein referred to as the RERA Act, which aims to protect the rights and interests of consumers by minimizing the malpractices done by the developers and promoting uniformity business practices and transactions in the real estate sector. The RERA Act came into effect on and from 1 May, 2016. At the time of passing of the Act, only 69 out of 90 Sections were notified and all other provisions were effective on and from 1 May 2017. On 31st October 2016, the centre, through the Housing & Urban Poverty Alleviation Ministry, released the general rules of the Real Estate (Regulation and Development) Act, 2016. The Act was legislated under entry 6 and entry 7 of the concurrent list of the Indian Constitution.

The 2016 Real Estate (Regulation and Development) Act's importance:

Real estate's working was previously unregulated. The enforcement of RERA intends to protect the buyers or investors and in turn boost their confidence. It requires transparency and authority to keep track of its functioning approach. In reality, it now serves as a spotless ground for buyers as well as reducing the risk of those buyers or investors who bought or invested in the real estate before the implementation of the Act. The Act clarifies the relationship between property buyers and developers. It lays down the process of establishing trust between suppliers and purchasers. It has even created a state agency to oversee real estate and business transactions. The RERA Act is now assisting home buyers in receiving their real estate projects on schedule which is a huge comfort for Indian homebuyers.[237]

- **Consumer Protection Act, 2019**

The Consumer Protection Act, 2019 is an important legislation passed by the Indian government to strengthen consumer rights and protection in the country. It was introduced during the Modi government's tenure and received presidential assent on August 9, 2019. The Act replaced the older Consumer Protection Act, 1986, with updated provisions and expanded the scope of consumer protection.

The 2019 Consumer Protection Act's main characteristics are as follows:

CCPA, the Central Consumer Protection Authority: The Act creates the CCPA, granting it the authority to look into, recall, and punish manufacturers and sellers that engage in unfair business practices, false advertising, and consumer rights abuses.

Consumer Disputes Redressal Commission: The Act establishes the CCPA, which has the power to investigate, recall, and impose penalties on manufacturers and sellers for unfair trade practices, misleading advertisements, and violations of consumer rights.

Product responsibility: The Act introduces the concept of product liability, making manufacturers, sellers, and service providers responsible for any harm caused to consumers due to defective products or deficient services.

E-commerce and Direct Selling: The Act also covers consumer protection in the e-commerce sector and introduces provisions to regulate direct selling and protect consumers from unfair practices in this domain.[238]

- **Citizen amendment Protection Act, 2019**

The Citizenship Amendment Act (CAA) is an act passed by the Indian Parliament on December 11, 2019. It was intended to amend the existing Citizenship Act of 1955 to provide a path to Indian citizenship for certain religious minorities from neighboring countries. The CAA grants eligibility for Indian citizenship to six religious minority communities - Hindus, Sikhs, Buddhists, Jains, Parsis, and Christians - who entered India on or before December 31, 2014, from Afghanistan, Bangladesh, or Pakistan.

The Bill contains two new clauses regarding citizenship for undocumented immigrants.

Consequences of acquiring citizenship: The Bill says that on acquiring citizenship: (i) such persons shall be deemed to be citizens of India from the date of their entry into India, and (ii) all legal proceedings against them in respect of their illegal migration or citizenship will be closed.

Exception: Further, the Bill adds that the provisions on citizenship for illegal migrants will not apply to the tribal areas of Assam, Meghalaya, Mizoram, or Tripura, as included in the Sixth Schedule to the Constitution. These tribal areas include Karbi Anglong (in Assam), Garo Hills (in Meghalaya), Chakma District (in Mizoram), and Tripura Tribal Areas District. It will also not apply to the areas under the Inner Line" under the Bengal Eastern Frontier Regulation 1873. The Inner Line Permit regulates visit of Indians to Arunachal Pradesh, Mizoram, and Nagaland.

Grounds for cancelling OCI registration: The Act provides that the central government may cancel registration of OCIs on five grounds including registration through fraud, showing disaffection to the Constitution, engaging with the enemy during war, necessity in the interest of sovereignty of India, security of state or public interest, or if within five years of registration the OCI has been sentenced to imprisonment for two years or more. The Bill added one more ground for cancelling registration, that is, if the OCI has violated any law that is in force in the country. When the Bill was passed in Lok Sabha, this was amended to limit the disqualification to violations of the Citizenship Act or of any other law so notified by the central government. Also, the cardholder has to be given an opportunity to be heard.

Citizenship by naturalisation: The Act allows a person to apply for citizenship by naturalization, if the person meets certain qualifications. One of the qualifications is that the person must have resided in India or been in central government service for the last 12 months and at least 11 years of the preceding 14 years. The Bill created an exception for Hindus, Sikhs, Buddhists, Jains, Parsis and Christians from Afghanistan, Bangladesh and Pakistan, with regard to this qualification. For these groups of persons, the 11 years' requirement will be first reduced to six years then into 5 years.[239]

Abrogation of Article 370

The abrogation of Article 370 refers to the revocation of Article 370 of the Indian Constitution, which granted a special autonomous status to the region of Jammu and Kashmir, allowing certain degree of self-governance. This provision was originally included in the Indian Constitution to recognize the unique circumstances of Jammu and Kashmir's accession to India in 1947. Article 370 granted special autonomous status to the region of Jammu and Kashmir, allowing it to have its own constitution, flag, and autonomy over various matters except foreign affairs, defense, and communications.

On August 5, 2019, the Government of India, led by the Bharatiya Janata Party (BJP) and Prime Minister Narendra Modi, took a significant step by revoking Article 370 through a presidential order and a subsequent resolution passed by the Parliament of India. This move effectively ended the special status that Jammu and Kashmir had enjoyed for decades, removing its autonomy in many aspects including governance, property rights, and laws. Additionally, the state of Jammu and Kashmir was reorganized into two separate union territories: Jammu and Kashmir, and Ladakh. This move was accompanied by significant political, legal, and constitutional changes. The decision was a major departure from the previous policy and aimed to integrate Jammu and Kashmir more closely with the rest of India.

The abrogation of Article 370 led to significant changes in the governance of Jammu and Kashmir:

- **Decline in violence**: There has been a **significant decline in violence** in Jammu and Kashmir since the abrogation of Article 370.
- According to official data, the **number of terrorist incidents has decreased** by over 50% and security forces have killed over 300 militants in the last four years.
- This can be attributed to a combination of factors, including increased security measures, better intelligence gathering, and a decline in public support for militancy.

- **Improved Economic Development:** The government has implemented several initiatives to boost economic development in Jammu and Kashmir, such as the **Prime Minister's Development Package (PMDP)** and the **Industrial Development Scheme (IDS).**

- These initiatives have led to increased investment, job creation, and economic growth in the region. The UT witnessed **tax revenue growth of 31%.** During 2022-23, the **GSDP of J&K grew at 8%** at constant prices, as against 7% at the national level.

- **Enhanced Infrastructure**: The government has also invested heavily in infrastructure development in Jammu and Kashmir. This includes projects such as the construction of new roads, bridges, tunnels, and power lines.

These improvements have made it easier for people to travel and do business within the region.

- **Increased Tourism:** The number of **tourists visiting Jammu and Kashmir has increased significantly** since the abrogation of Article 370. This is due to a combination of factors, including improved security, better marketing, and the launch of new tourism initiatives.

- According to a report, the region of Jammu and Kashmir has **seen 1.62 crore tourists in 2022, the highest** in India's 75 years of independence.

Reorganization of the State: The state of Jammu and Kashmir was reorganized into two separate union territories – Jammu and Kashmir, and Ladakh. This change aimed to bring these regions under the direct administration of the central government and increase development and governance efficiency.

Changes in Legislative Powers: The abrogation of Article 370 effectively ended the special autonomous status of Jammu and Kashmir. The region now follows the Indian Constitution, and the central government has more authority in areas that were previously under the state's jurisdiction.

Integration with the Rest of India: The Indian government's rationale for abrogating Article 370 was to integrate Jammu and Kashmir more closely with the rest of the country and promote economic development, investment, and infrastructure projects in the region.

Security and Administration: The central government's move was also expected to improve security and counter-terrorism operations in the region by allowing better coordination between state and central security agencies.

Land and Citizenship Laws: Following the abrogation, non-residents were allowed to purchase land and property in Jammu and Kashmir, which was restricted under Article 370. Additionally, the region now follows the central government's citizenship laws, which means that people from other parts of India can settle in Jammu and Kashmir.[239a]

Legal System: IPC, Criminal Procedure Code and the Indian evidence Act

The Indian Penal Code (IPC), the Code of Criminal Procedure (CrPC), and the Indian Evidence Act were passed under British rule in India and are being repealed and replaced by three legislations that the union Home minister submitted in the Lok Sabha. These bills:

The IPC, 1860 will be replaced by the Bharatiya Nyaya Sanhita Bill, 2023

- The bill specifies terrorism as well as crimes like separatist, armed rebellion against the government, and undermining national sovereignty that were previously specified under separate legal rules.
- It does away with the crime of sedition, which was widely decried as a remnant of colonial times that stifled criticism and free speech.
- The maximum sentence for mob lynching, which has become a serious problem recently, is set at the death penalty.
- It suggests a 10-year sentence for engaging in sexual activity with a woman under false pretenses of marriage, which is a frequent type of fraud and exploitation.
- The major feature is community service as a form of punishment for particular offenses, which can aid in prisoners' rehabilitation and lessen prison congestion.
- Another major feature is maximum 180-day to file a charge sheet, which can speed up the trial process and prevent indefinite delays.

The CrPC, 1898 will be replaced by the Bhartiya Nagrik Suraksha Sanhita Bill, 2023.

- It encourages the use of technology in trials, appeals, and the recording of depositions, enabling hearings to be conducted via video conferencing.
- According to the bill, police must notify a complaint status within 90 days. This requirement can increase accountability and openness.
- The CrPC's Section 41A shall henceforth be known as Section 35. With this amendment, a new safety measure is included, stating that no arrests may be taken without prior consent from an officer with at

least the rank of Deputy Superintendent of Police (DSP), especially in cases where the maximum sentence is less than three years or where the suspect is older than 60.

- To guarantee that justice is not tainted or withheld, the measure mandates that police contact the victim before dropping a case that carries a sentence of seven years or more.

The Evidence Act of 1872 will be replaced by the Bharatiya Sakshya Bill of 2023.

- According to the bill, electronic evidence that data produced or sent by a system or device that can be kept or accessed in any way.
- In order to avoid the misuse or alteration of digital data, it lays down particular requirements for the admissibility of electronic evidence, such as authenticity, integrity, and reliability.
- It includes unique guidelines for DNA evidence admissibility, including consent and custody chain requirements, which can improve the precision and dependability of biological evidence.
- The Bharatiya Sakshya Bill, 2023 (BSB) replaces the Indian Evidence Act, 1872 (IEA). It retains most provisions of the IEA including those on confessions, relevancy of facts, and burden of proof.
- The IEA provides for two kinds of evidence - documentary and oral. Documentary evidence includes primary (original documents) and secondary (that proves the contents of the original). The BSB retains the distinction. It includes electronic records in the definition of documents.
- Under the IEA, electronic records are categorised as secondary evidence. The BSB classifies electronic records as primary evidence. It expands such records to include information stored in semiconductor memory or any communication devices (smart phones, laptops).
- Under the IEA, secondary evidence may be required under various conditions, such as when the original is in the possession of the person against whom the document is sought to be proved or has been destroyed. The BSB adds that secondary evidence may be required if the genuineness of the document itself is in question.[239b]

Modi Government's Reforms in Education Sector

The Modi administration in India has implemented a number of educational reforms with the goal of modernizing the educational system and expanding access to high-quality education. Key educational reforms implemented by the Modi administration include the following:

One of the most significant reforms introduced by the government was the NEP 2020, which replaced the 34-year-old National Policy on Education (NPE) of 1986. The NEP 2020 aims to bring transformational changes in the education system by focusing on holistic and multidisciplinary education, reducing The NEP intends to raise the current GER (Gross Enrollment Ratio) to 50 by 2035. It is estimated that 3.5 crore more places for higher education will be added, according to the NEP. The emphasis on rote learning, promoting critical thinking and creativity, and enhancing vocational education. NEP 2020 is one of the biggest reforms of the education sector implemented by the Modi government as the policy focuses on the skill-based learning system and has stratified the school education system from 10+2 to 5+3+3+4. The NEP will work right from the roots of the Indian education system i.e. the pre-school strata or as known in rural India, "Anganwadi." NEP focuses on seamless aims at providing a system that facilitates seamless transition and coordination across institutions and across all stages of education.[240]

Key highlights of the National Education Policy 2020 include:

•**Early Childhood Care and Education (ECCE):** The goal of the policy is to ensure that all children up to the age of six have access to high-quality early childhood education and care. The policy places a strong emphasis on this subject.

•**School Education:** The policy suggests changing the current 10+2 structure of the school education system to a 5+3+3+4 structure, in which the foundational stage lasts for the first five years, then a total of three years of elementary school, three several decades of higher elementary school, and a total of four years of secondary schooling.

•**Flexibility and Multidisciplinary Education:** The NEP 2020 promotes a multidisciplinary approach to education, permitting students to select topics from a variety of streams that interest them. It encourages flexibility and provides several options for leaving the academic career.

•**Higher Education:** NEP 2020 anticipates extensive reforms in higher education, including the creation of the Higher Education Commission of India (HECI) as a single, all-encompassing regulator to replace other regulatory agencies. Additionally, it intends to boost higher education's gross enrollment ratio.

•**Language Policy:** The policy encourages studying many languages for holistic development while emphasizing the native or local dialect as the medium of communication until Grade 5.

•**Technology Integration:** To improve student achievement and access to high-quality education, NEP 2020 promotes technology integration in the classroom.[240a]

Skill India Mission: Launched in 2015, the Skill India Mission aims to provide vocational training and skill development opportunities to millions of youths across the country. The mission seeks to bridge the gap between industry requirements and the skills possessed by the workforce. Skill India Mission is a government scheme launched in 2015. It is an umbrella scheme that has many skilling schemes and programmes under it. The chief objective is to empower the youth of the country with adequate skill sets that will enable their employment in relevant sectors and also improve productivity. Features of Skill India are:

The Skill India Mission has a variety of features, including the following:

- The emphasis is on enhancing youth entrepreneurship and increasing their employability so that they can find jobs.
- The mission provides education, direction, and assistance for all conventional occupations, such as those of artisans, cobblers, woodworkers, welding technicians, masons, metalworkers and healthcare professionals, etc.
- New fields including real estate, transport, building, the gem industry, textiles, finance, jewelry design, tourism, and other industries with low skill levels will also be prioritized.
- Training imparted would be of international standards so that India's youth get jobs not only in India but also abroad where there is demand.
- An important feature is the creation of a new hallmark 'Rural India Skill'.
- Customised need-based programmes would be started for specific age groups in communication, life, and positive thinking skills, language skills, behavioural skills, management skills, etc.

Digital Initiatives in Education

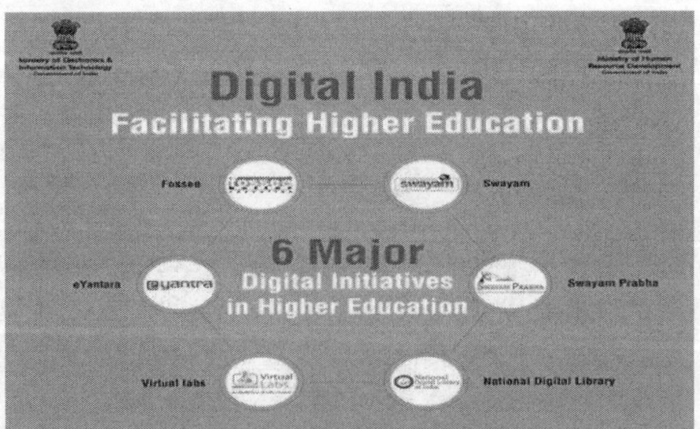

The government has emphasized the use of technology in education through initiatives like Digital India and Digital Education. It has promoted the use of online learning platforms, digital content, and e-learning resources to improve accessibility and quality of education, especially in remote and underserved areas. The growth of GER will be significantly influenced by open and distance learning. There will be initiatives like digital repositories and online courses, research funding, enhanced student services, and credit-based MOOC recognition, among others.

Online, open, and multi-modal learning have been strongly encouraged by both schools and higher education institutions. This programme has significantly reduced the learning loss brought on by the Covid-19 outbreak and will significantly aid in bringing education to rural and hostile areas of the nation. The number of students registering for SWAYAM, DIKSHA, SWAYAM PRABHA, Virtual Labs, and other online resource portals has increased significantly.[241]

Atal Innovation Mission (AIM): The AIM was established to encourage students to be innovative and entrepreneurial by establishing Atal Tinkering Labs (ATLs) in schools all around the nation. These labs give students practical experience in problem-solving and innovation. The Atal Innovation Mission (AIM), NITI Aayog, was established in 2016 as the Government of India's flagship program to encourage an environment of innovation and entrepreneurship across the nation.

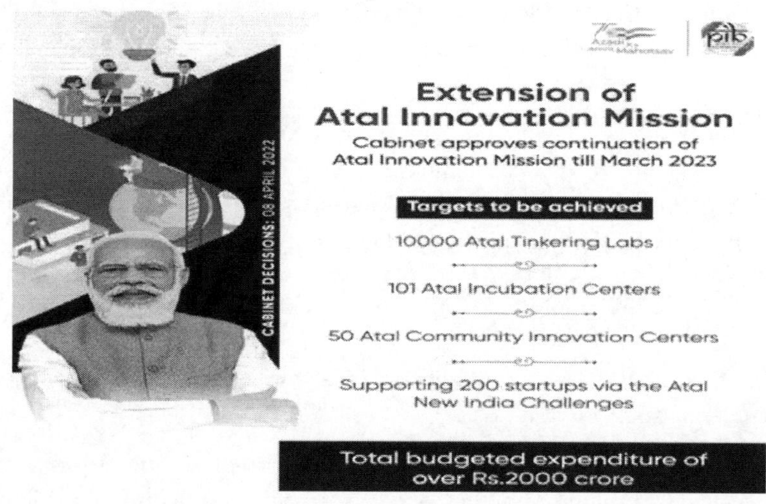

•Atal Tinkering Labs - at school level

AIM has been running the Atal Tinkering Lab (ATL) program for the past four years. With the help of cutting-edge tools and technologies from the 21st century, such as the World Wide Web, 3D-printed rapid design tools, robotics, miniature electronics, DIY kits, and others, ATL aims to inspire innovation and curiosity in young people in grades 6 to 12 across the country. The objective is to encourage children in the ATL and surrounding regions to think creatively and innovatively while solving problems. 10,000 schools in more than 680 districts around the nation have already been chosen by AIM for the creation of ATLs. More than 7000 schools are funded till now and over 2 million students have access to ATLs.[242]

Revamping Examination Systems: The government has taken steps to reform the examination systems to reduce stress on students. Changes in the exam patterns, reducing board exam syllabus, and introducing competency-based exams are some of the measures taken to promote a more holistic assessment of students' abilities. Common University Entrance Test (CUET). Earlier students who wished to get admission to various undergraduate and postgraduate academic courses had to apply separately for different universities and often the dates of various exams clashed making it hard for students to appear for the test.

With the execution of CUET students are now spared from applying for various universities separately and paying thousands of rupees for various applications as they get eligible for various universities by qualifying for just one exam, CUET. The National Testing Agency (NTA) is an autonomous organization established by the Government of India to conduct various entrance examinations for admission to higher educational institutions in the country. The NTA operates under the Ministry of Education (formerly the Ministry of Human Resource Development) and is responsible for conducting examinations like the Joint Entrance Examination (JEE), National Eligibility cum Entrance Test (NEET), Common Management Admission Test (CMAT), Graduate Pharmacy Aptitude Test (GPAT), and more.[243]

Study in India: The Ministry of Education (MoE), Government of India, created the Study in India (SII) program as one of its flagship initiatives. On April 18, 2018, a joint launch of the Study in India portal (www.studyinindia.gov.in) took place. The "Study in India" project was started in order to get more international students to attend Indian universities. It seeks to make India a popular choice for international students and further the internationalization of Indian higher education establishments

The Study in India Project has the extra benefit of quality assurance, where it collaborates with institutions:

It has an Institute of National Importance (INI) or Institute of Eminence (IOE) designation, or it has a National Assessment and Accreditation Council (NAAC) accreditation score of 3.26 or higher. It is also among the top 100 institutions in any category besides medicine according to the National Institutional Ranking Framework (NIRF).

New Institutes and Schemes: In order to concentrate on particular facets of education and evaluation, the government established a number of new institutions, including the National Testing Agency (NTA) and the Indian Institute of Skills (IIS). 62 new medical schools were constructed. Modi government has "sanctioned 692 Eklavya schools" in all tribal and backward districts of the country in just nine years.

• New Delhi's All India Institute of Ayurveda (AIIA) - Ayurveda, or traditional Indian medicine, is an independent institute that was established in 2017.

• The Indian Institute of Skills (IIS), based in Mumbai, was established in 2018 with the goal of offering training and skill development for a variety of businesses.

• National Institute of Mental Health Rehabilitation (NIMHR), Sehore – NIMHR was founded in 2018 and focuses on the treatment and rehabilitation of those who have mental health disorders. The 2016-founded Indian Institute of Petroleum and Energy (IIPE), located in Visakhapatnam, offers undergraduate, graduate, and doctoral degrees in petroleum and energy.

• The Indian Institutes of Technology (IIT) in Bhilai, Goa, Jammu, Dharwad, and Palakkad were founded to increase the access to technical education and research in various geographic areas.

• Berhampur, Tirupati, and Nagaland Indian Institutes of Science Education and Research (IISER) – These IISERs were founded to advance scientific education and research.

• Indian Institute of Information Technology (IIIT) in various locations - Several new IIITs were established under the government's initiative to boost IT education and research.

•Atal Innovation Mission (AIM) – Introduced in 2016, AIM is a flagship program to encourage entrepreneurship and innovation in young students.

• National Sports University, Manipur – National Sports University, Manipur - Established in 2018, this university focuses on sports education and research.

This 2018 establishment focuses on research and education in the field of sports.

• National Institute of Teachers' Training (NITTTR), Bhubaneswar – This institution was established in 2019 with the goal of enhancing the nation's teacher preparation program.

• In order to encourage a startup and innovation environment, 2,774 Institution Innovation Councils have been created set up by HEIs throughout 28 States and 6 UTs. In order to ensure that students' academic performance is not impaired by a lack of English comprehension, multilingualism has been highlighted in education and assessment.

• The Central Universities (Amendment Act) of 2021 established Ladakh's first Central University, Sindhu Central University, which is governed by the Ladakh UT's territorial boundaries. [244]

PM Shri School

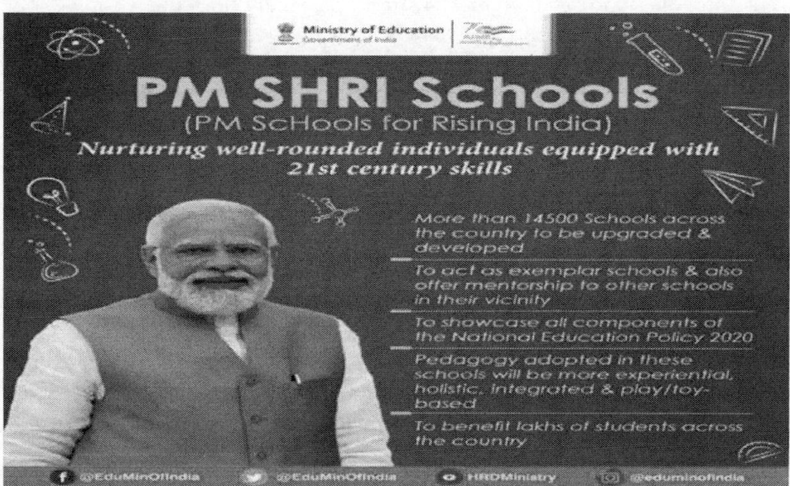

A new central funded program called PM SHRI Schools (PM Schools for Rising India) was authorized by the Union Cabinet, which is presided over by Prime Minister Shri Narendra Modi. This would be a new initiative to reinforce selected current schools run by the Central Government, State Governments, UT Governments, and local governments in order to build in excess of 14500 schools throughout the nation as PM SHRI Schools. PM SHRI Schools will serve as model schools, display every aspect outlined in National Education Policy 2020, and mentor other schools nearby. The PM SHRI schools will deliver quality teaching for the cognitive development of students and will strive to create and nurture holistic and well-rounded individuals equipped with key 21st century skills.[245]

Key features of PM Shri Schools:

• PM SHRI will provide high-quality education in an equitable, inclusive and joyful school environment that takes care of the diverse background, multilingual needs, and different academic abilities of children and makes them active participants in their own learning process as per the vision of NEP 2020.

• PM SHRI Schools will provide leadership to other schools in their respective regions by providing mentorship.

• The PM SHRI Schools will be developed as green schools, incorporating environment friendly aspects like solar panels and LED lights, nutrition gardens with natural farming, waste management, plastic free, water conservation and harvesting, study of traditions/practices related to protection of environment, climate change related hackathon and awareness generation to adopt sustainable lifestyle.[246]

National Institutional Ranking Framework

The National Institutional Ranking Framework (NIRF) was launched by the Government of India in September 2015. It is an initiative by the Ministry of Education (formerly known as the Ministry of Human Resource Development) to rank higher education institutions in India based on various parameters. NIRF aims to promote quality in education and help students and parents make informed choices while selecting colleges and universities for higher studies.

The NIRF rankings take into account a set of parameters that include Teaching, Learning & Resources, Research & Professional Practice, Graduation Outcomes, Outreach & Inclusivity, and Perception. These parameters assess the performance and overall excellence of higher education institutions in the country. The NIRF rankings are updated and released annually, and educational institutions, including universities, engineering colleges, management institutions, pharmacy colleges, and overall institutions, are ranked in different categories based on their performance.[247]

National Medical Commission Act, 2019

The National Medical Commission (NMC) has been constituted by an act of Parliament known as National Medical Commission Act, 2019 which came into force on 25.9.2020. The Aim of the National Medical Commission are to (i) improve access to quality and affordable medical education, (ii) ensure availability of adequate and high quality medical professionals in all parts of the country; (iii) promote equitable and universal healthcare that encourages community health perspective and makes services of medical professionals accessible to all the citizens; (iv) encourages medical professionals to adopt latest medical research in their work and to contribute to research; (v) objectively assess medical institutions periodically in a transparent manner; (vi) maintain a medical register for India; (vi) enforce high ethical standards in all aspects of medical services; (vii) have an effective grievance redressal mechanism.

It has been billed by the government as the "biggest reform" in the medical profession and a "pro-poor legislation" that shall make quality medical care more accessible to the people. The Act seems to bring governance reforms in the medical field, addressing the needs of health services, standardizing quality to be maintained in medical education, etc

Functions of the National Medical Commission:

The NMC's duties include: (i) formulating guidelines for the regulation of hospitals and medical professionals; (ii) determining the need for human resources and infrastructure in the healthcare sector; (iii) ensuring that the State Medical Councils follow the regulations made under the Bill; and (iv) formulating standards for the calculation of charges for up to 50% of the seats offered by private medical organizations and deemed universities that are subject to the Bill's regulation.

• Medical Advisory Council: The central government will set up a Medical Advisory Council in accordance with the Bill. The Council will serve as the main forum for the states and union territories to express their opinions and grievances to the NMC.[248]

Rashtriya Shiksha Aayog (National Education Commission)

The Modi administration suggested establishing a National Education Commission, which would function as a single, all-encompassing authority in charge of establishing educational standards and regulations throughout the nation. In close cooperation with the relevant apex bodies of states, RSA shall be in charge of creating, outlining, reviewing, and modifying the national vision for education on a constant and ongoing basis.[249]

National Testing Agency (NTA)

The Joint admission Examination (JEE) Main, the National Eligibility Comprehension Entrance Test (NEET), and other admission exams of higher learning institutions are all administered by the NTA, an independent organization that was created in 2018. The organization aims to administer exams more effectively and transparently. The Joint Entrance Examination - Main (JEE Main), the National Eligibility Cumulative Entrance Test-Undergraduate (NEET UG), the National Eligibility Test (NET), the Graduate Pharmacy Aptitude Test (GPAT), the Common University Entrance Test (CUET), and the All-India Ayush Post Graduate Entrance Test (AIAPGET) are administered by the National Testing Agency (NTA).[250]

Healthcare Reform Initiatives under Modi Government

The most important healthcare reform in the manifesto stated that the party would assure health care assistance to all Indians, and reduce the excessive spending on healthcare with the help of state governments. Along with this, they also intended to focus on the key factors that are detrimental to our health, such as sanitation and drinking water, to help reduce the number of water-borne diseases in the country.

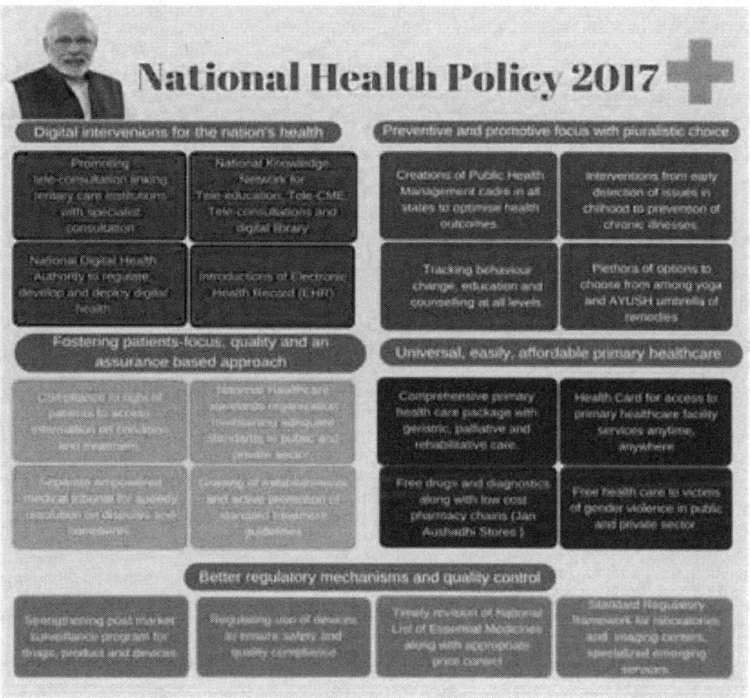

The National Health Policy (NHP) 2017 was formulated during the tenure of Prime Minister Narendra Modi's government. It was approved by the Union Cabinet on March 15, 2017, and it replaced the previous National Health Policy, which was formulated in 2002. The NHP 2017 aimed to provide a comprehensive and strategic framework for the healthcare sector in India. The Union Cabinet chaired by the Prime Minister Shri Narendra Modi in its meeting on 15.3.2017, has approved the National Health Policy, 2017 (NHP, 2017). The Policy seeks to reach everyone in a comprehensive integrated way to move towards the wellness. It aims at achieving universal health coverage and delivering quality health care services to all at affordable cost.

The main objective of the National Health Policy 2017 is to achieve the highest possible level of good health and well-being, through a preventive and promotive health care orientation in all developmental policies, and to achieve universal access to good quality health care services without anyone having to face financial hardship as a consequence. The policy envisages strategic purchase of secondary and tertiary care services as a short-term measure to supplement and fill critical gaps in the health system.

Here are some of the key features and highlights of the National Health Policy 2017:

•**Universal Health Coverage (UHC):** The policy aimed to provide access to affordable, comprehensive, and quality healthcare services to all citizens, irrespective of their economic status. Achieving Universal Health Coverage was one of the primary objectives of the policy.

•**Increasing Public Health Expenditure:** The policy aimed to increase public health expenditure to at least 2.5% of the country's Gross Domestic Product (GDP) in a time-bound manner. This was intended to enhance the availability of resources for the healthcare sector.

•**Preventive and Promotion of Healthcare:** The NHP 2017 emphasized the importance of prevention and promotion of healthcare measures, focusing on wellness and disease prevention. This included awareness campaigns, vaccination programs, and lifestyle interventions.

•**Strengthening Primary Healthcare:** The policy advocated for strengthening the primary healthcare system as the foundation of the healthcare delivery system in India. It aimed to provide comprehensive healthcare services at the grassroots level through the establishment of Health and Wellness Centers (HWCs).

•**Mental Health:** The policy recognized the importance of mental health and aimed to integrate mental health services into the mainstream healthcare system. It focused on promoting mental well-being, providing affordable mental health services, and reducing the stigma associated with mental illness.

•**Digital Health:** The NHP 2017 emphasized the use of digital health technologies and electronic health records to improve healthcare delivery, enhance data management, and ensure better accessibility and efficiency of services.

•**Strategic Purchasing:** The policy highlighted the need for strategic purchasing of healthcare services, which involves buying services from public and private healthcare providers based on predefined criteria and quality standards.

•**Regulation and Accreditation:** The NHP 2017 emphasized the importance of robust regulation and accreditation mechanisms for healthcare facilities and services to ensure quality and safety standards.[251]

National Health Mission (NHM)

The National Health Mission is an ongoing initiative aimed at improving healthcare services, especially in rural and underprivileged areas of India. It focuses on reducing maternal and child mortality, improving immunization rates, promoting family planning, and enhancing access to primary healthcare services. The National Health Mission is an overarching initiative that encompasses various health programs, including the National Rural Health Mission (NRHM) and the National Urban Health Mission (NUHM). It aims to improve the availability and accessibility of quality healthcare services, especially in rural and urban areas. The following programmes/ schemes are run by government under National Health Mission:

- ✓ Reproductive, Maternal, Neonatal, Child and Adolescent health
- ✓ Janani Shishu Suraksha Karyakaram (JSSK)
- ✓ Rashtriya Kishor Swasthya Karyakram(RKSK)
- ✓ Rashtriya Bal Swasthya Karyakram (RBSK)
- ✓ Universal Immunisation Programme
- ✓ Mission Indradhanush (MI)
- ✓ Janani Suraksha Yojana (JSY)
- ✓ Pradhan Mantri Surakshit Matritva Abhiyan (PMSMA)
- ✓ Navjaat Shishu Suraksha Karyakram (NSSK)
- ✓ National Programme for Family planning
- ✓ LaQshya' programme (Labour Room Quality Improvement Initiative)
- ❖ National Nutritional Programmes
- ✓ National Iodine Deficiency Disorders Control Programme
- ✓ MAA (Mothers' Absolute Affection) Programme for Infant and Young Child Feeding
- ✓ National Programme for Prevention and Control of Fluorosis (NPPCF)
- ✓ National Iron Plus Initiative for Anaemia Control
- ❖ Communicable diseases
- ✓ Integrated Disease Surveillance Programme (IDSP)
- ✓ Revised National Tuberculosis Control Programme (RNTCP)
- ✓ National Leprosy Eradication Programme (NLEP)
- ✓ National Vector Borne Disease Control Programme (NVBDCP)
- ✓ National AIDS Control Programme (NACP)
- ✓ Pulse Polio Programme
- ✓ National Viral Hepatitis Control Program (NVHCP)
- ✓ National Rabies Control Programme
- ✓ National Programme on Containment of Anti-Microbial Resistance (AMR)
- ✓ Non-communicable diseases

Union Health Dr, Mansukh Mandaviya expressed that more than 5 crore, Ayushman Bharat Health accounts (ABHA) have been created through NCD Portal under the national programme for non-communicable diseases.

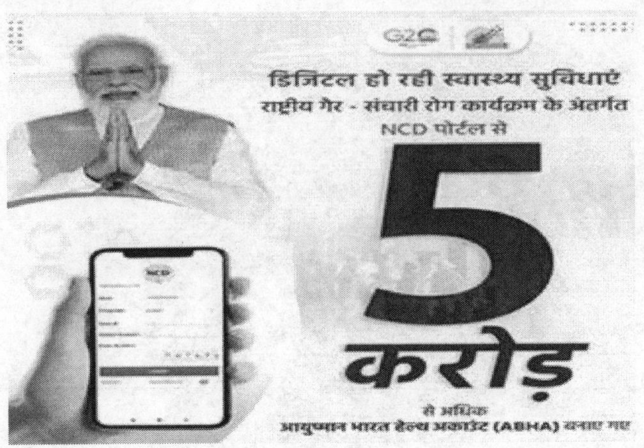

- ✓ National Tobacco Control Programme (NTCP)
- ✓ National Programme for Prevention and Control of Cancer, Diabetes, Cardiovascular Diseases & Stroke (NPCDCS)
- ✓ National Programme for Control Treatment of Occupational Diseases
- ✓ National Programme for Prevention and Control of Deafness (NPPCD)
- ✓ National Mental Health Programme
- ✓ National Programme for Control of Blindness & Visual Impairment (NPCB&VI)
- ✓ Pradhan Mantri National Dialysis Programme (PMNDP)
- ✓ National Programme for the Health Care for the Elderly (NPHCE)
- ✓ National Programme for Prevention & Management of Burn Injuries (NPPMBI)
- ✓ National Oral Health programme [252]

Ayushman Bharat – Pradhan Mantri Jan Arogya Yojana (AB-PMJAY): Launched in September 2018, Ayushman Bharat is a significant healthcare scheme under the NHM. The AB-PMJAY aims to provide health insurance coverage of up to Rs. 5 lakhs per family per year for secondary and tertiary care, hospitalization to over 50 crore vulnerable and economically weaker families in India. It is one of the world's largest health assurance schemes. Ayushman Bharat, a flagship scheme of Government of India, was launched as recommended by the National Health Policy 2017, to achieve the vision of Universal Health Coverage (UHC).

Ayushman Bharat is an attempt to move from sectoral and segmented approach of health service delivery to a comprehensive need-based health care service. This scheme aims to undertake path breaking interventions to holistically address the healthcare system (covering prevention, promotion and ambulatory care) at the primary, secondary and tertiary level. Ayushman Bharat adopts a continuum of care approach, comprising of two inter-related components, which are –

- Health and Wellness Centres (HWCs)
- Pradhan Mantri Jan Arogya Yojana (PM-JAY)

•Health and Wellness Centers (HWCs)

In February 2018, the Government of India announced the creation of 1,50,000 Health and Wellness Centres (HWCs) by transforming the existing Sub Centres and Primary Health Centres. These centres are to deliver Comprehensive Primary Health Care (CPHC) bringing healthcare closer to the homes of people. They cover both, maternal and child health services and non-communicable diseases, including free essential drugs and diagnostic services. Health and Wellness Centers are envisaged to deliver an expanded range of services to address the primary health care needs of the entire population in their area, expanding access, universality and equity close to the community.

Pradhan Mantri Jan Arogya Yojna (PM-JAY)

Benefit cover under various Government-funded health insurance schemes in India have always been structured on an upper ceiling limit ranging from an annual cover of INR 30,000 to INR 3, 00,000 per family across various States which created a fragmented system. PM-JAY provides cashless cover of up to INR 5, 00,000 to each eligible family per annum for listed secondary and tertiary care conditions. The cover under the scheme includes all expenses incurred on the following components of the treatment.

Benefit Cover under PM-JAY

Benefits within multiple Government-funded medical coverage systems in India have consistently been capped at an annual maximum of INR 30,000 to INR 3,000,000 per family across different States, which has led to a disjointed system. For the mentioned tertiary and secondary healthcare conditions, PM-JAY offers each qualified family a paperless coverage of no less than INR 5, 00,000 annually. The following costs related to the treatment are all covered by the scheme's insurance.

- ✓ Medical evaluation, treatment, and advice
- ✓ Prior to hospitalization
- ✓ Prescription drugs and related supplies
- ✓ Services for both non-intensive and intensive care
- ✓ Investigations in the diagnostic and laboratory
- ✓ Services for medical implantation, if required
- ✓ Issues that develop during treatment
- ✓ Follow-up care after hospitalization for up to 15 days

Mission Indradhanush: This immunization program was launched as a part of NHM to strengthen and expand immunization coverage for children and pregnant women. It focuses on increasing vaccination coverage in areas with low immunization rates. Mission Indradhanush aims to achieve full immunization coverage for all children and pregnant women in India against seven vaccine-preventable diseases. It focuses on reaching the unreached and under-served areas. Launched on 25 December 2014, this seeks to drive towards 90% full immunization coverage of India and sustain the same by year 2020. The ultimate goal of Mission Indradhanush is to ensure full immunization with all available vaccines for children up to two years of age and pregnant women. The Government has identified 600 high focus districts across 28 states in the country that have the highest number of partially immunized and unimmunized children .[253]

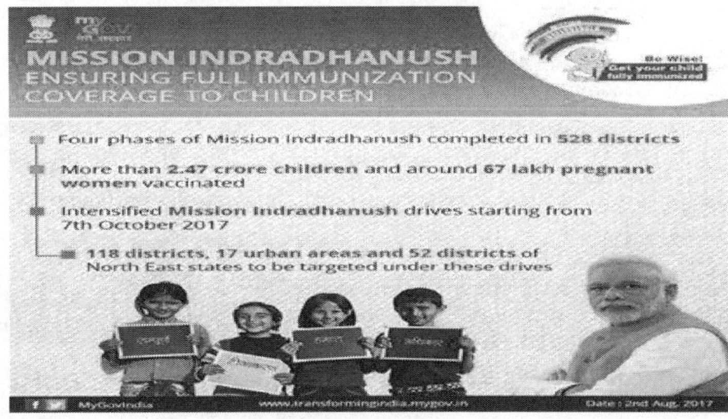

Poshan Abhiyaan (National Nutrition Mission): Launched in 2017, this program aims to reduce malnutrition and stunting among children and improve the nutritional status of pregnant and lactating women. Poshan Abhiyan was launched to address the issue of malnutrition in India. It aims to reduce the prevalence of stunting, under-nutrition, anemia, and low birth weight babies through a targeted approach and convergence among different ministries and departments. The Abhiyaan targets to reduce stunting, under nutrition, anemia (among young children, women and adolescent girls) and reduce low birth weight by 2%, 2%, 3% and 2% per annum respectively.[254]

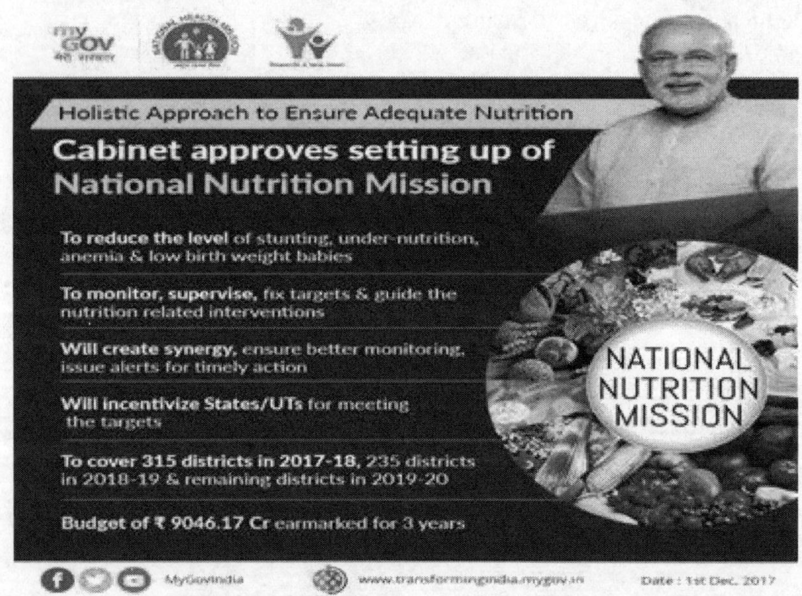

The National Medical Commission Act (NMC Act): In 2019, the government proposed and approved the NMC Act, which aims to reform medical education and establish the National Medical Commission in place of the Medical Council of India (MCI). The NMC Act seeks to make substantial changes to medical education. It also offers rules and procedures for recognizing and regulating medical institutions, making sure they adhere to the defined criteria.[255]

Swachh Bharat Mission (Clean India Mission): The Swachh Bharat Mission, which was established in 2014 but is not solely a health initiative, seeks to advance sanitation and hygiene standards throughout the nation. By lowering the prevalence of waterborne infections, improved sanitation facilities have a considerable positive impact on public health. The project was started by the Indian government, with the goal of making India "open-defecation free" (ODF) by 2 October 2019, marking the 150th year of Mahatma Gandhi's birth.

The second phase of the mission aims to sustain the open defecation free status and improve the management of solid and liquid waste, while also working to improve the lives of sanitation workers. The mission is aimed at progressing towards target 6.2 of the Sustainable Development Goals Number 6 established by the United Nations in 2015. By achieving the lowest open defecation-free status in 2019, India achieved its Sustainable Development Goal (SDG) 6.2 health target in record time, eleven years ahead of the UN SDG target of 31 December 2030.

Pradhan Mantri Bhartiya Janaushadhi Pariyojana (PMBJP: Jan Aushadhi Kendras (generic drug stores), project aims to offer high-quality generic medications at reasonable prices. It tries to lessen people's financial burden from healthcare costs. The Department of Pharmaceuticals established the Pradhan Mantri Bharatiya Janaushadhi Pariyojana Kendra (PMBJK) to distribute high-quality medications to the general public at reasonable costs.[256]

Financial Sector Reforms: Initiatives by Modi Government

Goods and Services Tax (GST): The GST, which is among the nation's most important economic changes, was implemented in July 2017. It established a single tax system by replacing various indirect taxes imposed by the central and state governments. GST aims to make taxation simpler, lessen the burden of compliance, and promote more productive corporate climate.[257]

Insolvency and Bankruptcy Code (IBC): The IBC, enacted in 2016, aimed to address the issue of mounting non-performing assets (NPAs) and improve the ease of doing business. It provides a time-bound process for the resolution of insolvency, bankruptcy, and liquidation cases, leading to better debt recovery and increased investor confidence. The government enacted the Insolvency and Bankruptcy Code, 2016 that allows lenders to immediately suspend the board, strip promoters' powers and enable time-bound recovery of loans. The Code, which has undergone several amendments, creates time-bound processes for insolvency resolution of companies and individuals. If insolvency cannot be resolved, the assets of the borrowers are allowed to be sold to repay creditors.

Banking Reform: India's banking industry has become one of the strong sector under the Modi administration. The Economic Survey 2015–16 advised the four R's – Recognition, Recapitalization, Resolution, and Reform – to handle the issue of non–performing assets.

• **Public Sector Banks (PSBs) Recapitalization:** To bolster PSBs' capital bases and increase their capacity for lending, the government introduced a number of recapitalization schemes. This action was taken to address the problem of defaulted loans and increase the flow of credit into the economy.

• **Public Sector Bank Mergers:** To build stronger and more effective banks, the government consolidated a number of PSBs. The combination sought to improve risk management and cut operational expenses.

Production Linked Incentive (PLI) Scheme

Production Linked Incentive (PLI) scheme was introduced in 2020–21 across 14 important manufacturing industries. In strategic growth industries wherein, India has an unfair advantage, the PLI Scheme encourages domestic production. The Government of India has also started a USD 10 billion incentive program to develop a semiconductor, exhibition, and design ecosystem in India, recognizing the crucial role of semiconductors in the global economy.

Unified Payment interface

India's business practices have undergone a change because of the universal payments interface (UPI). UPI has emerged as the go-to payment method for everything from paying street sellers to shopping for food in a store to paying for luxury items and transferring money. Its enormous popularity can be demonstrated by the fact that UPI processed approximately 19.65 billion activities in volume and 32.5 lakh crore in value during the third period of this year. Over the years, UPI has grown rapidly. About 19.65 billion transactions were recorded using UPI, with a total value of Rs 32.5 lakh crore.

JAM Trinity

The Jan Dhan-Aadhaar-Mobile (JAM) trinity, which was first suggested in the Economic Survey of 2014–15, is another significant reform of the Modi administration. In 2016, the Jan Dhan Scheme, Aadhaar, and cellphone numbers of all participants would be linked, per a declaration made by the then-finance minister Arun Jaitley. It helped the government stop subsidy leakages and ensures the poor get the full benefits of the schemes intended for them. It brought many who were financially excluded into the banking fold. The scheme proved to be a game changer during Covid times as the government could provide direct help to the people.[258]

PM Jan Dhan Yojana

The ambitious Pradhan Mantri Jan Dhan Yojana (PMJDY), introduced by Prime Minister Narendra Modi on August 28, 2014, aims to eradicate "financial untouchability" by implementing the largest banking-for-all program in history. The plan called for financial literacy, access to credit, insurance, and pension services, as well as universal access to banking services through a minimum of one fundamental bank account for every household. This financial inclusion program aims to give all households access to banking resources and financial services. It promoted the opening of bank accounts with little paperwork required and provided account holders with incentives including overdraft capabilities, coverage for insurance, and retirement benefits.[259]

Direct Benefit Transfer (DBT)

To distribute various subsidies and social benefits directly to beneficiaries' bank accounts, the government expanded the use of DBT. It has also helped the government in better targeting and monitoring welfare schemes, ensuring that the benefits reach those who need them the most. Significant advantages, including decreased leakages, the removal of redundant beneficiaries, and enhanced financial inclusion, have resulted from the introduction of DBT.

Here are some key aspects and highlights of the DBT scheme during the Modi government:

•**Aadhaar Integration:** For the purpose of identifying beneficiaries specifically avoiding fraud and duplication, the government connected the DBT program with Aadhaar, a biometric identification system. By using Aadhaar as the foundation for authentication, the benefits are guaranteed to reach their intended users.

•**LPG Subsidy:** The LPG (liquefied petroleum gas) subsidy was one of the DBT's earliest and most well-known applications. The government began paying the subsidy money immediately to the banking accounts of qualified beneficiaries rather than selling LPG cylinders at reduced prices.

•Public Distribution System (PDS): In order to ensure that beneficiaries receive their allotted food grains and commodities, the DBT scheme has been connected to the PDS for sending food subsidies automatically to the beneficiaries' bank accounts.

•Scholarships and Educational Plans: DBT has been expanded to include a number of educational plans and scholarships in order to directly deposit financial aid into students' bank accounts.

•Fertilizer Subsidy: To guarantee that fertilizer subsidies reach farmers more effectively, the government has been looking into the possibilities of implementing DBT in the fertilizer sector.

•Cash Transfer During COVID-19 Pandemic: During the COVID-19 pandemic, the government used the DBT platform to offer financial support to disadvantaged groups in society through programs like PM-KISAN (Pradhan Mantri Kisan Samman Nidhi), Jan Dhan Yojana, and other relief measures.[260]

National Single Window System

The National Single Window System (NSWS) is a digital platform to guide you in identifying and applying for approvals according to your business requirements NSWS was soft launched to all stakeholders and the public on the 22nd of September 2021 by the Union Minister of Commerce and Industry, Consumer Affairs, Food and Public Distribution and Textiles, Shri Piyush Goyal. NSWS was created by Department for Promotion of Industry and Internal Trade (DPIIT) as per the budget announcement of creation of an Investment Clearance Cell (ICC) to provide a single platform to enable the identification and obtaining of approvals and clearances needed by investors, entrepreneurs, and businesses in India.

The system is envisioned to reduce duplicity of information submission to different ministries, reduce compliance burden, promote sector specific reforms and schemes, reduce gestation period of projects, and promote ease of starting and doing business. NSWS enables the identification, applying and subsequent tracking of approvals for all integrated States and Central Departments, making it a true National Single Window System

Significance of National Single Window System

• It would transform into a "one-stop shop" for union and state government compliances and improve the ecosystem's transparency, accountability, and responsiveness.

• In addition, it will include a “Know your permissions service”, a common registration form, a document repository, and an e-communication module to help firms understand the specifics of all the permissions they must receive.

• It will provide other programs—such as Make in India, Startup India, the PLI scheme, etc.—strength with only a click.[261]

Ujjwala Scheme

The "Pradhan Mantri Ujjwala Yojana" (PMUY) is a flagship social welfare scheme launched by the Government of India during the tenure of Prime Minister Narendra Modi. The scheme was launched on May 1, 2016, with the aim of providing free LPG (liquefied petroleum gas) connections to women belonging to Below Poverty Line (BPL) households. Under the Ujjwala Yojana, eligible women from BPL households are provided with a financial support of Rs. 1,600 to cover the cost of the security deposit for the LPG connection, pressure regulator, and a basic gas stove. The scheme also allows EMI (Equated Monthly Installment) facility for meeting the cost of the gas stove or first refill.

The primary objectives of the Ujjwala Yojana are:

Empowerment of Women: By substituting traditional cooking fuels like wood, coal, or kerosene with clean and contemporary LPG and lowering their exposure to hazardous smoke and fumes, the program aims to empower women.

Health Benefits: The program attempts to enhance the health of women and their families by lowering indoor air pollution, which is a serious health concern, particularly for women and children. This is done by providing clean cooking fuel.

Environmental advantages: By promoting the use of LPG, which is a cleaner fuel compared to traditional biomass fuels; the scheme contributes to reducing deforestation and mitigating climate change. LPG cooking saves time and effort since it eliminates the need to gather firewood or other traditional fuels, which frees up women to pursue other economic or educational opportunities.[262]

Demonetization in India by Modi Government

Demonetization," refers to the act of stripping a currency unit of its status as legal tender. In the context of India, during the tenure of Prime Minister Narendra Modi's government, there was a significant demonetization move that took place in November 2016. On November 8, 2016, the Indian government, led by Prime Minister Narendra Modi, announced the demonetization of all ₹500 and ₹1,000 banknotes of the Mahatma Gandhi Series. These were the highest denominations in circulation at that time and accounted for a substantial portion of India's cash economy.

Key objectives of demonetisation:

Curbing Black Money: Demonetization's main claimed goal was to reduce the amount of black money (unreported, unaccounted-for, or unlawfully acquired) in the economy. The measure was intended to flush out the black money and bring it into the established banking system since the government thought that a sizable amount of it had been kept in cash.

Fighting Corruption: Since cash transactions were frequently used for bribes and other criminal activities, demonetisation was also considered as a method to combat corruption.

Reducing Counterfeit money: The action was intended to stop the circulation of fake money notes, which were raising issues with both economics and security concerns.

{Note: ***Long-term impact: Assessing the long-term impact of demonetization on curbing black money, corruption, and the promotion of digital transactions remains a subject of debate. Some argue that demonetization led to increased formalization of the economy and a boost in digital transactions, while others***

contend that the overall impact on black money and corruption might not have been as significant as initially expected}[263]

Atmanirbhar Bharat Abhiyaan

In May 2020, Prime Minister, Mr. Narendra Modi launched the Self-reliant India (Atmanirbhar Bharat Abhiyan) mission to promote Indian goods in the global supply chain markets and help the country achieve self-reliance. The mission was announced amid the pandemic when the government allocated funds worth Rs. 20 lakh crore (US$ 268.74 billion), which amounts to ~10% of India's GDP, as a stimulus package to help recover the economy by promoting incentives for domestic production. It encompasses themes such as 'Local for Global: Make in India for the World' and 'Vocal for Local'. The aim is to make the country and its citizens independent and self-reliant in all senses. He further outlined five pillars of Atmanirbhar Bharat – Economy, Infrastructure, System, Vibrant Demography and Demand. Finance Minister further announces Government Reforms and Enablers across Seven Sectors under Atmanirbhar Bharat Abhiyaan.

During the epidemic, the government launched the mission and provided funding totaling Rs. 20 lakh crore (US$ 268.74 billion), or 10% of India's total economic output, as a stimulus package to aid in the resurgence of the nation's economy by fostering opportunities for domestic production. It covers topics like **"Vocal for Local" and "Local for Global: Make in India for the World."** Making the nation and its people autonomous and self-sufficient is the goal. Aatma Nirbhar Bharat is supported by **five pillars: economy, infrastructure, system, vibrant demography, and demand.** He further described these pillars.

The following are the main goals of PM Narendra Modi's (Atmanirbhar Bharat Abhiyan) project, which he described in his speech on May 12, 2020, as the "Five Pillars" for building an independent India:

- Encourage India to become a hub for the global supply chain.
- Infrastructure - Gain the government's confidence in the abilities and prospects of the private sector.
- Build the government's trust in the private sector capabilities and prospects. Establish 'good force multipliers' for Indian manufacturers.
- Demand - Using the FY22 budget, assess the sufficiency of each area (such as defense, agriculture, healthcare, infrastructure, etc.) in order to attain self-reliance.[264]

The following are the main components of the Atmanirbhar Bharat initiative:

Strengthening the Domestic Economy: The major objective is to foster economic independence and lessen India's dependency on imports, particularly in crucial industries like military, electronics, and other necessary items. The program aims to increase domestic production and manufacturing capacity across a range of industries.

Boosting Manufacturing and Industries: To make India a centre for global manufacturing and increase export competitiveness, the plan intends to support local manufacturing and industrial growth. The government has implemented Production-Linked Incentive (PLI) Schemes in a number of industries to offer financial incentives to businesses for improving production and boosting exports.

Assistance to MSMEs: Atmanirbhar Bharat involves a number of initiatives to help Micro, Small, and Medium-Sized Enterprises (MSMEs) by giving them access to capital, credit, and markets. The Atmanirbhar Bharat program aims to empower MSMEs, which are essential to the Indian economy, by giving them financial support, facilitating simple access to finance, and creating an atmosphere that encourages company growth.

Agricultural Reforms: By implementing changes that increase farmers' incomes, increase agricultural production, and provide an effective supply network for agricultural products, the program aims to develop the agriculture sector. The Indian government has carried out a number of agricultural reforms as part of the Atmanirbhar Bharat plan to strengthen and increase the independence of the agricultural sector. To enable online trading of agricultural goods, the government broadened the platform's functionality known as "e-NAM." Through E-NAM, farmers can sell their goods in any market in the nation, fostering transparency and improving finding affordable prices.

Infrastructure Development: The initiative focuses on investing in infrastructure projects, such as roads, railways, ports, and airports, to create a robust and modern infrastructure network.

•**Road and Highway Development:** According to enormous government investment, the country's roads and highways are being built and renovated. In this regard, the Bharatmala Pariyojana is a big project to construct and improve transportation networks.

•**Railways:** Infrastructure development has placed a lot of emphasis on the Indian Railways. The government is putting high-speed trains on the rails, updating train stations, and developing new rail networks to connect outlying communities. To increase trade and economic activity and enhance connectivity, ports and airports have been developed and modernized as a priority.

•**Public-Private Partnerships (PPPs):** The government promotes involvement from the private sector in the construction of infrastructure using PPPs to amplify the development.

Digital India: To build a digital ecosystem and enhance governance and service delivery, Atmanirbhar Bharat places a strong emphasis on the development of technological innovations and e-government activities. Expanding the digital infrastructure developing a strong electronic core for delivering digital services, and enabling broadband connectivity in rural and distant locations.

• **Promoting digital skills and literacy** among the populace, particularly in rural and distant locations.

•**Online Service Delivery:** Reducing paperwork and revolutionizing government offerings by through rendering them accessible online through a variety of channels.

• **Mobile Connectivity:** Increasing connectivity to mobile devices and digital services' accessibility via mobile platforms.

Export Promotion: Atmanirbhar Bharat aims to expand exports and look into new international markets for Indian products and services. Export marketing under Atmanirbhar, the Indian government has put forth a number of initiatives to support and encourage exports. Under Atmanirbhar Bharat, some of the major projects and plans to encourage exports include:

Market Diversification: The program encourages exporters to go beyond conventional markets. Export destination diversification decreases reliance on particular markets and creates chances in new areas.

•**Development of Export Infrastructure:** To increase the effectiveness and competitiveness of Indian exports, the government makes investments in constructing and renovation in export-related amenities which includes ports, airports, and logistical facilities.

•**Support for Export Finance:** Atmanirbhar Bharat encourages exporters' access to export financing through a number of initiatives and programs aimed at making sure exporters have the operating capital to complete their export orders.

Foreign Policy Strategies under Modi Government to Achieve Economic Strength for India

The Modi administration is defined by a number of important values and goals. It's critical to remember that foreign policy is a vibrant topic that constantly changes. The main tenets of India's foreign policy under the Modi administration:

Neighborhood First Policy: A top objective was to improve ties with South Asian neighbors. With its close neighbors, including Nepal, Bhutan, Bangladesh, Sri Lanka, and Maldives, India sought to improve economic cooperation, connectivity, and interpersonal ties.[265]

Act East Policy: The Modi administration pursued the Act East Policy to increase India's involvement with Southeast Asia and East Asia. The emphasis was on expanding economic and geopolitical ties with ASEAN regions.

Relationships between Major Powers: India worked to keep a balance in its interactions with powerful nations like the US, China, and Russia. India maintained cooperative connections with Russia while fortifying its ties with the US through strategic alliances, and it worked to navigate its intricate connection with China.

Multilateralism and international forums: India wanted to take a more assertive position in these institutions. It aimed to strengthen its position and influence in institutions including the SCO, BRICS, G20, and UN.

Economic Diplomacy: The Modi administration highlighted economic negotiation as a crucial instrument for fostering business and investment ties with foreign nations. Make in India and Start-Up India was established in an effort to draw in international capital and expand India's industrial and technological industries. India seeks to involve its sizable diaspora community, which is dispersed throughout the world.

Counterterrorism and Security Cooperation: India persisted in working with other nations to combat terrorism and strengthen security cooperation, particularly in the context of maintaining regional peace and combating international terrorism.

Climate Change and Renewable Energy: India reaffirmed its dedication to combating climate change and advancing renewable energy programs on a global scale. The Bhadla Solar Park in Rajasthan state, which is close to the Pakistan border, is a well-known symbol of Prime Minister Narendra Modi's enormous goal to turn India into a centre for renewable energy production. By the year 2030, Modi would convert 50% of India's energy to green.

Vaccine diplomatic efforts: During the COVID-19 epidemic, India started a program named "Vaccine Maitri" to give COVID-19 vaccines to other nations in need, helping to boost its reputation as a responsible international participant.[266]

Economic Core Momentum Build up by Modi Government

Goods and Services Tax (GST): The government implemented the GST in July 2017 to replace the convoluted network of indirect taxes. The GST was designed to promote economic efficiency and lower tax-related barriers by unifying the market and streamlining taxation. Among the largest and most important economic changes was the GST's implementation in July 2017.

Infrastructure Development: The building infrastructure, such as roads, trains, ports, and airports, was prioritized by the government. To improve connectivity and logistics throughout the nation, projects like "Bharatmala" and "Sagarmala" were initiated. Through a number of initiatives, the government placed a focus on infrastructure development, including the building of roads, highways, trains, and smart cities.

Make in India: The "Make in India" project was started to encourage both domestic and international businesses to produce goods in India. The objective was to increase manufacturing, create jobs, and establish India as a centre for global manufacturing. This project, which was started in 2014, sought to increase domestic manufacturing and draw foreign direct investment (FDI) through facilitating commercial transactions and fostering knowledge of transfer.[267]

Financial Inclusion: Through initiatives like Jan Dhan Yojana, which sought to offer financial amenities to the unbanked people and advance financial literacy, the government placed a strong emphasis on financial inclusion.

Digital India: The goal of the Digital India program was to increase the use of electronic technologies and services throughout the nation while also strengthening digital infrastructure, information access, and service quality.

Entrepreneurship and startups: The government helped start-ups and entrepreneurs through initiatives like Startup India, which provided funding, mentorship, and other types of support to promote invention and the development of jobs. This policy was created in 2016 with the goal of encouraging innovation and entrepreneurship by providing several incentives and support to enterprises.

Ease of doing business is simple: The government attempted to improve India's standing on the index of the World Banking Organization to simplify, how to conduct business in India. Several reforms were put into place to streamline corporation registration procedures, promote global investment, and minimize governmental impediments.

Foreign Direct Investment: To promote economic growth and job creation, the government sought strategies to draw foreign direct investment (FDI) into a variety of industries, including manufacturing, retail, and defense. In order to encourage more foreign investment, the government has liberalized the rules for foreign direct investment (FDI) in a number of areas.

Banking and Financial Sector Reforms: To address problems in the banking industry and encourage financial sector changes for stability and growth, the government adopted a number of actions.[268]

Atmanirbhar Bharat (Self-reliant India): A policy that was introduced in 2020 during the COVID-19 epidemic, aimed to increase domestic production and decrease reliance on imports in order to make India self-sufficient.[269]

Merger of Ministries and Departments by Modi Government

Need of Creating or Merging the Ministries and Departments

In order to increase effectiveness, governance, and coordination, the Modi government in India undertook a number of substantial administrative changes, including the merging and restructuring of numerous ministries and departments. It is significant to remember that organizational reconfiguration is a continuous process, and it is possible that the government has implemented other alterations and mergers. Administrative reforms are frequently implemented to improve the efficiency of the government's policies and programs by streamlining governance, removing duplications, and ensuring greater cooperation among different ministries and departments.

The Government of India (Allocation of Business Rules) of 1961, which are a part of Article 77 of the Constitution, state that the President may establish new ministries or departments on the advice of the Prime Minister. According to these regulations, the President, acting on the Prime Minister's recommendation, appoints a minister to each ministry. The officer in charge of each department in the ministry typically serves as the minister's advisor on general policy issues.

Ministry of Finance: In 2017, the Modi administration combined the Railway Budget with the General Budget. The Rail Budget was previously presented separately before this merger. The Department of Economic Affairs (DEA), Department of Expenditure, and Department of Revenue came underneath the management of a single Secretary when the Ministry of Finance underwent reform.

Ministry of Overseas Indian Affairs: In order to better serve the requirements of the Indian diaspora overseas, the Ministry of Overseas Indian Affairs and the Ministry of External Affairs were combined in 2016.

Ministry of Human Resource Development: To put a stronger emphasis on educational reforms, the Ministry of Human Resource Development was renamed the Ministry of Education in 2020.

Ministry of Water Resources, River Development, and Ganga Rejuvenation: In order to streamline water-related challenges and conservation efforts, the Modi administration consolidated the Ministries of Jal Shakti and Water Resources, River Development, Ganga Rejuvenation, and Drinking Water and Sanitation in 2019.

Ministry of Information and Broadcasting and Ministry of Youth Affairs and Sports: In order to create the Ministry of Youth Affairs and Sports and Information and Broadcasting in 2021, these two departments were combined.

The Ministry of Power and Renewable Energy was created by the merger of the Ministries of Power and New and Renewable Energy. Promoting renewable energy sources and energy security are the main objectives.

Ministry of Skill Development and Entrepreneurship: The National Skill Development Agency, National Skill Development Corporation, and other skill development programs were combined to form the Ministry of Skill Development and Entrepreneurship, which was established to improve skill training and encourage entrepreneurship.

Ministry of Corporate Affairs: Serious Fraud Investigation Office (SFIO) and the Competition Commission of India (CCI) have been placed under the administrative jurisdiction of the Ministry of Corporate Affairs, which has undergone organizational changes.

Department of Public Enterprises: As a think tank for public sector businesses, the Department of Public Enterprises (DPE) was reorganized and repositioned.

Ministry of External Affairs: To improve India's diplomatic outreach and involvement with the foreign world, the Ministry of External Affairs went through the reform.

Urban development and housing and urban poverty reduction were combined into one ministry, the Ministry of Housing and Urban Affairs, by the Modi administration in 2017.

Ministry of cooperation: The establishment of the ministry and its mission statement, "Sahkar se samriddhi" (prosperity through cooperation), were both announced on July 6, 2021. The ministry supports the growth of Multi-State Cooperatives (MSCS), tries to simplify procedures for "Ease of Doing Business" for cooperatives, and strengthens cooperatives at the grassroots level.[270]

Modi Government Advancements for Space Sector

Indian Space Research Organisation (ISRO) Achievements: During the Modi administration, ISRO continued to make great strides in satellite launches and space exploration. The Mars Orbiter Mission (Mangalyaan) was successfully launched in 2014, making India the first Asian nation to enter the orbit of Mars and one of four space agencies in the world to do so.[271]

Navigation and Communication Satellites: Under the Indian Regional Navigation Satellite System (IRNSS), referred to as NavIC, ISRO launched a number of navigation satellites. With this technology, precise positional data would be made available throughout India and its neighboring regions. In order to improve India's communication infrastructure, the government also supported the launch of multiple communication satellites.

Mission Gaganyaan: Under the Modi administration, ISRO started making plans for the grandiose Gaganyaan mission, which aimed to launch Gagannauts—Indian astronauts—into space. The mission aims to advance India's space program by focusing on crewed spaceflight. In accordance with the Gaganyaan program, India intended to launch astronauts into orbit. India was to become the fourth nation to send people into space, and the objective was to show spaceflight capabilities.

PM Modi watches Chandrayaan 2 lift off, gave applause

Chandrayaan-2: Chandrayaan-2, India's second lunar exploration mission, was launched in July 2019. Its objectives included investigating the Moon's South Polar Region, doing in-depth remote sensing investigations, and looking for water ice on the lunar surface.

SATNAV Guidelines: The strategy encourages the achievement of self-reliance in satellite-based navigation and augmentation services, with an emphasis on assuring availability and quality, promoting usage, working towards the services' progressive evolution, and fostering interest in research and development.

Mars Orbiter Mission: Mangalyaan was the nation's inaugural extraterrestrial mission, and it was launched in November 2013. In September 2014, it successfully entered Mars' orbit and carried out a number of tests to learn more about the atmosphere of Mars, its surface, and minerals.[272]

Navigation with Indian Constellation (NavIC): India's regional satellite navigation system, NavIC, was created to give users precise position data of the surrounding data.

Series of RISAT: In order to improve India's all-weather surveillance capabilities and to aid in agriculture, forestry, and disaster management, ISRO conducted a number of Radar Imaging Satellite (RISAT) missions.

Chandrayaan 3 Achievement

On July 14, 2023, Chandrayaan-3 was put into orbit. India became the fourth nation to safely land on the Moon and the first to close to the lunar South Pole after the spaceship reached the moon's orbit on August 5 and the lander made contact with the moon on August 23 at 12:32. It is the third lunar exploration mission undertaken by India as part of the Chandrayaan program of the Indian Space Research Organization (ISRO). Its components are a base named Vikram and a rover named Pragyan. The mission objectives of ISRO for Chandrayaan-3 were:

•Achieving a safe landing of a lander on the Moon's surface.

•On the Moon, observing and showcasing the rover's driving abilities.

•Experimenting with and watching the results of the materials that are available on the better comprehend the lunar surface and its composition.[273]

Modi Government Initiatives to Propel Energy Capacity in India

COMPARING 2016 AND 2022

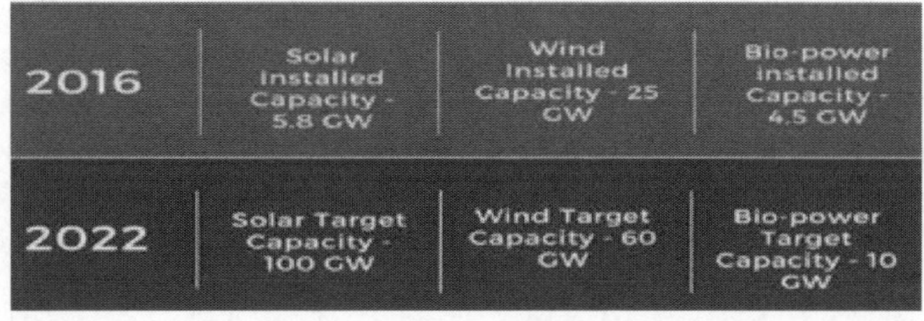

2016	Solar Installed Capacity - 5.8 GW	Wind Installed Capacity - 25 GW	Bio-power installed Capacity - 4.5 GW
2022	Solar Target Capacity - 100 GW	Wind Target Capacity - 60 GW	Bio-power Target Capacity - 10 GW

Renewable Energy Push: The government ensures the growth of large proportion from renewable energy within the nation's energy mix high priority. By 2022, it was intended to have 175 GW of renewable energy capacity, which would include projects for solar, wind, biomass, and minor hydropower. This program was designed to lessen India's carbon footprint and fight global warming. The administration set high goals for expanding the use of renewable energy. By 2022, 100 GW of solar electricity generation was the goal of the National Solar Mission, and the government also set goals for wind and other renewable energy sources.[274]

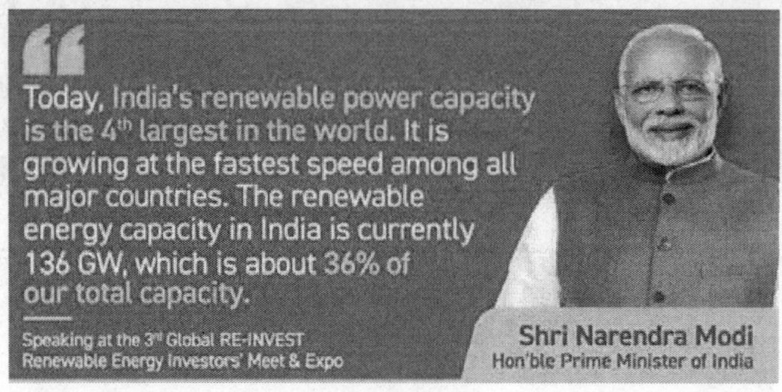

Solar Power Initiatives: The "Solar Parks and Ultra Mega Solar Power Projects" program, that sought to establish substantial solar parks all across the nation, was one of the government's vital solar energy efforts. Various incentives and subsidies were also used to promote rooftop solar installation.

Wind Power Development: In order to draw investments in the wind energy sector, the Modi administration supported the creation of wind power projects by easing regulations, supporting policies, and providing financial incentives.

Electric Mobility: Faster Adoption and Manufacturing of Hybrid & Electric Vehicles (FAME) is a government initiative to encourage clean mobility and lessen reliance on fossil fuels. This program aims to promote the use of electric vehicles and aid in the construction of a charging infrastructure.

Efficiency in Energy: The government put a lot of effort into increasing energy efficiency in many businesses, structures, and appliances. One such program that sought to increase energy efficiency in sectors with high energy costs was the Perform, Achieve, and Trade (PAT) programme.

Reforms in the Coal Sector: While placing a focus on renewable energy, the government also took action to change the coal industry. To promote competition as well as productivity in the coal sector, commercial coal mining was opened up to private parties.

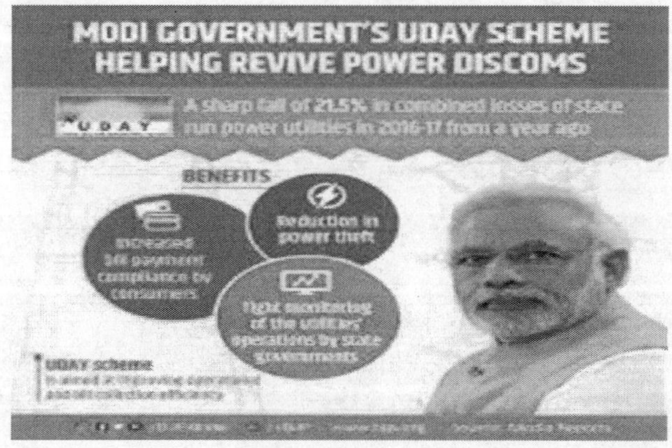

Ujwal DISCOM Assurance Yojana (UDAY): To improve the financial stability of government-owned power distribution firms (DISCOMs) and boost their efficiency in operation, the government introduced UDAY. The goal was to minimize financial losses and make sure that electricity generators received their payments on schedule.

International Solar Alliance India: Modi administration, took the lead in establishing the International Solar Alliance (ISA), a group of nations intending to encourage the use of solar energy and cooperation in the development of solar technology. In order to promote the utilization of solar energy and lessen dependency on fossil fuels, a group of nations with abundant solar energy, including India, formed the International Solar Alliance (ISA).

UJALA (Unnat Jyoti by Affordable LEDs for All): With the UJALA program, LED lights were provided free at discounted prices in an effort to encourage energy conservation. The goal of this effort was to lower energy usage and encourage the installation of lighting that is energy-efficient. To ensure the financial stability of the power industry, the UDAY scheme concentrated on the fiscal reorganization and operational development of power distribution firms (DISCOMs).

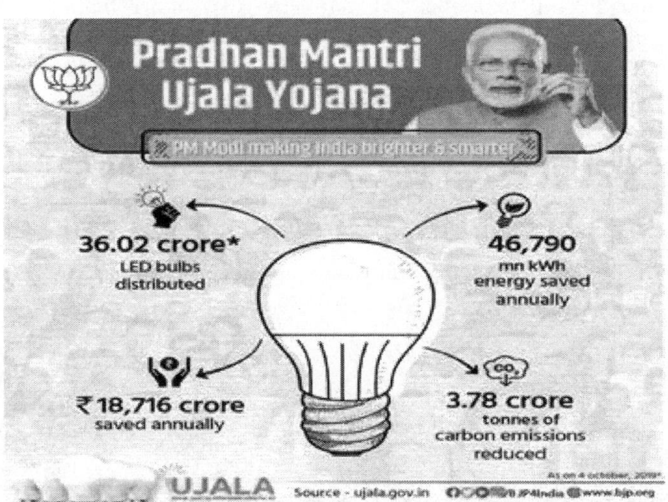

Electric Vehicles (EVs) and FAME India: To encourage the use of electric vehicles, the government introduced the Faster Adoption and Manufacturing of Electric Vehicles (FAME) India scheme. In order to promote the usage of electric vehicles and lower emissions from the transportation sector, FAME offered incentives to both electric vehicle makers and purchasers.

The Saubhagya Yojana: In order to attain universal electrification, the Pradhan Mantri Sahaj Bijli Har Ghar Yojana, additionally referred to as the Saubhagya Yojana, sought to give access to electricity to all families in India, particularly in rural and isolated areas.

National Biofuels Policy: To encourage the use of biofuels, that are 100% renewable and considerably more environmentally conscious than traditional fossil fuels, the government created a National Policy on Biofuels.

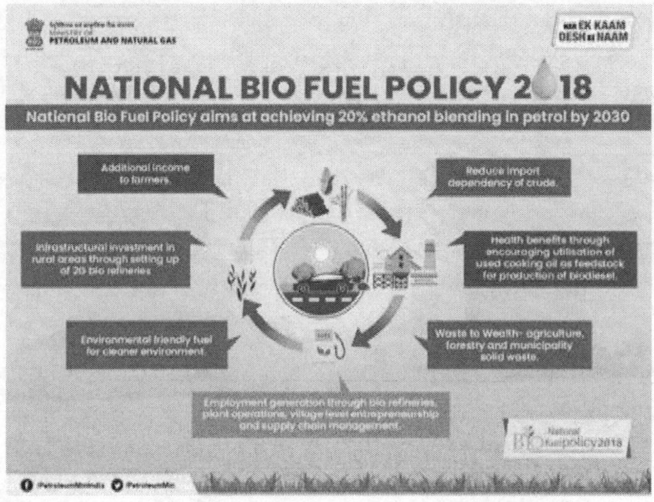

Paris Agreement and Climate Change Commitments: The Modi administration upheld its commitment to combat climate change while lowering emissions of greenhouse gases under the terms of the Paris Agreement.

Development in Science & Technology Sector

The policy actions of Prime Minister Modi have been essential in increasing self-reliance in the defense industry by encouraging native creativity in the creation and production of weapons and ammunition. The state governments were urged by Prime Minister Narendra Modi to develop cutting-edge science and technology programs. India is moving forward with the motto "Jai Jawan, Jai Kisan, Jai Vigyan, and Jai Anusandhan," according to Modi. To turn India into a leading worldwide hub for scientific and technological advancement in this "amrit kaal," we must collaborate on a number of fronts. Our scientific and technological research ought to be conducted locally.

National Quantum Mission: The National Quantum Mission (NQM) supports the advancement of research in quantum technologies in both academia and industry. The Ministry of Science & Technology's Department of Science & Technology (DST) will be in charge of carrying it out. The mission is design from 2023 to 2031, intends to advance scientific and commercial R&D while developing a thriving and creative habitat for quantum technology (QT). From 2023–2024 through 2030–2031, the National Quantum Mission (NQM) will cost a total of Rs. 6003.65 crore. India will become the eighth nation following the US, Austria, Finland, France, Canada, and China to have a dedicated quantum mission with the launch of this mission. (QTA) spanning industries like data security, energy, defense, and healthcare.

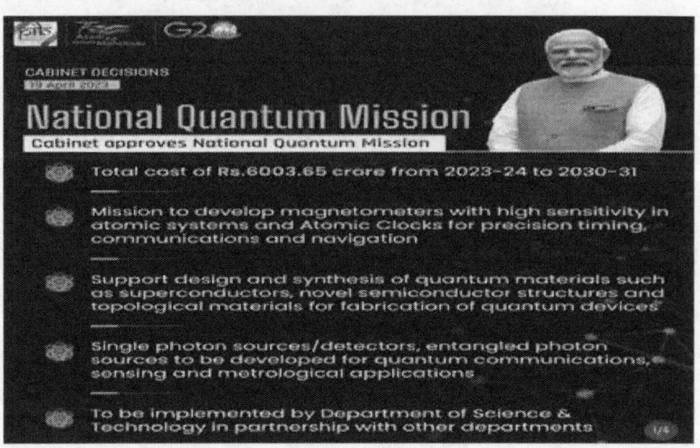

Features of National Quantum Mission:

•The expedition will aid in the creation of atomic clocks for precise time, communication, and navigation as well as magnetometers with a high degree of sensitivity in atomic systems. Additionally, it will aid in the development and manufacturing of quantum materials for the production of quantum devices, such as superconductors, innovative semiconductor architectures, and topological materials.

•Four Thematic Hubs (T-Hubs) on the topics of quantum computation, quantum networking, quantum detection and metrology, and quantum materials and devices will be established in prestigious educational and national R&D institutions. The hubs will boost R&D in areas that are assigned to them and will concentrate on producing fresh understanding using both fundamental and applied studies.[275]

National Hydrogen Mission: To make in India a centre for the production and export of green hydrogen, Prime Minister Narendra Modi unveiled the National Hydrogen Mission on the occasion of the country's 75th Independence Day. India's energy landscape is at a turning point, and green hydrogen will be essential for making the country self-sufficient and energy-independent. The Union Cabinet, led by the Honorable Prime Minister Shri Narendra Modi, authorized the National Green Hydrogen Mission on January 4, 2022.

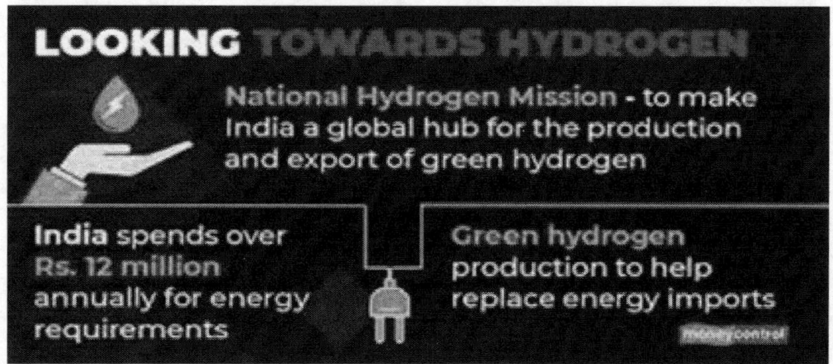

•A sustainable way to generate alternative fuel is hydrogen. The only byproduct when employed in a fuel cell, which creates electrical power from a chemical reaction, is water. Because of this, it is very appealing as an alternative to fossil fuels. A range of energy sources, including biomass, natural gas, nuclear power, and other renewable energy sources like wind and solar energy, can be used to make hydrogen.

•Use Cars with hydrogen fuel cells cars and trucks, as opposed to traditional vehicles, which operate on gasoline or diesel, mix hydrogen and oxygen to create electricity, which powers a motor. Fuel cell vehicles are classified as electric vehicles ("EVs") since they are totally powered by electricity; yet, despite conventional EVs, the mileage and refilling procedures are equivalent to those of regular automobiles and trucks.

•The Mission will have many beneficial outcomes, including the development of export markets for Green Hydrogen and its derivatives, the decarbonization of the industrial, transportation, and energy sectors, a reduction in reliance on foreign imports for feedstock and fossil fuels, the enhancement of domestic manufacturing capabilities, the creation of job opportunities, and the advancement of cutting-edge technologies. India's potential to produce green hydrogen is anticipated to increase to at least 5 MMT annually, adding more than 125 GW of renewable energy capacity in the process.[276]

X Band Doppler Weather Radar: The parabolic dish antenna and foam sandwich circular radome of the radar are used to increase reliability in far-reaching weather prediction and surveillance. The DWR has the necessary tool to pinpoint the center of a storm, the path of a severe thunderstorm or gust front, and the intensity and velocity of the wind. The Doppler Weather Radar (DWR) Systems in Jammu & Kashmir, Uttarakhand, and Himachal Pradesh were unveiled by the Ministry of Earth Science on the 148th anniversary of the establishment of the India Meteorological Department (IMD). For more precise forecasts, the Ministry of Earth Science is also getting ready to extend the Doppler weather radar infrastructure across the entire nation by 2025.[277]

Consumer Protection Measures Under Modi Government

Consumer protection has had an important role in the country for thousands of years. It is mentioned in the Atharva Veda that there must be no wrongdoing while weighing commodities. The rules of consumer protection have been mentioned in books which were written thousands of years ago. Punishment for trading in a wrong way has also been laid down," said PM Modi in Delhi.

Consumer Protection Act, 2019: The Consumer Protection Act (CPA), 2019, was adopted by the Indian government in July 2019 to replace the previous Consumer Protection Act, 1986. The purpose of the new law was to strengthen consumer rights, streamline the dispute resolution procedure, and impose harsher penalties for deceptive advertising and unfair business activities.[278]

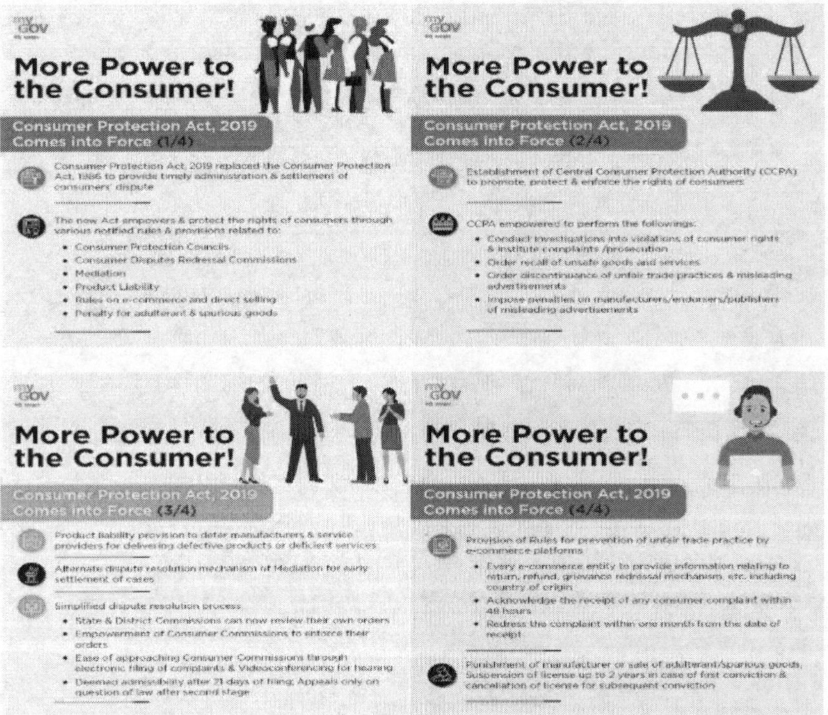

Central Consumer Protection Authority (CCPA): The CCPA, a regulatory organization tasked with promoting, safeguarding, and upholding consumer rights, was founded by the CPA in 2019. The CCPA has the power to look into and take legal action against deceptive or unfair business practices.

Product responsibility: The CPA, 2019, added provisions for product responsibility, holding producers, sellers, and service providers accountable for any harm consumers may have endured as a result of decent goods or services.[279]

E-Commerce Regulations: The new consumer protection act also contained clauses to control e-commerce platforms and guarantee openness, responsibility, and safety for online buyers.

ADR (alternative dispute resolution) and mediation: The CPA, 2019, stressed the significance of ADR (alternative dispute resolution) and mediation tools for quickly and affordably resolving consumer issues.

Enhancing Consumer Forums: Initiatives were taken to improve the way consumer forums work to render them more effective in resolving customer complaints.

Digital Consumer Protection: The government concentrated on safeguarding online shoppers, addressing concerns about data security, privacy, and online transactions.

False Advertising: There has been a greater emphasis on reducing false advertising and penalizing businesses discovered to have engaged in dishonest marketing techniques.

Consumer Complaint Resolution Process Simplified: The government sought to make the registration and resolution of consumer complaints more accessible and simpler to use.

Consumer Awareness Campaigns: Several consumer awareness efforts were run to enlighten customers of their rights and obligations and motivate them to make educated decisions. The Government of India launched the "Jago Grahak Jago" consumer awareness campaign that aims to educate and strengthen customers about their rights and obligations. The campaign's objectives are to increase consumer protection awareness and motivate people to shop with knowledge. It places emphasis on the necessity of exercising caution, knowledge, and assertiveness when interacting with goods and services.[280]

Consumer Protection (Listen to Consumer approach)

Several venues for a redress mechanism

Consumer courts, a three-tier quasi-judicial system, have been formed at the national, state, and district levels to provide straightforward, efficient, and cost-effective resolution of consumer disputes under the CP Act. These tribunals were established to offer no-cost remedy for consumer complaints against any goods or services, including any that entail unethical or deceptive company activities. The following organizations make up the system for resolving consumer disputes:

- The District Consumer Dispute Resolution Commission (abbreviated DCDRC), commonly referred to as the "district commission";
- The State Consumer Dispute Resolution Commission (SCDRC), commonly referred to as the "state commission," and
- The National Consumer Dispute Resolution Commission, or NCDRC, is referred to as the "national commission."

Consumer Protection (Human centric Approach and Public grievances

- National Lok Adalats are organized through the Integrated Grievance Address Mechanism (INGRAM) Portal in collaboration with the National Legal Services Authority.
- The 2019 Consumer Protection Act, in order to rapidly and effectively address consumer complaints, the government should set up adequate redress systems.
- Through a Public-Private Partnership (PPP) model, the government can use the infrastructure and platforms already developed by Alternative Dispute Resolution (ADR) and Online Dispute Resolution (ODR) organizations and regard them as digital public assets.
- Establishing a National Consumer Lok Adalat helpline with a focus on technology can aid in coordinating the actions of complainants, businesses, commissions, legal services authorities, private ADR and ODR providers, and Non-governmental Organizations (NGOs) throughout the Lok Adalat process.

The previous Consumer Protection Act of 1986 has been superseded with the Consumer Protection Act of 2019. It aimed to strengthen consumers' rights by offering them better protection. The act's essential components include the following: The creations of the Central Consumer Protection Authority (CCPA) to safeguard, advance, and uphold consumers' rights. Introduction of the idea of product liability, which holds producers, retailers, and service providers accountable for any damages consumers suffer because of indecent quality of goods or subpar services. [281]

G – 20 Summit in India 2023

G20 held its 18th Leaders of governments and states Summit in New Delhi, India, in September 2023. The G20 meeting in 2023 was center on the theme ***"One Earth, One Family, and One Future"*** under the Indian Presidency. The subject upholds the importance of people, animals, plants, and microorganisms as well as their interdependence on Earth and throughout the cosmos. The culmination of the G20 process and the work done during the course of the year for Ministers Conversations, Discussion of Organizations, and Interaction Committees. In 2023, the Bharat Mandapam International Exhibition-Convention Centre (IECC), Pragati Maidan, New Delhi, hosted G20 Meeting. It marked the inaugural of G20.

The theme of the G20 would ***be "Vasudhaiva Kutumbakam,"*** which is derived from the Sanskrit saying from the Maha Upanishad that means "The World Is One Family," and would direct the theme of the G20. The topic essentially emphasizes the importance of all life—human, animal, plant, and microorganism—as well as their interdependence on Earth and across the universe.

A number of efforts took place at the forefront in the manner of governmental and Participation Group meetings under the aegis of India's G20 Presidency and Amitabh Kant's leadership as CEO of NITI Aayog. They encompassed illuminating discussions at Health20 and Pharma20 Summits, philosophical discussions at G20 Think20 summits, and creative meetings at G20 Startup20 events.[282]

G20 India has put forth six agenda priorities for the G20 dialogue in 2023

LiFE, Climate Finance, and Green Development

India is putting a lot of effort into combating global warming, with a focus on climate financing and technology as well as ensuring equitable energy transitions for poor nations. The LiFE movement, which supports ecologically responsible behavior.

•Accelerated, Inclusive & Resilient Growth Focus on areas that have the potential to bring structural transformation, including supporting small and medium-sized enterprises in global trade, promoting labour rights and welfare, addressing the global skills gap, and building inclusive agricultural value chains and food systems.

• Advancing SDG progress Reaffirmation of commitment to attaining the goals outlined in the 2030 Program of Action for Sustainable Development, including a special focus on tackling the COVID-19 pandemic's effects.

• Public Digital Infrastructure & Technological Transformation, encouragement of a human-centric view of technology and improved information exchange in areas like financial inclusion, digital public infrastructure, and technologically development in industries like agriculture and education.

• 21st-century multilateral institution efforts to modernize multilateralism and build a more accountable, inclusive, and representative global order capable of facing the challenges of the twenty-first century.

• Development by women, in order to promote socioeconomic development and the fulfillment of the SDGs, emphasis should be placed on comprehensive growth and advancement, with a focus on women's empowerment and representation.[283]

Outcomes of G – 20

1. Global Biofuels alliance
2. Admittance of African union
3. India – Middle East European Economic Corridor (IMEC)
4. G20 Global Partnership for financial Inclusion Document
5. Tripling the Global renewable Energy Capacity by 2030
6. Commitment to Global Food security & nutrition
7. Healthcare resilience and research
8. Finance Track agreements
9. India US Tech collaboration

Modi Government Action to Increase the Productivity in Agriculture Sector

With the intention of enhancing the agricultural industry, raising farmers' incomes, and encouraging responsible agricultural methods, the Modi government in India has carried out a number of agricultural policies and projects. Under the Modi administration, some of the most important agricultural programs include:

Mantri Kisan Pradhan PM-Kisan Samman Nidhi: PM-Kisan is a financial assistance program that was introduced in 2019. In accordance with this program, qualified farmers receive a yearly financial aid of Rs. 6,000 splits into three equal portions.[284]

Agriculture Infrastructure Fund: The creation of infrastructure after harvest and agri-entrepreneurship received financial backing with the creation of the Agriculture Infrastructure Fund. It aims to support value addition and boost the agriculture supply chain.

National Agricultural Market or E-NAM: A uniform national market for agricultural products is what the e-NAM platform seeks to establish. With fewer middlemen and greater price discovery, it makes it possible for peasants to make money selling their produce online.

Soil Health Card Scheme: This program offers farmers individualized soil health cards that, based on soil testing, make suggestions for the proper use of nutrients and fertilizers.

Pradhan Mantri Fasal Bima Yojana (PMFBY): A crop insurance program called PMFBY offers farmers financial protection against crop loss brought by pests, illnesses, and natural disasters.

Paramparagat Krishi Vikas Yojana (PKVY): PKVY advocates for organic farming and environmentally friendly agriculture methods. To use fewer pesticides and chemicals, farmers are urged to embrace organic methods of cultivation.

Mega Food Parks: To build up modern facilities for the meals production sector, the government has concentrated on constructing mega food parks. These parks encourage value addition and lessen post-harvest loss.[285]

Kisan Credit Card (KCC) Scheme: Farmers can access finance under the KCC system for farming and associated applications. It attempts to guarantee farmers have access to loans in a timely and sufficient manner.[286]

Agricultural Export Policy: To increase agricultural exports and encourage the international trade of high-value agricultural products, the government established the Agricultural Export Policy.

National Bamboo Mission: The National Bamboo Mission promotes the sustainable production and use of bamboo resources by concentrating on the sector's overall growth.[287]

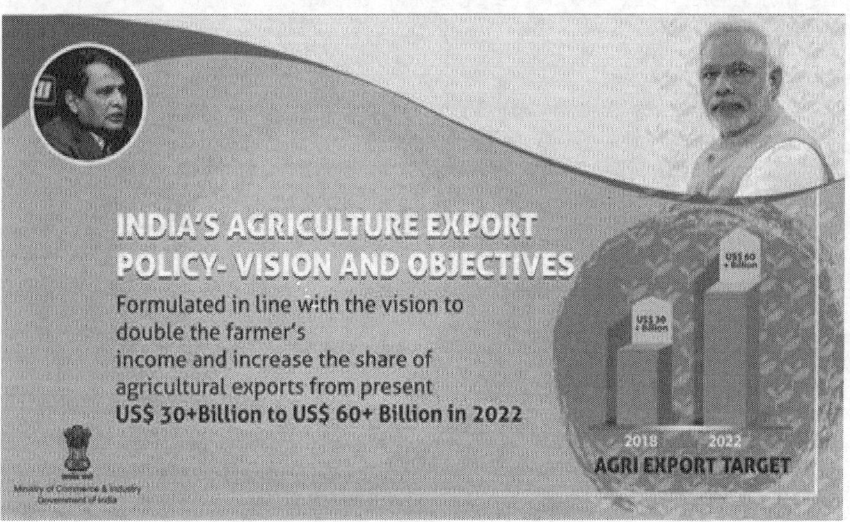

Jal Shakti Abhiyan: The Jal Shakti Abhiyan, while not only concentrating on agriculture, seeks to improve water management and conservation, which is essential for the sustainability of agriculture.

Electronic National Agriculture Market to establish a unified national market for agricultural products, the e-NAM platform was introduced. It enables farmers to sell their produce online, improving price discovery, lowering transaction costs, and removing barriers associated with physical markets.[215] Amendments to the Essential Commodities Act (215) 2020 to Modify Essential Commodities: Only in extraordinary situations, such as during a war, natural disaster and famine give a sharp increase in prices. It is possible for the government to control the supply of some commodities. The objectives of this reform are to encourage venture capital in the agricultural sector, ease limits on stock ownership, and curb excessive price volatility.[288]

Infrastructure Development by Modi Government to Expand Modernization

In order to help with economic expansion, communication, and development, the Modi government has launched a number of infrastructure programs and projects targeted at updating and extending the nation's infrastructure networks. These regulations span a range of industries, such as those related to transportation, energy, urban planning, internet connectivity, and more. The objective is to raise the standard of infrastructure in a number of industries, promote economic growth, and increase living conditions for people all around the nation.

Some key infrastructure policies and initiatives introduced by the Modi government include:

National Smart Cities Mission: By enhancing infrastructure for urban conveyance, disposal of waste, and technology adoption, the Smart Cities Mission, which was introduced in 2015, seeks to transform 100 chosen communities across India into smart cities. The National Smart Cities Mission is an urban rehabilitation initiative by the Government of India with the goal of creating sustainable, smart cities across the nation. The initiative originally targeted 100 cities, and the projects had completion window from 2019–2023. As of 2019, 11% of all projects were effectively completed. 3577 operations out of a total of 6939 submitted proposals on March 2022.

An adequate water supply, an uninterrupted supply of electricity, adequate water and sanitation, which includes solid waste management, effective urban mobility and public transportation, accessible housing, particularly to those with limited incomes, robust internet access and electronic commerce, good governance, particularly e-Governance and citizen participation, sustainable environment, protection and safety foremost women, children, and the elderly, and a smart city's core infrastructure would include all of these amenities.[289]

Pradhan Mantri Awas Yojana (PMAY) - Urban: PMAY-U aims to give urban disadvantaged people access to affordable housing. The program's main goals are house construction and infrastructure development for urban housing. The plan applies to the entire country's urban region, comprising Notified Planning/ Development Areas and all statutory towns as of the Census of 2011. The four verticals that make up the implementation of the program are Beneficiary Led Construction (BLC) and Affordable Housing Partnership (AHP).

The Pradhan Mantri Awas Yojana (PMAY) - Gramin (Rural) is a landmark housing initiative started by the Indian government, which is led by Prime Minister Narendra Modi. This program's main goal is to deliver "Housing for All" in remote regions, with the intention of giving pucca (permanent) dwellings to qualified rural households. To help those who are eligible in rural regions build pucca homes with the amenities they need, PMAY-Gramin offers financial support. The program targets particular beneficiary groups, such as homeless households, those residing in kutcha (temporary) housing, members of Scheduled Castes (SCs), Members of Scheduled Tribes (STs), and various other vulnerable populations.

Bharatmala Pariyojana: Using new, improved highways and road networks, this initiative for road and highway development seeks to improve connectivity throughout the nation. A nationwide highway development project is called the Bharatmala Project. It will be made easier to travel between the Char Dhams of Kedarnath, Badrinath, Yamunotri, and Gangotri.[290]

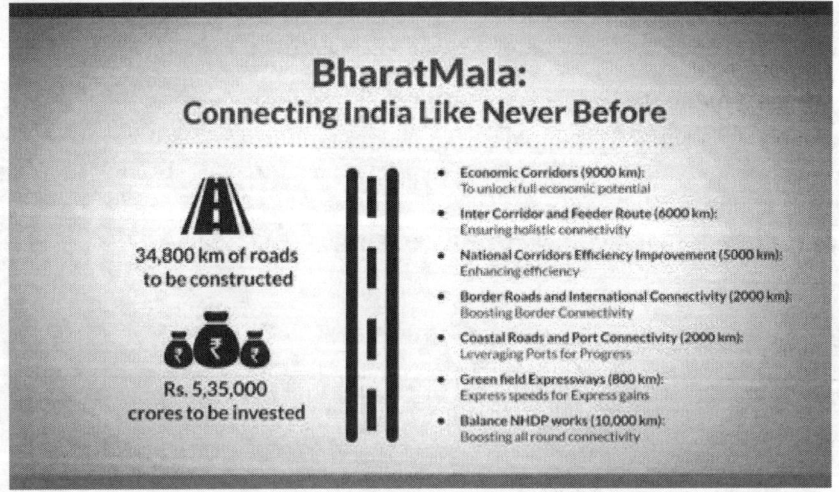

Sagarmala Project

The Sagarmala plan aims to improve port connectivity, upgrade ports, and support coastal economic zones through developing the nation's coastal and naval infrastructure. The Union Cabinet adopted the Sagarmala Programme in 2015 with the goal of developing the port infrastructure holistically along the 7,516 kilometers of coastline through technological advancement and automated processes. The Sagarmala Programmer's goal is to lower logistics costs for domestic and EXIM (Export-Import) trade with a minimum investment in infrastructure. By 2025, Sagarmala could increase India's exports of goods to 110 billion USD and add approximately ten million new jobs. With potential airline operators, the Ministry has begun the ambitious Sagarmala Seaplane Services (SSPS) Project. These are the four main categories of Sagarmala are:

- Framework for Coastal Infrastructure

- Coastal Tourism

- A coastal industrial building

- Incorporation of Coastal Communities [291]

Udaan Scheme: Udaan promotes accessible and inexpensive airfare to unserved and underutilized airports in an effort to improve regional air connectivity. The Regional Connectivity Scheme (RCS), a project to upgrade underserved air connections, It is an airport area development program of the Indian government. Its objectives are to lower the cost of air travel and advance India's economic growth.

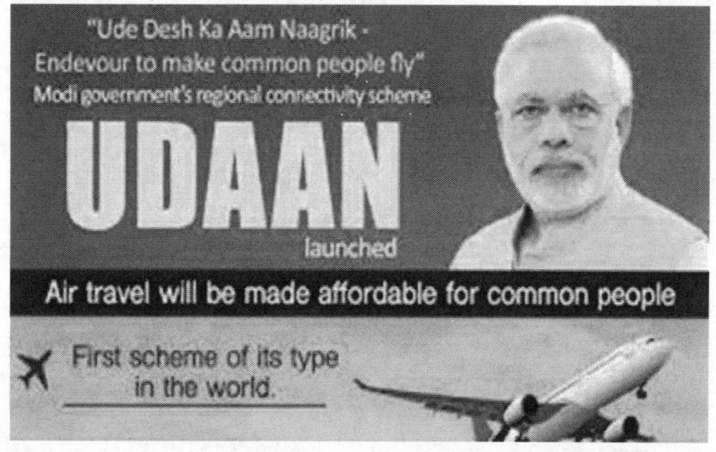

The scheme has been implemented in five phases so far:

36 new airports were opened as part of **UDAN 1.0**, while 5 airline firms received funding for 128 flight routes for 70 locations.

Utilization of a helicopter was discovered using **UDAN 2.0.** 73 subserviced airports were reported in 2018.

UDAN 3.0: Several modifications were made, including tourist routes, seaplane connections between water aerodromes, and routes under the "UDAN" brand in the North-East.

UDAN 4.0: In 2020, 78 additional routes were added. The Lakshadweep islands of Kavaratti, Agatti, and Minicoy was additionally be interconnected by new routes during this phase.

UDAN 4.1 consists of connecting regional airports and developing specialized seaplane and helicopter services. Sagarmala seaplane services have also announced new routes.[292]

Pradhan Mantri Gram Sadak Yojana (PMGSY): With the help of all-weather roads, PMGSY hopes to improve rural connection and ease the flow of both people and commodities. A nationwide program called Pradhan Mantri Gram Sadak Yojana (PMGSY) aims to connect India's unconnected villages with good roads. As of December 2017, 82% of the 178,000 (1.7 lakh) communities with populations over 500 in the plains and over 250 plains in the hills.

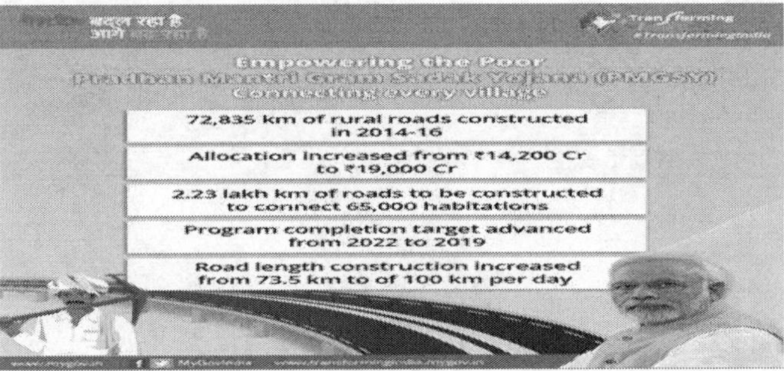

AMRUT, the Atal Mission for Rejuvenation and Urban Transformation to enhance the quality of life in cities, AMRUT focuses on providing essential urban services like water distribution, waste products, and transportation in cities. The Government of India's Atal Mission for Rejuvenation and Urban Transformation (AMRUT) was introduced in June 2015 by Prime Minister Narendra Modi.

The Atal Mission for Rejuvenation and Urban Transformation (AMRUT) aims to: (i) guarantee that every home has access to a water source with a guaranteed supply of water and a sewer connection; (ii) improve the amenity value of cities by creating greenery and well-maintained open spaces (such as parks); and (iii) minimize pollution by switching to public transportation or building facilities for non-motorized transport (such as walking and cycling).

The following advancements have been accomplished under this program, according to information provided by the Ministry of Housing and Urban Affairs (MoHUA) in June 2021:

- 1,240 MLD worth of sewage treatment plant (STP) capacity has been built, and of that, 907 MLD is being recycled or reused. Another with a 4,800 MLD STP potential is in the works.

- Water pump energy audits have been carried out accomplished in 396 cities throughout 27 States and UTs. The Online Building Permission System (OBPS), which seamlessly integrates with internal and external agencies, has been made functional in 2,465 towns, including 452 AMRUT cities. India's ranking for ease of doing business (EODB) in terms of construction licenses increased to 27 from 181 during 2018.[293]

PM Gati Shakti

In order to accelerate Indian economic growth, Narendra Modi, the country's prime minister, unveiled this project on August 15, 2021. To offer multimodal connection infrastructure to all of India's economic zones, the plan was introduced on October 13, 2021, and it was approved by the Cabinet Committee on Economic Affairs on October 21, 2021. Breaking down inter-ministerial silos and integrating the preparation of construction endeavors is the main goal of this program. The plan aims to improve coordination between the many ministries participating in these projects and streamline the execution of infrastructure enhancements across the nation.[294]

In the budget of 2022, Finance Minister Nirmala Sitaraman mentioned the program and said that the master plan's cornerstone would be world-class, contemporary infrastructure and logistical synergy among all means of transportation for people.

Objectives of PM Gati Shakti Project:

• To improve supply chains and lower the cost of logistics, which will increase the competitiveness of Indian products on the world market.

• The investment from around the globe for enhancing the nation's infrastructure.

• To deal with the matter of high supply chain and logistics costs, which in India account for almost 12% of GDP, vs the worldwide median of 8%.

• To decrease the underutilization of the waterways, air, and rail networks and the undue reliance on road transportation.

• To facilitate greater cooperation between various ministries, states, and divisions and to concentrate construction efforts along designated corridors.

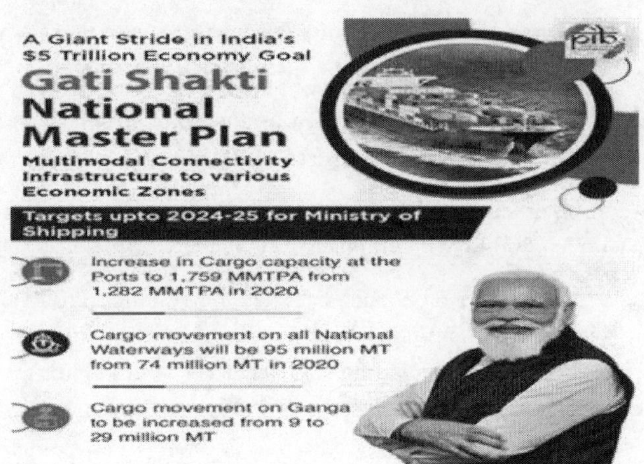

By integrating together 16 ministries, including roads and railroads, the Gati Shakti digital platform aims to consolidate the scheduling and implementation of infrastructure connectivity projects. It aims to address persistent problems such fragmented planning, a lack of standards, obstructions, and the timely production and usage of infrastructure capacities. The portal offers more than 200 layers of geographic data, including details on the state of the infrastructure, enabling multiple government agencies to monitor the advancement of many different initiatives.

National Infrastructure Pipeline (NIP)

Over a five-year period, the NIP plans to invest in a variety of infrastructure projects to promote economic growth and open up job possibilities. The NIP is a project that will build top-notch infrastructure all around the nation to raise everyone's standard of living. For the Indian economy, the program will improve project planning and draw from domestic as well as foreign direct investments.[295]

The NIP will meet every need that is necessary for India to reach its goal of having a $5 trillion GDP by its fiscal year 2025. The initiatives will include both social and economic infrastructure. To create the National Infrastructure Pipeline (NIP) for every single one of the fiscal years running from 2019–20 to 2024–25, a task force was established. Around 70% of India's estimated capital investment on infrastructure is expected to come from industries like energy (24%), roads (19%), urban (16%), and railways (13%) between the fiscal years 2020 and 2025.[296]

Jal Jeevan Mission: Every rural household will have access to tap water as part of the goal, which also encourages the development of water infrastructure and water conservation. By 2024, every residence in rural India is expected to have access to Jal Jeevan Mission's particular household tap connections with safe and sufficient drinking water. The program will also incorporate upstream conservation efforts as requirements, such as water saving, rainwater collection, and replenishment and recycling with grey water management.[297]

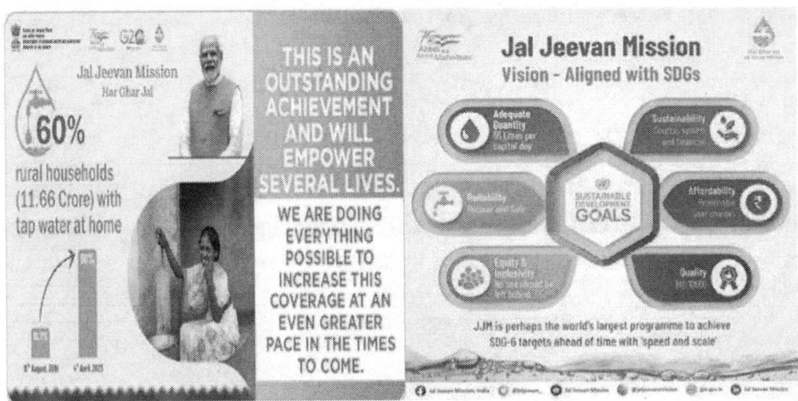

Under JJM, the following elements are supported:

The National Waterways Act, 2016: In order to improve logistics and transportation productivity through inland water transport, the legislation aims to develop and control the national waterways. The National Waterways Act, 2016, which went into effect on April 12, 2016, designated 111 waterways, comprising 5 already-existing and 106 new ones, as National Waterways (NWs) in order to encourage Inland Water Transport (IWT) in the nation. 25 NWs have been identified by the Inland Waterways Authority of India (IWAI) as viable for cargo/passenger movement based on the results of techno-economic feasibility and Detailed Project Reports (DPRs) of NWs. These 25 NWs are listed at Annex-1. Out of the 25 potential NWs, development operations have been started in the first 13 NWs.[298]

Environment Friendly Policies Introduced by Modi Government

To address environmental issues, encourage sustainable development, and protect natural resources, a number of environmental statutes and bills were proposed or revised in India under the Modi government. Here are some key environmental laws and acts passed by the Modi administration:

The National Clean Air Program: NCAP is a comprehensive program that was introduced in 2019 with the goal of reducing air pollution in Indian cities and regions. In many polluted cities, it establishes goals for lowering particulate matter (PM10 and PM2.5) and other air pollutants.

Rules for the Management of Plastic Waste, 2016: These regulations were developed to deal with the nation's mounting plastic waste issue. They seek to develop Extended Producer Responsibility (EPR) for the management of plastic waste, encourage recycling, and lessen the production of plastic trash.

The E-Waste (Management) Rules, 2016, have been enacted for handling electronic debris efficiently, including e-waste recycling and disposal of electronic products in a way that is sustainable.

The Wetlands (Conservation and Management) Rules, 2017, were passed to protect and manage wetlands, vital ecosystems that are crucial to the provision of numerous ecological services.

The 2019 Notification for the **Coastal Regulation Zone (CRZ):** To safeguard coastal ecosystems and control activity in coastal areas to stop environmental damage, the CRZ notification was modified.

The CAMPA Act (Compensatory Afforestation Fund Management and Planning Authority) was updated in 2016 to use resources efficiently raised for compensatory afforestation and wildlife conservation.

The Indian Forest (Amendment) Act, 2017: This amendment sought to simplify the process of transferring forest land for developmental projects while ensuring appropriate compensatory afforestation.

Under the Modi administration, some of the important environmentally friendly changes and initiatives have included:

International Solar Alliance (ISA): Under Prime Minister Modi's direction, India was instrumental in the establishment of the ISA in 2015. The ISA is a group of nations that wants to encourage the use of solar energy and lessen reliance on fossil fuels.[299]

Swachh Bharat Abhiyan or the Clean India Mission: A national initiative to promote cleanliness, the Swachh Bharat Abhiyan aims to improve sanitation, waste disposal, and hygiene standards throughout the nation.

National Clean Air Programme (NCAP): To address air pollution in metropolitan areas and establish goals to lower particle matter (PM) levels, the government introduced the NCAP in 2019.

Management of Plastic Waste: The Modi administration has taken action to reduce the problem of waste made of plastic with programs that include the Swachhata Hi Seva programme and by encouraging the usage of substitute materials.

Renewable Energy Promotion: To lessen reliance on fossil fuels, the government has established goals for the production of renewable energy and is currently proactively promoting the development of wind and solar energy projects.

Green India Mission (GIM): To lessen the effects of global warming and encourage the preservation of biodiversity, the GIM seeks to increase the number of trees and forests in the nation.

National Mission for Clean Ganga (Namami Gange): The Ganga River, a source of life for many people in India, is the focus of the Namami Gange initiative, which aims to clean and revitalize it.

Conservation of Wildlife

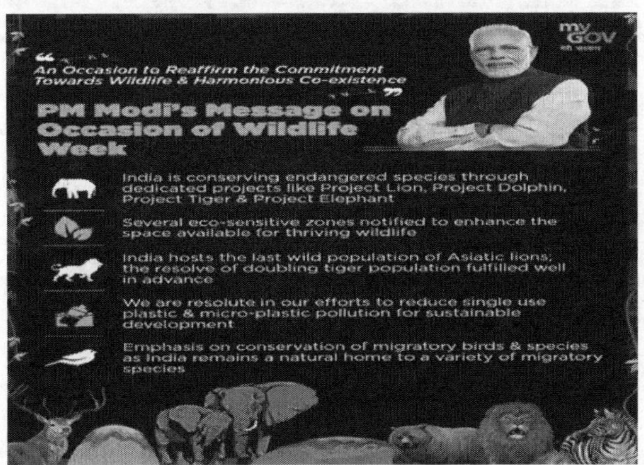

Modi Government promotes Cultural Diversity

To encourage India's rich cultural diversity and develop a sense of oneness among its population, the Modi government has launched a number of cultural integration programs. These programs seek to promote inclusivity and sense of national pride while preserving India's cultural traditions, heritage, languages, and art. Listed below are some cultural integration programs implemented by the Modi administration:

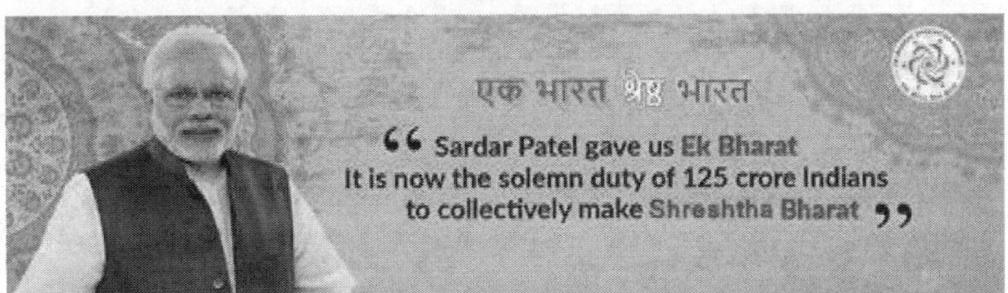

Ek Bharat Shreshtha Bharat: The project, which was started in 2015, aims to facilitate cross-cultural interactions and exchanges amongst residents of various Indian states and union territory areas, to foster greater understanding and appreciation across states, cultural gatherings, festivals, workshops, and other. The states engage in activities to foster a sustained and cohesive cultural connection in the fields of sports, culture, traditions, music, tourism, gastronomy, language learning, and sharing best practices, among others.[300]

National Cultural Heritage Mission (Puratattva): The ultimate objective of this initiative is to safeguard and encourage cultural heritage, which includes traditional arts, historical places, and archaeological sites.

Adopt a Heritage Scheme: The "Adopt a Heritage Scheme" is a novel initiative of the Ministry of Tourism in close cooperation with the Ministry of Culture and the Archaeological Survey of India (ASI) to adopt historical attractions, landmarks, and museums with the goal to support their maintenance, conservation, and development.

List of 10 Monuments adopted under the Adopt a Heritage scheme:

- Red Fort
- Gandikota Fort
- Area surrounding Gangotri Temple and Trail to Gaumukh
- Mt. Stok Kangri Trek in Ladakh
- Jantar Mantar
- Suraj Kund
- Qutub Minar
- Ajanta Caves
- Leh Palace
- Hazara Rama Temple in Hampi[301]

Rashtriya Sanskriti Mahotsav: This cultural festival emphasizes traditional music, dance, artwork, crafts, and delicacies from several Indian areas to honor the diversity of Indian culture. Every year, Rashtriya Sanskriti Mahotsav is held in several Indian states to encourage national cohesion and integrity. The Rashtriya Sanskriti Mahotsav promises to be an ode to India's artistic legacy as well as a celebration of the country's cultural diversity.

It is an exceptional opportunity for different people to gather together to participate into the account of best cultural traditions of India.[302]

Promotion of Yoga and Ayurveda: The entire world commemorates the International Day of Yoga on June 21 to draw attention to India's historic yoga tradition. Ayurveda is additional indigenous medical system that the government supports in order to promote holistic health and wellness. The 'Project Collaboration Agreement' was signed in Geneva on May 13, 2016 by Ajit M. Sharan, Secretary of the Ministry of AYUSH, and Marie Kieny, Assistant Director General of Health Systems and Innovations, WHO.

Promotion of Indian Language

By fostering linguistic diversity through projects like "Bhasha Sangam," the government promotes the usage and maintenance of Indian languages. The Ministry of Education has launched a program called Bhasha Sangam as part of Ek Bharat Shreshtha Bharat to teach the fundamentals of 22 Indian languages. The goal is for individuals to learn the fundamentals of a conversation in an Indian language in addition to their native tongue. Initiatives started under Bhasha Sangam are: [303]

- A program for schoolchildren that is made accessible through 22 books, ePathshala, and DIKSHA
- MyGov and a startup called Multibhashi collaborated to create the Bhasha Sangam mobile app.

Defence and Military Strength under Modi Government

Under the Modi administration, India's military strategy has helped to improve national security, equip the armed forces, and enhance India's standing on worldwide level.

Modernization of Armed Forces: The government providing financing for the procurement of cutting-edge defense technologies, tools, and platforms the highest priority in its plan for modernizing the military's arsenal.

Rafale Aircraft Deal: The acquisition of 36 Rafale fighter planes with France's Dassault Aviation was one of the most famous defense transactions. The Indian Air Force's operational capacity was to be strengthened as a consequence of this deal.

S-400 Air Defense System Deal: India and Russia entered into an acquisition arrangement for the advanced S-400 Triumf air defense missile system. The goal of this partnership is to improve India's air defense competence.

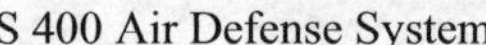

S 400 Air Defense System

Apache and chinook Helicopter

Apache and Chinook Helicopter: For the purpose of enhancing its rotary-wing capabilities, India procured CH-47F Chinook heavy-lift aircraft and AH-64E Apache helicopters from the US.

Aatmanirbhar Bharat in Defence: The government has set a high priority on sovereignty in the development of technology for defense whilst encouraging indigenous production.

S

K9 Vajra Guns

K9 Vajra Guns: An autonomous howitzer system called the K9 Vajra was created for the Indian Army. The objective is to strengthen the Indian armed forces mechanized and armored divisions with artillery. A South Korean defense firm, Hanwha Techwin, and Larsen & Toubro (L&T) collaborated to develop the K9 Vajra. The K9 Vajra howitzer was purchased for the purpose of the India's initiatives to upgrade the Indian Army's artillery capability.

Strategic Partnerships: The Strategic Partnership (SP) model, encompassing partnerships between Indian private firms and foreign original equipment suppliers (OEMs), was established by the government for the objective of manufacturing defense equipment. The Indian government devised the "Strategic Partnership (SP) Model" as a framework for policy that promotes the capabilities of the domestic defense sector by stimulating interaction between Indian private enterprises and international Original Equipment Manufacturers (OEMs) for the military industry.[304]

New Version of OFB: To boost the utility, capacity, and output of the defense commercial businesses, the Indian government has set an enormous premium on the advancement of the Ordnance Factory Board (OFB). The primary organization in charge of making weapons, ammunition, and defense gear for the Indian armed forces is the OFB. With the goal to attain autonomy, meet the armed forces' defense needs, and lessen the reliance on imports, OFB needs to get reformed.

Appointment of Chief Defense of Staff: For the Indian armed forces, selection of the Chief of Defence Staff (CDS) is a momentous and crucial choice. In order to enhance collaboration and synergy. between the Army, Navy, and Air Force—India's three main armed services—the CDS position was established. A big step toward improving India's military capabilities while encouraging better and more effective coordination among the military forces is the establishment of the position of Chief of Defence Staff.

Women's Power in Army: In the Army, there are 557 female officers with permanent commissions. For the first time ever, 83 female soldiers were named to the Army's Military Police Corps. Five female officers were promoted to colonels. Abhilasha Barak, a captain, was the first female combat aviator. Captain Bhawna Kasturi received assistance from the military service corps during the 2019 Republic Day parade.

INS Vikrant: India's defense capabilities have improved substantially with the completion of the INS Vikrant. It is India's first manufactured aircraft carrier warship. Under the Modi administration, the building of INS Vikrant represents a turning point in the nation's attempts to bolster its maritime security and increase its naval power. Additionally, INS Vikrant, as part of the Indian Navy's fleet, paves the way for fleet technological advancement and extension in the future, to make sure the state's naval capabilities remain up with changing geographical conditions and concerns.

Surgical strikes: An armed forces tactic in which an accurate target gets attacked to achieve an operational purpose whilst reducing collateral damage. There have been two significant examples of surgical strikes utilized by the Indian armed forces in response to security threats during the term of the Modi government.

September 2016 Surgical Strike (Uri Attack): The Indian Army deployed surgical strikes across the Line of Control (LoC) in Pakistan-administered Kashmir in retaliation for a fatal terrorist attack on an Indian Army post in Uri, Jammu and Kashmir, on September 18, 2016, which claimed the lives of 19 Indian soldiers. The attacks aimed terrorist launch pads and severely damaged terrorist organizations. The primary objective of the operation was to outright denounce global terror.

February 2019 Surgical Strike (Pulwama Attack): Suicide bombing that killed over 40 people on February 14 in Pulwama, Jammu and Kashmir, which was directed against an entourage of Indian auxiliary soldiers, the Indian Air Force carried out airstrikes on Pakistan's Balakot region on February 26. Terrorist training sites were the focus of these airstrikes. The main goal of this operation was to eradicate possible risks preemptively.

National War Memorial: On February 25, 2019, the Modi administration formally dedicated the National War Memorial in India. The memorial commemorates the bravery and contributions made to India's defense by the troops who dedicated their lives while serving the country. In the centre of New Delhi, next to India Gate, is the location of National War Memorial. It serves as a principal site where Indian soldiers who have died are commemorated. The Army, Navy, Air Force, and Paramilitary forces are the primary branches of the Indian Armed Forces that have been symbolized by the memorial's architecture.

The memorial's main pillar is called the Amar Chakra. It symbolizes the soldiers' eternal souls who gave the ultimate sacrifice for the nation. The Param Vir Chakra, Maha Vir Chakra, and Vir Chakra are the highest gallantry medals in India. The Braveheart Gallery pays tribute to the sacrifices made by the warriors who were awarded these decorations. The names of troops who died in combat are listed on the Wall of Valor, along with information about the operations they took part in. The National War Memorial is a silent sentiment of a nation’s gratitude towards its Bravehearts. The National War Memorial's construction highlighted the government's dedication to honoring the efforts and achievements of the armed services while also marking the brave warriors' place in Indian history.[305]

CoWIN: Strength to Control Global Pandemic in India

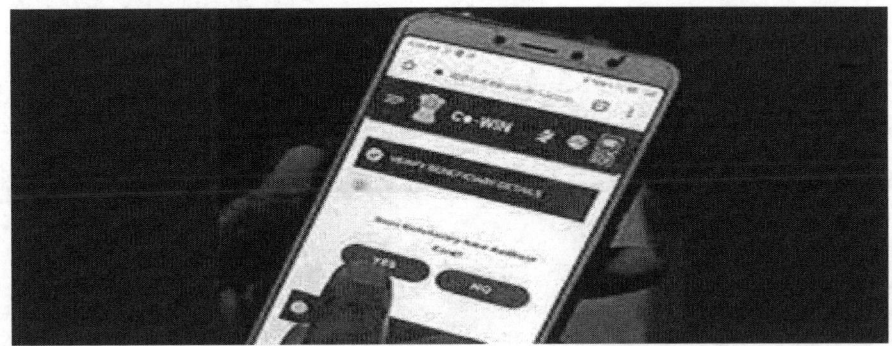

The *"COVID Vaccine Intelligence Network," or "Co-WIN,"* is a crucial component of India's COVID-19 immunization campaign. The Indian government created this cutting-edge digital platform to organize and streamline the process of handling of COVID-19 vaccines throughout the nation. The important accomplishment in the nation's battle against the epidemic, Co-WIN performed a crucial part in the vaccine campaign.

India's impressive vaccination campaign showed accomplishments, including the accurate policy implementation of vaccine doses for millions and demonstrate the effectiveness of Co-WIN. Co-WIN was crucial in expediting the procedure, providing transparency, good governance in crucial times, and avoiding vaccination treatment and dissemination failures. While Co-WIN is a remarkable success story, it's crucial to remember that India's fight against COVID-19 also includes a number of other components, including workers in primary healthcare of Central & States Management, Services in Regions & Local regions, public cooperation, and international collaborations. Co-WIN was one of these initiatives, and together they have helped India manage and lessen the effects of the pandemic. Most significant was the Vande Bharat Mission "Air Bubble" Civilian Evacuation Mission.[306]

Key features and contributions of Co-WIN in India's COVID-19 response:

Vaccination Registration and Scheduling: Using a web-based interface and smartphone application, Co-WIN allowed people to sign up for the COVID-19 immunization. Users had the option of choosing the best time for their immunization appointments.

Dosage	*Vaccination (% of entitled Population Vaccinated)*
Partly Vaccinated	*1, 025, 789, 302 (94.61)*
Fully Vaccinated	*952, 033, 158 (87.61)*
Preventive (Booster) Dosage	*228, 593, 024*

Source: Covid Dashboard [307]

Real-Time Data Management: The technology made it possible to track vaccination coverage, availability, and distribution in real time at the union, state, and local levels.

Co-WIN created electronic vaccination certificates for everyone who received the vaccine, offering a safe and convenient record of a person's immunization status.

Supply Chain Management: The online system assisted in managing the complete vaccination supply chain, from distribution and administration to storage and procurement, resulting in a smooth and well-planned procedure.

Co-WIN assisted in the identification and prioritization of several target populations for immunization, including healthcare professionals, frontline workers, and particular generations.

Data confidentiality and Protection: The platform protected the privacy and security of user health data while enabling authorized workers to access necessary data for management and monitoring.

Scalability and Accessibility: Co-WIN is digital, it is scalable and accessible, allowing it to manage an extensive and varied population across the nation.

Population Consciousness: The platform also aided in raising awareness among the general public about vaccinations, advantages, and significance of vaccination.

Vande Bharat Mission

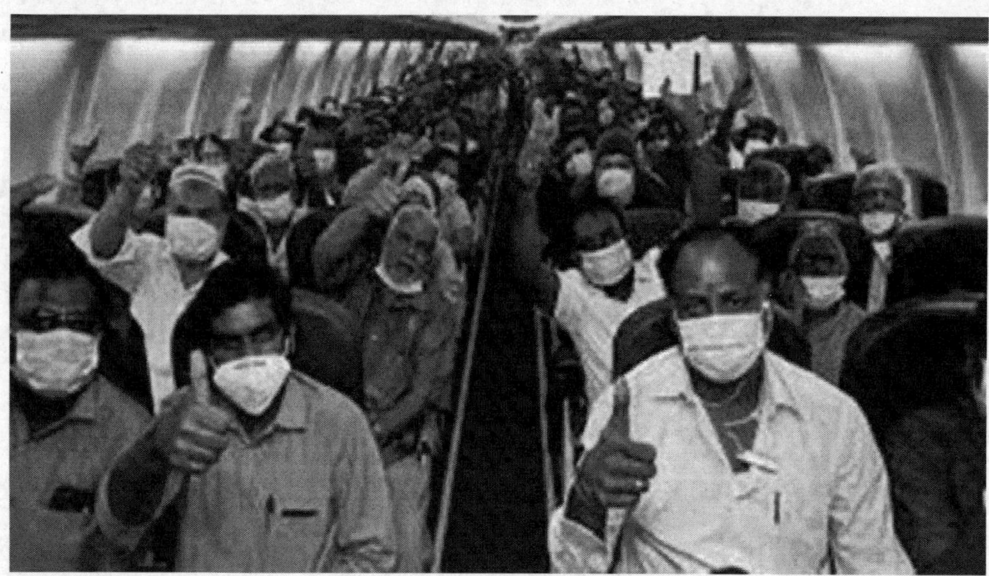

The Vande Bharat Mission: which was introduced in May 2020, is the nation's largest-ever repatriation effort. It attempts to repatriate Indian nationals who are stuck abroad as a result of travel prohibitions and lockdowns. In order to evacuate Indian nationals from various locations, special aircraft must be organized. Flights conducted by Air India alongside other Indian airlines have formed for the operation.

Air Bubble Arrangements: Air bubble partnerships are intergovernmental pacts that permit only a certain amount of cross-border travel. Flights between the participating nations are made possible by these agreements, subject to specific restrictions and safety guidelines. Air bubble agreements seek to reduce the risk of COVID-19 spreading while partially restoring international travel. According to the regulations of the individual nations, passengers flying on air bubble arrangements typically have to follow strict testing and quarantine standards.[308]

Government Ensured Policies & Services to manage Covid

In order to combat the COVID-19 pandemic, the Central Government of India launched a number of policies and actions, which included health, economy, and social efforts to lessen the virus's effects. These programs and initiatives were an aspect of the government's comprehensive reaction to the epidemic, which had three main objectives: to protect public health, offer economic relief, and promote social well-being. The following are some of the crucial policies and actions:

Nationwide Lockdown: To stop the virus's spread, the authorities enacted a lockdown nationwide in March 2020. To combine the requirements for the economy and society with health concerns, the lockdown was gradually eased in phases. Announcement of the "total lockdown," as Prime Minister Narendra Modi called it, was declared on March 24, 2020, and would last for 21 days. The initial timeframe for the shutdown was from March 25 to April 14, 2020. The statewide shutdown was a dramatic and audacious move to deal with the problems of the pandemic. Its goals were to boost the potential to conduct testing and medical treatment, avoid the healthcare system from becoming overburdened, and slow the virus' spread.

The main goal of the closure was to stop the COVID-19 transmission chain by limiting social connections and forbidding meetings.

Restrictions: Companies, educational facilities, public transit, public spots and the majority of government buildings were shut down as a result of the lockdown. Movement was banned save for necessities like buying food and medications, and people were told to stay at home.

Impact: The economy, those who work for a living and other industries were all significantly affected by the lockdown. Those in vulnerable demographics, such as migratory workers faced difficulties.

Phases: Following the original lockdown for 21 days; the authorities modified and gradually prolonged it. In certain regions, the lockdown had progressively eased, but in zones of containment and areas with a high COVID-19 caseload, stringent safeguards were still in place.

Coordination with States: Although the national lockdown was declared by the federal government, state and local administrations were in charge of enforcing it. This made administration possible according to local conditions and needs.

Social Welfare Initiatives: Throughout the period of lockdown, the government started a number of social welfare programs, including the distribution of food grains, cash transfers, and assistance to vulnerable groups.

Phases of "Unlock": As the lockdown deepened, governments instituted "unlock" phases to progressively relax restrictions and restart the economy. The COVID-19 circumstance determine the implementation of lockdown unlock phase.

Testing and Tracing: The Central Government tried to increase the capacity for COVID-19 testing and track down contacts of positive cases. Under the Modi administration, monitoring and identification have been crucial parts of India's COVID-19 pandemic response plan. To increase testing and improve contact tracking, the government has put in place a number of initiatives to increase Testing Capacity. The government vastly increased the nation's COVID-19 testing capacity in numerous states and districts. Testing stations, comprising both RT-PCR and fast antigen tests.[309]

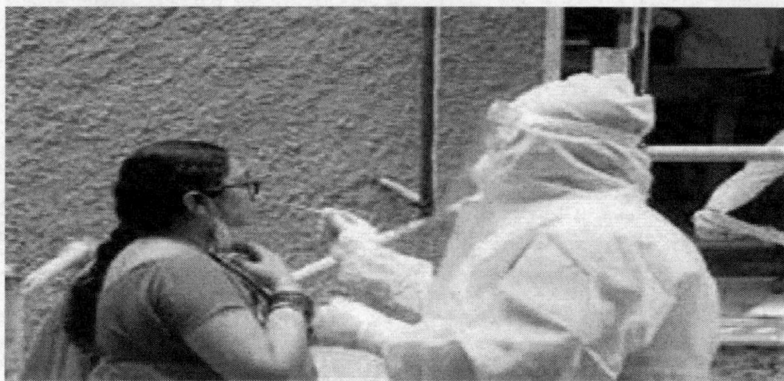

Jan Aushadhi Kendras: The accessibility of medication for patients throughout the pandemic was ensured by providing necessary medications at reasonable prices. A program was started by the Indian government to encourage the general public, especially the economically underprivileged groups of society, to have access to affordable generic medications. Although this effort was initiated prior to the Modi administration, it has been extensively promoted and developed throughout his tenure. Aushadhi Kendras make access to essential medical care less expensive for the general people by offering top-notch generic medications at much lower prices.[310]

COVID-19 App: The Aarogya Setu and UMANG apps were introduced by the government to assist citizens in determining their COVID-19 risk and to encourage contact tracing. In order to address many facets of the COVID-19 pandemic, such as public health, information distribution, and contact tracing, Modi government introduced a number of smartphone applications. The purpose of these apps was to inform the public, monitor the virus's transmission, and encourage safety precautions. Aarogya Setu is an application for mobile devices created to assist citizens in determining their risk of exposure to COVID-19.

COVID-19 Vaccination Drive: A considerable segment of the population was to be immunized as part of the government's extensive COVID-19 vaccination effort in order to develop immunity to the virus.

Economic Assistance Packages In order to assist people, businesses, and different sectors affected by the pandemic-induced lockdowns, the Central Government offered many economic relief packages. A comprehensive economic plan called "Self-Reliant India" was introduced to support diverse industries and encourage self-reliance.

PM CARES Fund: To provide financial support and aid COVID-19 relief efforts, the government launched the Prime Minister's Citizen Support and Relief Fund in Emergency Situations. The Prime Minister's Citizen Assistance and Relief in Emergency Situations Fund, or PM CARES Fund, is a public charitable trust that was founded by the Indian government under the direction of Prime Minister Narendra Modi. The fund was established to offer support and help during emergencies, especially during the COVID-19 epidemic. The PM CARES Fund was established to accept charitable contributions from private citizens, groups, and businesses in order to aid the government's fight against the pandemic and aid people afflicted by it.[311]

Pradhan Mantri Garib Kalyan Yojana: This program was designed to help disadvantaged groups in society during the epidemic by giving them free food and monetary transfers. This program aims to offer urgent assistance to the most vulnerable members of society, such as low-income people, migratory workers, and women. It featured programs like the free distribution of food grains, payment transfers, and coverage for insurance.

Unlock Phases: To strike a compromise between the necessity for economic recovery and worries about public health, the gradual reopening of commercial and social activity was implemented. Unlocking lockdown phases were introduced in stages, with recommendations and choices based on whether the pandemic situation was changing in various areas.

Services To Local Government During Covid

Both the Central and State Governments in India collaborated with local administrations (municipalities, panchayats, etc.) to provide a range of services and support during the COVID-19 pandemic. In order to address public health requirements, guarantee basic services, and manage the socioeconomic effects of the pandemic, various support services were provided. Collaboration across all tiers of government was essential to successfully addressing the problems brought on by the pandemic. The central government as well as the state government worked with local governments in the following ways:

Measures for public health:

• The federal and state governments gave local government instructions and tools for putting public health measures like lockdowns, confinement areas, and social estrangement procedures into practice.

• The health departments coordinated testing, tracking contacts, and isolation activities for several levels.

Medical Infrastructure and Supplies:

• In order to establish specialized COVID-19 healthcare facilities, containment centers, and testing facilities, the Central and State Governments provided assistance to local governments.

• Local healthcare facilities received medical supplies, such as personal protective equipment (PPE), masks, ventilators, and medications. Included in this were containment plans and guidelines on a variety of topics, such as travel, behavioral and psychosocial health, surveillance, laboratory support, hospital infrastructure, clinical management, rational use of Personal Protective Equipment (PPE), etc., as well as motivational advice for medical staff. [312]

Awareness Campaigns:

• Every branch of government worked together to start awareness efforts about COVID-19 prevention, proper sanitation, and safety precautions.

• A communication campaign that is conducted through venues like markets, train stations and anganwadi centers will be useful for the campaign.

• All participants will make a Covid-19 pledge. Provincial and UT departments as well as central ministries will carry out a coordinated action strategy.

Relief Measures:

• The federal and state governments established relief programs for disadvantaged groups, including food distribution, cash aid, and basic necessities. These projects were monitored and implemented with assistance from local governments.

• The federal and state government's unveiled rescue measures for the economy. Local governments helped in beneficiary selection, program implementation, and financial aid distribution.

Coordination and Reporting:

• For accurate case reporting, monitoring the application of policies, and suggestions from the ground, both the central and state governments utilized local administrations.

Anubhav

Anubhav Portal is a place for retirees to treasure memories from their working lives and direct improvements to internal procedures by the Department of Pension & Pensioners' welfare under the Ministry of Public and personnel grievances & Pensions, Anubhav is a dream pursuit of the honorable Chief Executive. It offers a podium to retired workers to communicate their experiences working with government and provide a few key recommendations for motivating the existing personnel. An important initiative by the government is the Pension MMP, which enables retirees to discuss their professional experiences and make improvements to many areas. Anubhav is a website where former government employees can share their experiences with working for the government. This technique aids in fostering a feeling of belonging and happiness in the participants.

Objectives and Mission

It aims to give departing Central Government personnel a forum to highlight their exemplary service. The retiring employee would feel satisfied, and it would also serve as inspiration for current workers. Additionally, this would be a fantastic opportunity to recruit departing employees to make voluntary contributions to nation-building after retirement. Along with their biographical information, Anubhav records the field experiences, types of experiences, skills, and suggestions of his staff. The Head of Office evaluates these write-ups before sending them to the Head of Department for final evaluation. Retiree suggestions are forwarded to the relevant organization. Before the assessment, retiring staff can revise their write-ups using PAN and OTP, build a database of noteworthy, ideas and professional experiences and channel the personnel of retiring workers to create the country. Initiatives like ANUBHAV make possible for Ministries/Departments to implement important steps while weighing helpful and suggest relevant recommendations.

The following features are available to retirees and pensioners: uploading images; uploading articles and suggestions in PDF and audio formats; and editing articles and suggestions before publication.

Awards Program

Along with other officials, the recipient was present with the Honorable Minister. Jitendra Singh

In order to promote the submission of writings by retired government employees, an annual awards program was launched in 2016. Dr. Jitendra Singh, Union Minister of State (Independent Charge), Development of North-Eastern Region (DoNER), MoS PMO, Personnel, Public Grievances & Pensions, Atomic Energy and Space, presented awards to six pensioners at the third Anubhav Awards Ceremony on September 18, 2018.

Implementation

Department/Ministry on boarding HoO and HoD of the Ministries/departments have been given login credentials. Additionally, a department can create logins for any affiliated or subordinate offices. Boarding new hires after retirement. Employees who are retiring don't need a login name or password to upload write-ups. Using PAN and OTP, they can edit their writing before publication.

Helpdesk

To offer regular support, telephonic and email-based helpdesks have also been established.

Procedure

1. The retiring staff can provide a write-up of up to 5000 words, as well as any necessary attachments. To make sure the submission is in the proper format, the Head of Office will verify the input before submitting the results to the administrative head or authority assigned to this task.

2. The retired person's article will be printed after it has been properly verified by the relevant organization.

3. By clicking the "Anubhav" link on the website **http://persmin.gov.in/pension**.asp, retiring personnel, administrative offices, and people can access the facility. By providing the necessary information, employees will be able to provide personal information as well as a write-up. Administrative offices are able to log in and process the supplied inputs. The top executives of offices will confirm that that staff member is a legitimate worker under their supervision and that the write-up supplied complies with all requirements.

4. If he is satisfied, he will send the write-up to the Head of Department (HOD) who is the designated authority. Before "approving," the designated representative Head of Department (HOD) can verify that the submission is appropriate. The article can then be "Published" in a formal manner. People can examine the documents that have been published under **"Anubhav"** and provide comments on them.[313]

References

1. Maheshwari, S R., (2012). Indian Administration, Orient Blackswan, New Delhi
2. Laxmikanth, M., (2022). Indian Polity, McGraw Hill, New Delhi
3. Maheshwari, SR., (2012). Indian Administration, Orient Blackswan, New Delhi
4. Ignou Book, Chapter Continuity after Post Independence
5. Laxmikanth, M., (2011). Public Administration, McGraw Hill, New Delhi
6. Laxmikanth, M., (2022). Indian Polity, McGraw Hill, New Delhi
7. Singh, Hoshiar &Singh, Pankaj (2011). Indian Administration, Pearson, New Delhi
8. Dr Agarwal. P.K & Dr Chaturvedi. K.N., (2022). Constitution of India. Prabhat Exam, Asaf Ali Road, New Delhi
9. Laxmikanth, M., (2011). Public Administration, McGraw Hill, New Delhi
10. Chandra, Bipan., Mukherjee, Mridula & Mukherjee, Aditya., (2008). India since Independence. Penguin Books, India.
11. Laxmikanth, M., (2022). Indian Polity, McGraw Hill, New Delhi 6th edition *p 13.3*

11a. Laxmikanth, M., (2022). Indian polity, McGraw Hill, New Delhi *p 12.3*

12. Maheshwari. S.R., (2012). Indian Administration, Orient Blackswan, New Delhi.
13. Laxmikanth, M., (2011). Public Administration, McGraw Hill, New Delhi

13a. *ibid reference 13*

14. Maheshwari. S.R., (2012). Indian Administration, McGraw Hill, New Delhi (Prime Minister Office importance Since Jawaharlal Nehru)
15. Maheshwari.S.R., (2012). Indian Administration, McGraw Hill, New Delhi (Gorwala Report)
16. Maheshwari.S.R., (2012). Indian Administration, McGraw Hill, New Delhi
17. Laxmikanth, M., (2022). Indian Polity, McGraw Hill, New Delhi

17a. https://en.wikipedia.org/wiki/Planning_Commission (India)

17b. https://fincomindia.nic.in/

17c. https://en.wikipedia.org/wiki/Finance_Commission

17d.https://en.wikipedia.org/wiki/Pay_Commission#:~:text=Pay%20Commission%20is%20set%20up,structure%20of%20all%20civil%20and

18. Maheshwari, S.R., (2012). Indian Administration, McGraw Hill, New Delhi
19. Singh, Hoshiar & Singh, Pankaj, Indian Administration, Pearson, New Delhi

19a.https://prepp.in/news/e-492-administrative-reforms-commission-indian-polity-notes

20. Maheshwari.S.R., (2012). Indian Administration, Orient Blackswan, New Delhi
21. Laxmikanth., (2022). Indian Polity, McGraw Hill, New Delhi
22. Laxmikanth. M., (2011). Public Administration, McGraw Hill, New Delhi
23. *Ibid, Reference 23*
24. Laxmikanth. M., (2022). Indian Polity, McGraw Hill, New Delhi
25. Bandhopadhyay, Sekhar. (2004). From Plassey to Partition, Orient Longman, Asaf Ali Road, New Delhi
26. Laxmikanth, M., (2011). Public Administration, McGraw Hill, New Delhi
27. Laxmikanth, M., (2022). Indian Polity, McGraw Hill, New Delhi
28. Bandhopadhyay, Sekhar. (2004). From Plassey to Partition, Orient Longman, Asaf Ali Road, New Delhi
29. Laxmikanth, M., (2022). Indian Polity, McGraw Hill, New Delhi
30. Laxmikanth, M., (2011). Public Administration, McGraw Hill, New Delhi
31. Laxmikanth, M., (2011). Public Administration, McGraw Hill, New Delhi *P 405*

32 Laxmikanth, M., (2022). Indian Polity, McGraw Hill, New Delhi

33. Constituent Assembly Debates, Volumes VII, *P.34*
34. Laxmikanth, M., (2022). Indian Polity, McGraw Hill, New Delhi
35.https://www.legalservicesindia.com/article/589/Position-of-Fundamental-Rights-during Emergency.html#:~:text=The%20Fundamental%20Rights%20under%20Article,of%20war%20or%20external%20ag gression.
35a.https://en.wikipedia.org/wiki/Forty-second_Amendment_of_the_Constitution_of_India
36.https://www.scobserver.in/journal/how-many-times-has-the-senior-most-judge-of-the-supreme-court-been-superseded/
37. https://www.bbc.com/news/world-asia-india-30040790
38.https://organiser.org/2023/05/03/124131/bharat/when-freedom-of-speech-and-press-were-by-completely-curtailed-by-congress-and-indira-gandhi-during-emergency/
39. Laxmikanth, M., (2022), Indian Polity, McGraw Hill, New Delhi
40. Laxmikanth, M., (2011), Public Administration, McGraw Hill, New Delhi
41. *Ibid, Reference 40*
42.https://www.jagranjosh.com/general-knowledge/new-economic-policy-of-1991-objectives-features-and-impacts-1448348633-1
43. Bandhopadhyay, Sekhar.,(2004). From Plassey to Partition. Orient Longman, Asaf Ali Road, New Delhi
44.https://unacademy.com/content/wbpsc/study-material/polity/jvp-committee/
45. Laxmikanth, M., (2022). Indian Polity, McGraw Hill, New Delhi
45a. *Ibid Reference 45 p 5.5*
46. *Ibid Reference 45 p 5.4*
47. Laxmikanth, M., (2011). Public Administration, McGraw Hill, New Delhi
48. Ignou Book, Chapter Impact of Decentralized Development
49. *Ibid, Reference 40 p 186*
50. Laxmikanth., (2011). Public Administration, McGraw Hill, New Delhi *p 531*
51. Laxmikanth, M., (2012). Indian Polity, McGraw Hill, New Delhi
52. *Ibid Reference 9 p 41.3*
53. Laxmikanth, M., (2011). Public Administration, McGraw Hill, New Delhi *p 40*
54. Laxmikanth, M., (2022). Indian Polity, McGraw Hill, New Delhi *p 39.10*
55. Laxmikanth, M., (2022). Indian Polity, McGraw Hill, New Delhi
56. Laxmikanth, M., (2011). Public Administration, McGraw Hill, New Delhi *p 212*
57. https://www.ifioque.com/library/accountability
58. Laxmikanth, M., (2011). Public Administration, McGraw Hill, New Delhi *p 53*
58a. *Ibid, reference 54 p 38.12*
59. Ibid, Reference 53 *p 532*
60. Ibid, reference 53 *p 531*
61. Laxmikanth, M., (2022). Indian Polity, McGraw Hill, New Delhi *p 38.12*
62. Laxmikanth, M., (2011). Public Administration, McGraw Hill, New Delhi *p 232*
63. https://byjus.com/free-ias-prep/citizens-charter/
64. Laxmikanth., (2022). Indian Polity, McGraw Hill, New Delhi *p 29.1*
65. *Ibid Reference 9 p 29.3*
66. https://www.clearias.com/social-audit/
67. https://blog.ipleaders.in/role-of-bureaucracy-in-india/
67a. Firstpost - How Civil Servants Built Modern India
68.https://unacademy.com/content/upsc/study-material/ncert-notes/polity-class-11-part-2-bureaucracy/
69. Laxmikanth, M., (2011). Public Administration, McGraw Hill, New Delhi *p 479*
70. Laxmikanth, M., (2022). Indian Polity, McGraw Hill, New Delhi *p 66.1*

71. Laxmikanth, M., (2022). Indian Polity, McGraw Hill, New Delhi *p44.1*
72. Laxmikanth, M., (2011). Public Administration, McGraw Hill, New Delhi
73. Maheshwari.S.R., (2012) Indian Administration, Orient Blackswan, New Delhi *p 579 – 582*
74. https://en.m.wikipedia.org/wiki/Superintendent_of_police_(India)
https://testbook.com/ias-preparation/how-to-become-sp-in-police
75. Laxmikanth, M., (2022). Indian Polity, McGraw Hill, New Delhi *p 36*
76. Report of the committee to identify the central acts which are not relevant or no longer needed or require repeal/Reenactment in the present socio-economic context.
77.Guha, Ramcharan., (2017). The History of the World's Largest Democracy, Macmillan, New York, United States.
78.https://www.drishtiias.com/to-the-points/paper3/green-revolution-1
79.https://en.wikipedia.org/wiki/Minimum_support_price_ (India)
80.https://en.wikipedia.org/wiki/Green_Revolution_in_India#:~:text=The%20Green%20Revolution%20was%20a,faciliti9. https://byjusexamprep.com/upsc-exam/economic-planning-in-india
81.https://en.wikipedia.org/wiki/Five-Year_Plans_of_India
82. https://en.wikipedia.org/wiki/Public_sector_undertakings_in_India
83.https://www.drishtiias.com/to-the-points/paper3/india-s-industrial-policy
84 https://en.wikipedia.org/wiki/National_Policy_on_Education
85.https://onlineschoolsindia.in/school-guide/key-features-of-national-education-policy-1986/
86. https://en.wikipedia.org/wiki/Women_in_India
87.https://mea.gov.in/Speeches-Statements.htm?dtl/9285/Indias_Foreign_Pol-icy_Successes_Failures_and_Vision_in_the_Changing_World_Order_Talk_by_#:~:text=Immediately%20after%20the%20independence%20of,as%20the%20realism%20of%20tomorrow.
88.https://www.economicsdiscussion.net/articles/progress-of-health-services-in-india-after-independence/2297
89. https://en.wikipedia.org/wiki/Alma_Ata_Declaration
90.https://prepp.in/news/e-492-nationalisation-of-banks-indian-economy-notes
91. https://en.wikipedia.org/wiki/Economic_liberalisation_in_India
92. https://byjus.com/free-ias-prep/economic-reforms-1991/
93.https://www.linkedin.com/pulse/5-major-milestones-shaped-indian-economy-since-1947-sandeep-jadhavs%2C%20pesticides%2C%20and%20fertilizers.
94. https://en.wikipedia.org/wiki/National_Policy_on_Education
95.https://www.thehindu.com/news/national/upa-endorses-governments-economic-reform-measures/article3941838.ece
96.https://nhm.gov.in/index1.php?lang=1&level=1&lid=49&sublinkid=96
97. https://en.wikipedia.org/wiki/Accredited_Social_Health_Activist
98.https://scroll.in/article/1025029/manmohan-singh-vs-narendra-modi-who-handled-the-indian-economy-better
99.https://m.economictimes.com/news/economy/infrastructure/government-to-start-new-infra-projects-including-8-new-airports-prime-minister-manmohan-singh/articleshow/21839892.cms
100.https://www.ndtv.com/business/opinion-11-big-trade-deals-for-india-under-manmohan-singh-none-after-2712298
101.https://mea.gov.in/Portal/ForeignRelation/India-Russia_Relations.pdf
102. https://thewire.in/security/fact-check-india-china-border-roads
103.https://www.investindia.gov.in/foreign-direct-investment#:~:text=Total%20FDI%20inflows%20in%20the%20country%20in%20the%20FY%2022,into%20India%20FY%202022%2D23.
104.https://ncdc.gov.in/WriteReadData/l892s/27505481411548674558.pdf
105. https://indiaculture.gov.in/world-heritage

106.https://en.wikipedia.org/wiki/Jawaharlal_Nehru_National_Urban_Renewal_Mission#:~:text=JNNURM%20 primarily%20incorporates%20two%20sub,redevelopment%20of%20old%20city%20areas.
107.https://www.thehindu.com/sci-tech/science/manmohan-formally-announces-indias-mars-mission/article3775271.ece
108.https://www.isro.gov.in/MarsOrbiterMissionSpacecraft.html#:~:text=Mars%20Orbiter%20Mission%20(MOM)%2C,orbit%20on%20Sept%2024%2C%202021.
109. https://dot.gov.in/national-telecom-policy-1994
110.https://m.economictimes.com/industry/energy/power/india-to-double-renewable-energy-capacity-by-2017-manmohan-singh/articleshow/19595092.cms
111. https://darpg.gov.in/arc-reports
112. https://en.wikipedia.org/wiki/Administrative_Reforms_Commission
113.https://dpar.mizoram.gov.in/uploads/attachments/91a04af8e661b87c447ccfbacc8f48d5/pages-51-presentation-on-the-2nd-arc-and-its-recommendation.pdf
114.https://scroll.in/article/1025029/manmohan-singh-vs-narendra-modi-who-handled-the-indian-economy-better 101. Bagchi, Indrani, (2011). A Tale of Two Manmohan Singh, JSTOR.ORG, Vol. 110, No. 735, South Asia pp. 131 – 135
115. https://www.reuters.com/article/idINIndia-54761320110209
116.https://www.bbc.com/news/world-asia-india-46902935
117. Viswanathan. KG., (2010). The Global Financial Crisis and its impact on India, Journal of International Business and Law, Vol 9 Issue 1
118. Laxmikanth, M., (2011). Public Administration, McGraw Hill, New Delhi
119. Singh, Hoshiar & Singh, Pankaj (2011).Indian Administration, Pearson, New Delhi
Laxmikanth, M., (2022).Indian Polity, McGraw Hill, New Delhi *p 38.8*
120.https://m.economictimes.com/news/india/why-govt-is-moving-slowly-on-lateral-hiring-of-experts-from-private-sector/articleshow/94272831.cms
121. https://www.iipa.org.in/cms/public/training_course/1
122. https://www.iipa.org.in/new/cbc.php
123.https://dopt.gov.in/schemes/national-programme-civil-services-and-capacity-building-npcscb-mission-karmayogi
124. https://igotkarmayogi.gov.in/
125. https://cbc.gov.in/
126. https://byjus.com/free-ias-prep/reform-attempts-in-recruitment/
127. https://en.m.wikipedia.org/wiki/National_Recruitment_Agency
128. Civil Services Reforms – VISION IAS p 3
129. Specialists/1602543/ https://www.mygov.in/campaigns/agniveer/
130.https://unacademy.com/content/notification-updates/agneepath-army-scheme/
131. https://gem.gov.in/gem-advantages
132.https://en.m.wikipedia.org/wiki/Human_resource_management_in_public_administration
133. Burns, P John., (2022). Human Resource Management in Public Administration: Key Challenges, Oxford University Press
134.https://www.yourarticlelibrary.com/personnel-management/top-6-changing-roles-of-personnel-department/75336
135. Laxmikanth, M., (2011). Public Administration, McGraw Hill, New Delhi
136. *Ibid, Reference 22 p 480*
137. Laxmikanth, M., (2022).Indian Polity, McGraw Hill, New Delhi p43.1
138. Laxmikanth, M., (2011). Public Administration, McGraw Hill, New Delhi *p481*
139. Laxmikanth, M., (2011). Public Administration, McGraw Hill, New Delhi *p 483*

140. Laxmikanth, M., (2011). Public Administration, McGraw Hill New Delhi
141. Laxmikanth, M., (2011). Public Administration, McGraw Hill, New Delhi p486 – 487
142. https://blog.ipleaders.in/administrative-tribunals-in-india/
143. https://cgat.gov.in/
144.https://prsindia.org/billtrack/prs-products/the-tribunal-system-in-india-3750
145 Laxmikanth, M., (2011). Public Administration, McGraw Hill, New Delhi *p486 – 487*
146. Jain, Chandra Sures., (2000). Making Indian Bureaucracy Responsible, Accountable and Result Oriented. Indian Journal of Public Administration, Sage Journals Vol. 46. Issue 2
147.https://ndma.gov.in/Capacity_Building/Admin_Coordination/LBSNAA
148. https://www.niti.gov.in/cooperative-federalism
149. Laxmikanth, M., (2011). Public Administration, McGraw Hill, New Delhi *p485*
150. Laxmikanth, M., (2022). Public Administration, McGraw Hill, New Delhi *p57.1*
151. Laxmikanth, M., (2011). Public Administration, McGraw Hill New Delhi
152. Laxmikanth, M., (2011). Public Administration, McGraw Hill New Delhi *p326*
153. Government of India document on NITI Aayog entitled as "Form Planning to NITI – Transforming India's Development Agenda," February 8, 2015
154. Laxmikanth, M.,(2022). Indian Polity, McGraw Hill, New Delhi *p 54.1*
155.https://www.drishtiias.com/daily-news-editorials/democratic-decentralisation-in-india
156. Ignou unit 26 decentralization Debate
157.https://byjus.com/question-answer/what-are-the-features-of-decentralization/
158.http://www.ciesin.org/decentralization/English/General/Different_forms.html
159. https://www.acubeias.com/article/rajamannar-committee
160. https://en.wikipedia.org/wiki/Sarkaria_Commission
161. https://www.iasabhiyan.com/punchhi-commission/
162. https://www.niti.gov.in/cooperative-federalism
163. Laxmikanth, M., (2022). Indian Polity, McGraw Hill, New Delhi p *46*
164.Types of good and Services Tax – https://www.bajajfinserv.in/insights/types-of-gst-in-india
165. Impact of GST on Economy – https://gstcouncil.gov.in/
166. https://cleartax.in/s/gst-rates
168. https://www.trai.gov.in/
169. https://www.fssai.gov.in/
170. https://en.m.wikipedia.org/wiki/Reserve_Bank_of_India
171. https://www.sebi.gov.in/
172.https://en.m.wikipedia.org/wiki/Securities_and_Exchange_Board_of_India
173.https://en.wikipedia.org/wiki/Board_of_Control_for_Cricket_in_India#:~:text=The%20Board%20of%20Control%20for,of%20cricket%20in%20the%20world.
174.https://en.m.wikipedia.org/wiki/Central_Board_of_Film_Certification
175.https://m.timesofindia.com/india/from-economy-to-politics-how-india-has-changed-during-9-years-of-modi-govt/articleshow/100619638.cms
176. https://www.mygov.in/campaigns/
177.https://www.makeinindia.com/about#:~:text=PROGRAM,response%20to%20a%20critical%20situon
178. https://dbtbharat.gov.in/
179.https://drive.google.com/file/d/1LxtdU3knRnVrt-hqKkX1mJtZo4bP9sfp/view?usp=drive_web
180.https://newsonair.gov.in/News?title=9-years-of-Modi-Govt%3A-Introduction-of-GST-brings-tax-transparency-in-the-country&id=461145
181.https://www.livemint.com/companies/news/modi-govt-s-new-e-commerce-rules-have-amazon-flipkart-jiomart-on-its-toes-11624408242028.html

182.https://www.thehindu.com/news/national/prime-minister-narendra-modi-addresses-digital-india-week-2022-in-gandhinagar/article65600061.ece
183.https://www.mygov.in/overview/#:~:text=MyGov%20has%20been%20established%20as,of%20public%20interest%20and%20welfare.
184. https://pmwani.gov.in/
185. https://www.india.gov.in/spotlight/ek-bharat-shreshtha-bharat
186. https://hi.vikaspedia.in/social-welfare/social-awareness/schemes/ek-bharat-shreshtha-bharat
187.https://www.hindustantimes.com/cities/others/pm-modi-urges-temple-managements-to-further-the-vision-of-vikas-bhi-virasat-bhi-at-itcx-2023-in-varanasi-101690039975474.html
188.https://www.pmindia.gov.in/hi/%E0%A4%AE%E0%A4%A8-%E0%A4%95%E0%A5%80-%E0%A4%AC%E0%A4%BE%E0%A4%A4/
189. https://newsonair.gov.in/Mann-ki-Baat.aspx
190. https://pib.gov.in/PressReleaseIframePage.aspx?PRID=1920766
191.https://www.pmindia.gov.in/en/news_updates/pms-address-in-the-100th-episode-of-mann-ki-baat/
192. https://swachhbharat.mygov.in/
193.https://sulabhenvis.nic.in/Database/SwachhBharatAbhiyan_7101.aspx
194. https://amritmahotsav.nic.in/har-ghar-tiranga.htmlIbid
195. https://harghartiranga.com/
196.https://m.economictimes.com/news/india/pm-modi-to-celebrate-international-day-of-yoga-at-un-events-planned-across country/articleshow/101148426.cms#:~:text=Synopsis,with%20the%20wider%20international%20community.
197.https://www.livemint.com/news/india/yoga-an-idea-of-pm-modi-that-is-now-a-worldwide-phenomenon-11655713858698.html
198.https://www.narendramodi.in/yoga-remains-ray-of-hope-in-covid-hit-world-says-prime-minister-narendra-modi-555817
199.https://m.timesofindia.com/city/lucknow/pms-call-for-sabka-saath-sabka-vikas-ensured-social-justice-for-all-says-cm/articleshow/101441718.cms
199a. https://www.niti.gov.in/aspirational-districts-programme
200. https://www.digitalindia.gov.in/
201. https://usof.gov.in/en/bharatnet-project
202.https://www.bbnl.nic.in/index1.aspx?lsid=249&lev=2&lid=21&langid=1
203. https://pib.gov.in/PressReleseDetail.aspx?PRID=1547309
204. https://pib.gov.in/Pressreleaseshare.aspx?PRID=1847837
205. https://www.meity.gov.in/divisions/national-e-governance-plan
206. https://pib.gov.in/PressReleaseIframePage.aspx?PRID=1897272
207. https://nielit.gov.in/ajmer/content/national-digital-literacy-mission
208. https://www.pmgdisha.in/
209. https://www.makeinindia.com/sector/electronic-systems
210. https://en.wikipedia.org/wiki/Make_in_India
211. https://www.drishtiias.com/daily-news-analysis/national-policy-on-electronics-2019
212. http://cashlessindia.gov.in/aeps.html
213.https://health.economictimes.indiatimes.com/news/health-it/how-india-can-benefit-from-digitalization-in-healthcare-delivery/98524762
214.https://covid19.trackvaccines.org/country/india/
215.https://en.wikipedia.org/wiki/Identity_documents_of_India
216.https://uidai.gov.in/en/media-resources/uidai-documents/parliament-questions/lok-sabha/3864-aadhaar-project.html

217. https://en.wikipedia.org/wiki/Personal_Data_Protection_Bill,_2019
218.http://164.100.47.4/BillsTexts/LSBillTexts/Asintroduced/373_2019_LS_Eng.pdf
219. https://www.pib.gov.in/PressReleasePage.aspx?PRID=1877030
220. https://svamitva.nic.in/
221.https://vikaspedia.in/social-welfare/rural-poverty-alleviation-1/svamitva-scheme
222. https://www.surveyofindia.gov.in/pages/svamitva
223. https://www.nic.in/products/egramswaraj/
224. https://panchayat.gov.in/eGramSwaraj/
225. https://byjusexamprep.com/bank-merger-list-india-i
226.https://www.bankbazaar.com/ifsc/list-of-merged-public-sector-banks-in-india-2021.html
227. https://www.gktoday.in/constitution-100th-amendment-act-2015/
228. https://gstcouncil.gov.in/gst-council
229.https://byjusexamprep.com/upsc-exam/102-constitutional-amendment-act
230. *Ibid Reference 229*
231.https://en.wikipedia.org/wiki/One_Hundred_and_Third_Amendment_of_the_Constitution_of_Indi
232.https://indianexpress.com/article/opinion/columns/ravi-shankar-prasad-law-minister-103rd-constitutional-amendment-was-passed-8263212/#:~:text=It%20enjoins%20the%20state%20to,to%20all%20the%20weaker%20sections.
233.https://blog.finology.in/Legal-news/105th-amendment-of-indian-constitution
234.https://en.wikipedia.org/wiki/Muslim_Women_(Protection_of_Rights_on_Marriage)_Act,_2019
235. https://en.wikipedia.org/wiki/Aadhaar_Act,_2016
236.https://en.wikipedia.org/wiki/Insolvency_and_Bankruptcy_Code,_2016#:~:text=An%20Act%20to%20consolidate%20and,the%20interests%20of%20all%20the
237. https://blog.ipleaders.in/real-estate-regulation-and-development-act-2016-2/
238. https://byjus.com/free-ias-prep/consumer-protection-act-2019/
239. https://prsindia.org/billtrack/the-citizenship-amendment-bill-2019
239a.https://en.wikipedia.org/wiki/Article_370_of_the_Constitution_of_India
239b. https://indianexpress.com/article/india/amit-shah-bills-reforming-indias-criminal-justice-system-8887532/
240. https://en.wikipedia.org/wiki/National_Education_Policy_2020
240a. https://pib.gov.in/PressReleaseIframePage.aspx?PRID=1847066
241.https://zeenews.india.com/india/narendra-modi-turns-72-major-changes-in-education-sector-under-pm-and-way-ahead-read-details-2511063.html
242. https://pib.gov.in/PressReleaseIframePage.aspx?PRID=1937948
243. https://pib.gov.in/newsite/PrintRelease.aspx?relid=193388
244.https://en.wikipedia.org/wiki/Sindhu_Central_University#:~:text=Sindhu%20Central's%20was%20established%20by,university%2Dlevel%20institutions%20in%20Ladakh.
245. http://dsel.education.gov.in/pm-shri-schools
246. http://dsel.education.gov.in/pm-shri-schools
247. https://www.nirfindia.org/
248. https://www.nmc.org.in/
249. https://www.news18.com/news/india/draft-nep-proposes-rashtriya-shiksha-aayog-apex-body-for-education-to-be-chaired-by-pm-modi-2167691.html
250. https://www.nta.ac.in/
251.https://main.mohfw.gov.in/sites/default/files/9147562941489753121.pdf
252. https://nhm.gov.in/
253.https://main.mohfw.gov.in/sites/default/files/21684629120148966518 2.pdf
254. https://poshanabhiyaan.gov.in/

256. http://janaushadhi.gov.in/pmjy.aspx
257.https://timesofindia.indiatimes.com/blogs/economic-update/gst-a-great-fiscal-reform/
258. https://en.wikipedia.org/wiki/JAM_Yojana
259. https://pmjdy.gov.in/
260. https://en.wikipedia.org/wiki/Direct_Benefit_Transfer
261.https://www.businesstoday.in/latest/economy/story/what-is-the-national-single-window-system-and-how-will-it-work-355372-2022-12-06
262.https://wcd.nic.in/schemes/ujjawala-comprehensive-scheme-prevention-trafficking-and-rescue-rehabilitation-and-re
263.https://en.wikipedia.org/wiki/2016_Indian_banknote_demonetisation
264. https://www.investindia.gov.in/atmanirbhar-bharat-abhiyaan
265.https://www.brookings.edu/wp-content/uploads/2015/05/modi365_final-book.pdf
266. https://www.orfonline.org/research/indias-vaccine-diplomacy/
267. https://www.careerlauncher.com/upsc/make-in-india/
268.https://timesofindia.indiatimes.com/blogs/voices/modis-midas-touch-turnaround-from-telephone-banking-to-profitable-banking/
269.https://blog.mygov.in/major-announcements-and-policy-reforms-under-aatma-nirbhar-bharat-abhiyan/
270.https://www.financialexpress.com/policy/economy-recasting-ministries-several-govt-departments-likely-to-be-merged-or-pruned-1591948/
271.https://www.deccanherald.com/india/india-achieving-new-feats-under-pm-modis-leadership-carving-a-unique-identity-for-itself-bjp-2658231
272.https://www.narendramodi.in/pm-witnesses-historic-successful-insertion-of-mars-orbiter-mission-into-martian-orbit-6640
273.https://indianexpress.com/article/india/chandrayaan-3-moon-landing-salute-scientists-bjp-notes-modi-leadership-congress-nehrus-vision-8906532/
274.https://www.thehindu.com/news/national/seeking-investments-pm-modi-says-indias-potential-in-green-energy-no-less-than-a-goldmine/article66543695.ece
275.https://www.deccanherald.com/india/india-to-become-seventh-nation-to-have-national-quantum-mission-1211108.html
276. https://www.cnbctv18.com/economy/india-cabinet-approves-green-hydrogen-mission-explained-narendra-modi-15578611.htm
277.https://www.business-standard.com/article/economy-policy/india-to-have-doppler-weather-radar-network-by-2025-jitendra-singh-123011501016_1.html
278. https://consumeraffairs.nic.in/acts-and-rules/consumer-protection
279. https://blog.ipleaders.in/product-liability-and-consumer-protection/
280. https://www.vedantu.com/commerce/consumer-awareness
281. https://consumerhelpline.gov.in/convergence-request.php
282. https://www.g20.org/en/g20-india-2023/new-delhi-summit/
283.https://moes.gov.in/g20-india-2023/moes-g20?language_content_entity=en
284. https://services.india.gov.in/service/detail/pm-kisan-samman-nidhi
285https://www.drishtiias.com/daily-news-analysis/mega-food-park-scheme
286. https://www.indianbank.in/departments/rupay-kisan-card/
287. https://www.sarkariyojnaa.com/national-bamboo-mission/
288. https://www.enam.gov.in/
289.https://www.india.gov.in/spotlight/smart-cities-mission-step-towards-smart-india
290.https://www.india.gov.in/spotlight/bharatmala-pariyojana-stepping-stone-towards-new-india
291.https://www.drishtiias.com/daily-news-analysis/sagarmala-projects

292.https://byjus.com/free-ias-prep/udan-scheme/
293.https://www.india.gov.in/atal-mission-rejuvenation-and-urban-transformation-amrut
294.https://www.india.gov.in/spotlight/pm-gati-shakti-national-master-plan-multi-modal-connectivity
295.https://en.wikipedia.org/wiki/National_Infrastructure_Pipeline
296.https://www.clearias.com/national-infrastructure-pipeline/\
297.https://www.drishtiias.com/daily-news-analysis/jal-jeevan-mission-11
298.https://www.indiacode.nic.in/handle/123456789/2159?sam_handle=123456789/1362
299. https://mnre.gov.in/isa/
300. https://tourism.gov.in/ek-bharat-shreshtha-bharat-action-plan
301. http://adoptaheritage.in/
302.https://indiaculture.gov.in/complete-schedule-rashtriya-sanskriti-mahotsav
303.https://www.india.gov.in/spotlight/bhasha-sangam-celebrating-linguistic-diversity-india
304. https://www.orfonline.org/research/momentous-changes/
305.https://www.thehindu.com/news/national/pm-modi-inaugurates-national-war-memorial-in-new-delhi/article61538825.ece
306.https://www.indiatoday.in/coronavirus-outbreak/vaccine-updates/story/cowin-all-you-need-to-know-about-india-s-digital-push-behind-covid-19-vaccination-1759121-2021-01-14
307.https://dashboard.cowin.gov.in/
308.https://m.economictimes.com/industry/transportation/airlines-/-aviation/vande-bharat-mission-air-india-to-operate-additional-repatriation-flights-to-six-countries/articleshow/76091402.cms
309.https://timesofindia.indiatimes.com/india/pm-modi-stresses-on-containment-contact-tracing-testing-to-win-war-against-covid-19/articleshow/77494900.cms
310.https://m.economictimes.com/industry/healthcare/biotech/healthcare/janaushadhi-kendras-rendered-essential-services-in-covid-19-pandemic-union-health-minister/articleshow/81378255.cms
311https://pmnrf.gov.in/
312.https://pib.gov.in/Pressreleaseshare.aspx?PRID=1737184
313.https://www.india.gov.in/anubhav-portal-ministry-personnel-public-grievances-pensions

BUREAUCRATS ANUBHAV

2021

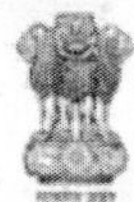

भारत सरकार
GOVERNMENT OF INDIA
कार्मिक, लोक शिकायत तथा पेंशन मंत्रालय
MINISTRY OF Personnel, PUBLIC GRIEVANCES & PENSIONS
पेंशन एव पेंशनभोगी कल्याण विभाग
DEPARTMENT OF PENSION & PENSIONER' WELFARE

ANUBHAV

2021

Contents

ANUBHAV Write-Ups

1. 2021 Anubhav

Purnimaa TN
IPOS, LSG Postal Assistant

I Had Joined the department on 14 .4.1981, Those were the days when the public have the impression of the post office only meant for sending the money orders and registered orders. Then I was posted to SB branch. 1 tried my level best to educate and make public believe in post office financial Investments comparing the interest rates and safety measures when compared banks, share markets and MFs 1 was never in the habit of coming late to the counter and I never closed the counter as soon as the time was up. 1 always used to stand in the shoes of the public and help them to the extent possible.

When I was working in Fraser town ln SB counter one gentlemen got his wife and daughter to the office and introduced me to his family saying "see this is the girl who serves with smile". This made me very confident. I have never made any differences between caste creed and religion during my service with the public. I was good terms with the public; they felt very happy to come to the Post for services rendered by me at the counter, our administration that is ASP called me and I was transferred to. YST PO and for the first time I was independent in charge of the PO. I got an opportunity to excel myself. I used to call the investors to the cabin and explain them about all the schemes.

This made remarkable difference after my joining YST as SPM I have visited RWF and defense offices to educate them about postal savings and PL\s and conducted several carnivals to promote postal schemes. I have enclosed two such appreciation letters. I am heart fully satisfied for the service rendered by me all these years to the department. Also, my sincere thanks to one and all who have been so supportive all these years.

****

Ms. M Vijaya Rajeshwari

DRTC, Technical Officer 'C'

I have joined low noise amplifier division of microwave group on 5th March 1991. As a part of my first

assignment. I have learnt gold wire bonding on a bonding machine. As a bonding expert I used to carry

out bonding work for all the divisions of microwave group. My primary job responsibilities were component assembly and testing which includes electrical card assembly die attach, wire bonding and connector integration and generating mechanical and electrical card drawings for microwave components. I have performed wire bonding of large couplers FET devices, MMICs and numerous others. ICS and assembly and integration of mainly C - band, Ka band low noise amplifiers and power amplifiers.

I have carried out assembly & testing of 18 - 40 GHz high pass filter, diplexers, triplexers, quadraplexes in suspended stripline, configuration and also carried out assembly, integration and testing of 2 - 4 GHz and 2 - 6 GHz switched filter Banks in pass hand steps of 250 MHz and 500 MHz for channelized receiver. I have designed and developed 850 - 960 MHz Band reject filters and 20 NOS such notch filters have been delivered to project Samyukta.

In project ***MIDAS***, I have carried out assembly and testing of lumped low pass, high pass and band pass filters in different frequency bands, 18 -26 GHz phase correlators and 2 -18 GHz DIFM receiver.

In project ***GARUDA***, I have designed and developed lumped high pass filters. I was also involved in ESS, Soft and EMI/EMC testing of phase measurement units productionized at Astra Microwave products limited.

In project ***VARUNA***, I have carried out assembly integration and testing of diplexers, switched filter Banks using different lumped low pass and high pass filters.

In project ***NGARM***, I was involved in assembly and testing of prototype hardware development and

Participated in ESS and Soft tests of 1 - 10GHz and 818 GHz microwave system developed by M/S Astra Microwave products limited.

In project ***AEWACs,*** I have also carried out assembly and testing of 1.0 - 1.1 GHz and 3.1- 3.5 GHz Notch filters with a pass band up to 18 GHz.

I received laboratory cash award during 1999, 2005, 2011 and 2018.

Technology group award for critical microwave technologies in the year 2016.

****

Mr., Ramesh Kumar
CAPF, Sub inspector (GD)

By the grace of the God, I Ramesh Kumar joined SSB on 16/03/1989 as Constable (GD) at erstwhile GC Jammu (J&K) and intending to proceed on Voluntary Retirement w.e.f 30/09/2021. I completed BRTC during 1990 from TC SSB Haflong (Assam). I had performed duties under Cabinet Secretariat sincerely on various general duty and I.S duty at Jammu, Punjab & NIP duty at Leh Ladakh at during the year 1992 to 1994. The central Government has changed the role of SSB and SSB came under MHA from Cabinet Secretariat The name of erstwhile G.C Jammu (J&K) was also changed and established as 7th Bn and performed duties of Border guarding on Indo-Nepal Border. In my service period, I always got good support and love from seniors and my colleagues. Nobody gave any bad opinion during the service. All assigned tasks assigned by my superiors have been completed timely with my experience and the guidance of my superiors and help of my colleagues.

During the long span of service of 32 years, I experienced that things have changed very much since 1989 to 2021 the atmosphere of service life, thinking of personnel, life styles and many more have changed. Now, everything is new and I too have learned to march with new generation side by side.

I am very grateful to all officers and colleagues who have given support/guided me in my journey and I will always remember all of you in future.

****

Mr. Alam Singh Rawat
CAPF, Assitant Sub inspector

By the grace of the God, I Alam Singh Rawat joined SSB on 22/06/1991 as Constable (GD) at erstwhile GC Srinagar, Garhwal. (Now 1st Bn SSB Sonapur) and intending to proceed on Voluntary Retirement w.e.f 31/07/2021. I completed BRTC during 1992 from TC SSB Salonibari (Assam). I had performed duties under Cabinet Secretariat sincerely on various general duty and I.S duty at Punjab during the year 1993 to 1994 & 1998 to 1999 & J &K 2001-2002.

The central Government has changed the role of SSB and SSB came under MHA from Cabinet Secretariat the name of erstwhile G.C Srinagar (Garhwal) was also changed and established as 1st Bn Didihat and performed duties of Border guarding on Indo-Nepal Border. In my service period I always got good support and love from seniors and my colleagues. Nobody had given any bad opinion during the service. All assigned tasks assigned by my superiors have been completed timely with my experience and the guidance of my superiors and help of my colleagues.

During the long span of service of 30 years, I experienced that things have changed very much since 1991 to 2021 the atmosphere of service life, thinking of personnel, life styles and many more have changed.

I am very grateful to all officers and colleagues who have given support/guide me to till journey and always remember all of you in future.

****

Ms. Indira Agrawal
IRPS, Office Superintendent

With an approximate 40 years of career span in railways, I can truly say that I have not only learnt and grown professionally but also grew as a better human being. I joined railways when I was all of 19 years and got a chance to learn various facets of life by serving in Reservation office, NDLS, Type Section- P Branch and finally in Welfare Section. During this long tenure, I was given a chance to supervise Employees' Camps, Spouse Camps, Physically Challenged Workshops/Seminars, Children Camps, arrangement of Cultural functions, GM Award Functions.

Apart from these, I have learnt a lot from my duties in Pulse Polio programmes and St. John Ambulance duties also. I have a lovely small family comprising of my husband (retired from Railways), son, daughter-in-law, 2 grandsons and a daughter. Now, I think, God has given me a chance to devote fully towards my family. I can go on and on describing my wonderful Anubhav but I would end by simply saying that I am always ready and willing to serve my organization - Northern railway, as and whenever required.

****

Mr. Ramesh Trikha
RBSSS, STENO

I joined Indian Railways on 18.02.1988 through RRB/Chandigarh.

The first placement was in COFMOW, Indian Railways, Tilak Bridge, New Delhi. I was posted in Stores Department and was attached with Dy.COS/COFMOW. After watching the quality of my work, I was shifted and posted with Controller of Stores/COFMOW. It is quite gratifying, when I look back that I had spent almost 14 years in COFMOW a very small organization with most of the time with SAG Officers even if I was not that senior. Since COFMOW was mostly dedicated Workshop Modernization involving procurement of high-handed State of Art Machinery and Equipment. I developed that dexterity of drafting the Tender Committee Minutes. A stage came when I use to prepare the drafts of my own which prove very useful to my officers who could devote their time to the other demanding issues. As is well known tenders and contracts being more sensitive work, involving public dealing with contractors and suppliers but I never divorced my integrity and honesty as such I earned a lot of respect and motivation. In recognition beyond my meritorious services. I was awarded seven times by Chief Administrative Officer. My example inspired other clan to work with similar tenacity. Even as the output of the Stenographers is associated with the similar trait of the officers with whom they are attached but I always took initiative to contribute and complement the output of my boss.

After a long time of 14 years, I was posted out on the ground as working on sensitive seats. Another useful period working with Medical Director/Northern Railway Central Hospital where I had to utilize my expertise in drafting and I had acquitted myself excellently. I had to manage the entire Cell attached with Medical Director/NRCH office. My all-round multi-purpose skill was rewarded with my elevation when I was posted with PCMD/Northern Railway as PS-II in Northern Railway Baroda House, New Delhi. My sincerity of purpose and loyalty to my bosses was always appreciated in the entire Medical Department where I was also awarded many times. My next posting was under PCSO/NR/Baroda House/New Delhi till date.

When I look back at my career, spanning over 33 years, I get lot of satisfaction and contentment in that I have given back to the Indian Railways the most valuable services. I do not have any regrets or remorse but just goodwill and harmony.

I owe my sincere thanks to all my colleagues/Seniors/Officers for my spotless and successful career.

****

Mr. Rajesh Chandra Sharma
IRSS, Chief office Superintendent

With an approximate 39 years of career in Railways, I can truly say I have not only learnt and grown professionally but also evolved as a better human being. I joined Railways when I was 21 years old and got a chance to learn various facets of life by serving in Store Branch, HQ Office, Baroda House, New Delhi. During this long tenure, I was given a chance to supervise various Purchase and Non-Purchase Sections, IT Cell. I have also got a chance to work on deputation in CRIS from 2007 to 2011. I had good learning of IT field. I have one daughter studying in10th class. Now, I think, God has given me a chance to devote fully towards my family. I can go on and on describing my wonderful experience but I would end by simply saying that I am always ready and willing to serve my organization- Northern Railway, as and whenever required.

****

Ms. D Jyothi
DRTC, Technical Officer D

I have joined DLRL on 18th September 1979 and worked in various departments like pilot plant, Trishul Wing and microwave wing. I have contributed towards design, development, testing, integration, Lab demonstration and user evaluation. During the tenure of my service in DLRL, I have been involved in various technical & techno managerial activities for various projects. The following are the details of my assignments.

1) Project CIPHER

I worked for Project Cipher. My team members are Mr. B.B Pillai and Mr., K. K Mallik. I have worked in the assembly lines of ECL – 2A 7 CC – 2A circuits. I have worked in team towards productionalisation of 295 equipments and handed over to the users and ISPW (Inter State Police Wireless) and Intelligence Bureau. I have also contributed during final inspection of GOLF Rx Project.

2) Project Trishul

In May 1984, I was transferred to newly formed wing called TRISHUL> My team members are Mr. S. Sathyanarayan, Mr. P Raghavendra Rao, Mrs G. Krishna Leela. I have Contributed towards the development of Ground electronics system for project 'Trishul' of Programme IGMDP> I am actively involved in the Development, Assembly and testing of missile channel Receiver (MCR) and Performance evaluation of various Millimetric wave components mm W components used in receiver chain such as mixer pre amplifiers, VOO's, Low noise amplifiers, 4 port circulators, Band Pass Filters, Isolators, Variable attenvators, SPDT Switches and Ka Band W/G plumbing components. MCR is integrated with fly catcher radar, breaking the chain of radar antenna and Radar Receiver.

First Trials: I made the subsystem MCR ready for flight trials being conducted at ITR, Balassore. Prior to that I have actively participated in local link trials (for Trishul Project) at RCI campus. At this juncture electrical Support system. Here, MCR is a part of ground Electronics Support system. During the link trials the necessary modifications were carried out on MCR to suit the updated Mission requirements.

3) Project MIDAS & Project GARUDA

I have been associated in the development and testing of RF front end for channelised Receiver subsystem in 0.5 – 18 & 18 -40 GHz band for technology demonstration projects, i am an active team member for development, testing and successful evaluation of the Ch. Rx covering 0.5 – 18 GHz & 18 – 40 GHz frequency band. I have successfully evaluated and integrated the unit in the laboratory system configuration successfully tested.

4) Project HIMRAJ

I have been actively involved and associated during development and testing of channelised Receiver front end 18 -40 GHz dual channel. I have participated and successfully completed ATP. Quantity 24 Nos wee productionised and integrated to the system and is being exploited by the users.

5) Project SAMUDRIKA, Project SARANG

I have been actively involved and associated during development and testing of channelized receiver front end 18 – 40 GHz quad channel. I have been actively involved in testing and evaluation of 4 units of ch.Rx for the rate wed specifications. I have been actively involved in ESS and SoFT including EMI/EMC tests, Pre and Post FTP were completed successfully with the involvements of project team, internal QA, RCMA & ORDAQA reps as per approved documents. Data is consolidated and prepared Test report document with approval of all the members. I was actively involved during the integration of channelised Receiver 18 -40 GHz unit in ESM/ ELINT chain form Project SARANG. I have participated and carried out the integration checks and performance testing along with other systems. Testing for sensitivity parameters measurements & DF accuracy. I was involved continuously during trouble shooting and problem rectification of the sub modules both at integration and at M/S AMPL, Hyd and successfully evaluated the chain. I have participated during Lab Demonstration and user evaluation at DLRL and completed successfully.

6) Project VAMANA

I was associated with the pre-project activities like PEER, PDR meetings. Associated in testing of prototype wide bend RF Unit up to 18 GHz frequency range and maintained the project registers and associated during quarterly audits along with project manager. Presently, associated during PMRC, EB & Project meetings.

During my tenure I have received the following awards; Received IGMDP cash award project TRISHUL in 1989, Received Laboratory cash award during 2001,2007, 2016 & 2018 for my contribution in the field of MN, mmW and EW system.

****

Mr. G Basavaiash

DRDS, Scientist 'F'

I, G BASAVAISH joined DLRL on 18.10.1982; I am T division Head to Mechanical Engineering Division. I am responsible for technical Administration of All chops of MED and fabrication of Mechanical Hardware for various projects of DLRL, like PANTHER, Ultraviolet, falcon (RPV), Prog. SANGRAHA KITE ON WHEELS, ELINT ON AEROSTAT, RFPS, DISHA, GBMES VARUNA, GARUDA, SARWAGNA, RUSTOM- 11, HIM$_2$ KAJ, HIM SHAKTI, A EW2 C, system for ARC. Systems Development and Demonstration At User sites and DLRL Responsible for integration & Installation of Mechanical Hardware for various Outgoing Projects for Ew System for Lab Demonstration like.

Project PANTHER: Design and Development of Air Born POD for MIG-21

Project, Ultraviolet: Design and Development of Ground Based system for VVIP security.

Project Falcon (RPV): Design and Development of ELINT and Comint Payloads for Remotely Piloted vehicle.

Project SANGRAHA: Design and Development of MBTU cooling system, ESM systems

KITE ON WHEELS: Design and Development of vehicle mounted GSM system.

Project RFPS: RADAR finger printing system for EW system.

Project DISHA: Design and Development of ESM system on TATA Vehicle.

Project GARUDA: Design and Development of ELINT and COMINT Payloads UAV and Acrostat.

Projects ARWAGNA: Design and Development of ECM systems for ship some platform

Project VARUNA: Design and Development of Esm system for ship Borne platform.

Project RUSTOM I: Development of ELINT payloads DAV platform.

Project HIMRAJ: Ground based ESM system.

Project HIMSHAKTI: Design and Development and installation of ESM & Esm system for Ammy at LEH Ladakh.

Project AEW & c: Design and Development ESM system for Air borne pattern.

ARC Ground based: High Performance ESM & ECM system for Army.

Ms. A Sudha
DRTC, Technical Officer, D

I joined in a group named OPAL PRODUCTION which was involved In the development of 6 Nos of Ecom receivers as add on facility to P30 RAPAR Number of PCB circuits were wired and tested by me. Interconnection diagrams and PCB layouts were also part of my job. After the production was complete and all the receivers were deployed at the respective Air force stations. I was transferred a lot working with a team of 24 members All my superiors and seniors guided me and trained me in the new cork environment.

In RF Group I have actively participated in the development of ESM systems for project 'COIN –B' and Project 'CATCH - M. My specific assignment was in the development of front-end receiver subsystems in 1 to 18aH frequency range. Though I was new to RF and MW Systems and measurements with the help of collegues. I could learn everything needed. COIN system integration in the vehicle was carried out and tested I evaluated. Similarly for project CATCH-M. I have taken part in the electrical environment and EMI / EMC testing of the subsystem. All the subsystem were also integrated and evaluated and handed over to IAF. Participated in TOT to M/S BEL.

Our group involved in the design and development of ESM Entity for project SAMYUKTA. As subsystem manage for RP distribution units of front-end receiver of Esm system. I have taken the responsibility of concurrent TOT to TOT to M/s. BEL and development of the subsystem Testing, evaluation and integration was completed in Esm system at ELSEC. Entity along with other entities handed over to Army.

I was also a part of the Technology Development project ALERT and carried out various activities like project proposal feasibility study etc. As this was a render developed project. I have actively participated in development, testing, evaluation and integration of math switching matrix Network, RF Distribution whit and Quad superhot Receives modules. Many modules developed in this project were used in other projects of DLRL at a later stage. Our team is involved in project 'SARANG' ESM system for installation on komov 31 Helicopter this system evaluated by various committers internally and by users and shitted to Goa for field trials. It is presently undergoing field trials at God.

All through the service of 40 years in the same division, I was working with very humble and great people who trained me and helped me in my growth. All my superiors and seniors were very considerate to me. Working in DLRL was a happy memory for me. Not only the work, I met many friends here who have supported me from the beginning. I am thankful to God for everything he bestowed upon me.

****

Mr., Shyam Lal Silan

DRTC, Technical Officer C

I joined TBRL DRDO in Oct'1983 as a Junior Scientific Asstt – I and was posted in Warhead Group. Which has the prestigious project of IGMDP.

Evaluation of Critical energy of fragment of IMGDP Warheads against stimulated M.S target

I have been assigned the job to work out the critical energy of different fragments of pre-Fragmented warheads. To work out this critical energy of fragments, a number of trials were conducted with fragment launching gun against different M. S stimulated target plates with fragment sent by ARDE. Fragment pre 7 post perforation velocity data was recorded with help of electronic digital counters. AI foil sensor rear side flower appears and sensor does not work. To overcome this problem, I have replaced rear side AI foil with higher thickness.

Fabrication of Multilaver Aluminum foils Sensor:

In the warhead trails Pre & Post performance velocity of fragments was to be recorded at the distance of 100, 150, 200-meter distances. At such distance fragment hit density assumed to be one hit per sq. meter& to record this fragment velocity sensor size required is 6ft by 8ft. To meet this requirement, I have made sensor of 3ft by 4ft on available paper size and then used four sets of 3ft by 4ft sensors and combined them & connect parallay to make bigger size of sensor. It has been also observed that two-layer AL foil sensor having success rate of 60%. To improve this I have made triple layer AL foil sensor which has the success rate of 99%. One set of multi-layer sensor required four layers of brown paper sheets and three layers of AL foil and quick fix as an adhesive.

Range & Fire Safety

I was assigned the task of Range safety and five safety. As range officer my responsibility was to look out the range & fire safety for high explosive trials, liasoning with outer agencies like Air traffic control and civil administration for safe conduct of high caliber Bomb trials, nearly 250 Nos. of High explosive trials have been conducted every year.

Fire & Safety training

Every year during fire safety week, fire safety demo's (theory and Practical) were given to 300 employees of the lab in more than 10 batches and were trained to capable to handle office building as well as domestic fire incidents. Disaster Management training was also given to 240 lab employees for handling manmade & natural disasters.

Jungle Fire Protection

TBRL Range has huge jungle area of 5500 acre. Jungle fire incidents are frequent is summer season as well as after high explosive trials. The jungle fire spreads fast with supporting wind and burns a lot of wild growth and creates enormous pollution in environment. High explosive trials are regular phenomena and to control this jungle fire necessary measures are to be taken:

To control this jungle fire, I have suggested the concept of 30-meter-wide fire lane so that fire cannot jump this lane and is contained in limited area. For this I have planned three types of fire lane:-

1) **Parameter Fire Lane** – Along with parameter so that outside jungle fire could not enter inside range boundary.
2) **Cross Fire Lane** – Range core area divided in four quadrants so that fire outbreak in one quadrant remains only in that quadrant.
3) **Technical zone fire lane** - Fire Lane along with technical zone parameter will protect in two ways i.e., does not allow outside fire in zone. Secondly fires inside zone due to trial with not cross the zone parameter to spread in whole Range.

****

Dr. (Mr). Y Ravi Kumar
DRTC, Technical Officer 'C'

Working as a Team Leader (Development) in Programme SAMYUKTA (Non – Com) Engineering Group which was headed by S/Sri A Gangadhara Rao, Sc, G, B.S Kishore Sc E, D Prabhakar, Sc E, G V Prabhakar Rao Sc F and Dr. P Rajendran, Sc F, under their valuable guidance, contributed significantly in a noteworthy way for electronic packaging of vehicle mounted ARSS structures, prototype development of OMNI stacked antennae, BLI and DBD antennae of defined frequency range and their support mechanical hardware led to successful development. The Modular development part of OMNI slacked antennae which is consisting of three antennas as one electronic unit retainer ring method for ach antenna so that each antenna can be used independently or with one another, ensuring fully co axial, interconnectivity along with environmental safety and maintainability. The modularity features of stacked nature have got wide applause from all system managers for its high success.

In 1996, the development of BLI antenna for three different frequency ranges is another jewel of Mechanical engineering. Each BLI antenna system was developed in such a way that four modularized antenna were electronic packaged finned panels fitted to either one or two tier light weight open housing with all inner connected hundred electronic items with different sets of super components. Ensured inter connectivity cabling along with stability, perfect assembling, proper cooling requirements, maintainability as well as environmental protection. This unique structured modular development for three BLIs has got wide applause from all system managers for their high success.

In this process of design and development, some notable problems come across and are solved, resulting in saving of time and resources for example;

1. Mismatching of angular polarizers of all the OMNI stacked solved by development of matching the same angle alignment method of angular polarizer's and
2. Development of swiveling of ATR horns on fixed swiveling base for accommodating one set of ATR horns of an antenna system into ARSS bay for clear hoisting and retraction. All these efforts were highly appreciated and awarded.

As a leading member of a design team led by S/Sri N. Divakar Sc. G, Shri G Shanta Ram Sc F, working in design engineering group headed by S/Sri K Raghunathan Sc G, Muthusamy Sc f, CVH Prasad Sc G, I have made deep imprints by engineering design, development and draughting of all the servo drives of 1 to 3 axes pedestals made in DLRL for radar antenna on different platforms for projects like Ajanta, IFF , Coin, indigo and prestigious TRISHUL of integrated guided Missile programme (IGMDP).

These works include critical understanding study of electro mechanical engineering aspects of design specifications, housing geometry, drive elements like gears and pinions, shafts, bearings, servo motors, synchros, rotary joints and related cable routing which resulted in high quality huge engineering layouts leading to many assemblies, sub-assemblies and detail drawings. All the engineering layouts, assemblies and engineering detail drawings generated in non-CAD era, are so clear in draughting, much easier to understand for any technical information to fabricate was the highlight of each pedestal work. All these efforts are highly appreciated on record and earned the IGMDP award in 1989 announced by Sri V. S Arunachlam, Scientific Advisor to Ministry of Defence and Direction of the LAB.

****

Ms. Josyula Usha Rani
DRDS, Scientist E

1) I have been working in Defence Electronics Research laboratory (DLRC) for the past four decades in various. Programme / Projects.

2) Over the years, I have acquired in depth - Knowledge and immense exposure to the design & development of various microwave RF Broadband components, super components and subsystems in microwave wave frequency bands up to 40 GHz frequency range.

3) The following are major Contributions:

a. Design, development and production of microwave Control Components such as switches, Limiters and attenuators & wing PIN Diodes & MMIC Devices.

b. Design, development and productionization of Microwave Super components such as RF switch Super components modulator super components etc.

C. Design, development and productionization at Microwave such as RF switch Super components, modulator super components etc.

d. Design development and productionization of Micro- wave & mm wave subsystems such as down / UP GR- verters, RF BITE Sources etc.

4. I have been responsible for imparting transfer of Technology (TOT) of different control components like PIN Diodes Switches units, mw & mm Wave down Converter subsystem, switch matrix units & RF BITE sources etc.

5. The following one some of the important components & sub- systems used in different programme projects.

Programme SAMUDRIKA

1.MM Wave down converter 18-40 GHz. I have carried out the design & development of mm Ware down Converters for ship borne project Shakti and Airborne Project SARA- KSHE NIKASH. The 18-40 GHz frequency band is Split into two frequency bands 18-29 GHZ & 29-40 GHz by using diploxer and these two Sub bands are down converted to 6-17 GHz by mixing with 35 GHz 9 46 GHz Local Oscillators.

Generated design details document and continuously involved during the development of Qty 2 Nos. for ship borne project & Qty 24 Nos for Air borne projects. Total quantity 26 Nos. was successfully qualified and the units were integrated in LRU as per system configuration.

2. Switch matrix Units 2-189H2, 2-6 & 6-18 GM2; success; fully developed Qty to Nos of 2-18 GHz switch matrix units and completed Electrical & Environmental fests for the total quantity. Switch matrix units of Qty 2 Nos. in each frequency band of 2-

6 9H2 & 6-18.

Project VANUNA

I was instrumental in finalization of Configuration of Down Converters 6-18 GH_2 to 2-6 QH 2 -6 GHz (DC-H) & 2-6 GHz (DC –L), Local Oscillators (LO –H & LO –L) for Narrow band ESM Receiver. I was associated during the testing & Evaluation of production qualities of DC H, DC – L and LO –H & LOL units for 4 systems along with production & project teams. Prototype switch filter bank (SFB) 2-^ GHz to suppress the interference signals was developed in house and production quantities were developed through Vendor.

Development of RF Front and subsystem for Project DISHA

I was involved in the Development of down Converter – I, II, III and Channelizer subsystem covering split frequency bands over 0.5 to 40 GHz. Each down converter 1 & 2 super components for CW Repeater Chain.

Programme 'CODE'

I have carried out the design & development of SPDT, SP4T, and SP6T & SP8T Pin code switches and TOT was imparted to a vendor for Qty 5 Nos. each. Indigenous development of 17 GHZ DRDOS of Qty lo Nos and sty EDLVA Super components were productionized through private industry.

Project PRITHVI

Assembly & Testing of SPST Switches and 9.75 GHz Dielectric Resonator Oscillator for RAS 1500 and Tot imparted to BEL, Ghaziabad.

Project Trishul

Associated in the design & development of 35 GHz DRDO and repaired imported DRDS used in project.

Project COIN & VISHAL

Actively associated in the design & development of SPST switches DROS 9GHZ 11 GHz & 169Hz for project COIN and TOT was imparted to MIS ECIL. DRDO in 26 GHz, 35 GHz using doubles & SPST & SPDT Switches from 18- 90 GH_2 were designed & developed for VISHAL Project- were designed.

Granted PATENT in 2009 for High-Speed High Power Single Pole Sixteen Throw Switch (SP167) for a period of 20years.

****

Ms. KB Subha Lakshmi
DRTC, Technical Officer D

I have joined DE RE as ISA-11 28th April, 198 Then I was Posted to RAPAR- 11 Division and reported to Shri e Madhusudan Rao Guru Division head, RADAR -n division. Since then, I served the laboratory in various capacities, i.e. ISA-11, USA 1, SSA, TO 'A' and now To 'D'. I have continued to work in the same division for about 361/2 year and played a vital role in various projects viz., AJANTA. CANNON COIN, VIKRAM, Complex Emitter classifier (CEC). DOLPHAN FLINT for integrated Ew Programme SAMYUKTA Worked by ECM-L ECM-M, ECM-H & ESM entities of noncom segment and for projects VARONA, DOLPHIN-11, HIM- SHAKTI, GARUDA of my contributions also go to GAV and Aerostat platform of RUSTUM-11 and Airborne & ship Borne projects of programme SAMUDRIKA.

The following are some of my commendable Contributions and works.

I have carried out the development testing Integration and documentation of the major subsystems and systems such as Receives processing. Real Time Crate (RTC) generation. Conical scan Extraction and measurement boards for project Ajanta, CANNAN CEC, DOLPHIN, FLINT, SAMYUKTA etc.

My Contribution also goes to project COIN in the area of development and testing of video extractor and 32 bits To A generator Cards, DMA interface cards for 8086 CPU and high Speed Amplitudes Digitization cards

I have carried out the chasis wiring and documentation for project VIKRAM. I have worked for development and testing of font End Hardware and Carried out documentation with Packages such as Harvard Graph Picture makers under DOS & UNIX environment and developed required software in C and C++ language.

Project VARUNA

Associated in design, development, testing 2 integrations of EST Subsystem Developed Software using VHDL Programming design and development of stimulator hardware e software for EST subsystem testing. Development of Embedded application software wing X LINX EDI quit for establishing Ethernet link.

Project DOLPHIN II: Development and testing of EST Subsystem hardware and Receiver processor subsystem hardware.

Project GARUDA Design, Development, testing, integration, evaluation and documentation of Rx processor and ESS -Subsystem hardware for UAV and Aerostat platforms. Gyro & Blanking interface - hardware & software. Connector and cable harness details for both UAV and Aerostat

Project HIMRAJ (HIMSHAKTI)

Development testing and documentation of Realisation of interface Control Unit (ICU) hardware. Configuration & development of Receiver Processor Hardware.

Project SAMUDRIKA:

Design, development testing, Integration, evaluation and documentation of ESI Subsystem hardware for ship drone and Airborne project Implemented the VHDL coding, ported and texted Receives processes subsystem hardware for ship borne project. Broad processor subsystem hardware for ship borne project.

Project SARANG:

Design, development testing and documentation of wide-open RA LRU - Back plane, front Panel PCBs, Connectors & Cable harness details.

Project Rustom II

Wide Band Processor board hardware, will band processor LRU hardware, Generation of software. Generation of related document for the aboveboard and LRU

For the past 3 years, I am associated with TSO's office of director's secretariat and contributed for smooth functioning of the project. Some of activities include: processing of APAR's of DRDS and DRTC cadres, processing of security clearances for foreign nationals, maintaining Database of all employees and projects of PLRL; extending logistic support for Smooth Conduct of project review meetings. And other lab meetings, coordinating with treats and other sister labs.

In recognition of my outstanding work. I have received laboratory awards and Best Performance Awards in DRTC category at DRDO Harts awards ceremony.

****

Ms. Usha Kiran U Shetty
DRTC, Technical Officer C

Working for LCA FCS Software development of Flight Control System with FCS Software. Major work involved:

DFCC-OFP, ADC-OFP & LADC-OFP Design: I was responsible for preparation of Software Design Document for Digital Flight Control Computer (DFCC), Air Data Computer (ADC); Levcon Air Data Computer (LADC Operational Flight Program (OFP) releases of various versions. This work involved: -

1) Updating foreground scheduling jobs w.r.t design - Preparation & Updation of Unique identifier table which contains more than 650 procedures ; functions of 31 packages of OFP. Generation of design document w.r.t changes in design for all the packages of DFCC, ADC & LADC-OFP software.

2) Verification of Pressure Transducer Coefficients for ADC & LADC Boxes: Each of the ADCs and LADCs has four pressure transducers. For converting the transducer frequency input to pressure values in engineering units, the set of coefficients are required to be loaded in EEPROMS. This work involved - Verifying the coefficient files in Ada used for romable code generation used for fusing the data in EEPROMS with respect to manufacturers data. - Preparation of Version Description Document (VDD) for the corresponding pressure transducers coefficient for every release.

3) Software Configuration Management Activity: I was responsible for the entire Configuration management process of DFCC, ADC & LADC-OFP software releases of different versions. This work involved, verifying & reviewing the release process of configuring the design and test files in Tele logic Synergy database which provides various control for the configured files. Also verifying the build process for local, engineering and formal releases of DFCC, ADC & LADC-OFP.

4) Preparation of Functional changes & Impact Analysis for each of the releases of OFP: This work involved preparation of Impact Analysis and functional changes by extracting the information from the database for functionality changes and corresponding Test IDs for each release which is used for Hardware Software Integration Test.

5) Tracking Of Software Changes: This work involved creation and updation of databases on day-to-day basis w.r.t Software Problem Reports & Software Design Change Report for various versions. Generation of reports into open & closed SPRS for design and test to track schedule.

6) Version Description Document (VDD): This work involved - Preparation of functional changes from the previous releases by extracting information from the closed SPRS and corresponding SDCRS from the database. - Open SPRS from the database for particular release. Waiver preparation of the procedures which exceed 100 executable statements for ever release.

7) SCM Library: This work involved -configuration of all the soft and hard copies of the documents in library and maintenance of the database.

8) OTHER Activities: Involved in the procurement activities of the stores and also other activities which is assigned by the lab as and when required. Outcome: Maintenance of the database for SPRS, SDCRS has helped the releases without any errors and it has led to successful flight trials of Tejas. Impact analysis has lead for the smooth conducting of smooth Hardware Software Integration tests. Maintenance of the SCM library has helped the easy access to the documents for the users.

****

Dr. Mr. Sanjay Kumar Singh
DRDS, Scientist G

I worked on numerous projects/ assignments after joining as Scientist on 05 June 1987 at CASSA, Bangalore, subsequent to completion of one year training at IAT, Pune in Ballistic Space Mechanics Fellowship Course during 1986-87. Subsequently, I had the opportunity to work at ISSA, Delhi and ADE, Bangalore. Some of the important/ significant contributions are as follows:

1. Weapons Systems Analysis: Worked for nearly twenty-four years in various aspects of weapons effects modelling: to include a few- conventional high explosive weapons/ warheads, fuel- air explosive warhead (as a subproject from HEMRL, Pune for modelling various stages of functioning of the warhead). Bunker buster weapons for underground hardened targets, etc. Numerous targets were considered- metallic and fibre reinforced composite panels of airborne structural parts (wings, fuselage, etc.). Derived damage criterion for damage of such structural elements (for both metallic/ composite structures). Developed elaborate models for various phases of functioning of fuel-air explosive warhead- models for fuel cloud formation subsequent to rupture of container (near field and far field models) and subsequent detonation of the cloud over target area using suitably chosen numerical techniques of computational fluid dynamics. Pressure- impulse criterion for numerous targets (including ear- drum rupture/ lung rupture criterion of human beings) was used for evolving a suitable damage criterion of targets. Models were also developed for dispersion of parachute borne canisters from the mother bomb/warhead.

2. Information/ Decision Support Systems: Led a team of scientists for the development of strategic information/ decision support system. Models based on blast wave propagation, interaction of these waves with structures, numerous models for damage assessment and damage criterion were established. Also guided team members to develop models based on game theory for formulation of deterrence policy. Was awarded Team award by the then SA to RM.

3. Basic research: Used Shock Ray Method; (also known as new theory of Shock Dynamics) for prediction of location and strength of curved shocks. A computational scheme was developed and its computational efficiency in comparison to existing analytical formulations as well as computational schemes was demonstrated in numerous international/ national publications. Was awarded Ph. D. from IISc for this work. Later the same technique was generalized for propagation of detonation (reactive wave in two-phase medium) wave through a combustible mixture of air and fuel-droplets.

4. Later shock wave propagation theories were extended to consider such materials as numerous types of rocks, soils (dry and wet with varying degrees of water saturation), etc. Detailed mathematical models were also developed for propagation of seismic waves due to an air-blast by team members under my guidance. A large number of well written reports were prepared and forwarded to concerned authorities.

5. Managerial and corporate responsibilities: Worked in MALE UAV TAPAS programme office; was engaged in managerial/ corporate activities- co-ordination with DRDO HQ, Services HQ, Production Partners, etc.; preparation of replies to parliamentary queries, periodic progress reports (weekly, monthly, bi-annually. etc.);

Co-ordination with stake holders by Board level reviews, documentation for these reviews and their dissemination to all stake holders, etc.

****

Ms. Hama P Hiremath
DRTC, Technical Officer C

I began my career in ADE in Receiver group of Avionics division as TM-A in April 1983. My first assignment was to develop the Range unit for Pilotless target Aircraft - Lakshaya. Lange unit measures the slant Range of Ground Control Station and the PTA (Pilotless target Aircraft). I was involved in the design and carried out complete development opportunity to learn a lot technically while developing the Range Unit with independent responsibility and it helped me through my career. I have configured the unit into Rack mountable and got the units qualified functionally and electronically for meeting the requirements.

The Range Unit was successfully used in several flights' trials of Lakshaya. It is still useful in Lakshaya ground Station. The Range Data and Azimuth Data of PTA were plotted on XY plotter to indicate the exact location of Lakshaya during flight. This parameter is of significant importance for Lakshaya mission and Control point of view. I have been involved in process the ToT to TATA Electronics for production and subsequently carried out acceptance tests for the project. I have taken part in evaluation trials of Lakshya at ITR, Chandipur.

I was also assigned for development of Azimoth offset correction of Antenna position angel with true north position. I joined Antenna design group FTTT in 2005. In this place, I got opportunity to associate in the development activities of various indigenous Antennas for ongoing UAV programme of ADE. I have supported by creating I have of antenna of different types such as slotted blade and monopole, Yagi Microstrip antennas arrays. I have carried out critical VSWR and Radiation pattern measurements to ensure functionality of these antennas. I have been responsible for clearing of all antennas and associated RF Coaxial cables before all field trials of UAV such a Lakshya, Nishant, Rustom -I, Tapas, Nirbhay etc.

In addition, I have participated as GCs & Datalink team member in evaluation trials of various UAV.

I thank almighty for giving me the opportunity to serve the nation as a team member of ADE, DRDO fraternity. I wish ADE to be successful in all its endeavours for the Country's progress and Defense security.

****

Mr. Sagayam Backyanathan
DRTC, Technical Officer B

1) Providing support for all project assembly activities in PAAC assembly.

2) Lakshaya: Supporting of mechanical work in all in including Rivitting, grinding, driving Taping etc in preciroo components.

Nirbhay: I carried out LRV Scheme GLO1G LIGL02 air Vehicle and Carried out Supporting of technical work to assist all technicians.

- Fixing of name boards for all divisional heads.
- Dispatching and helping in pattern works in carpentory.
- Contribution is sports: Represented ADE football team in A, B, C and super division (State level).
- Participated in DRDO South outer & Intra zone tournaments. Supported in Conducting All India Defence Initiation foot ball tournament (Argin cup) and south Inter and Intra Zone tournaments.

****

Mr. S Sampath
DRDS, Scientist, H

System integration of missile, testing trials Coordination between DRDL and BEL UAV system integration customer support. Design, fabrication and testing of onboard power supply switching units, pyro environmental units and its testing. Evolving system integration plan for missile, Fabrication of onboard cable fabrication, Design and execution of Missile to checkout interface, Flight trials at ITR balasore for AGNI. Prithvi war head Test vehicle integration and development of ground testing setup. Procurement and planning for the system integration activities

Project management work related to coordination between DRDL and BEL regarding Trishul projects/s System integration and testing of Lakshya, Limited series production, user training, customer support for Lakshya users namely Airforce. Navy, Army. Nishant system integration and user trials at Pokhran Project Director of Lakshya 2 from Nov2009 to March 2012 Conduct of four launch campaigns and demonstration the all the objectives of Lakshya 2 as per JSQR requirements notable low level flight at 15 meter in clean and 25meterin tow configuration and Autonomous flight Joint project Director Project management systems, coordination for conduct of flight trial, organizing reviews, coordination with HQ for JSQR formalization Group Director for three major divisions of ADE namely (A)FTTT division- the area of RF.

Communication, Data link, flight instrumentation Flight systems (B) USD division - dealing with system Integration & flight trials of UAVS- Lakshya 1,2 Nishant Rustom 1, Rustom 2 Cruise missiles Nirbhay. LGB Project Sudharshan and the development of Check out systems ground systems and (C) MST divisions dealing with development, testing of EO Payloads for Nishant, Rustom 1 Rustom 2 and Laser seeker for Sudharshan LGB. Preparatory for ATOL Corporate management Budget - Group Director for three divisions management, accounting and Mechanical transport & Audit Aeronautical Test Range ATR Chitradurga Aeronautical Test Range by leading team at ATR is being undertaken - a vast infrastructure project consisting of latest Radar, Telemetry, Fibre Optic networked stations, Communications local, ATC Air Traffic Control management to cater UAV flights particularly about 60 flights of TAPAS (Rustom 2) Rustom 1 Panchi. Also, VVIP aircraft movements and Air force flight testing Wes facilitated. Also, other major testing activities of DRDO labs such as MTRDC, LASTEC R & DE (E). CAIR LRDE is being facilitated.

ISRO RLV project related trials are also facilitated and support provided A project proposal Project PDS - ATR was made and sanctioned for the operation. Maintenance of ATR Programme director (Cruise missiles) From 27 September 2019 functioning as

Programme director Cruise Missiles) leading the two cruise missile projects SLCM Submarine launched cruise missiles and Project ITCM - Indigenous Technologies for Cruise missiles Project Management Project Nirbhay ITCM - Project Director for Project Nirbhay Interacted with 7 partner labs and numerous Technology divisions of ADE to conduct flight trials of NGL 05 in Nov2017 and NGL 06 in April 2019. Important technology of complete mission in Way Point Navigation and particularly low-level sea skimming flight at 5 meter above the ground/ sea was demonstrated. Also, was show cased in Def expo 2018 at Chennai and in Republic Day parade of 2018. It was show cased in Def expo in Feb2020 at Lucknow. New project proposal to integrate indigenous engine indigenous RF seeker was made and a multi lab Project ITCM was sanctioned in July 2019. Closer interaction with GTRE to integrated ingenious engine run and detailed preparation and realisation of first flight was made ready in September 20 for flight trial.

****

Mr. Chandrasekhar
DRDS, Scientist G

1. NPOL from May 1987 to May 2007 (Sc B to Sc F) Involved in mechanical design, development and packaging of underwater acoustic Transducers of low frequency, high power handling of active sonars (Projectors) such as Tonpilz Transducers, Flex tensional Transducer. In addition to conceptualization, design and development of Obstacle Avoidance Sonar including array, under water communication Transducers with (Dual band widths) for ships and submarine (Indian make) application. Also carried out design, development and testing of underwater connectors & junction box. A part form this taken up design and development of spacing kit for on board application where in the underwater cables can be joined in-situ was completed on board a submarine.

In addition, carried out setting up of facilities like pressure testing, pressure cycling, hydro-vulcanizing units & hydrophone assembly in vacuum for transduces production. Established vibration testing facility in the division for carrying out the hydrophone sensitivity and transducers are being tested. Conceptualization, design development of special purpose hydraulic machines for assembly of projectors such as boot assembly with vulcanizing facility. Biasing unit, Stacking machine, Fiber winding machine (Circumferential Biasing Machine for Piezoelectric cylinders with online tension reading facility) and Vacuum assembly etc., These facilities are established in house and at production agency for the assembly and mass production of transducer for least rejection of transducers in the production line.

Head Transducer Engineering Division from 2005 to 2007

1. DRDO Technology Award (Medal & Certification) by SA to RM on National Technology Day (11 May 2002) for developing Flex tensional Transducer for Towed array project.

2. ADE from June 2007 to Dec 2020 (Sc F to Sc G) - Project Rustom-1 UAV Joint Project Director from June 2007 to Aug 2010 and Project Director from Sept 2010 to May 2020.

Some of the land marks/achievements are:

1. First UAV in the country to prove and demonstrate conventional take-off and Landing.

2. To fly at above 20,000 flights with Gimbled pay load (40 kg) ADE make flying it took place from Kolar Airfield.

3. UAV to fly for 10 hrs. endurance with EO Pay load (40 kg) form Kolar Airfield.

4. To fly 220 km Range with 40 kg EO Pay Load from ATR, Chitradurga.

5. Demonstrated first in the country the Use of Li-ion batteries as secondary power source in R1.

6 Integrated WOW, Radio Altimeter for DGPS for future ATOL application.

7. Integrated of OPATS a secondary system for ATOL.

8. Integrated Pico SAR and Wireless Datalink system to prove a Datalink system and Ethernet for future UAVS application.

9. Demonstration of high-speed taxiing with external store. 10. ATR runway was made Operational by conducting flight of R1 UAV.

Conducted demo flights at INS Parandu, Air defence. Navy also at Bhilai Airport for paramilitary forces Technology Group Award (cash and certificate) - Team 2012 (on 11 Jan 2012) in recognition for the excellent team work for the successful flight of Rustom-1 UAV.

3. TDF Scheme

Chairman, PMMG for the Development of Drones for carriage of stores in High Altitudes as part of TDF Scheme, a requirement projected by Indian Army. Three Indian Industries are identified under Engine, Hybrid and Electrical categories and recommended DRDO HQ to place orders to vendors to initiate development.

****

Mr. Sridhara Rao
DRDS, Scientist F

I was involved in the design, development, testing of various electronic components, LRUS, sub-systems, systems and launching of various air vehicles throughout my career spanning over 38 years.

LCA/ DISPLAYS PROJECT

#Hybrid Micro-Circuits:

Buffer hybrid; 2.Sync hybrid; 3.Raster hybrid; 4. Cursive hybrid: These hybrids have been developed, produced in quantities and handed over to the user group.

FALCON PROJECT

#Hybrid Micro-Circuits:

1. Antenna Switching Unit (ASU), 2. Flasher Unit (FU): These hybrids have been developed, produced in quantities and handed over to the user group.

TEMPEST PROJECT (DARE)

Microwave Integrated Circuits: For ESM systems.

1. Power dividers. a) 1Gc b) 4Gc to 56c: Designed the Power dividers using Wilkinson technology: Using HPEESOF S/W simulated each of the circuit independently; combined them and tuned them for optimum performance.

2. Band Pass Filter, Pass band: 4Gc to 5Gc Stop band: a) DC to 4Gc; b) 5Gc to 18Gc. Designed the BPF using Generalized Chebyshev technology. This circuit contains three low pass filters operating at 5Gc, 7.5Gc and 9Gc and a high pass filter operating at 4Gc. Each of the circuit was independently designed using In-house CAD software package and was simulated using HPEESOF package. They were cascaded and tuned for optimum performance. This circuit uses Microstrip technology.

3. Two-way Power divider, 750MHz to 1250MHz: Design, development of Power divider which uses Microstrip technology: Er=10; produced in quantity using thin film process 4. Parallel coupled filters: Developed six types of band pass filters with pass band freqs: 6-8GHz, 7.3-10.1GHz, 9.4-12.2GHz, 11.5-14.3GHz, 13-15.8GHz, 15.1-18GHz; Microstrip technology; Er=2.2;

LAKSHYA/LSP PROJECT

Microwave Integrated Circuits:

Power divider/combiner; 3input, 2output; Fre=1486 MHz: Designed & developed for Scan converter; dual hybrid ring, Sports, Microstrip technology; Er=2.2. 2. Low pass filter; Fre=1486 MHz: Developed LPF using Microstrip technology; Er=2.2; Produced in quantity & handed over to the user.

NIRBHAY PROJECT

Senior Scientist of Nirbhay PO of ADE heading electronics group.

Responsible for providing qualified, QA cleared LRUS; # Fulfill the requirements of integration

#Conduct of NGL03, 04 and 05 trials at range; # Committees & gt; 40 Nos; # Finance, transport, manpower, other logistics for the above DIVISIONAL ACTIVITIES, MICRO-CIRCUITS TECHNOLOGY CENTRE Carried out extensive upgradation of microcircuits facility. Lab has been expanded, technical interiors carried out, about eight machineries bought. Lab has been extensively used for development of HMCS and MICS for various developmental and project activities as mentioned above.

DIVISIONAL ACTIVITIES, ELECTRONIC ENGINEERING TECHNOLOGY CENTRE

Head of EETC division: Responsible for electronics packaging and qualification testing activities which include Assembly of components on to printed circuit boards, Wiring Subsystems, Preparation of auxiliary looms & RF cables, Environmental tests, Dynamic tests, EMI-EMC tests for various ongoing projects. Involved in the in-house D & D activities. # Printed Circuit Boards, # Subsystems, # Auxiliary Looms, RF Cables handled thousands of Work Orders

DIVISIONAL ACTIVITIES, MECHANICAL TRANSPORT SECTION

Head of MT section: Handled the functioning of MT section. Took care of overall activities including operation, maintenance. # 901s honored: 22958 Nos., # KMs Run: 391000, # Drivers recruited: 12Nos. # Vehicles bought: 8Nos, # Preventive/ Breakdown maintenance done: 348 Nos. # No. of requests able to handle: 40 per day, # Trial campaigns supported: 20 Nos.

DIVISIONAL ACTIVITIES, KNOWLEDGE CENTRE

Head of KC division: Guiding all the activities pertaining to library including physical holdings and e- resources.

FUNCTIONAL MANAGEMENT

(i)Infrastructure up gradation: # Challenging tasks of infrastructure up-gradations successfully carried Out in EETC, MT and Nirbhay divisions. Latest facilities are available now.

(ii) Human resource: # Member-Secretary: Various boards of HRD.

LEADERSHIP RESPONSIBILITIES

Head of team Nirbhay (electronics) (Project), DH, EETC (Technology division), DH, MT (Corporate division), DH, Knowledge Centre (Corporate division).

****

Ms. Sunita G Khedekar
(A & A) Administrative Officer DRDO

I joined DRDO in 1/10/1983 in one of the oldest laboratory 37 years which was named NCML at that time. Presently I am retiring from NMRL on 31/10/2020. In my Service was my pleasure that whichever responsibility I was given, span, it I tried my best for completion of the same. In 37 year major responsibilities given to me, were maintaining services. Book Appointment- Retirement documents papers, preparing Do Part II. In dispatch section, worked on Telegram machine in nineties.

Preparation the task as ac ledges which comprises (RV/DCIV/Ledger Action stock verification/TRVR/CV disposal (condemnation) EXIV / Items transferred from project to build-up / Gate passes Retornable / Non-Retornable. It would always remain my memorable pride, 9 honors for myself that I could serve my nation by performing my duty in a dignified manner and in a healthy & supporting environment. For this, thank all of you.

****

Mr. BK Chandrasekhar
DRTC, Technical Officer, C

I joined LRDE, Bangalore as D/M II on 28 July 1988 and I was posted to MED, I was engaged in drafting work on Radar Group from there I learnt drafting package software and started work on computer. Again I posted on public interest to Defence Bio Engineering and Electro Medical Laboratory (DEBEL) Bangalore on 15.09.1989. I started drafting work on Automatic Inflatable Life jacket, and learnt AutoCAD software started working on Anti G Suit, Life jacket, Bladder, Helmet, mask & Etc and also all the manual drafting which was done on the board & fed in to the computer by using AutoCAD software.

During in the year 1992 I joined in Department of Life support system was engaged on Drawings of components and assembly drawings on 3D Modeling by using Ideas & UG software on work station and 2D drawing by using AutoCAD Software of the following LRUS of ILSS Project. Demand Oxygen Regulator (DOR), Anti G Valve, Personal Equipment Connector (PEC), Back up Oxygen System (BOS), Emergency Oxygen System (EOS), Solenoid Valve Oxygen sensor (O2 Sensor).and On Board Oxygen System (OBGS).

1) Carried out the inspection of the component, checking and correction of the drawings and giving the tolerance by considering the functional aspect of the component. Of the following project work TDLAS Base Oxygen Sensor, Electro Pneumatic Demand Breathing regulator (EPDBR), Dilution demand Oxygen Regulator (DDOR-MK-3) Apart from the above supervision of the drawings related assignments given to the contract engineers & carried out the verification & correction of the same. With the entire above task I have also been involved procurement of stores initiated / processed various demand pertaining to the stationary, AMC of the design Center that the latest version of the software available to the users arranging timely updates training courses during upgrade of the software. Co-ordination with the Service Engineer for maintenance of PCs Peripherals, UPS, & Colour copier ensures the proper functioning with the AMC groups with the vendors & by arranging preventive maintenance activities.

I was happy & satisfied with my work assignments of the various projects activities related by using latest CAD tools has given me an ample opportunities and challenging to demonstrate my capabilities, the support & guidance offered by my Group Heads was highly motivating.

During my tenure I have worked under 7 Directors, I express my sincere thanks to DEBEL for giving me an opportunity to serve, I thank Director madam, Associated Directors, Joint Directors, Division Heads, Senior officers and DEBEL Family for providing all encouragement & support in discharging my duties, while in service I have gathered lots of good memories to carry with me at the time of my superannuation. DEBEL has allowed me to grow from D/M II to TO & C; in the category of DRTC. I wish my organization very best in all its future endeavors in the years to come.

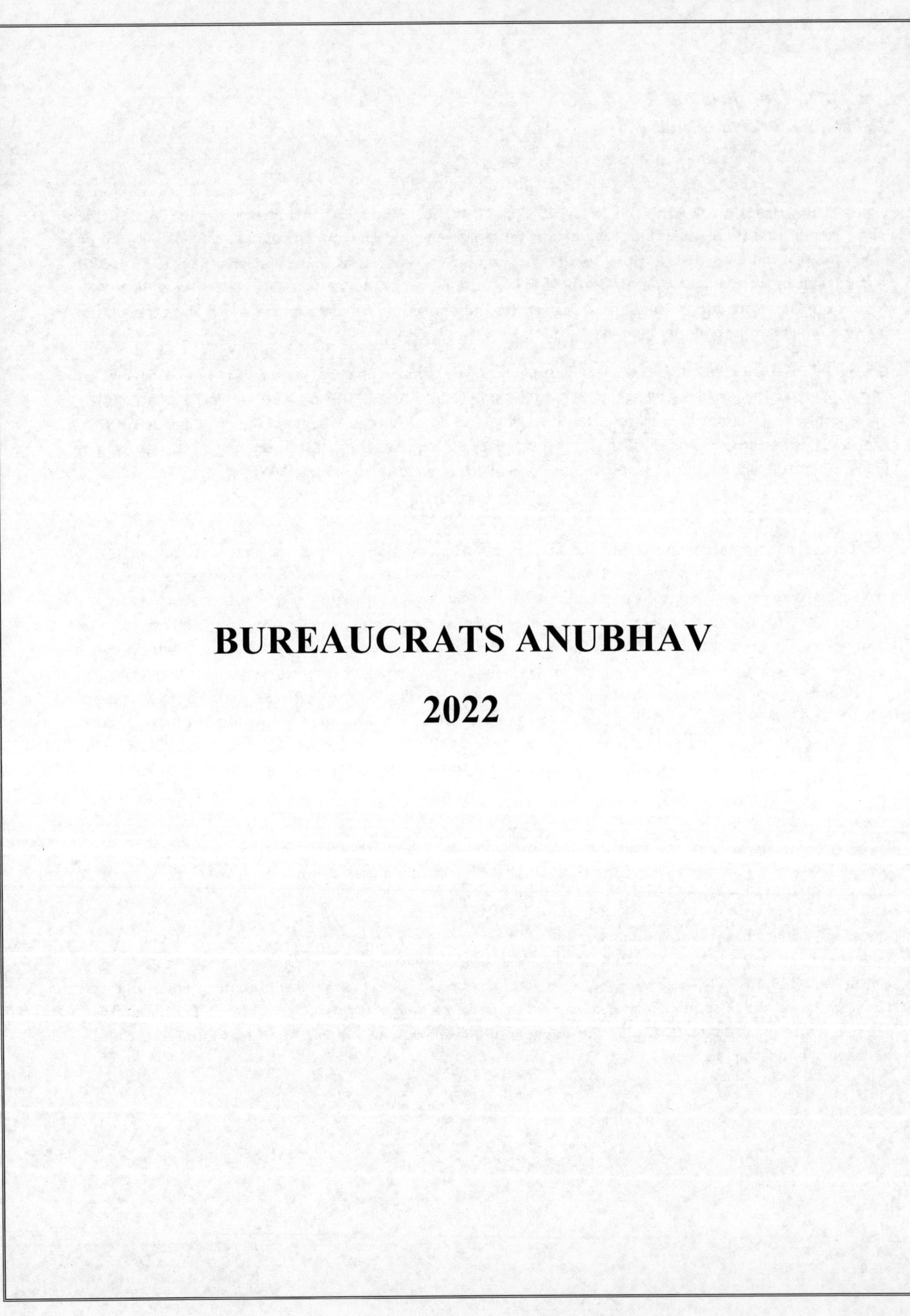

BUREAUCRATS ANUBHAV

2022

भारत सरकार

GOVERNMENT OF INDIA

कार्मिक, लोक शिकायत तथा पेंशन मंत्रालय

MINISTRY OF PERSONNEL, PUBLIC GRIEVANCES & PENSIONS

पेंशन एव पेंशनभोगी कल्याण विभाग

DEPARTMENT OF PENSION & PENSIONERS' WELFARE

ANUBHAV

2022

Contents

ANUBHAV Write-Ups

2. Anubhav 2022

Mr. Tallavajhula Venkat Narsimha
GCS, Assistant Registrar

March 1997 to October '1999 - worked as PA to Union Minister for Environment & Forests I Prof. SaifuddinSoz & Sri Suresh p. prabhu] , New Delhi. March, 96 to Feb, 97 - worked as PA to Director (Joint secretary level), project Tiger. ln the Project Tiger Directorate, New Delhi.

Jan 1994 to Feb, 96 - Worked as PA to Ex. Governor Hon. Sri S.N. Dwivedi, (in the status of Union cabinet Minister) of Arunachal Pradesh & Convenor of National Committee ofl25th Birth Anniversary of Mahatma Gandhi under the Deptt. Of culture, Ministry of Human Resource development, Govt. of India, New Delhi.

1993 - Worked as PA to Director (Admn / conservation & Survey) in the Ministry of Environment & Forests, Govt. of lndia, New Delhi. Feb 1991- Dec, 1992: Worked as PA to Development Commissioner (in the Rank of Joint Secretary), Export Processing Zone, (VEPZ), Ministry of Commerce, Govt. of lndia, Ministry of Commerce, Visakhapatnam.

1989 – 90: Worked as PA to Union Minister of Environment & Forests I Sri Nilamani Routray New Delhi

1986 - 89: Worked as Stenographer attached with Under Secretary (Admn) / (Finance) in the Ministry of Environment & Forests., New Delhi. Assisted in conducting including international Forestry Forum Meet held in New Delhi in the year 1989 and also various international /National Meetings of the Ministry.

Assisted in organizing all lndia PCCFs/chief wildlife wardens/Field Directors, Project Tiger meet at Corbett National Park, Ramnagar, up and other places. Assisted in organizing various National Committee meetings on 125th Birthday Celebrations of Mahatma Gandhi under the Ministry of Human Resource Development in New Delhi and toured all over the country along with the Convenor to propagate and convene the event.

Actively assisted in organizing various events like ozone Day, world Environment Day and other important events in the Ministry. Discharged the duties of Central Public information Officer under RTI Act Nodal Officer in the Tribunal and also served as Drawing & Disbursing Officer of the Tribunal intermittently from 2008 till date during the tenure.

Mr. Kantilal Rambhai Rathod
IPOS, Sub Master

I Feel Proud to be a part of Department of Post; I have completed my 34 years of service as a postal employee. During my entire career, I personally found that the department becomes better with the time.

On the day of appointment, I still remember there were a small building two wooden chairs and tables and today on the day of retirement, I am the sub postmaster of fully computerized CBS office having departmental building.

Once we could never even imagine that, Post office will have an ATM facility in future. Today we feel proud that we have a banking license. During the implementation of project arrow and CBs, I feel many difficulties and also applied for VRS to get out from the situation. But, during the notice period of VRS I feel that this change to become a part of pioneers. I made up my mind to accept the challenge and today I am retiring on superannuation.

I will be always thankful to the Department for better social life and helping in the evolution of me and my family.

****

Mr. Vijay Shanker
CSS, Section officer

I, Vijay Shanker, had joined the Government of India as an LDC in the year 1981. I was posted in the FCRA Division of the Ministry of Home Affairs w.e.f. 31.08.1981 till 05.02.1989. Thereafter, I joined the SSO Section, MHA on deputation basis, where I worked as a JRO w.e.f. 06.02.1989 till 15.04.1990. On being promoted as an UDC, I worked in the Foreigner's Division, the Freedom Fighter's Division and the Indian Citizenship Division in MHA from 16.04.1990 till 19.09.2001. Later, on being promoted as Assistant, I was posted in Ministry of Statistics& Programme Implementation w.e.f. 20.09.2001 till 20.05.2003.

I have been working in DoPT since 21.05.2003. I was initially posted as an Assistant in the SM-II Section in the EO Division, where I worked from 30.05.2003 till 04.09.2012. I was promoted as Section Officer in 2012 and for a brief period I was posted in EO(SM-I) Section. Since 2013, I have been working as Section Officer in the EO (ACC) Section in the EO Division.

IN EO Division, the work is mainly related to proposals which are submitted to the Appointments Committee of the cabinet relating to Board level appointments/extensions, etc in Public Sector Banks, Central Public Sector Enterprises. I also looked after work relating to elections/general elections, etc.

Throughout my career I had the pleasure of working with some great officers and even better colleagues. The support I got from my superiors and my colleagues, I can say that I completed my service to the satisfaction of my heart. For this I will always be thankful to God and my second family in office.

****

Mr. Sunil Kumar
CSS, Section Officer

I will be retiring as Section Officer from Government service after completing 37 years & 9 months of service in November, 2017. I joined as L.D.C. on 18th Feb, 1980 in Ministry of Home Affairs and posted in RGI. I worked there from 1980 to 1988.

In the year 1988, I was promoted as U.D.C. and posted in Joint Intelligence Committee which was further renamed as National Security Council Secretariat. It is a secret Department and it was mandatory for every person in NSCS to maintain secrecy. The national security issues are discussed in NSCS. I was involved in the work of National Security Advisory Board. Being a sensitive organisation, the work allotted to me cannot be described here.

In the year 2003, I became Assistant and transferred in Department of Telecom. From 2003-2008, I dealt within the work of technical cadre along with court cases, RTI, Parliament Questions etc. In the year 2008, I sought transfer from DoT and further transferred in DoPT. From 2008- 2009, I worked in the office of MOS (PP).

In the year 2009, I was transferred from DOPT to Public Enterprises Selection Board. I was given there the work related to shortlisting of Candidates for Board level posts in CPSES, Confirmation, and Extension, creation of Posts, RTI, and Parliament Questions etc. I became Section Officer in 2011 and dealt within the same work which I was earlier doing as Assistant. I worked there from 2009 to April, 2017. In April, 2017, I was transferred from PESB to DoPT and posted as S.O. R with additional charge of S.O (CR & Record) in May, 2017.

I would like to add here that the proper training is required for every employee on Administrative, finance and other official matters. The lack of training initially hampers the working of any Individual as he has to learn from precedents. Proper training in all issues should be imparted to all in order to increase the efficiency of the system. On this Occasion, I feel proud and content in serving the Govt. of India for such a long period, I tried my best to give maximum output.

****

Mr. Ashok Kumar Verma
CSSS, Private Secretary

I am thankful to DoPT for giving an opportunity to share my Anubhav – showcasing the work done during service.

First of all, in the year 1980, I joined Public Health Engineering Department (PHED) of Government of Rajasthan after clearing shorthand test and interview at Jaipur. I was posted in Ajmer, Rajasthan as Personal Assistant from4.4.1980 and worked there upto March, 1982. In PHED, Ajmer I worked with Superintendent Engineer and Chief Engineer, both the officers were very intelligent and cooperative in nature. There, I gained lot of experience and made many friends. That was the best time of my bachelor life.

In the year 1981 I cleared SSC Examination for the post of Steno Grade D. My journey in Central Government of India started on 25.3.1982 when I joined Central Electricity Authority (CEA), Ministry of Power, R.K. Puram, and New Delhi-110066. I was posted with Director, Training and Manpower Directorate of CEA which was located in Vasant Vihar, New Delhi. I worked there till 1985. Then, I was transferred to Thermal Operation Input-II Directorate (TOI-II Dte.) which dealt with supply of coal to all the Thermal Power Station in the country.

In the year 1987, I applied in the Narmada Control Authority (NCA) for the post of Personal Assistant on deputation basis and selected. In June, 1987, I joined NCA, Palika Bhawan, and R.K. Puram as Personal Assistant on deputation basis. In NCA, I worked with Under Secretary (Admn), Secretary and Member (Power), NCA. In the year 1990, NCA was shifted to Indore. I also had to join there and posted with Executive Member who was head of NCA and performed the duties of PS. It was my first experience as Private Secretary which helps me in performing my duties now when I am working as Private Secretary. I was in NCA up to June, 1991.

In June, 1991 I was again transferred back to my parent Department i.e. CEA and was posted in Coordination Division of CEA. In the year 1995, I was promoted as Personal Assistant (Ad hoc) and was posted with Chief Engineer (Coordination), CEA. I was posted with Secretary, CEA and worked there with 10 nos. of Secretaries for14 years and performed duties of PPS/PS as there was no PPS/PS.

In the year 2014, my name was selected for training in ISTM for the post of Private Secretary and in 2015 I was promoted as Private Secretary in the seniority list of 2013. I was transferred and joined DoPT on 1.6.2015 and posted with Deputy Secretary (Lokpal). Since February, 2016, I am working in the Establishment Reservation-II Section OF DoPT.

****

Mr. Debashis Kumar Sengupta
CSS, Deputy Secretary

I got the opportunity to serve under the Central Government when I successfully qualified in the Assistants & Grade Examination held in 1983 and started working in 1985 picking up three promotions along the way to the posts of Section Officer, Under Secretary and Deputy Secretary in 1993, 2007 and 2016 respectively. There are three Ministries where I have worked, i.e., Ministry of Labour & Employment, Ministry of Health & Family Welfare and finally in Department of Personnel and Training

During the course of my 33 year long service, I found myself having dealt with a wide array of subjects not a small part of which can be characterized as administrative, vigilance-related, overseeing of the administrative aspects of Central Government Industrial Tribunal cum-Labour Courts Public health institutes including their in-house procurement matters, their upgradation, handling JCM matters are some of the other activities in the discharge of which I was and still am intimately associated.

Needless to say, I have hugely enjoyed each of them plunging myself, as I did, headlong into each of these activities. Modesty forbids me to mention however, in generic terms it must be said that unless one immerses himself/herself completely in the job assigned to him/her, the performance becomes at best lackluster, at worst perfunctory. And why should a person with a modicum of sincerity and sense of proportion not do it, paid as he is, from the taxpayer's money. Whether I have been able to acquit myself creditably is for my senior officers to comment on; suffice it to say that wherever I have worked, I have always inspired myself to give of my best. The love, affection and cooperation that I have received from my colleagues are something that will remain forever etched in my mind, unique as they are in every sense of the words.

Therefore, I will call it quits with a tremendous sense of fulfilment hoping for a bright future for our beloved country. My country has given me much more than what I have given to her. During my Level-E training before my promotion to the post of Deputy Secretary, I visited 4 European countries two years ago as part of the overall training format. The experience was unique as it gave me a rare opportunity to see, firsthand how the various government institutions function there, their social life, governance and so on. All these varied experiences perhaps would not have been possible had 1 not got a chance to work under the Central Government. Therefore, on balance, and to sum up, my association with the Central Government as an employee has been extremely fruitful and unforgettable.

****

Mr. N Sriraman
CSS, Director

I joined Central Government service as Assistant in Central Secretariat Service in the month of January 1982. My initial posting was in Department of Posts, Ministry of Communications and served in the said department for nearly 12 years as Assistant and on promotion as Section Officer. While working as Assistant in Establishment Branch, Section Officer in Postal Policy and Operations Branch and thereafter as Desk Officer in Building projects Desk, I was able to gain knowledge of rules and regulations and experience as regards creation of posts in the field formations of Department of Posts, postal operations and policy and on processing of building projects including its monitoring. Work culture in Department of Posts was very good and with cooperation from my sub-ordinates and guidance of my seniors I could contribute significantly in all my assignments. My tenure in Department of Posts was very eventful and I really enjoyed my work fully, as due to excellent cooperation of my sub-ordinates and guidance.

2. I was thereafter transferred to Department of Telecom as Section Officer in December 1994 and was initially assigned the task of managing the affairs of Telecom Commission. This was the time when the Telecom sector in India was going through a big transformation. My assignment in the Telecom Commission was understandably very arduous and demanding. As Telecom Commission had to consider and deliberate on various crucial issues relating to privatization, regulations etc. of the Telecom sector, meeting of the Commission were to be organized at very short intervals and the decisions of the Commission followed up.

2.1 The matter regarding setting up of a Regulator for Telecom sector was also being considered at that point of time. This involved enactment of a statute. I was very closely associated with the drafting and enactment of statute and after many deliberations at various levels, the Telecom Regulatory Authority of India Act was enacted in the year 1997 paving the way for establishment of the Regulator the Telecom Regulatory Authority of India (TRAI). Subsequent to the establishment of TRAI, various rules under the said Act were to be framed to enable The Regulator to function smoothly. II was assigned the task of notification of various rules which I completed within the time stipulated. My assignment also involved attending to court cases, establishment matters of TRAI etc.

2.2 In addition to the above, a need was felt to provide a level playing field in Telecom Sector and therefore it had become necessary that operations wing of Department of Telecom be hived off. Accordingly, it was decided to set up a corporate body as a separate Government service provider of telecom services. The process involved engagement of a consultant to suggest the ways and means of effecting corporatization and thereafter based on the recommendations of the Consultant process the matter for seeking approval of the Cabinet. On approval of the Cabinet to the proposed setting up of a Corporate Body under Companies Act, the process of incorporation of the Company with Registrar of Companies was to be undertaken involving finalization of Memorandum of Association and Articles of Association. I was associated in the entire process of incorporation of the Corporate Body and finally Bharat Sanchar Nigam Limited was incorporated in the year 2000.

2.3 Simultaneously, there was a need to amend to TRAI Act 1997 to provide more clarity which included establishment of Appellate Body called Telecom Disputes Settlement (TDSAT). I was closely associated in the process of amendment of TRAI Act in the year 2000 and the establishment of TDSAD.

2.4 It was also proposed that there be convergence of Telecommunication, Broadcasting and IT. For this a fresh legislation on the lines of enactments in other connection is drafted. I was involved in the task of drafting of the legislation and then its introduction in Parliament.

****

Mr. Sunil T Shah
DRDs, Scientist G

Development at Gujarat University.(Prior to Joining DRDO): Data acquisition for Balloon Experiments. Developments of microprocessor-based code for collection of data from balloon payload in the space and transmit of the data to ground system. Development of programs for statistical application. Instrumentation and Development of Gun Concept:

Microprocessor based data acquisition system. Development of code for microprocessor. Sensor Integration and interface with digital electronics for Instrumentation was done. This microprocessor setup was used for evaluating illuminating candles and pressure and velocity measurements. Development of liquid propellant (LP) electro- thermal chemical (ETC) gun. Development of servo system for AD Gun. PC based instrumentation using digital storage oscilloscope (DSO) for LP gun. Development of internal ballistic code for regenerative loaded liquid Propellant Gun (RLPG).

Design and Development of Armament system for infantry combat vehicle: Development of Electrical firing control of three weapon system namely, main gun, machine gun, automatic grenade launcher. Development of feeding system of main Gun for two types of ammunition namely conventional shell and FSAPD Development of 40mm FSAPDS. The firing control unit was successfully evaluated for all the three weapon systems in a turreted configuration.

Weapon Sensor Interface Module (WSIM) for Individual Weapon system (IWS): As a team leader, I was responsible for development of the weapon sensor interface module (WSIM) for rendering sensor integrated electronic monitoring of IWS. At present three weapon parameter, namely Firing mode, caliber type, Numbers of round in magazine were monitored. The main challenge was incorporation of the electronic monitoring in the existing weapon-INSAS. I worked out the details for development of sighting system simulator (SSS) which displays the weapon status. The SSS was developed to carry out evaluation of the monitoring system and to study the output of ballistic code in terms of fuse-set-time & other parameters for firing air burst grenade. Identified & incorporated sensors on the weapon.

Integrated and evaluated WSIM on INSAS.

Development of 40mm Air Burst Grenade: I was responsible for design and development of the Air Burst Grenade (ABG) to enhance range, lethality and effectiveness of the grenade. I led the team for this multi-disciplinary project. The main challenge was to keep the existing dimension same and render air burst capability to grenade. ABG with wireless programming configuration was worked out and mechanical integrity of grenade body was established. ET Fuze with Safety Arming Mechanism and wireless fuze setter realized.

The ABG will be fired from the existing UBGL weapon. 40mm ABG for individual weapon was developed and successful firing evaluated. Development of 152/52 cal Advanced Towed Artillery Gun System (ATAGS). I was responsible for development of automation and control subsystem for ATAGS. The automation and control subsystem aims to incorporate all electric gun laying, ammunition handling and breech & firing operation. I led the team and successfully completed design calculations and modeling and simulation analysis for the gun automation and control. I also successfully finalized the technical specifications for the development of the subsystem. I have envisaged controller to provide various sequential operations with necessary safety interlocks. Automation and control subsystem for ATAGS was developed and successful firing evaluated. Now the ATAGS is under acceptance evaluation stage.

****

Mr. Shashi Shekhar Mahto
CSSS, Private Secretary

I got opportunity to serve in the Secretariat of Government of India. During the period of 37 years of long service, I have learnt file language and process and its management. During the period of service, I had been given training of office procedure which had helped me a lot. With the help of honest approach and determination I learnt operation of computer and other electronic instruments introduced in Government offices from time to time. Now entire office is working as e-office. I have got training of this and not felt any difficulty during working in e-office system. It is a good experience.

I had got opportunity to get experience of working in Administrative Section of Public Sector Undertaking & Parliamentary procedure etc. in Government of India. The experience of work was entirely different from one to other sections. With strong will power and sincere efforts I had justified the work allocated to me. Govt. of India is an ocean and its experience cannot be written and measured. What I experience in service was good. I personally cannot explain the experience in words. But I can say that sincere efforts, punctuality, responsibilities and honest towards their duties always helps us to create better understanding among officers, seniors and staffs.

****

Mr. Santosh Sikka
CSSS, Private Secretary

I Joined Government of India on 23 November, 1978 as an LDC in the erstwhile Ministry of Supply and Rehabilitation (DGS&D) and worked there for 14 years. It was a very long period that I spent in that office. In 1982, I joined as Stenographer Grade-D in 1983 in the same Ministry on qualifying the Departmental Examination. I joined Ministry of Defence in May, 1992 after decentralization of DGS&D.

In the year 2006, I was promoted as Personal Assistant in the Ministry of Defence. I served Government of India for 39 years 9 months. I performed so many tasks here; I took every new task as a new challenge whether it was punctuality or dedication to work. I gave my best. In the year 2010 I was transferred under Rotational Transfer Policy in the Ministry of Heavy Industries & Public Enterprises as Personal Assistant. In 2014, I was promoted as Private Secretary in the Ministry of Heavy Industries & Public Enterprises. I will retire in the month of August, 2018from Ministry of Heavy Industries & Public Enterprises.

During my service period, I have worked under various officers from time to time. They were actually my guides. Without their guidance, I could not have completed my tasks and completely my service remarkably for which I will remain indebted. Once again I would like to thank Government of India Ministries and colleagues under whom I have served.

****

Ms. Bhaswar Gangopadhyay
CSS, Deputy Secretary

My experience of 38 years of Government service.

I consider that it is a privilege to work for the Government of this vast country having more than 700 districts spread over in 29 States and 7 Union territories, no less than other big countries like China, USA, Russia, Canada, Australia or, Brazil etc. Having served in eight Ministries/ Departments / Divisions like Railways, Home Affairs, Cabinet Secretariat, Official Language, Women and Child Development, Information and Broadcasting, and lastly in Heavy Industries made me mature enough to undertake the journey for the rest of my life in a pragmatic way. Right from the early days in Accounts Department of two zonal Railways in Eastern India, the public service has taught me the lessons of life from a very grass-root level by interlinking activities of various arms of an organisation and indicating how they are dependent upon each other. It has made me realize the face of a beneficiary behind the figures of accounts and how it can change a situation from grim to encouraging. I remember how the release of funds for plantation drive in an arid region of a division of zonal Railways can bring about significant changes by introducing afforestation and help in restoration of ecosystem through conservation of flora of the region.

My long association with Home Affairs brought me in close contact with citizenship issues, security scenario of the country in general and effectiveness of being alert to a situation in order to prevent an untoward incident or, unwelcome situation. It has also made me aware about the contribution of Non-Government Organisations in nation building and huge areas of activities undertaken by them both at micro and macro levels. To share some of my experiences, I remember the involvement of these organisations (NGOs) in looking after not only orphan or, disabled children, men and women but also injured animals, birds and maintaining environmental equilibrium through nature conservation activities. Their activities in spreading education in the remotest part in the northern tip of the country close to the international border in Jammu and Kashmir to the southern tip of the country in the tsunami affected regions of the coastal districts of Tamil Nadu and Kerala are not only exemplary but also testimony to their commitment to the society. It was not possible for me to witness or, experience these without being a part of the public service team.

As a matter of fact more I have seen and experienced, more I have discovered myself among the victims of natural calamities, disabled persons, orphan children, senior citizens who are detached from their families. One of the greatest learning experience of my life came through my association with Ministry of Women and Child Development when I visited series of child care centres of rural West Bengal in 2009 known as 'Anganwadi' where expected mothers are given appropriate lessons for childbirth and given basic medicines and pre-school children are taught the basic lessons prior to going to school. I had witnessed focused attention of Anganwadi workers and Anganwadi helpers in running the Anganwadi centres with minimal support from government, often working selflessly for long hours for making a better future for the beneficiaries from makeshift arrangements often without a proper roof and basic necessities of life. I have seen in them the real concern for the would-be mothers, lactating mothers and their children in the respective areas. Their enthusiasm, zeal and dedication in some of the centres are exemplary. It is a different issue that both the quality and quantity of materials supplied to the centres do not commensurate with the demand. It is a gap which needs to be addressed at the appropriate level. The Integrated Child Development Services Scheme is one of the largest and unique programmes of its kind in the world for the benefit of young mothers and children in the age group of 0- 6 years.

My next posting was in the Central Board of film certification under Ministry of Information and Broadcasting is an unique experience in the sense that it took me to a virtual world and its connectivity with important issues of the society like impact of political disturbances, menace of terrorism, poverty, rich cultural heritage and history of this country, romance and storytelling through the medium of films of different categories like short, feature and research oriented documentary films of exceptionally enriching content. This is an eye-opening experience and rare occasion in the life of serving government servants to get acquainted with the film industry and different kinds of films with variety of audio-visual contents being made every day in many languages all over India.

My tenure in the Department of Heavy Industry gave me knowledge about how the Central Public Sector Enterprises are contributing to the national economy and various problems being faced by them. Lastly, being a part of Jal Shakti Abhiyan, which is aimed at improving water availability in draught affected, water stressed and over exploited areas of the country through different interventions like water conservation and rain water harvesting (through roof top structures etc.), renovation of traditional and other water bodies, reuse and recharge structures, watershed development and intensive afforestation, is another unique experience.

****

Mr. Singam Yadagiri,
GCS Engineer SG

I joined as Engineer SB in NRSA on 08/AUG/1984 after completion of my BE degree in 1983 from Osmania University. Initially I was involved in developmental activities of "hardware development division (HDD)" under Technical Group headed by Mr. ML Mittal. There I was working for development & testing of FSDU (Frame sync and de-commutation Unit) which was a Front-End hardware unit.

This FSDU unit was interfaced to Vax 11/730 Computer System. The serial data along with synchronized clock from the Bit Synchronizer unit was fed to the FSDU unit and data was stored in the computer for pre-processing of remote sensing data. The outputs of this pre-processed data in the form of ADIF, OAT, browse files along with RAW data recorded on the High Density Digital Tape Recorders are sent to further level of processing at NRSA Headquarters.

During year 1987, I was transferred to Earth Station Group where I was involved in IRS-1A data acquisition, recording and pre-processing operations. IRS-1A was first remote sensing project from ISRO and I was involved in the project as "deputy operational manager" for IRS-1A project. I have contributed to various IRS projects such as Project/Operations Manager IRS-1B, Project/Operations Manager Cartosat-2, and Project/Operations Manager oceansat-2, Project Manager for Cartosat-2C/2D/2E/2F and Dy. Operations Director for Cartosat-2Series. I also contributed to all the projects T&Es and the latest one is Hysis Project.

I was design team member of SPS data acquisition and processing System which was operationalized in 2012. I was involved in frequent up-gradations of SPS System as per the requirement. Currently I am superannuating in the capacity of Manager Real-time Data Archival Systems Facility (RDASF) of RDAS Group of SDR & ISA area.

****

Mr. Sharad Sharma
GCS, Scientist

I Joined Vikram Sarabhai Space Centre (VSSC) in 1982 and worked extensively on physical metallurgy, heat Treatment and welding of high temperature super alloys, ultra-high strength maraging steels, High Strength Low Alloy (HSLA) steels, and special stainless grades of steels for Indian space programme. Carried out extensive research on & Disorder entrapment in NiAl based intermetallics for enhancing their deformation characteristics and use at high temperature and & Development of microstructures in Fe-Al system under micro-g conditions & as Visiting Scientist at German Aerospace Establishment, Cologne, Germany from Jan. 1992 to Oct. 1992. Designated as the Project Leader, Special Purpose Materials Development Project in 1998 and under this assignment, successfully led the indigenous development programme for a series of import-critical special purpose alloys for inertial and navigation systems of satellite launch vehicles and satellites.

Guided the development of powder metallurgy based products, ferrous & non-ferrous alloys and special foundry and investment casting activities for Indian space programme, as Head, Materials Processing Division and subsequently Head, Special Materials Division of Materials and Metallurgy Group (MMG), VSSC from 2005 to 2011, Concurrent to the above responsibilities, spearheaded the efforts spanning over years to nurture the exotic field of micro-g materials processing in the country first as Project Manager and subsequently as Dy. Project Director, Micro-g Scientific Payloads, Space Capsule Recovery Experiment Project (SRE) of Indian Space Research Organization (ISRO). In addition to my own experiments, also coordinated various space experiments from India and abroad, keeping pace with the advanced space programmes world over, ISRO conceived and success.

Fully implemented one of its most formidable projects viz. Reusable Launch Vehicle-Technology Demonstrator (RLV-TD) wherein thermal protection of the space vehicle during atmospheric reentry is the most critical phase of the whole mission. As Associate Project Director (TPS), RLV-TD Project led the development of silica tiles, flexible surface insulation and other high temperature materials for RLV programme.

As Group Director, Materials & Metallurgy Group of VSSC from 2011 to 2016, was responsible for the development and supply of a range of ferrous and nonferrous materials/components and process- technologies for on-going as well as emerging programmes of ISRO, including performance-critical powder metallurgy products, complex-shaped investment casting, ignition resistance coatings, brazing technologies, special titanium alloys and materials processing and characterization support for cryogenic engine, semi-cryo engine and other projects. From 2016 to 20, as Dy. Director, Propellants, Polymers, Chemicals and other Projects. Materials (PCM) Entity, successfully led the important technical activities of PCM Entity in the areas of energy systems including development, qualification and delivery of Li-ion cells for launch vehicle and satellite projects, polymeric products such as modified foam insulation for cryo tanks of C-25 stage in GSLV MkIII and polyimide pipes for cryo stages in GSLV MkIII & GSLV, lab-scale development and scaling up of high burn rate propellant (PEDCEM-86) upto 1200 kg level for Crew Escape System, environment friendly asbestos-free PEDIN C inhibition system for solid motors, igniter grains for Crew Jettisoning motor/Low altitude Escape motor for Gaganyaan, etc. Also ensured timely supply of more than fifty schedule-critical project-deliverables from PCM Entity to LVs and satellite missions including HTPB, PF 106 and PF 108 resins, thermal control films & paints, igniter grains, a variety of adhesives & sealants, TPS coating materials, nozzle enclosures, thermal screens, etc. Technology of eight in-house developed PCM products was transferred to industries. Steered Indigenization of Space Materials (ISM), an inter-centre programme of ISRO from 2016 to 2019, as Chairman, ISM Steering Committee. Major thrust was put on indigenous development of new strategic materials such as electronic ceramics, powder metallurgy products, coating techniques, special rubber and polymeric products, critical requirements in satellite area such as Au plated Mo mesh for large aperture unfurlable space antenna, complex-profile based extruded Al alloy heat pipes etc.

Currently as Associate Director, R&D, VSSC since February 01, 2020, was focusing major efforts towards catalyzing research environment and synergizing R&D activities in VSSC. As Chairman of the VSSC Research Forum (VRF) which is constituted for the first time in the Centre, guiding and steering entire range of research process in VSSC. As Chairman, VSSC Standing Committee for Review of Adv. R&D and TDP Activities, putting in major efforts for steering 779 activities of the Centre in this area, in terms of meeting their technological objectives and time- lines.

****

Mr. Shanmugnathan
GCS, Scientist/Engineer G

I got the opportunity to work as Product Engineer from Oct-1983 to as on date in every area of Composites for both Launch vehicle and Spacecraft Projects. Details of my contributions are given below. RSR -Nozzle for RH-125,200,300,560 Sustainer & Booster. RH- 300 MK-II Nozzle new development and inducted for replacement of Centaure rocket. ASLV – Ablative Nozzles & Filament wound products like Motor cases, Igniter cases & Pressure vessels are realized and delivered for four ASLV. PSLV – PSO Ablative Nozzles & Igniter cases for all solid stages including out-sourcing of Nozzle liners to BHEL, Trichy for thirteen numbers of PSLV. Interstage – ¾ is developed and inducted with composites for replacement of metallic with payload gain of 130 Kg. INSAT & GSAT – Communication Antenna Reflector for various satellites are developed and delivered and met all project requirements.

GAGAN & NAVIC – Navigation Antenna Reflectors are developed and delivered for GAGAN Payload requirement and the payload is implemented for Aircraft Navigation. Antenna Reflector for Regional Navigation requirement are developed & delivered including outsourcing of 10 Nos. to Kineco, Goa and the payload is implemented. System Engineering –Contributed in Composites System Engineering area and uniform System is implemented for all products of Composites Entity. Encouragement and support given by all concerned staff for carrying out my activities as Product Engineer is acknowledged.

****

Mr. Ramesh Arora
CSS, Assistant Section Officer

1984 Joined as Lower Division Clerk (LDC) in the Ministry of Information and Broadcasting (I&B Ministry), Shastri Bhawan, and New Delhi on 04.02.1984 and posted in TV Section of I &B Ministry.

1985 After the new Government came, posted in I &B Minister's Office (Shri V N Gadgil) in January 1985. Worked also in I & B Minister's Office (Shri Ajit Kumar Panja). I served there for around 2 years.

1986 In November 1986, transferred to Publications Division, Patiala House, New Delhi, an attached office of the I&B Ministry and posted in Admn. I Section.

1988 In February 1988, transferred in I &B Ministry. Joined I &B Ministry again on 04.02.1988 and posted in Admn II Section (later on Admn. IV Section w.e.f. 01.01.1989).

1990 Again posted in I &B Minister's Office

(Shri Subodh Kant Sahay).

1991 Posted in Admn. IV Section after I &B Minister's Office left.

1994 Promoted as UDC w.e.f. 24.05.1994.

1996 Posted in Cash Section of I &B Ministry

1996 Posted again in Admn. IV Section of I &B Ministry

2000 In May 2000, transferred to Press Information Bureau, Shastri Bhawan, New Delhi, an attached office of the I&B and posted in Budget & Accounts Section.

2006 In August 2006, promoted as Assistant and transferred to I & B Ministry and posted in PC Cell dealing with Plan Schemes.

Ministry of Finance, Department of Financial Services (DFS)

2013 In March 2013, transferred to Ministry of Finance, Department of Financial Services on rotational transfer policy (RTP) and posted in Banking Operation-III Section (BO.III Section) dealing with public grievances of Banking Sector and Insurance Sector. Still continuing in BO.III Section at the time of retirement.

I have come a long way from working on manual typewriter to personal computer in my whole service. Initially, I worked on manual typewriter with big roller for typing seniority lists, stencil, red fluid, and carbon paper for typing upto 10 copies, typing rubber (eraser), white fluid, photo copier, electronic typewriter, and electronic type writer with daisy wheel in English and Hindi, UNIX, personal computer, scanner, e-mail and internet. I learnt everything in office itself i.e. electronic typewriter, electronic typewriter with daisy wheel in

English and Hindi. I worked on UNIX in office. We had to remember all the commands of UNIX. Then Personal Computer came and we learnt PC. In the beginning, we feared touching mouse of the PC. We learnt MS Word for simply typing letters etc. Then gradually, I learnt MS excel to work in the Budget and Accounts Section and PC Cell. I saw change of system from File Tracking System (FTS) to e-office.

There was a time when we were unable to see any important order related to us like DA order, Bonus order etc. We used to take photo copy of order available with any of our friends. Now, everything is available on websites of Ministries / Departments. The information related to other Ministries /Departments like their work allocation, contact numbers of the officers is now available which has made it easier to contact any other office of the Ministries/Departments.

There was a time when we wished our salary to be in five figures. The time has come and we are very happy to see our salary in five figures. I have seen four Pay Commission Reports in 1986, 1996, 2006 and the last one in2016 in my entire service span.

We used to get our pay from cash section in cash on last working day of the month. We used to be happy since morning of the last working day of the month. One person from the section used to bring salary for all the staff members of the section. Sometime, we used to stand in queue and wait for payment. We used to note pay particulars from the cash section available in PBR. Then our pay slips were hung outside of the cash section. One person could take pay slips for all. Then, the time came we took our pay slips from the computer system using numbers allotted to us for pay slips. Now, the time has changed and we can get our pay slips through e-office individually.

We apply for our Earned Leave, Casual Leave, RH and station leave etc. and the same is approved and sanctioned in e-office only. The attendance is marked in biometric system.

I am very thankful to Government of India for the LTC facility given to employees. I along with my family travelled to various destinations in East, West, North and South as well as North-east India. I could travel by air to North East because it is permitted as per LTC Rules.

This is a general notion among all people that transfer during service is a punishment but this is not always the case. After transfer in the new offices, I met very nice people. I had very nice experiences and learnt a lot from my all colleagues in the new offices.

I am going to retire on 31.03.2018. I thank Government of India that I could serve my country and my colleagues and friends who helped me sail through my service life successfully.

****

Mr. Ashish Kumar Chattopadhyay
DRTC, Technical Officer C

a. SASE (Mar-1988 to Oct - 1991)

Worked for Project MASCOT

Weather Forecasting Group - Gathering of Weather Parameters for Avalanche Forecast/Undertaking Reccee Electronics Group - Checking & Calibration of Automatic Weather Station situation at remote. Locations including Inaccessible Snow bound Regions of about 5000 meters above sea level. Development of Software programs for the support of Admin and Finance groups. Development of computer model for Avalanche Forecasting Group

b. IAT/DIAT (Nov - 1991 to Oct - 1998)

Development of computer Software programs for G-Branch (Office of Registrar Academics) for the smooth functioning of the Establishment as it was conducting lots of Long & Short Courses for the Defence Services/ DRDO Officers on regular basis including some post-graduate courses of University of Poona. For the computerization of the Group

i. Developed Software programs that helped about 10-Admin Staffs manning different desks in streamlining to avoid duplication of work

Manual typing errors in generation of various reports such as letters sent to various Estt. for local as well as outstations tours of the various courses both long and short

ii. Important Events Program

iii. Weekly Instruction Schedules Program for both Long & Short Courses

iv. Instructors Lecture Load Program for Each Instructors for Each Month

V. University Exams - Number of Reports for Conduct of University Exams and software Program for the automatic display of the Seating arrangements for each course Exam according to the seating capacity of Each Exam Hall

c. ARDE, Pune.

• Development of Web Site on IIS Web Server for ARDE Intranet using HTML, DHTML and ASP for Personnel Information System & Computer Information System.

• Compilation of Information for consolidated AMC of different software packages, Computers, Printers and UPS in ARDE

• Campus Wide Networking - Installation of individual LANs. Integration of various LANS into the Campus Wide Network consisting of about 620 nodes and 30 servers. The backbone of this network are three high-end servers, which provides 24 X 7 connectivity to the campus using a Backbone Chassis Switch - 3Com 4007, now upgraded to Nortel 8610 Chassis Switch.

• E-Mail Connect Server - Implementation of Third-Party Software on Campus Network: E-Mail Connect Server is an in-House E-mail multi-lingual communication system with a Web calendaring facility (appointments, Tasks, diary, etc).

• Network Administration - As Network Administrator for CAMPUS WIDE NETWORK of ARDE, setting up, maintaining and sharing hardware and software facilities. Installation and Implementation of Network Access Storage (NAS), Backup Tape Library, KVM switch, and Power strip on the Campus Network.

• DRONA - Implementation of DRONA facilities to all clients of Campus Network. Implementation of 34 Mbps leased line between ARDE and R&DE (E) for the implementation of Video Conferencing.

• Internet Facility through ADSL- Setting up of Internet Access to about 350 Senior Officers using ADSL technology. It is a implementation of a parallel Network for access to Internet using 10 Mbps leased line, Routers, Firewall, Switches, Bandwidth Management H/w & S/w, later Upgraded to 20 Mbps. Now implemented CIAG and transferred all clients to new CIAG network. Providing 24 x 7 up time.

• NKN Setup: Setting up of a separate 100 Mbps network for NKN - National Knowledge Network at ARDE, which is terminating at the Internet Room and forwarding Fiber connection to TIRC, for a separate LAN with Five nodes? Providing 24 x 7 up time.

• Virtualization Set up: Installed & Configured Six Blade Servers with SAN Storage and Implemented VMware vSphere 5.5 (Upgraded to 6.5) for Virtualization of Servers & Desktops. Virtualized all Production Servers i.e., Web Server, Database Server Mail Server, Antivirus Server, Information Security Server, Visitor Pass Management Server. Integration of this Setup with the Campus Wide Network. Migration of all existing PC/ Servers to Virtual Servers. Providing 24 x 7 up time.

****

Mr. Kamala Devidas Joshi
DRTC, Technical Officer B

IN 1982, Nov. I Joined ARDE, Pune-24 as D &man-III Post. i. e. for 18 years worked in PINAKA (LAUNCHER) gl. There I had experience in design development of Launcher system. BM-21 to SS-45. I played an important role in designing of launcher Pod, cradle, FRP Tubes etc. I also attended the gaspection 4 firing. Trials of the same my senior's guided me that the whole process; really learnt lot from them. Names: - 1) R. Bhattacharya, sca 2) S.V. Gode, Sc& H& 3) B. G. Gersjar, SC. D, 4) MD Sahy, SC.E This project was a great success & handed to the users. This launcher was used in Kargil 99.

(2) From 2000; I am working in MT section; as mTo I am looking after all the activities of MT section. Maintenance of unit vehicles for effective purpose. To keep the vehicle fleet in roadworthy condition at all times. Hiring of PMPML Bus for school going children of ARDE defence Personal & employees. FoL management, KPL work, Car diary, Ledger entries. Issue/ Receipt Vouchers. Authorized civil garages for effective maint Correspondence with DRDO HQ for condemnations Board;

3) After 38 years Services; now I am going to get Superannuation from duty; with my honest work. I got an opportunity to contribute in DRDO serve my country. It gives me immense pleasure to be a Part of ARDE. I am thankful to all my colleagues.

****

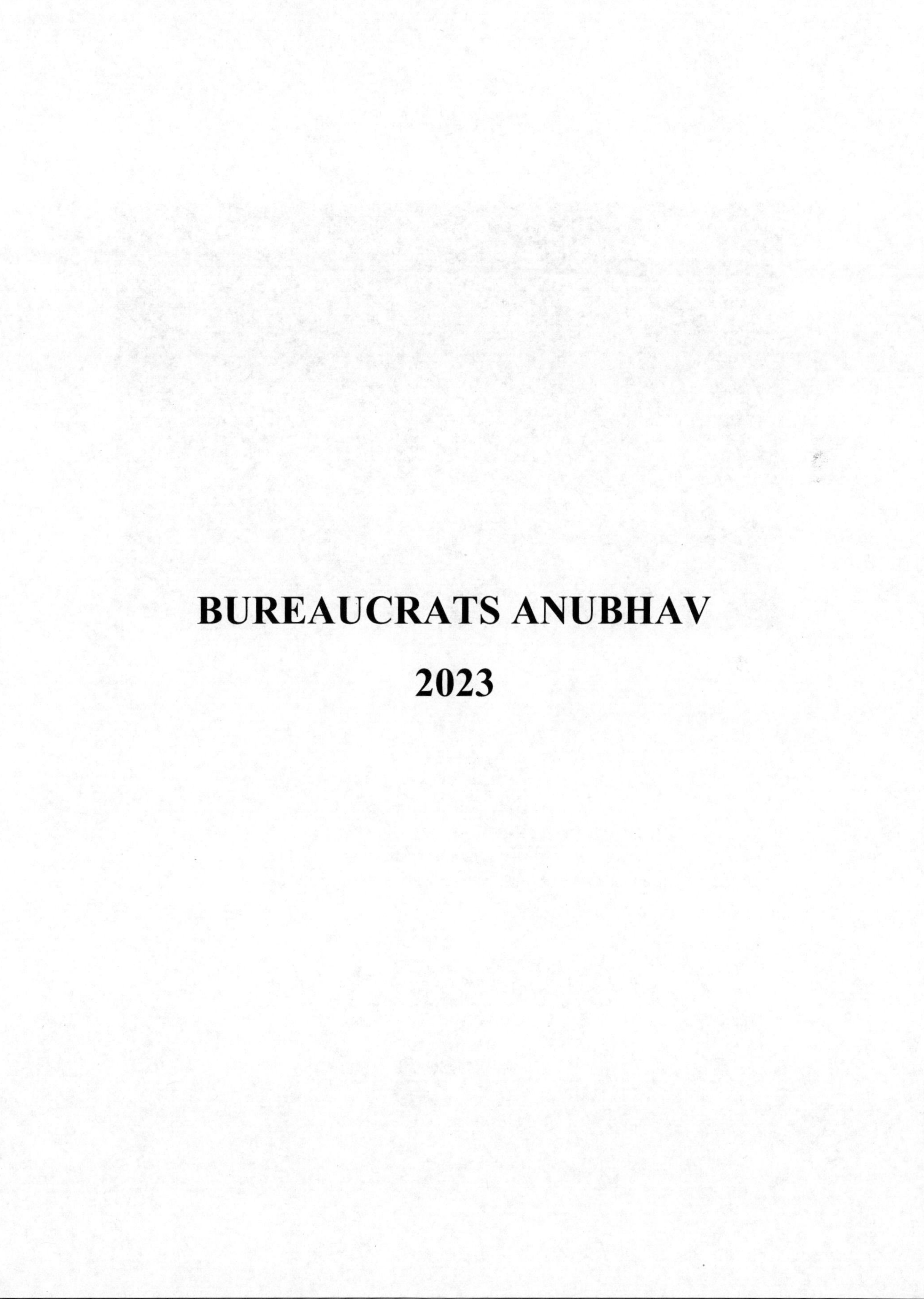

BUREAUCRATS ANUBHAV

2023

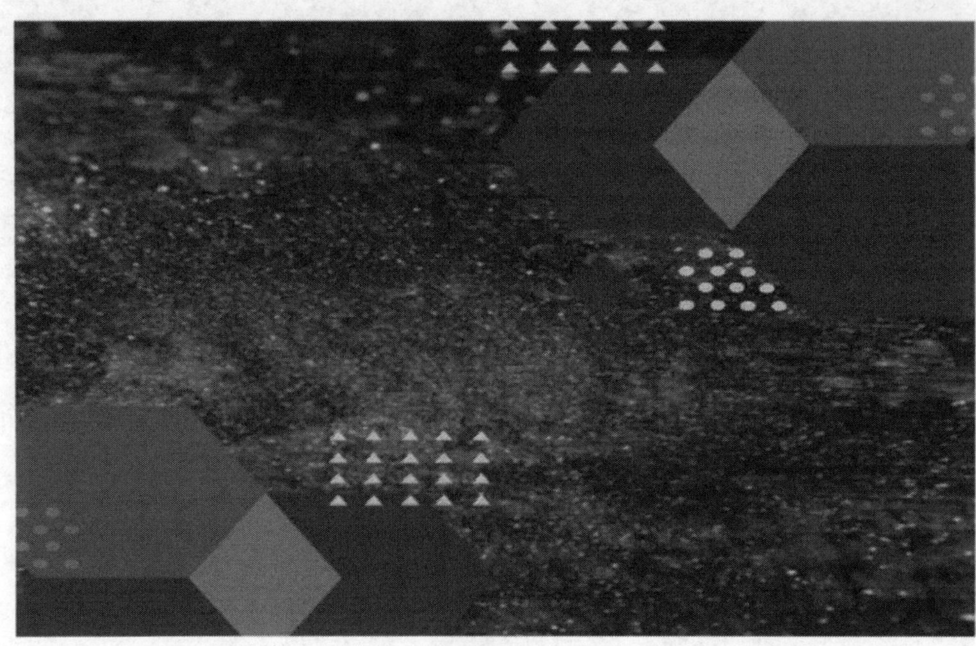

भारत सरकार
GOVERNMENT OF INDIA
कार्मिक, लोक शिकायत तथा पेंशन मंत्रालय
MINISTRY OF PERSONNEL, PUBLIC GRIEVANCES & PENSIONS
पेंशन एव पेंशनभोगी कल्याण विभाग
DEPARTMENT OF PENSION & PENSIONERS' WELFARE

ANUBHAV

2023

Contents

ANUBHAV Write-Ups

3. Anubhav 2023

Mr. Ramprasand
GCS, Junior, Technical Officer (Drawing)

I joined CQAL, Dept. of Defence Production on 10.08.1987 as TRACER possessing Qualification of ITI in Draughtsman ship and DIPLOMA In Mech engg. With 07 Years working experience as Draughtsman. I was promoted as DM III 1995, merged with DM II and re designated as Sr. Draughtsman. I was promoted as Junior Tech. Officer (Drawing) in May 2022. I have worked in Drawing section and CC Section. I am presently in PC group. During my tenure, I was responsible for the following

a) Preparation of Main eqpt. /Spares Drawing for indigenization of imported / stores manufactured by Pvt. Vendors.

b) Scrutiny / Vetting of Draft indents /Ordnance Demands and supply orders for Tech. Parameters and intimate likely source of supply for the stores by referring to various tech /scaling documents/drawings.

Scrutiny of Draft assignment lists for Designation, Drawing No. cat / part No. of the items /stores issued for Main eqpts, spares / SPL to Main eqpt for various Causality pertaining to different COS section. Update the records (super catalogue /makers' code index Etc.) on receipt of final assignment list.

Between 1998 to 2010 in connection with AERO INDIA and DEFEXPO conducted biennially by Ministry of Defence, the following works were carried out by me: writing of invitation cards for VVIP/VIPs/Ambassadors of different countries, preparation of seating plan, Route map etc.

****

Mr. Vinod Ananth
DRDO (AFHQ) Assistant Engineer

I joined DGQA in 1988 as CM-II; I was involved in Quality Assurance activities of Systems/sub systems of armed forces. In SQAE (L), I carried out QA checks on Gen sets, Ground systems of Missile systems under IGMDP, LRUs of EW Projects, and Project Shakti etc. During my tenure in CQA(AVL) I was involved in QA checks of Electrical/Electronic sub Assys of Main Battle Tank Arjun Mk-I. I was also involved in the evaluation of improvements implemented in Arjun Mk-II.

Analysis of Defects whenever reported was also carried out along with reps of HVF, MAG and CVRDE. In 2018, I was transferred to CQAL, wherein I was involved in Evaluation of Advance Samples of DG Sets, Defect investigation, Vetting of scales, Indents, Technical literatures, QTP, ATP etc. I was a test Engineer in GSTG lab of CQAL which is NABL Accredited for Testing DG sets.as a recognition to my meritorious service, I was awarded with DGQA Commendation 02 times and DGQA Commendation certificates 03 times in my total service of 33 years' service.

****

Mr. S Chandra
GCS, Sorting Postman

I had the pleasant to join the Postal department in 1983 as GDS BPM Ramagondanahalli B.O. I have worked as the B.P.M of the till June 1991. During this said period, I was awarded with an S.B incentive of Rs. 5000 per year by the departments. I was also placed in the second place by the department for my sincere work. From the July 1991 to December 2015, I had worked as a postman, vimanapura MDG, Bengaluru 560017. At that time, there was 1st&2nd delivery of speed post articles. I had taken maximum efforts to deliver almost all the articles entrusted to me. My hardwork was appreciated by the officer in charge of speed post section. The postmaster also had appreciated my hard and sincere work.

In the year 2014, I had in my best efforts by opening 1294 small savings accounts. The piece of good work got me second place in Bengaluru east division and was highly appreciated by senior superintendent. I was also awarded by commendation certification by the SSPOs. During my long tenure as postman, I did my job to the best of my efforts without inviting public complaints. All the addresses/customers had liked me for my amiable qualities. I may mention here that I had been a disciplined worker of the department. I have been working as sorting postman, vimanapura from 2015 till date.

****

Mr. A.M.A Khader
CSSS, Principal Private Secretary

I joined the Government Service in June 1982 as an LDC and rose to the Level of Principal Private Secretary. I had the distinction of qualifying the PS Examination conducted by UPSC three times (could not come finally due to a smaller number of vacancies in those days). Finally, I qualified the UPSC 2005 Examination and was appointed as Private Secretary.

As regards outstanding work, my experience used to be always aimed at good performance in each and every field /work. Regardless the nature of the job, I performed all kinds of work assigned to me in the best possible manner. June 1982 to December 1985 Worked as an LDC in the Electronic Switching Section of P&T Directorate (then it was) and now the Department of Telecommunications (bifurcated in the year 1985) during which period I was associated and assisted my superiors in the setting up of electronic exchanges throughout the country.

January 1986 to March 1992, Appointed as Grade D Stenographer on the basis of Bimonthly LDCE (August 1985) and continued to work in DoT. During this period, I was associated and assisting my Director in Integrated Digital Network – the unit which was instrumental in bringing the ISDN (Integrated Services Digital Network – like Video Conferencing), Internet, E-mail, Pager Service etc., in the country.

Prior to this, in the year 1990-91, I had been associated in the work of installation of one STD PCO in every Village Panchayat throughout the country. Thus, the STD PCO booths spread all over, in each and every village of the country. However, with the penetration of mobile telephones in large number the significance of STD booths lost its relevance.

April 1992 to August 2007

Appointed as Grade C Stenographer (LDCE 1990) and transferred to Ministry of Information & Broadcast where I worked till August1997 in the Media Units like Publications Division and Press Information Bureau. During my tenure in PIB I looked after the publicity work of Petroleum & Natural Gas and Ministry of Telecommunications. Two significant announcements in each of the Department were given wide publicity i.e. LPG on demand – across the counter and one paise per minute for mobile calls.

During my Tenure in Information & Broadcast Ministry I went on deputation to the Income-tax Appellate Tribunal as Sr. P.A., a Gazetted Post, (December 1994 to January

1997). I was also deputed as Haj Assistant to Saudi Arabia by the Ministry of External Affairs three times – during the Haj 1998, 2000 and 2005-2006

September 2007 to till date

Joined the Ministry of Chemicals & Fertilizers on being promoted as Private Secretary on the basis of LDCE 2005and was posted in the Department of Chemicals & Petrochemicals. In July 2008, a new Department i.e. Department of Pharmaceuticals was carved out and I continued to work in the Department of Pharmaceuticals till date. During my posting as PS in this Department I had the privilege of working with two seniors most IAS officers (who were Secretaries to the Government of India). I was promoted as Principal Private Secretary in the month of December 2015 and retained in Department of Pharmaceuticals only from where I will be retiring on 31.5.2016.

****

Ms. Anandalekshmy S
GCS, Scientist/Engineer SG

It is a great honour and privilege to me for being part of prestigious organization ISRO and the Contribution to meet the organization goals. I joined ISRO on October 12, 1988. During the initial period, I have contributed for optimal trajectory design and optimal payload assessment (GTO & SSPO) studies for PSLV & GSLV MKII. The major contribution was the optimal trajectory design for the first flight of GSLV – MKII and payload improvement studies for GTO mission. The next very important contribution was the vehicle configuration sizing and optimal trajectory studies for GSLV – MKIII during initial vehicle design phase, another contribution is towards the ascent phase mission and optimal trajectory design for Chandrayaan and mars orbiter mission (Mom) mission of ISRPO. Open loop steering program generation during launch, trajectory design for operational launch vehicle of ISRO, launch vehicle sizing and mission design for future missions, feasibility of launching PSLV from other launch sites and commercial launch services mission feasibility studies.

My Contribution also related to trajectory design for mars orbiter mission which involves performance assessment of launch vehicles with various launch opportunities. EPO (Elliptical Parking orbit) performance for mars orbiter mission with PSLV in 2013 launch. Open loop steering program generation during launch. Trajectory design and performance assessment for various launch vehicles and mission. Feasibility of launching PSLV from other launch sites. Solution for commercial launch services. Launch vehicle sizing – LVM3, SSLV, HLV (Heavy lift Launch Vehicle).

****

Mr. Sudhir George Verghis
GCS, Scientist Space

I started my career in October 1986 at SAC, Ahmedabad in my sensor electronics division of remote sensing area. My first assignment was to design the camera electronics for the VHRR payload of India's indigenous communication spacecraft INSAT 2A (INSAT IITs) Remote Sensing Electronics involved designing low noise electronics engineer. SAC was always at the forefront of new technology lessons were learnt in data acquisition and processing PCB layout using at work checking, checking design, data transfer and so on.

Those lessons proved a gift for me in future. I designed on board circuits, tested with GPIB automation instrument using HP controllers. I had opportunity to test electronics cards for visible & opportunity to test electronics cards for visible, IR cameras. This probability developed a penchant for automation in me. I am grateful to my bosses, Dr. George and Shri K Nagachenchia, who helped me tremendously & moulded me. I had the opportunity to test electronics cards for visible and IR cameras. I spent 6 years in SAC, which were some of the happiest times I spent, satellite remote sensing and communication application helped in understanding the social impact they had on society. From SAC, I moved to VSSC Quality Division - Avionics system in 1992. I was fortunate to associate with the team in its qualification of PSLV stage for PSLV D1. This was a totally new experience for me. It took me to understand the launch vehicle systems & system engineering concept was learnt. Facilities for transport and accommodation in SHAR were scarce and difficult, and then however, the struggle of those early days helped me later on when I had to oversee the campaign of LVM3.

I was involved in PS2 stage at Makendaragin and CHAR Concepts of Quality, red reliability, liquid propulsion compel systems, pyro, instrumentation and power were imbibed. This helped me later during my days. LVM3. I had the privilege of participating and ensuring the quality of the initial PSV & GSLV missions after my promotion, I was moved C/SLV MkIII Core project. Hence, I had the opportunity to configure the vehicle avionics architecture, get the subsystem designed, fabricated and delivered. Reviewed to low up ensured the qualification of 30 ne extend and fight and flight were tested in PSLV AAM and later inducted in PSLV &GSLU Mission. The fines aspects of project management among agencies Like ISTRAC SHAR were imbedded.

In August 2021, ESA Entity was formed and I was asked to lead the entity as the first Dy Director, which was great honour and privilege. Three and half decades in ISRO have been a great learning experience in establishing friendships and facilities, coordinating and leading teams. Solving problem, meeting Schedules and mentoring youngsters. My thanks and heartfelt gratitude to the excellent mentors I had in my career, the warm and well-meaning team which always gave their best.

****

Dr. (Mr.), Ganji Venkata Narayana
GCS, Scientist/ Engineer

1) I, Mastered testing of various rocket materials (M250 maraging steels, To alloys, Al alloys, steels, super alloys, ceramics, polymers and composites) over a wide temperature range from 270° C to 1500° C & helped in grading acceptance purpose.

2) Studied the fracture behavior of AA 2219- T87 aluminum alloy welded plates of cryo propellant tank at room temperature and cryo. Through this study, I have suggested a simple, low cost & most reliable procedure for proof pressure testing of cryogenic thanks for use in rockets.

3) Played a key role in selecting and certifying material for various ISRO projects such as PSLV, GSLV, LVM3, Chandrayaan, Mangalyaan & upcoming gangayaan.

4) Generated human rated material procurement specifications for the prestigious gangayaan project envisaged for carrying Indian astronauts on our own rockets from SDSC SHAR – Srihari Kota.

5) Contributed in the material selection design & realization of 1st Indian space suit for Gangayaan

6) Handled material management for crew module atmospheric Reentry experiment (CARE) mission and Pad abort test flight towards Gangayaan flight qualification.

7) Received best research award for fracture characteristics of AA2 219 AI Alloy.

8) Outstanding contribution award for space suit design and realization.

****

Mr. VS Radha Krishna
DRDO, Scientist 'B'

1. As scientist 'B' carried out a number of experiments to find out solution for effectively muting the radio – Controlled improvised explosive devices (RCIED), a potential threat VIP security from Anti National Elements.
2. Successfully designed muting techniques to then prevailing RCIED threat and development muting system for VIP convoy protection. Quality Numbers were produced by M/S Bharat Electronics, Hyderabad and delivered to the user agencies.
3. As core member of the operation team, actively participated in the installation, operation and maintenance of jammer stations in the forward areas of J&K for countering the malicious propaganda of the adversaries.
4. During the tenure of scientist 'C' as a team leader developed a 1500w high power VHF transmitter for communication jammer applications and its work proved the wary for indication of indigenously developed jammer amplifiers.
5. During the tenure of scientist D&E, shared the design developed of high-power jammer amplified based on completed indigenous technology and a vehicle mounted convoy protection jammer system for Indian army; planned, coordinated and guided the field trials of the jammer in the agency M/s Bharat Electronics , Hyderabad.
6. Successfully designed & developed a VVIP Convoy protection system against RCIEDs and QTY 60 Nos of the same were produced by MIS BE.
7. As Project Director, successfully planned, coordinated and generated the design & development of the state-of-the-art electronic counter measure system for jammer spoofing the satellite signal-based navigation system complying the requirements of Tri Services.
8. Trial Evaluation of indigenously developed ECM system at various locations as identified by the user agencies, quantity members have been produced by the industry partner/development partner and the same are under exploitation by the user agencies.
9. Established a comprehensive electronics warfare test range, over 3000 acres of land at Kurnool district of Andhra Pradesh. The open-air Range enables testing & evaluation of all types of electronic warfare systems intended for Tri services and other security agencies.

10. The National open-air Range (NOAR) also facilitates the testing of high energy laser systems and Anti-Tank guided missiles. The systems design and performance can be optimized with the help of stimulators.

The 34 ½ years of journey facilitated by the DRDO offered great opportunities and challenges in the design and development of EW system and equipment in related areas and to see the great team work getting culminated in the successful realization of sate of the art EW system equipment for Tri Services and other user agencies is truly a memorable and satisfying phase of life. I sincerely acknowledge the support received from my senior officers and team members and gratitude to the DRDO/DLRL for having given me opportunity to work in the capacity of designer, system coordinator, team leader, Group director and project director for technology development projects and a national infrastructure facility. Receipt of DRDO Agni Awards for indigenous technology development.

****

Ms. Manimozhi Theodore
DRDS, Scientist H

I Dr. Manimozhi Theodore, outstanding scientist & chief coordinator, ISRO – DRDO Gangayaan programme, Defence Bioengineering & Electro medical Laboratory (DEBEL) a Bangalore based Defence research & Development organization. I joined in Defence and Development organization and joined DRDO in LRDE in 1984 as scientist B contributed for development switching and communication equipment for Army radio engineering network (AREN) and are successfully inducted in Indian Army and are in use.

I contributed defense command control and communication intelligence system (31 system) from inception to induction covering design & Development, transfer of technology to production agencies and in various fields trials, induction to services successfully. She has extensively contributed quality assurance and standalization activities of equipment for all the three defense forces from CAIR and instrumental for obtaining ISO 9001:2015 first in DRDO and CMMI Dev 2.0 certification for CAIR. Later, she has contributed many medical equipment research & development production and installed successfully as the Director, DEBEL, Bangalore.

I served earlier as the chief executive officer of the society for Biomedical Technology (SBMT) started by APJ Abdul Kalam to help the common man with development of affordable biomedical devices. She is conferred Honory Doctorate for digital educational excellence &sustainability development at Bangalore by St. Mother Teresa University (SMTU).

****

Ms. KS Padmaja
DRDS, Scientist F

I worked at DRDO for 33 years 6 months, 13 years at DLRL and 30 years 6 months at NSTL joined as scientist B, worked, at DLRL from 8th Feb 1989 to 31st Dec 1991. Involved in signal identification and analysis using microprocessor-based systems. Took transfer to NSTL and working here since 1st Jan 1992. Design and Development of instrumentation systems (Embedded system) and identification of sensors for varunastra, ALWT, EHWT, HEAUV & Torpbuster. Team leader for fiber optic wire guidance technology (A highly critical and path breaking technology which was denied by foreign firms to part with).

Design & Development of Fiber optic wire guidance system, FO modems, winding machine & unreeling of various fiber, optic equipment, FO connectors, various variants of FO cables, underwater electrical connectors, FO bulk heads, winding methodologies, unwinding techniques, embedded and Test station software, resolved FO cable routing issue and evolved with an innovative unique splicing technique and splice joint protection scheme which is established in field trials.

Worked for projects like AET, WGT, Mareech, Manthan 1, Manthan 2, CRITECH, Mohini (Mobile Decoy), contactless communication moule based on IR and RFID system, for decoys, AUV, CARS projects, few R8D, IETE support activities. Associated many industries with NSTL. Production induction support partners for TAL and Varunastra, ALWT, maintenance of MSSS (Band hub station and procedures for channel acquisition. Design & Development of MSS transceiver for HEAUV, an Unique satellite/GPS based reporting terminal for varunastra, EHWT, sahayak – NG ADC – 150 & CET 65E (Russian Torpedo) Recovery did to locate articles after termination of mission gives critical information of surfaced article at C band hub station.

****

Mr. R. Panneer Selvam
DRTS, TO D

I joined as JSA – I to SSPL – DRDO, October 1987, responsible for operation and maintenance of 2000 KVA DG set integrated with Inverters & Battery Bank to provide UPS power to crystal growth system to grow NDYAG crystals for defense warfare warning systems. The system consists of the separate power source from a nominated transformer fed into the required electrical switch gears and controls to operate the main system and auxiliary system like compressors, vacuum pumps cooling plants, wafer cutting, lapping & polishing devices. In case of DSESU power failure, within 3 – 5 Nano second the DG set power was to be connected. A set a single crystal of 40 mm; I was attached to QAD of GTRE since my mutual transferee was working in QAD. I was assigned with the quality control inspection in particular on metrology.

All the components of combustion, after burner, Jet pipe and oil tank components were inspected from components stage to S/A stage and to total assembly of the concern modules pertain to GTX. The work recognition and timely promotion till T.O- B in QAD, GTRE was motivational reward transferred to vibration division of MBSI – GTRE, from installation, commissioning, demonstration, training and acceptance. First Kind in the nation dynamic rig facilities to spin & stimulate the LP & HP bladed routers to the maximum feasible parameters of the engine running condition was affected.

I obtained my MS in production Engineering evaluation of additive manufactured turbo rotor. I can never forget the entire team of VEG and their valuable technical & moral support. I salute SSPL, GTRE DRDO in total which was very instrumental to complete my 35 years of fruitful service in addition to 5 years of Non DRDO experience prior to DRDO. I pray & wish GTRE to achieve its final victorious milestone of its projects.

****

Mr. K Viswanathan
DRTS, TO D

I actively been involved in complete product development cycle i.e. configuration, layout study, detailed design, generation of manufacturing drawings, guidance, inspection, vehicle integration and participation in trial validation by both DEDO and users. Participated in the development of CVRDE products viz, Arjun main Battle Tank, MKI, EX Tank, Arjun MBT MKII, CATAPULT and configuration development for future MBTs and NGMBT.

I generated many technical documents for various sub systems of Armoured fighting Vehicles (AFVs). Material specification like CDA 99, CDA 101, DGQA related documents like CCES Technical repair manual. He has also published papers and won many commendations and awards during my career. During my long service from August 1985 at CVRDE, the officer has immensely contributed in the area of design and development of mechanical systems pertaining to turret and weapon system of India' Prestigious Armoured fighting Vehicle, Arjun MBT. The officer has developed core competence in the area of Armoured fighting Vehicle structure development. During the product development period, turret configuration had to be revised to suit various major sub systems like Gunner main sight procured from different vendors all over the world. Major Projects were:

a) Structurally improved Arjun MBT MKII: Towards weight reduction program of Arjun MBT MKII the officer has configured and modelled generated weight reduced Hull & Turret structure for research and prepared the manufacturing Gas cutting drawings of armour plates and provided guidance during the manufacturing activities of Hull & turret structure at manufacturers premises of OFMK and M/S Reliance Silvassa.

b) Contribution in Arjun CATAPULT the variant from Arjun MBT he has prepared complete illustrated spare parts list (ISPL) by generating drags and documents using the 3D models created. He has completed the task in a record time of one month.

c) Being part of the Next Generation Main Battle Tank (NGMBT) feasibility study team, the officer was tasked with generation of various external and internal hull & turret design options, which the officer accomplished in a very short period of one-month so as to enable the NGMBT team to complete the feasibility report and submit it to DRDO HQ within the stipulated time period. Extensive association during manufacture of the product at vendor's premises and trial evaluation at the field areas speak volumes about his laudable techno – managerial qualities.

****

Mr. Satya Narayana
DRTS, TOB

I provided safety coverage for various static Tests conducted at DRDL. Providing safety coverage for static tests, explosive integration, and Explosive inspection for projects of K4, K 15, LR Sam, QRSAM, AKASH, PJ 10, ASTRA, SFDR, and NGRAM & HELINA. Implemented safety requirements for the static tests conducted in HTF, MTF, and STF & 100 test bed. Co – ordinated and assisted the internal safety audit of Project ASTRA and HSTDV to identity the non-compliance as per STEC and Statutory regulations. Conducted emergency mock drills and the observed the non-compliance and sent recommendations to fire, medical and security for corrective action. Coordinated with MES for conducting load test of Cranes and forklifts at DRDL.

Conducted Load testing of 'D' shackles, wire Rope/Nylon Slings, forklifts, tools & tackles by competent authority of tools & tackles every year. Ensured safety requirements for internal transportation at various work Centres and provided safety coverage for transporting rocket motors IK4 missile PI, P2 motor from ACEM Nasik to INS Kalinga Vishakhapatnam by road. I am greatly thankful for everything.

****

Ms. Bhavirsetty Indira
DRTS, TOD

I joined as stenographer in March, 1996 worked in administration. Started with FORTRAN for mainframe, developed online quiz using GW – Basic, Conducted online exam for trainings. Developed around 15 applications for administration & finance using Dbase III plus; developed different modules for military hospital, patient information monitoring system. Around 2000, DNet DRDL internet website and some applications started under Dr. R.N Biswas using HTML, JavaScript & ASP, and oracle on windows platform with 3 tie architecture. I was an administrator for DNet, DRONA website and web & Database servers also. Later on, Development started using JSP, oracle as backend and Linux Platform for servers.

I was involved in all phases of software development like requirements & analysis, design, development, testing, implementation and maintenance for almost all DNet application. Now, I am working as O i/c for DNet serves administration, site maintenance and around 150+ applications. Which consists of administration, finance, test requisitions, management & information system etc. Some of the major applications are personal information system; leave management, Ta/Ba, LTC, HRMS trainings. All applications views & status, project management & information system, some test requisitions like SDRC/Waiver, TARB/PTARB etc.

I have very good satisfaction for the works whatever I have executed during my entire service as almost all applications are implemented and most useful to DRDL & missile complex employees in day-to-day transactions and also administration, finance functional groups and some of the directorates.

****

Mr. Ramesh Singh Negi
GCS, Senior Statistical Officer

I would like to thank you for giving me this opportunity to share my wonderful experience called Anubhav with the whole heart. I had put in more than 37 years of service in General Reserve Engineer Force (GREF) which an integral part of Armed Forces from September, 1983 to September, 1996 and in Ministry of Health and Family Welfare from October, 1996 to February, 2021. I dealt with matters related to administrative and welfare of GREF employees worked in remote and far-flung areas of the country. Thereafter, I have worked in Department of Health and Family Welfare under Ministry of Health and Family Welfare from October 1996 to February, 2021 where I dealt with plan and policy related matter concerning to the Department. It was a wonderful experience where I had learned a lot during my tenure in GREF as well as in Ministry of Health and Family Welfare. I would like to thank all my seniors and colleagues who helped me in my career.

****